The Origins of Religions

by
Julien Ries

William B. Eerdmans Publishing Company
Grand Rapids, Michigan

Contents

Foreword

RELIGIOUS FEELING touches the very depths of the human soul. Its exploration is arduous in the case of present-day man, and harder still when the subject is prehistoric man. Methodology presents the greatest challenge: what should be sought and which frameworks adopted in pursuing the history of religious feeling?

Only a century ago, when paleoanthropological evidence was still unavailable, the origins of religion, or rather of the religious phenomenon in early man, was reconstructed on the basis of various approaches (evolutionary, ethnological, sociological, etc.) that ended up by favoring a given ideological framework or by transferring religious feelings found in present-day peoples, primitive or advanced, onto mankind of the past.

This is not the method adopted by Julien Ries, who has referred to the historical, phenomenological and hermeneutical methods described by Mircea Eliade as being suitable for historians of religion, and thereby has set out from the currently available evidence regarding paleoanthropology, prehistory and protohistory, and their relative interpretations. In the space of one hundred years, the evidence has grown considerably regarding the conceptual activity expressed in the technology, the funerary practices, the pictographs in mural and miniature art and, in more recent times, in the cult of the mother goddess and the transmission of religious texts.

The evidence currently available attributes the birth of religions, that is of systems of beliefs and rites, to the relatively recent Neolithic period. Although it is still possible that the absence of certain evidence pertaining to religions in earlier periods can be explained by the lack of suitable tools for transmitting such rites and customs, it is nevertheless true that religions as such derive from a basic religious feeling that is innate in man. Whether this man lives in cities or is the hunter-gatherer of prehistoric times who decorated cave walls 15,000-20,000 years ago or practiced funeral rites much earlier still, it can be said that religious sense dates back to the very origins of humanity. This is Julien Ries's conviction, and I fully agree with it.

It is certainly true that the contents of religious experience prove to be extremely rich and diversified in the period that witnessed the flourishing of the great religions of both the West and the East. However, it is also possible to detect a line of continuity with previous experiences, gently following the Sumerian religious epics of ancient Babylonia back to the prayers of the Neolithic period, to the mythograms of the Upper Paleolithic, and to the funerary practices of the Middle and Lower Paleolithic.

Yet apart from showing how *homo religiosus* derives from the earliest human forms *(Homo habilis* and *Homo erectus),* Julien Ries also offers us a masterly conceptual and methodological framework for research into the history of religions, presenting religious experience in the various periods in faithful relation to the evidence available and with complete interpretative coherence.

I am honored to present a work that bears witness to the author's incomparable gift for transporting the reader back into the atmosphere of the past, involving him, as it were, in the religious experience presented, whether this be the contemplation of the firmament or the initiation ceremonies of the the Upper Paleolithic or Neolithic temples.

The power of the book is further increased by the magnificent illustrations that make it so attractive.

In approaching the religious phenomenon in this way we are able to appreciate the fact that religious feeling is a constant of mankind, insofar as he is endowed with abstractive and symbolic capacities. Reference to what is transcendent, merely glimpsed or implicit in Paleolithic man, is evident in various great religions of the last millennia B.C. and clearly manifest in original form in Christianity, which represents the highest expression of religious feeling in the meeting of divine and human.

— Fiorenzo Facchini

Glossary

Hermeneutics The science of interpretation. Hermeneutics takes proven evidence that has been critically reviewed and classified and sets out to render its meaning explicit, reveal its trans-historic dimension, and make it comprehensible and accessible in the present context by means of comparative analysis. Hermeneutics analyzes religious phenomena as significant. *Descriptive* hermeneutics tries to discover the message perceived by *homo religiosus* in his immediate environment, whereas *normative* hermeneutics aims at revealing the essential aspects of the human condition.

Hierophany The act of revelation of what is sacred. The sacred makes its appearance in the world of phenomena and can be humanly perceived. All hierophany is made up of three elements: firstly the object or being through which the sacred reveals itself — stone, tree, space, man, etc; secondly the invisible reality that transcends this world, the "totally other," the "divine" or the "nouminous," as R. Otto put it; and finally, the central mediating element, the being or object invested with a new dimension, that of sacredness. The person invested with this new dimension is the priest. The sacred tree is still a tree, but something has changed in the way *homo religiosus* relates to it.

Homo erectus The earliest examples of *Homo erectus* were discovered in eastern Africa, to the east of Lake Turkana, and date back one and a half million years. Characteristics are cranial capacity between 775 and 1250 cubic centimeters, and an elongated and fairly thick skull. *Homo erectus* populated the whole of the ancient world and disappeared around 300,000 years ago.

Homo habilis This is the earliest known appearance of the *Homo* species. It appeared in eastern Africa about two million years ago; the first specimen was found in the Olduvai Gorge in Tanzania in 1959. Characteristics are brain, teeth and bipedism. A cultural component and an inevitable increase of his cognitive capacity should also be noted: he is the creator of the first culture. *Homo habilis* fills in the hiatus between the Australopithecines and *Homo erectus.*

Homo religiosus At this point we leave the sphere of phylogenesis, or the way in which the species are formed, and instead enter that of anthropology, ethology and psychology. Created by contemporary historians of religion, the expression *homo religiosus* refers to man as the subject of the real experience of the sacred. *Homo religiosus* believes and claims to experience the sacred. The history of religions establishes him as historic and trans-historic.

Homo sapiens Descendent of *Homo erectus.* The characteristic brain size is 1400 cubic centimeters; the face appears reduced and is positioned beneath the cerebral cranium. The earliest examples of *Homo sapiens* appeared around 300,000 years ago. *Homo sapiens neanderthalensis* is a European subspecies; when it became extinct *Homo sapiens sapiens* took over.

Homo sapiens sapiens This branch of the *Homo* species derived from *Homo sapiens* and appeared around 100,000 years ago, presenting adaptive diversifications in relation to the geographical and climatic differences. The variations in present-day man derive from this diversification.

Homo symbolicus Expression by which anthropologists indicate the action carried out by a specific human faculty revealed in man's cultural creativity and perceived as resulting from his imagination. Thanks to his imagination man can grasp the invisible by means of the visible and can become the creator of culture and cultures.

Myth The myth is an account of events that took place at the very beginning, a story destined to supply models for human behavior. The myth establishes ways of thinking and acting that allow man to find his place in the world; it is both holy and exemplary for individual and collective life.

Mythogram System of representation characteristic of the art of the Upper Paleolithic, devoid of a narrative structure that would allow us to grasp the message. A key is required for such understanding, that is, the recital of a myth whose elements we have lost. Mythograms constitute the fundamental component of Franco-Cantabrian mural art.

Natufian This is an intermediate civilization between gathering and agriculture. The term derives from Wadi en-Natouf in western Judea, dating from 10,000 to 8,300 B.C. Beginning with the exit from the caves, it continued with the settlement of populations that continued to live off gathering wild vegetables and the immediate resources of the environment. Although agriculture is still unknown, man is already producing art and tools and creating the first villages.

Neolithic During the eighth millennium in the Near East a great transition took place in the way food was procured: man changed from being a predator to becoming a farmer, cultivating vegetable species and raising animals. He thus created a production economy, accompanied by new techniques (making pottery and smoothing tools). This important change in society derived from an ideological shift that has come to light through recent discoveries: the creation of the images of the deity, and a change in the conception of the sacred. Social and economic changes originated in a new ideology (Cauvin).

Paleolithic Term created in 1865 to indicate the Old Stone Age, when tools were chipped but not smoothed. The Archaic Paleolithic is the earliest period: it begins in Africa with the stone remains of human species similar to the Australopithecines. The Lower Paleolithic begins in Africa with the *Homo habilis,* Olduvai and the *pebble culture,* whereas in Europe it begins much later. The Middle Paleolithic dates from 200,000 to 35,000 B.C. In Europe we have *Homo sapiens* and Neanderthal man (80,000-35,000 B.C.). The Upper Paleolithic begins around 34,000 B.C. and ends toward 9500 B.C., by which time it is the age of *Homo sapiens sapiens.*

Rite This is an action thought up in the mind, decided by will and carried out by the body using words and gestures. Rites belong to a hierophanic event connected with the mediated experience of the supernatural and aim at establishing a link with a reality beyond that of this world. The ritual act is always related to a symbolic structure by means of which man is able to move from significant to signified, from sign to being.

Sacred The word *sakros,* derived from an archaic inscription in the Roman forum, takes us back to the origins of the sacred in Rome and in the whole of the Indo-European world, that is to the root *sak-* that gives rise to the verb *sancire* meaning "to confer validity, reality; to make something real." *Sak-* is at the root of what is real and touches the fundamental structure of things and beings. It suggests a metaphysical and a theological notion whose religious and cultural connotation will vary according to the different traditions of each people. The experience of the sacred implies discovery of an absolute reality which is perceived as transcendent.

Shamanism In the strict sense shamanism is a phenomenon specific to Siberia and central Asia, where the ultimate religious experience is considered to be that of the shaman, who possesses the special gifts of magical flight, ascent to heaven and the mastery of fire. Derivative forms of shamanism are found in China, Japan and the Magyar world.

Symbol A symbol is a sign that brings to mind something that is absent or imperceptible by means of a natural relationship (A. Lalande). The symbol is a representation that brings a hidden meaning to light; it is the epiphany of a mystery (G. Durand).

PART ONE
Research and Attempts at Explanation

1 Trying to Define Religion

THE EARLIEST meaning of the word religion is to be found in Cicero, who assumes a connection with the verb *relegere,* "to assemble": thus, religion is the assembling and transmitting of the ancestral worship of the gods. Since the third century, following Tertullian, the word *religio* has been adopted by Christians, who took the word to be derived from the verb *religare,* "to bind together." They thus gave the concept of religion its Western meaning: "a set of doctrines and practices that forms man's relationship with the divinity."

Beginning in the nineteenth century, the discovery and study of the religions of Asia and other countries prepared the way for a wider concept of religion and for definitions which varied according to the different cultural and religious contexts of the peoples involved, but also according to each author's ideology.

Sociologists identify three essential elements in religion: a system of beliefs, the sacred, and the community. Thus, according to E. Durkheim (1912), religion is "an integral system of beliefs and practices relative to sacred things . . . beliefs and practices that unite in a single moral community called the Church all those who adhere to it." On the other hand, psychologists underline three other aspects: man's aspiration to values; his conscious reliance on a force that maintains such values; and his behavior in pursuing them by means of this force.

The rediscovery and study of humanity's immense spiritual heritage have led twentieth-century historians to take the universality and importance of the religious phenomenon into consideration. This new perspective has focused attention on religion as a real experience of the sacred. At the center of this experience is man, who by virtue of it is called *homo religiosus.* As part of the various historic and cultural stages of the growth of humanity, *homo religiosus* has left innumerable traces of his beliefs and practices, his myths, rites and symbols that bear witness to his conception of the gods, the cosmos and human destiny. In this perspective, all religions are inseparable from *homo religiosus.*

1

1. Detail of sun worship with a praying man, his hands raised, beside a solar disk. This is a reproduction of a cave inscription dating back to the Camunian civilization of the Neolithic period. Valcamonica, Italy.

Christianity

Islam

Primitive Religions

China: Confucianism,
Buddhism, Daoism

Hinduism

Japan: Shintoism
Buddhism, New religions

Buddhism

Judaism

Areas of low
population density

Parseeism

Sikhism

2. This map gives an overall idea of the
present-day distribution of the main religious
confessions.

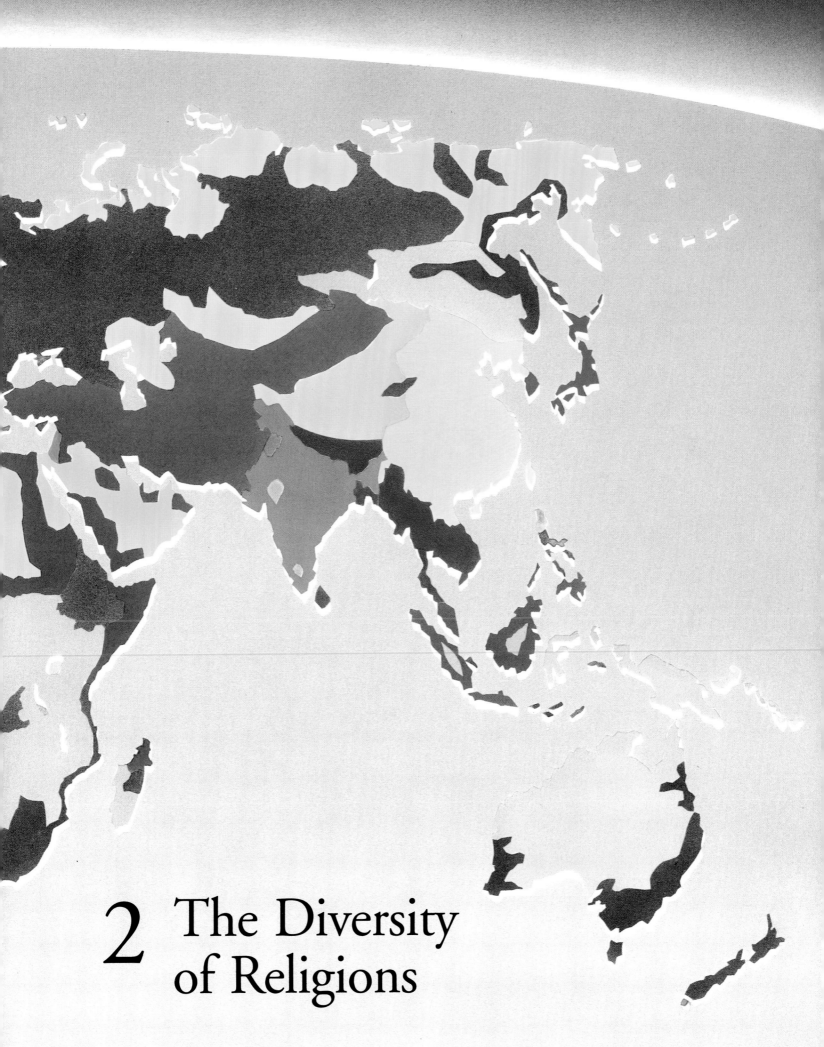

2 The Diversity of Religions

THE COMPARATIVE historical research begun by Max Müller and continued by the different schools of the history of religions has made it possible to compile two maps: the first indicates world religions according to geographical distribution, and the second classifies them according to type.

Each classification sets out from a series of principles, while disregarding certain elements considered to be secondary. Many typologies based on ideologies that were fashionable in the nineteenth century have since fallen into disuse. This is the case of the evolutionist typologies that were influenced by the positivism of Auguste Comte (1798-1857) and that understood the development of religions as occurring in three stages: the animistic religions which subsequently gave rise to polytheism, which in its turn generated monotheism.

A classification founded on the comparative method, modified by the theory of sociocultural influences, tried to establish a typology according to "religious horizons" (J. Murphy). Zoroastrianism, Judaism, Christianity, Islam, Buddhism and Confucianism were all said to belong to the prophetic and monotheistic horizon. As reflections of the political and social organization of the different peoples, the great polytheistic religions were said to correspond to the horizons of the ancient civilizations: Rome, Greece, Egypt, Sumero-Babylonia, and Indus. The so-called "monistic" religions are said to have originated within the agricultural horizon, whereas the animist religions are identified with the tribal horizon.

There is another typology that proceeds according to three elements: the importance of ethnological thought and the development of civilizations; the development of revelation in the religious history of humanity; and the originality of Christianity (A. Anwander). A first category comprises what are called natural religions, those of the peoples of central Asia who were still without writing. Next come the religions of the great world civilizations, which are based on writing. These are followed by the world religions: Buddhism, Judaism, and Islam. Finally there is Christianity, a religion that embodies complete originality.

R. C. Zaehner (1913-1974) of Oxford formulated a distinction between the great mystical religions and the great prophetic ones. In the mystical religions the accent is placed on the interior experience of transcendence: this is the case of Hinduism, Buddhism and Taoism. By contrast, the prophetic religions are characterized by a revelation perceived as the word of God. Zoroastrianism, Judaism and Islam are all of the prophetic type. Mystical theology and prophetism converge in Christianity.

In pursuing the historical and comparative research of Raffaele Pettazzoni (1883-1959), Ugo Bianchi of Rome has established a twofold historical typology. The first focuses on the constitutive phenomena of religion: beliefs, myths, rites, institutions. The second concerns historical and cultural processes that are active within the various religions and the religious forms that are specific to given periods and cultures: polytheism, the religiousness of prehistoric man, dualism, gnosticism. What clearly emerges from this research is the way religions can be divided up into two groups: the ethnic religions that arise in particular cultures and do not derive from a founder; and the religions that do have a founder, such as Buddhism, Zoroastrianism, Judaism, Christianity and Islam. The notion of analogy that appears again and again from the earliest documentary sources plays a part in the construction of this twofold typology.

Recent comparative research has placed the accent on two factors that are important in the religious history of humanity: culture and revelation. Religious events are linked to cultural events, and in particular to their symbolic aspect, since *homo religiosus* has also been a *homo symbolicus* since early prehistoric times. Thus we have a remarkable number of religions in which *homo religiosus* is bent on seeking the divine, the transcendent, the traces of God. From Abraham on, there is evidence to show how *homo religiosus* relates to God, from whom he receives a message, a revelation that is destined to orient his life, his behavior, his salvation. Culture and revelation are both fundamental for the typology of religions and the study of their origins.

3 The Discovery of Religions

THE CONQUESTS of Alexander the Great (356-323 B.C.) were crucial to the meeting of the Greek world with the religions of the Near and Middle East, those of Egypt, Anatolia, Syria, Canaan, Iran and India. The expansion of the Roman Empire further encouraged this process, favoring contacts with the religions of central Europe, Gaul and Germany. Thanks to the Christian apologists, the fathers of the Church and the writers of the first centuries of the Christian era, numerous documents and texts pertaining to these religions were saved. The evangelization of the Franks, the Germans and the Scandinavians preserved fragments of their beliefs and their forms of worship. The West first became acquainted with Islam through the Crusades, while the medieval universities contributed significantly to early evaluation of the documentation that had been brought together.

Pico della Mirandola's *De omni re scibili* (1486) contained considerable learning about ancient religions, and soon after it was published the Renaissance humanists engaged in what was to become a widespread resurgence of interest in antiquity, including a critical review of pre-Christian religions. Then, in 1492, the discovery of the New World introduced yet more unfamiliar cultures and religions. During the seventeenth century the missionary activity of the Jesuits opened up contact with the cultures of China, India and North America, and a huge quantity of documents were brought back to Europe. In France they were put to scientific use in the *Mémoires de Trévoux*, a comparative inquiry into ancient religions. In 1701 Louis XIV entrusted the Académie Française with the task of studying the religious thought of antiquity. Thus a movement begun by the Florentine humanists was continued by the Paris scholars. This was still the dawn of the science of religions, and it was greatly aided by the important contribution of the Christian missions in Asia, Africa and America during the course of the eighteenth century. Controversies that arose from the heated debates of the Enlightenment gave the movement further impetus.

J. F. Lafitau (1681-1746) and Ch. de Brosses (1709-1777) were the founders of religious ethnology, and G. B. Vico (1668-1744) embraced a wide range of mythological sources in presenting in his *Scienza Nuova* the first hermeneutic of myths, cultures and civilizations. During the eighteenth century two major discoveries were to unleash a wave of Orientalism. In 1730 the Jesuit Jean Calmette rediscovered two Veda; in 1732 he found the other two. By 1730 these first manuscripts had found their way into the Royal Library in Paris, where they gave impetus to a continual series of discoveries and ultimately to the birth of Indianism and the foundation of Asian societies in India, Paris and London. During one of his journeys, A. H. Anquetil-Duperron managed to gain access to the Parsee community in Bombay, and in 1762 brought a batch of 180 manuscripts back with him to Paris. In 1771 he then published the first translation of the *Zend-Avesta*, which provided access to the Zoroastrian religion.

In the wake of colonial expansion and the development of the Church's missionary activity, nineteenth-century Europe was able to rediscover an important part of the religious heritage of humanity. As in the case of Hinduism, it was the missionaries' discovery of Buddhism that prepared the way for the scientific discovery. The *pali* manuscripts of Siam, Tibet, China and Nepal and the works of Chézy, of Eugène Burnouf and Abel Rémusat in Paris, of B. H. Hodgson in London, and those of many other researchers were able to unveil the true face of Buddhism. Toward the middle of the nineteenth century the confusion between Hinduism and Buddhism was finally overcome.

3. *Jean-François Champollion (1790-1823), the founder of Egyptology.*
4. *Max Müller (1823-1900), founder of the study of comparative religions and eminent scholar of Hinduism.*

3

4

11

ATHARVAVEDA   YAJURVEDA

Upanishad   Upanishad

Aranyaka   Aranyaka

Brāhmana   Brāhmana

RIGVEDA   SAMAVEDA

Upanishad   Upanishad

Aranyaka   Aranyaka

Brāhmana   Brāhmana

6

5. Hammurabi in front of the stele being engraved with the famous codex in cuneiform writing that was named after him. This is the most complete Babylonian codex to have come down to us. Fundamental for our knowledge of Mesopotamian culture, it is now kept at the Louvre in Paris. It was discovered between 1901 and 1902 by J. De Morgan during the Susa excavations and was transcribed by V. Scheil.

6. The most important source of information about the earliest stage of the religion of India is known in short as the Veda (in Sanskrit it means "knowledge"). Here a tree symbolizes the various collections of the Veda that were written on rectangular sheets, as shown at the base. Below, a Brahman is shown meditating. Largely thanks to the works of R. Roth and M. Müller, the West became acquainted with the Veda in the mid-19th century, when the Rig-Veda was first published (1849-1874).

8

8. *Example of Egyptian hieroglyphic writing. In 1822 Champollion managed to decipher it, thus making the study of ancient Egyptian religion possible.*

9. *One of the two sides of the Phaistos disk (1700-1600 B.C.) discovered in 1908 by Pernier. The ideographic signs have still not been deciphered.*

9

7

7. *The Sanchi stupa (3rd century B.C., Bhilsa, India), discovered in 1818. It is the most famous of the characteristic Buddhist funerary monuments that were very widespread in the areas of Buddhist influence and have provided scholars with precious information regarding funerary practices.*

In 1822, Jean-François Champollion deciphered the famous Rosetta stone, thus revealing the voice of pharaonic Egypt. The stelae, sarcophagi, pyramids and tombs disclosed the secret of their inscriptions. In Germany the brothers Wilhelm and Alexander von Humboldt played an essential role in the rediscovery of the religions of the American Indians. Excavations began in Mesopotamia in 1840, and the archaeologists' discoveries followed one after another in quick succession. Thousands of cuneiform tablets ended up in museums, and then in 1857 H. Rawlinson, E. Hincks and J. Oppert finally managed to decipher cuneiform writing, thus providing Assyriology with a statute. The study of the *Avesta* continued, while in France Abel Rémusat and S. Julien began to study Confucianism and Taoism.

Sinology was to reach a decisive stage with the work of Paul Pelliot. In the Mediterranean area excavations were begun in Palestine and Syria, and explorers flocked to Egypt as new archaeological and epigraphical research was carried out in the Greco-Roman world. In France, Jacques Boucher of Perthes discovered a number of flints shaped to form tools, and in 1846 declared that prehistoric man had existed at the time of the great animal species long extinct. This was the beginning of prehistoric research. Religious ethnology gained new impetus from the continual discovery of preliterate populations in Asia, Africa and Australia.

At the start of the nineteenth century, the science of religions began looking for a path of its own. During the last two decades of the century the history of religion was recognized as a proper field of learning thanks to university chairs and the periodical reviews founded in England, Holland, France and Belgium. Outstanding among the dozens of specialists was Friedrich Max Müller (1823-1900), founder of a proper comparative science of religions. A pioneer in Indo-European studies, he also published the monumental *Sacred Books of the East* (51 vols., 1872-1895).

13

4 Peoples without Writing and Their Religiosity

IN HIS *Moeurs des sauvages amériquains comparées aux moeurs des premiers temps,* published in 1724, J. F. Lafitau suggested that contemporary primitive peoples should be studied in order to understand archaic man and his religion. In so doing he underlined the importance of human nature, of the role of mysteries and initiation, and of religion in primitive societies. Adopting the same method, Ch. de Brosses published *Du culte des dieux fétiches* (1760), in which he argued that the origins of religions should be sought in fetishism: the worship of upright stones, animals, trees, plants, rivers, the sun and the stars. In this context a fetish is not a symbol, as it is in polytheism, but an active presence for archaic man who hopes to attain salvation from his anguish by means of certain rites.

During the nineteenth century the discovery of hundreds of populations that still had no system of writing gave impulse to religious ethnology and anthropology as well as to various theories concerning "the religion of primitive man" and the origins of religion. Auguste Comte, the father of positivism, merely adopted the fetishist theory developed by Ch. de Brosses. During the course of the eighteenth century, J. J. Rousseau (1712-1778) in France and the Sturm und Drang movement in Germany rejected the *Aufklärung* and instead exalted nature and the rights of the heart. All the scholars who identified with the Romantic movement followed much the same path: Ch. Fr. Dupuis (1742-1809), J.-G. Herder (1744-1803), Fr. Creuzer (1771-1858), J. J. Gorres (1776-1848). F. Schleiermacher (1768-1834) considered intuition of the universe and experience of the infinite as the common origin of all religions. Max Müller's school of comparative mythology focused on Indo-European myths. Convinced that man has always had an intuition of the divine and an idea of the infinite, Müller suggested that the great phenomena of nature act as symbols that can stimulate a sense of the infinite in man. The religion of "primitive" peoples thus derives from and can be explained by the naturalist myths. At the end of the nineteenth century, the German school of astral mythology (H. Winckler, E. Stucken, F. Delitsch) drew inspiration from the Babylonion myths and showed appreciation for Mesopotamian astrology. The remarkable unity of mythology was held to prove that among primitive peoples the myths concerning the sky and stars constitute the fundamental elements of primordial religions.

In a series of notable works Lucien Lévy-Bruhl (1857-1939) tried to explain the religion of primitive peoples on the basis of their mentality, which he understood in terms of collective representations, of primordial relationships based on emotion, attempts at partaking in the mysterious powers of the mythical ancestor, and a uniformity of emotions in the presence of invisible beings. Masks, rhythms, dances and songs create a collective emotion aimed at establishing a communion with the "supernatural" powers. The function of the myth is to assure the presence of the mythical ancestor of the clan in order to imitate him and partake of his life.

In *L'expérience mystique et les symboles chez les primitifs* (Paris, 1938), Lévy-Bruhl tried to approach the religious experience of primitive man by means of symbolism. The symbolic function is seen as a way of representing the invisible being. Through this representation man partakes of the invisible powers, which would explain the permanence

10

of sacred sites, the multiplicity of the rupestrian inscriptions and prehistoric paintings, drawings and inscriptions, mysterious stones and ancestor symbols. It is by means of symbols that primitive man could unite with mysterious powers and with realities that do not belong to the sphere of nature.

Lévy-Bruhl argues that the mentality of primitive man was prelogical and that this is what differentiates him from civilized man. Primitive man would have had a form of magical and religious thought that eludes our categories and was not disoriented by contradiction. When the author talks about the supernatural or the mystical, he is not referring to the transcendent but to the supersensible. In fact, philosopher Lévi-Bruhl places religion on a horizontal level, without contemplating transcendency. What is interesting about his study, carried out on the basis of information gathered indirectly rather than from primary source material, is the way it insists on the role of the symbol as a means of participating in "mystical powers." This fact is useful for understanding *homo religiosus* in the prewriting stage for imagining his experience of the sacred. However, the author's position is undermined by his positivist presuppositions and the corresponding view that all religion is mere superstition.

Alongside such ideologically based studies, the late nineteenth century also saw the emergence of a historical movement within the sphere of ethnology. The authors of this movement favored fieldwork, the study of various peoples with no writing, the publication of monographs, and inquiries into human behavior and institutions. Among these ethnologists and anthropologists mention should be made of Summer Maines (1821-1881), A. Lyall (1835-1911), F. W. Maitland (1850-1906) and W. R. Rivers (1864-1928) in England; A. de Quatrefages (1810-1892), who worked out the "proof by the convergence of evidence" in France; and in Germany F. Ratzel (1844-1904), author of the theory of migrations, and Léo Frobenius (1873-1938), father of the concept of "cultural circle" in ethnology, a concept that was to have extraordinary repercussions on ethnological studies.

10. Left: Sanana mask (Touyogou).
11. Buguturu altar. These two works are products of Dogon culture that still occupies a region largely located in what is now Niger. The drawings are by M. Griaule, author of the most important study of Dogon masks (Masques Dogons, Paris, 1963). Griaule describes the Dogon religion as based on ancestor worship. "Totemism" is an expression of immortal ancestor worship, in the sense that they resuscitate after death (lébé): the altars are dedicated to the ancestors and the masks are a means for communicating with them.

11

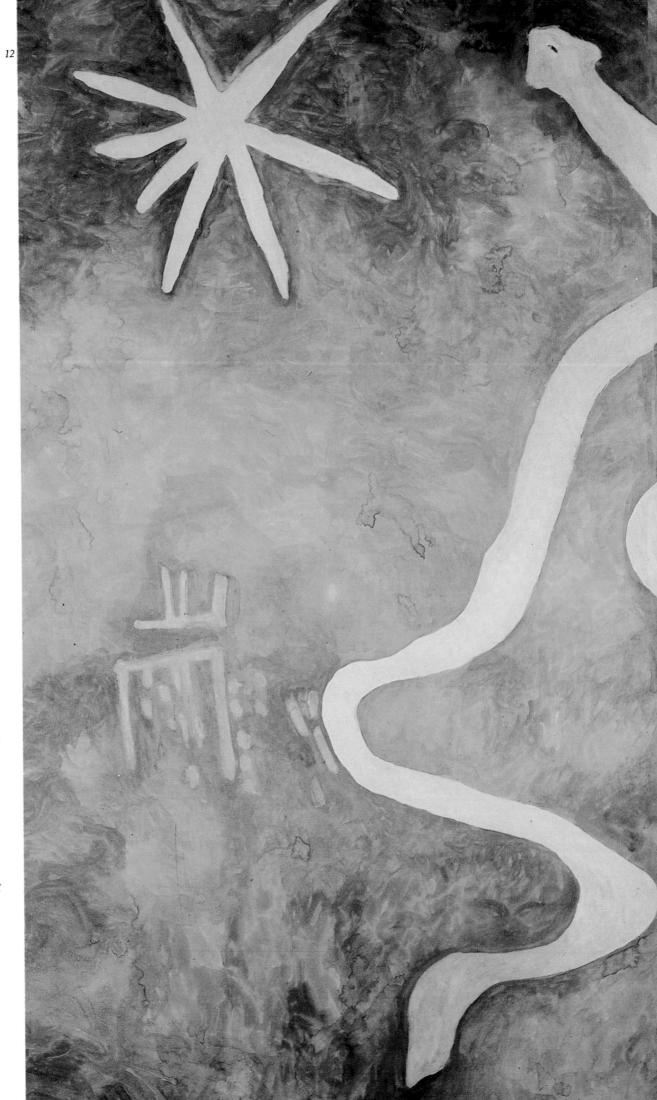

12

12. Example of an African "mythogram" (see glossary). This is a reproduction of a cave painting in Malawi, near Mphunzi. The archaeologist E. Anati relates how the Bantu guide described this painting as an origin myth. The snake and the iguana have mated, thus producing three eggs: one large, one medium, one small. From each egg a tribe is born: one large, one medium, one small. In Anati's view the radial sign at the top left could indicate the mythical place where the event happened.

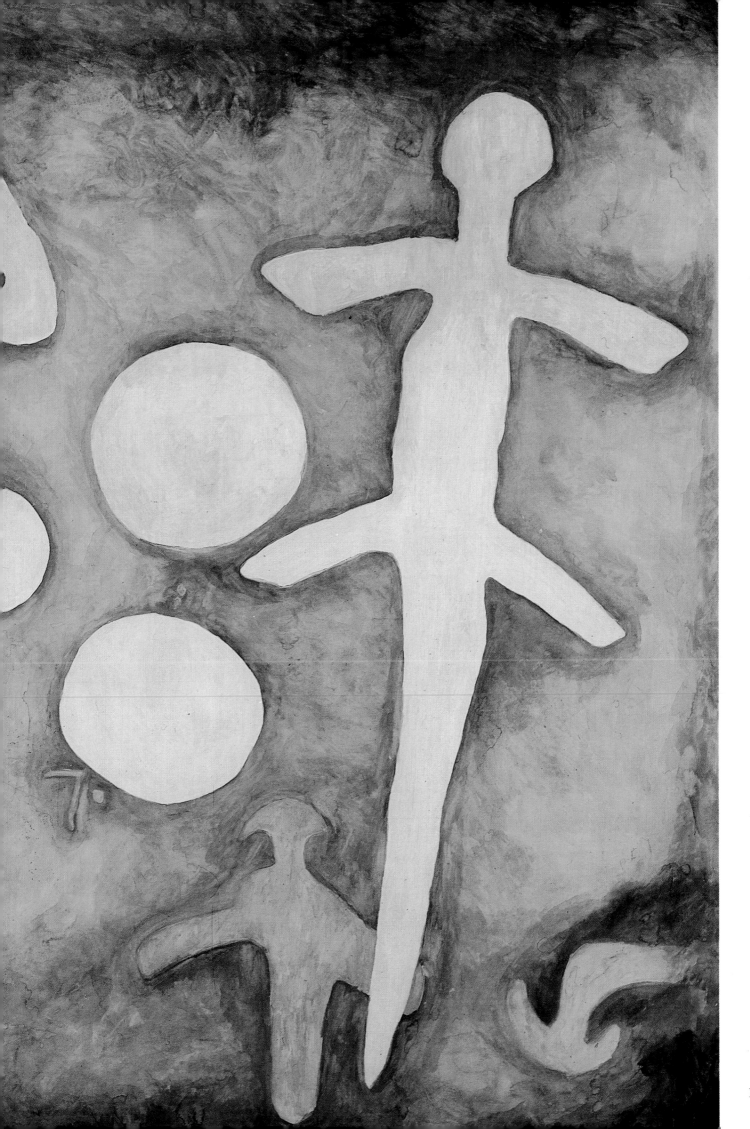

17

5 Mana, Totem and Taboo

The Vocabulary

Mana is a Polynesian term, first introduced to the West by W. Williams in 1814, then by R. Codrington, an ethnologist working in Melanasia. Codrington passed it on to M. Müller and considered it of generalized use in the Pacific. *Mana* indicates a force, an influence, an impersonal power possessed by spirits that can be communicated through water, a stone, or a bone. Since 1892, the term has been adopted by certain ethnologists and anthropologists (J. H. King, R. R. Marett) who have considered it as an important category in the religious experience of primitive peoples. It is thus identified with the *manitou* of the Algonquins, with the *orenda* of the Iroquois, or with the Hindu *Brahman*. The evolutionist movement considered it an essential concept in the development of religion. Recent archaeological research has shown that the interpretation provided at the beginning of the century is in fact erroneous: today in Melanesia *mana* stands for the efficacious power of a person who is able to accomplish extraordinary deeds.

Totem derives from the Ojibwa, an Algonquin tribe of North America, and indicates kinship while designating the exogamous clan in relation to a "guardian" animal. The term *totem* also indicates the guardian animal attributed to a person. These are ethnographic phenomena. Australian totemism involves a relationship between a natural species and a kinship group, Polynesian totemism a relationship between an animal and a kinship group. In *Le Totémisme aujourd'hui* (Paris, 1962), Cl. Lévi-Strauss shows that what is called totemism eludes any general definition, and that the relevant phenomena should simply be placed within the sphere of peoples without writing. In Oceania and America totem poles placed at the entrance to villages represent the succession of the clan's ancestors. In the history of religions, totemism may mean either the set of theories that have claimed to distinguish in the totem the origin of religion or the basis of behavior and institutions in archaic society.

Taboo is a Melanasian and Polynesian term. It stands for the limits pertaining to particular people (kings, priests), things (food, ritual objects), activities, sanctuaries and sacred places, and defines the rules to be observed whenever these limits are approached or neglected in order to ensure protection or prohibition. Introduced to the West by Captain Cook in 1777, the term became part of J. G. Frazer's inquiries. In 1911 Frazer used the term *taboo* as a universal religious category to indicate the negative or prohibitive dimension of the sacred: *taboo* thus stands for the separation that exists between the sacred and profane worlds. Freud referred to this concept in 1913 in *Totem and Taboo*. Current ethnological studies have become highly critical of such interpretations, showing that in Polynesia *taboo* also has many nonreligious meanings. Supporters of evolutionism in religion have used all three terms, *mana, totem* and *taboo*, almost interchangeably to develop their hypotheses concerning the origins and meaning of primitive religions. Such confusion regarding the experience of the sacred is now becoming a thing of the past.

The Theories

In *Primitive Marriage,* published in 1866, J. F. McLennan introduced the phenomenon of exogamy to the scientific world and claimed that it was religious in character. Then in 1869, in *The Worship of Animals and Plants,* he tried to show that totemism is a religion and the origin of all forms of animal and plant worship. J. G. Frazer (1854-1941) took over this theory: convinced of the absurdity of primitive beliefs, the British anthropologist, whose research was conducted exclusively in libraries, argued that totemism was a religious system comprising different archaic beliefs (*Totemism and Exogamy,* 4 vols., London, 1911). Frazer argued that such primitive religion must be the amalgam of clan organization, of the totemic denominations of the clans,

13. *Sigmund Freud (1856-1939), the father of psychoanalysis. His theories had a great influence on studies of religions in postwar Europe and America in particular.*

14. *Mircea Eliade (1907-1986) adopted a threefold approach in his studies of religion, taking into account history, phenomenology and hermeneutics. He described the historic and trans-historic figure of homo religiosus and showed the importance of his cultural and religious message.*

of belief in a relationship between the totem and the clan members, and of the prohibition to eat the totem animal or plant, except in sacrificial ceremonies. He obtained this last idea from W. Robertson Smith (*The Religion of the Semites,* London, 1889).

Following long discussions and much opposition, in 1927 Frazer published a summary of his views on totemic religion in *Man, God and Immortality* (London), claiming that the first stage of the evolution of religion was magic, that is, the personification of natural forces and the creation of a multitude of spirits. The gradual development of polytheistic religions and forms of worship ultimately leading to monotheism derived from the creation of kings, priests and divinities. In France Salomon Reinach (1858-1932) extended the reach of Frazerism through his *Orpheus. Histoire générale des religions* (Paris, 1909; 1931) and *Cultes mythes et religions* (Paris, 3 vols., 1905; 1922); the same was done in Germany by W. Wundt (1832-1920) in his monumental *Völkerpsychologie* (10 vols., 1910-1920).

Emile Durkheim (1858-1917) saw in totemism the religious system of primitive peoples, indeed the very origin of religion (*Les formes élémentaires de la vie religieuse,* Paris, 1912). Influenced by A. Comte, H. Spencer and W. Wundt, he envisaged society as a superior metaphysical reality, a mechanism that transcends the individual and is animated by a collective consciousness created by the set of beliefs and feelings common to a community. Religion he thus conceived as a natural manifestation of human activity. As a positivist, Durkheim maintained that the religious phenomenon was shaped by social behavior and was therefore bound to exclude the supernatural, mystery, and the divinity. According to religious thought, the world is divided into two realms, the sacred and the profane, such that the objective, universal and eternal cause of religious experience is society. As an emanation of the collective consciousness, religion is a universal fact and a necessary phenomenon. Its function consists in administering the sacred.

Durkheim chose to identify totemism as the most primitive and elementary religion. For totemism was the religion of the clan, for which the totem stood as the absolute representation of the sacred. The source, heart and energy of totemic religion was thus the mana, the sacred principle, the anonymous and impersonal force present in all members of the clan. Mana is therefore seen as the raw material of all religions and the source from which societies have created spirits, demons, genies and gods. The totem expresses and symbolizes the mana; it is the hypostasis of the clan. By means of a transfer of power, the latter creates the sacred and is destined to administer it. The sacred generates the form of worship with the rites and practices that continually tend to knit society together. Marcel Mauss (1873-1950) and Henri Hubert (1872-1927), both disciples of Durkheim, focused their inquiries on the study of the social functions of the sacred, making mana coincide with the sacred and extending the totemist concept to all religions, including the religions of the book. For two decades their ideas inspired a number of historians of religion.

Influenced by both Frazer and Wundt, in his studies of taboo S. Freud found analogies between taboo and obsessive neuroses. In fact, breaking a taboo creates feelings of remorse that in time give rise to the moral conscience. Moving from one subject to another, Freud then deals with totemism, which he conceives as an explanation of religion and its origins. Referring to Robertson Smith's notions of the importance of sacrifice and the totemic meal, Freud suggests a relationship to the origins of mankind, to the first feast of humanity that took place when the primitive horde of the sons assassinated the father in order to possess the women. Totemic religion is thus seen as the product of the sons' feelings of guilt: it consists of the effort made to suffocate such feelings and, at the same time, to bring about reconciliation. In Freud's view, this primordial event tied to the origins of totemic religion later effects all the religions of humanity (*Totem and Taboo,* 1913).

15

15. *Picture taken from a bas-relief on a platform surrounding a pelota court in the ceremonial center of Totonac culture at Tajín, Veracruz state, Mexico.*

Between 400 and 700 of the present era, Totonac culture expressed the fundamental religious elements that the Europeans found among the Aztecs and the Mayans of the Yucatan. Pelota was a ritual game that ended with the sacrifice of one of the two team captains, as described in this panel. The sacrificial blood was food for the gods. While the sacrificed man received the ritual pulque drink as he rose to the next world, the god of rain filled the vat of the sacred drink and guaranteed the fertility of the fields and the renewal of life. This is a clear example of a sacrificial rite aimed at ensuring divine intervention.

16. *Reconstruction of a Haida Indian dwelling and totem poles in the garden of the Museum of Anthropology, Vancouver, on the Canadian Pacific coast. In the tradition of the various Indian peoples of the northwest coast of North America (British Columbia), totem poles adopted a sequence of sculpted and painted animal (zoomorphic) and human (anthropomorphic) figures to express the sacral presence of the ancestors and their descendents for Indian populations and families.*

17. *Great monolithic sculpture of a moai on Easter Island in the Pacific, to the west of Chile. This was one of the foremost artistic expressions of the first long period of Rapanui civilization. The moai is a deified ancestor guardian of the universe. Having been discovered and populated in the 5th century A.D., Easter Island had no contact with other parts of the world for one thousand years.*

6 Evolutionism as an Explanation of Religion

THE SCHOLARS of the nineteenth century focused largely on the progress of humanity, the process of human development through the various stages of its evolution. In his *Phenomenology of Mind* (1807), G. W. F. Hegel (1770-1851) explained how history reveals an endless progress of the mind. Having adopted and adapted an idea expressed by G. B. Vico (1668-1744) in his *Scienza nuova* (1725) whereby the concept of the three ages of man is transferred to history, A. Comte (1798-1857) argued that the law of the three states (theological, metaphysical and positivist) is the law of the evolution of the mind and of society. Once free of myths and speculation about God, man could finally fully devote himself to science and the cult of humanity. Priests, the secularized sacraments, and the new dogma of positivist philosophy would guarantee the organic unity of society. Comte was thus preparing the way for positivism, perceiving evolution as the law shaping the religious history of mankind.

Herbert Spencer (1820-1902) was interested in the relationships between science, society and religion, and adopted biological evolution as a model in his research into society and religion. In his *Principles of Sociology* (3 vols., 1876-1896), he explained how initial atheism gave way to primitive religion founded on ancestor worship, in its turn supplanted by polytheism and then monotheism, which were followed by positivism. In primitive societies man thought of the hereafter as a place in which the ancestors make up a society of spirits able to influence living beings. During the course of the evolution of society, these spirits are transformed into gods. In Spencer's view, religion originates in ancestor worship, and the influence it exercises over man is due to the fear of the dead, thought of as spirits who can act in the world of the living. To influence such interventions man invented prayer, expiation, offerings of food, and all the other religious rites.

Already in 1767, N. S. Bergier had suggested that fetishism and idolatry should be explained in terms of the primitive mentality that saw nature as populated with genies and spirits *(Les dieux du paganisme)*. One century later this theory was taken up again by E. B. Tylor (1832-1917), the founder of British anthropology. A great traveler and an intelligent explorer, he collected wide-ranging evidence, analyzed it with insight, and classified it neatly. Tylor studied the vestiges of ancient cultures in order to compare them with the customs of his own times. In 1865 he published the outcome of his inquiries into the origins of the history of man, opposing the theory of degradation with that of transformism, taken from Darwin. In *Primitive Culture* (1971), he argued that primitive man can be placed at the beginning of a process of uninterrupted psychic evolution from the archaic stage to that of civilized man. This was tantamount to a manifesto of cultural and religious evolutionism and of animism seen as the integral explanation of religion and religions. The point of departure is primitive man's discovery of the notion of the soul. Tylor saw this as having come about through observations of sleep, sickness and death, and, somewhat differently, through dreams and visions. The primitive mentality applies this notion of soul to all the beings of the cosmos: thus we have animism, which begins with ancestor worship and then spreads into polytheism. Polytheism then generates the pantheon of great cultures, and ends up by flowing into monotheism. Tylor's animism was to achieve support from many ethnologists and historians of religion — even the biblicists — who held this religious stage to be at the origin of religion and religions.

Tylor's work comprises many laudable aspects: the insistence on the discovery of the soul on the part of primitive peoples and hence the importance of funeral practices that appeared very early and bear witness to faith in the afterlife; the acquisition of the idea of mind separate from matter that would ultimately lead to man's discovery of the Supreme Being as a personal God; the search for the psychic unity of humanity; the theory of the continuance of the past that makes comparative research possible; and the elimination of the insurmountable abyss separating civilized man from primitive man. Tylor's work gave rise to important research and many published monographs regarding peoples without writing. The notion of animism was to persist during the twentieth century, but with many new contributions and some fundamental adjustments.

The weakness in Tylor's work — as indeed in that of Spencer — lies at the level of transformist theory. Setting out from the Darwinian framework of biological evolution, Tylor maps the evolution from

18. The naturalist Charles Robert Darwin (1809-1882). In 1859 he expounded for the first time his theory of natural selection in biological evolution in The Origin of the Species. *This theory influenced the study of the origins of religion during the course of the 19th century.*

18

animism to monotheism with one straight hard line. The process is thus conceived in deterministic terms, without taking into account the numerous cultural influences involved in the development of *Homo sapiens*. The disciples and followers of Tylor were to turn such evolutionism into a dogma and an ideology that culminated in the totemism of Frazer, Durkheim and Freud. Frazer's *Golden Bough* of 1890 had grown to twelve volumes in 1911-1915: according to this work, religion and culture evolved from the totem in a deterministic, uniform manner. The entire output of Wundt, Durkheim and Mauss is conceived within this same evolutionistic perspective.

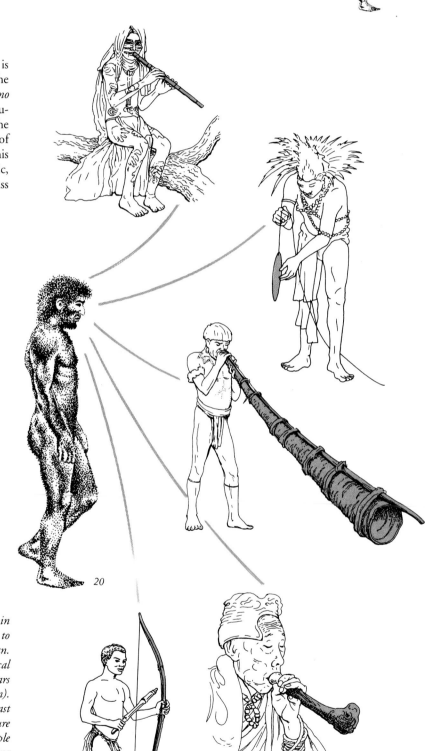

19. *The creatures portrayed above illustrate some of the major steps in biological evolution, from the invertebrates to the first vertebrates, then to fish, amphibians, reptiles, birds, mammals, and finally to man.*
20. *With man a new kind of evolution begins that is no longer biological in character. Since man's first appearance in Africa over two million years ago there has been no further variety in the species (biological evolution). Instead, the* Homo *species alone has persisted. Evolution and the vast differentiation that exists within humankind has been cultural in nature and cannot be explained in terms of biological evolutionism. The example illustrated here shows different musical stances and instruments. Starting from the top there is the Sioux flute player of South Dakota (United States), a rhomb player from Papua (New Guinea), a Tikuna Indian (Brazil) with a bark trumpet, a Tibetan musician playing a trumpet made from a human femur, and last a Basuto bow player (Lesotho). This same creativity and ability to generate different expressions, mythologies and rites is also to be found in the cultural and religious evolution of mankind.*

7 Toward New Paths: Beyond the Evolutionist, Ethnological and Sociological Hypotheses

TOWARD THE end of the nineteenth century, a number of scholars began to reject these explanations of religion and its origins. While the Romantic movement emphasized sentiment and argued that the divine derived from the language of nature and its influence on man's behavior, the supporters of positivist theories tried to turn philosophy into a sort of religion, denying all ideas of transcendence. Proponents of atheistic materialism such as Ludwig Feuerbach (1804-1872) and Karl Marx (1818-1883) considered religion to be an alienation of the human mind and claimed that God was dead. The evolutionist school applied the framework of biological evolu-

tion to religion, excluding all ideas of the supernatural in its effort to identify the origins of religion in elements such as mana and totem. Such elementary evidence was thus used to interpret the entire religious history of humanity. Numerous ethnologists and anthropologists undertaking fieldwork gave rise to a historical movement that focused on analyzing the religious, social, and cultural data pertaining to peoples without writing.

In Germany F. Ratzel (1844-1904) described surviving primitive peoples, creating the migration theory and illustrating the unity of the human species. In 1898 his pupil Léo Frobenius (1873-1938) published his seminal work *Der Ursprung der afrikanischen Kulturen* and launched the idea of cultural circles. The two ethnologists were looking for the geographical and cultural origins of such evidence: the material civilization, the institutions, myths and entire cultural symbology. Fritz Graebner (1877-1934) and Bernard Ankermann (1859-

21. The Sabean temple of Awwan, located south of modern Marib in Yemen. It is dedicated to the moon goddess Iluruquh and dates to around 500 B.C.

21

1953) used these results to create the historical cultural method in ethnology. The outcome was a positive method that studied and compared the evidence in order to identify relationships between civilizations. These latter were first studied from the point of view of their origins, emanations and interpretation. Next came analyses of the various types of civilization, their distribution in space, their alternation in time and the causes of their evolution. All this would lead to inquiries into the historic origins of cultural formations. Numerous research projects were carried out in Australia, Africa and America, and the data collected contradicted the evolutionist and sociological hypotheses.

In 1898 Andrew Lang made a crucial break with evolutionist theory in embracing the historical and cultural research method. In his book *The Making of Religion* he formulated the hypothesis of a primitive belief in a Supreme Being. The ethnologist Wilhelm Schmidt (1868-1954) wished to verify this hypothesis, and with a number of collaborators set out on a vast research project studying the Australian aboriginals. The resulting articles were published in the journal *Anthropos* between 1908 and 1912 and later collected in a book entitled *Der Ursprung der Gottesidee* (The origin of the idea of God) in 1912. They made an enormous impact on the scientific world. Research continued for many decades, and *Der Ursprung des Gottesidee* expanded into a weighty work in twelve large volumes that were published between 1912 and 1954. Schmidt founded the "Wiener Schule der Völkerkunde," and the number of ethnologists to embrace his thesis increased from year to year: "Belief in a Supreme Being is at the origin of the religious thought of many archaic peoples. We find this belief in the primitive cultures of the Pygmies of Africa and Asia, among the Bushmen, in Tierra del Fuego, in southeast Australia and in the primitive societies of the Arctic and North America." The works of the "Wiener Schule" made a mark on the first half of the twentieth century and gave rise to a new type of field research in religious ethnology with proponents such as W. Koppers, A. Closs and P. Schebesta.

Alongside religious ethnology, the history of religions was also developing, likewise focusing on archaic peoples and the origins of religious thought. A critical study of the hypotheses used to explain the facts observed by the ethnographers tried to specify how archaic man discovered the Supreme Being. In his first works Raffaele Pettazzoni (1883-1959) insisted on the heavenly aspect of the Supreme Being (*L'essere celeste nelle credenze dei popoli primitivi*, 1922). In his view the Supreme Being is not perceived as an initial cause, but as a mythical personification of heaven. On the one hand there are the creator beings, isolated in inaccessible regions; and on the other dynamic, omniscient beings that watch over human actions. A long discussion between Schmidt and Pettazzoni attempted to circumscribe the vision of ancient man. The dossier of this debate was then taken up by Mircea Eliade (1907-1986), who felt that Schmidt's identification of the *Urmonotheismus* with the belief in an omniscient, all-powerful Creator God was excessively logical and causal in its approach. In Eliade's view, not only does the primordial Supreme Being and Creator belong to the sphere of mythical thought, but *homo religiosus* also discovered symbolic meaning in the heavenly hierophany. The sky symbolizes transcendence, power, and immutability. Heavenly symbolism thus acts as a revelation. Thanks to the works of Eliade it has been possible to place the facts within a new framework, that of the symbolism of *homo symbolicus*.

Part Two
The Religious Facts

8 The First Tools, Fire, and Rites

SINCE 1959, the scientific expeditions in Tanzania, to the south of Lake Turkana, in the Omo and Awash Valleys, in the Rift Valley of Ethiopia and in many other parts of Africa have brought to light a prodigious quantity of paleoanthropological evidence dating the emergence of *Homo habilis* (see glossary) to more than two million years ago. The inventory and detailed study of this evidence show that he was able to devote himself to systematic tool-making. Later on, *Homo erectus* (see glossary) appeared throughout Africa, Java, China and Europe. His territory covered much of the three continents. The earliest traces attributed to the *erectus* stage, discovered in East Africa to the east of Lake Turkana, date back 1,600,000 years (Y. Coppens).

Tools from this period have been found all over Africa and Eurasia. Bifacial tools appeared with *Homo erectus* and became increasingly important. Chipping the two sides of a pebble implies an awareness of and a certain desire for symmetry. An examination of the tools and what remains of the places in which they were made shows that *Homo erectus* chose his materials carefully, taking their color into account and preferring one type of stone to another, which in its turn implies a sense of the aesthetic. The deposits found at Olduvai in Tanzania and Melka Kunturé in Ethiopia have produced a few rudimentary structures of circular dwellings: portions of flattened ground, pebbles placed in a circle to support poles, the framework of huts. There is evidence to suggest that *Homo erectus* was capable of building internally structured huts: there was an area in which tools were cut, another used for the preparation of animals, and a third that served as a place of rest (J. Piveteau). Tools and habitat are the significant features of the culture. In the areas inhabited by *Homo erectus*, among the bones numerous skulls have been found with remarkably regular breaks at the base, which means that there was ritual behavior with regard to death. Fire also made its appearance with *Homo erectus*: 700,000 years ago in China, and 450,000 years ago in Europe. The use of fire reveals a psychic development inasmuch as it indicates a certain social and ritual behavior.

The convergence of these archaeological documents and their meaning tells us that *Homo erectus* was a *homo symbolicus,* aware of symmetry, possessed of aesthetic sensibility and able to invent and engage in rites concerning death and fire. He was thus aware of his creative capacity, was conscious of symbols, and endowed with both an aesthetic sense and a certain awareness of the event that death represents. In the view of Yves Coppens, there are various grounds for suggesting that *Homo habilis* might also have used language: the development of the Broca and Wernicke cerebral areas that condition the use of words, and the hunting of big game and the making of tools, two activities that presuppose communication.

In the light of the recent African discoveries which actually confirm the considerable evidence collected earlier, we can be certain that an awareness of symbols is one of the characteristics of man. His presence in Africa and Eurasia bears witness to his mobility, his routes, and his changes of place. Able to control the territory around him, he contemplated the wide horizons and the vault of heaven. Once sensitive to symbols, the creator of the first culture, conscious of his situation in the cosmos, attended the rising and the sinking of the sun. He saw the movement of the stars and the moon in its waxing and waning. Contemplation of the firmament with its daz-

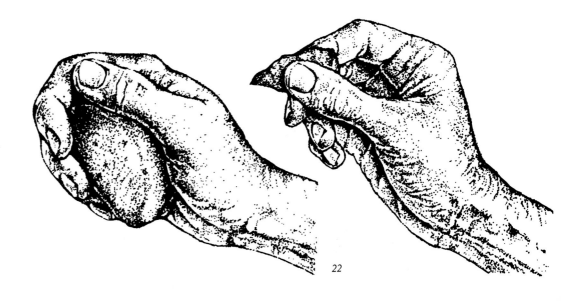

22. *The achievement of bipedism is considered one of the crucial factors in progress toward the human form. The first illustration shows the hand that develops a strong grasp once freed of its locomotor function. In the next one the thumb is pressed against the other fingers to create the precision grip necessary for the manipulation of objects.*

22

23

23. Reconstruction of the habitat of a European hunter of around 400,000 years ago, discovered by H. De Lumley at the Terra Amata site near Nice in 1966. The ground in various inhabited sites shows the mastery of fire, with the fireplace surrounded by low walls inside the huts. These dwellings had blocks of stone around the outer perimeter to keep the shape true and anchor the walls to the ground.

24. Reproductions of cave paintings at Barkly East (South Africa) by the archaeologist L. Williams. The scene shows a ritual with three sorcerers kneeling in trance. The one below, left, has antelope hooves instead of feet and arms held in the "flying" position; the one to the right holds his arms straight back, as though asking God for power.

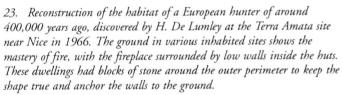

24

zling light by day and the movement of the stars and moon by night awoke in him the presentiment of the mystery of the infinite and of transcendency. Might this not constitute man's first awareness of the sacred? In Mircea Eliade's view (*Treatise*, p. 43), the heavenly vault has a heavenly meaning. Contemplation of it reveals its transcendency, power and sacredness to man, since the "symbolism of its Transcendency is deduced from the mere awareness of its infinite height." Evidence of the existence of a ritual concerning death seems to corroborate our hypothesis regarding the impact of transcendence on the consciousness of *Homo erectus*. As more discoveries have come to light there has been an increase in the evidence derived from symbols and rites, the cumulative weight of which suggests that there was indeed an experience, albeit rudimentary, of the sacred. So *Homo erectus,* who was unquestionably a *homo symbolicus,* was already a *homo religiosus,* and his presence was to establish itself during the course of the millennia of the Lower Paleolithic.

25. *Chopper pebble chipped on one side dating back around 1,700,000 years. It was found at Melka Kunturé in Ethiopia and is the product of* Homo habilis.

26. *Over one and a half million years separate the previous chopper from these skillfully chipped stones from Levallois that date back around 120,000-100,000 years. Such implements belong to Neanderthal man. In archaeological terms, this achievement signals the dawn of modern man.*

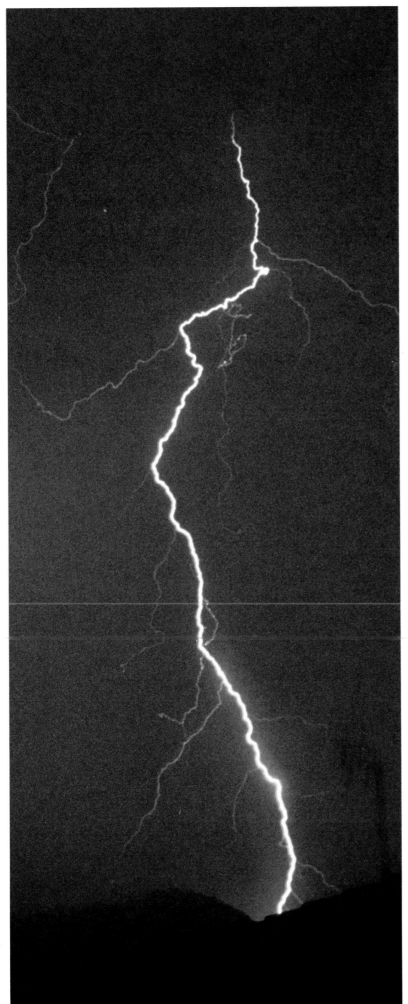

27. *Lightning. Prehistoric man's concern with the vault of heaven and atmospheric phenomena is likely to have inspired his interest in natural fires.*

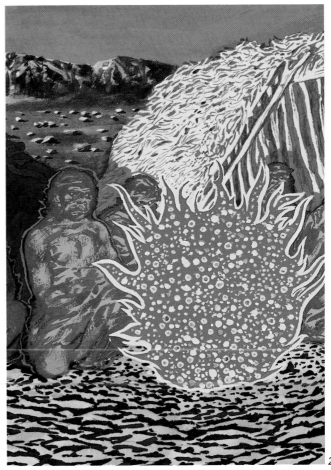

28. *Artist's conception of men gathered around the fire at night. Such occasions provided a means of social interaction.*

9 Archaic Funerary Rites: Neanderthal Man and Upper Paleolithic Man

IN 1857 some laborers found the remains of a human skeleton at Neanderthal, near Düsseldorf. Other similar-looking fossils were discovered in Belgium, at Spy, in various parts of France, including La Chapelle-aux-Saints and La Ferrassie, and in Italy at Monte Circeo. This *Homo sapiens neanderthalensis* populated Europe from 80,000 to 30,000 B.C. He differed from *Homo erectus* in various anatomical features; his characteristic activities were hunting, funerary rites and burial, and "skull worship." In 1933 R. Neuville and in 1965 B. Vandermeersch discovered some tombs at Qafzeh near Nazareth (Israel). The skeletons were accompanied by traces of ochre. The Qafzeh men take us back to 90,000 B.C. These two types of *Homo sapiens* both practiced burial and lived in the second part of the Middle Paoleolithic, which lasted from 200,000 to 35,000 B.C.

These men brought about a new culture that gave rise to the production of stone tools known as Mousterian. Characteristic items were points, scrapers (worked on one side only), and very flat bifacial implements. One of the concerns of the living was care of the dead. Because the dead were buried in specially dug ditches, numerous Neanderthal burial sites have been found revealing whole, well-preserved skeletons. At La Ferrassie, a child of three was laid in a tomb covered with a stone slab, which indicates an affectionate relationship with the deceased. Offerings were placed in some tombs: in many cases these would have been food offerings, but there were also other kinds, such as the three scrapers found in grave no. 5 at La Ferrassie and the well-cut flints at La Chapelle-aux-Saints.

The excavations at Teshik-Tash in Uzbekistan (central Asia) revealed "the skeleton of a Neanderthal boy aged about eight, whose body was surrounded by five ibex trophies" (G. Camps). In the famous no. 6 tomb at Shanidar in Iraq dating back 50,000 years, a skeleton was found surrounded by a circle of rocks and lying on a litter made of ephedra branches trimmed with flowers. A skull was also discovered at Monte Circeo in a secondary tomb, a reserved room that was not otherwise used.

The Upper Paleolithic covers the period from 34,000 years ago to 9000 B.C. With the appearance of *Homo sapiens sapiens* (see glossary), the production of stone tools improved (artifacts in bone, cervidae horn, ivory), and mural and miniature art pieces began to be created. In 1868 the discovery of five skeletons at Cro-Magnon in Dordogne (France) gave rise to research on a large scale and to the subsequent discovery of a great many tombs.

One of the first concerns of the living was the protection of the body of the deceased, especially the head. This fact is corroborated by the discoveries made by Grimaldi, Predmost, and Pavlov in Moravia. The presence of furnishings in the tomb — shells, teeth, deer canines — reveals progress in the symbolic concept of the hereafter. Although it was rare in the Middle Paleolithic, the use of red ochre now became more widespread. This yellowish iron oxide turns red when worked with fire. The production of red ochre for funerary purposes constitutes clear evidence of a precise desire on the part of the living. It may be that it was used for aesthetic and hygienic purposes, since ochre cleared the ground of parasites. Here again the concern was the protection of the deceased in the life to come, since cleanliness implied an improvement in the conditions of the deceased. However, a symbolic interpretation of the red ochre would point to the color of blood: red ochre was the symbol of blood and therefore of life, thus suggesting faith in the afterlife.

Toward the end of the Upper Paleolithic, parallel to the art of the Magdalenian period, we note the emergence of a series of funerary practices of evident symbolic significance: items in bone stripped of flesh, skulls placed on flat stones and decorated with shells, as at Placard, and skulls with small disks set into the eye sockets (Mas d'Azil). Such practices were to increase during the Mesolithic Age and

29, 30. The first two scientists to discover Neanderthal man were Johann Fuhlrott (left) and Hermann Schaafhausen (right). The remains of skeletons found in the Neanderthal valley near Düsseldorf in Germany in 1856 were considered by Fuhlrott, president of the local naturalists' society, to be of great interest. Schaafhausen recognized them as human remains, and on February 4, 1857, presented them to the Society of Medicine and Natural History of the Lower Rhine as belonging to an archaic human form.

29

30

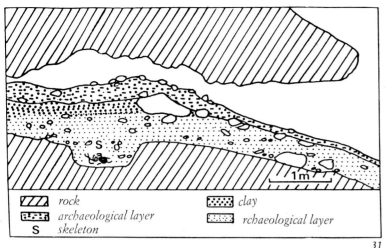

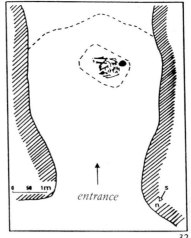

rock

archaeological layer

S skeleton

clay

rchaeological layer

31

entrance

32

31, 32. In 1908 Abbé L. Bardon and Abbé J. Bouyssonie discovered for the first time a Neanderthal burial in a cave at La Chapelle-aux-Saints near Brive (Corrèze, France). A complete skeleton was found. The site afforded evidence that humans of a much earlier period engaged in cultic practices comparable to our own, without aiming at any material benefit. Left, longitudinal section of the burial; right, plan of the cave.

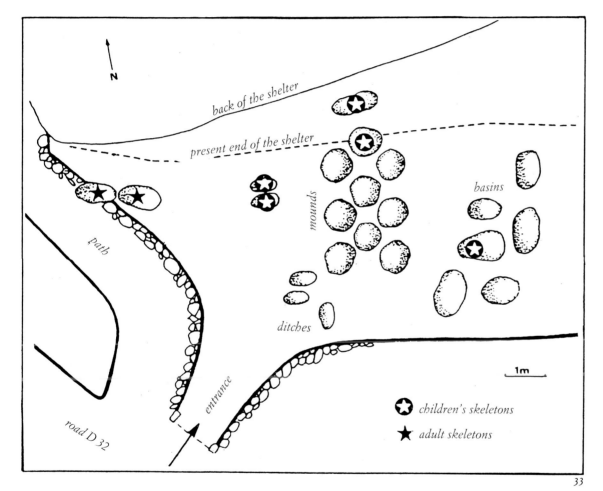

N

back of the shelter

present end of the shelter

mounds

basins

path

ditches

entrance

road D 32

1m

⭐ children's skeletons

★ adult skeletons

33

33. In 1908 L. Capitain and D. Peyroney discovered human remains in deliberate graves in a rock shelter at La Ferrassie in Dordogne (France). Excavation continued during the 1970s under H. Delporte. As the illustration shows, the cave contained remains of children and adults, with different structures for the positioning of the various skeletons.

34

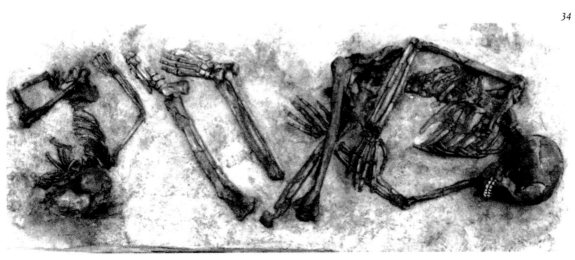

34. A wealth of human remains of the Mousterian period in the Middle East have been found in the Qafzeh cave just outside Nazareth (Israel). The photo shows a simultaneous burial of a girl and a child who were bent so that they fit into the grave.

35. With Neanderthal man we have the first clear evidence of burial of the dead. The corpse was often buried in a crouching position and sprinkled with red ochre as part of a symbolic and ritual procedure. Implements, weapons, ornaments and even flowers were often placed beside the dead.

36. Skullcap of the famous Neanderthal man that so impressed Schaafhausen (see previous pages). A few years earlier the prominently arched brow that particularly interested Schaafhausen had been considered by R. Owen to be an exclusive characteristic of monkeys, and the gorilla in particular.

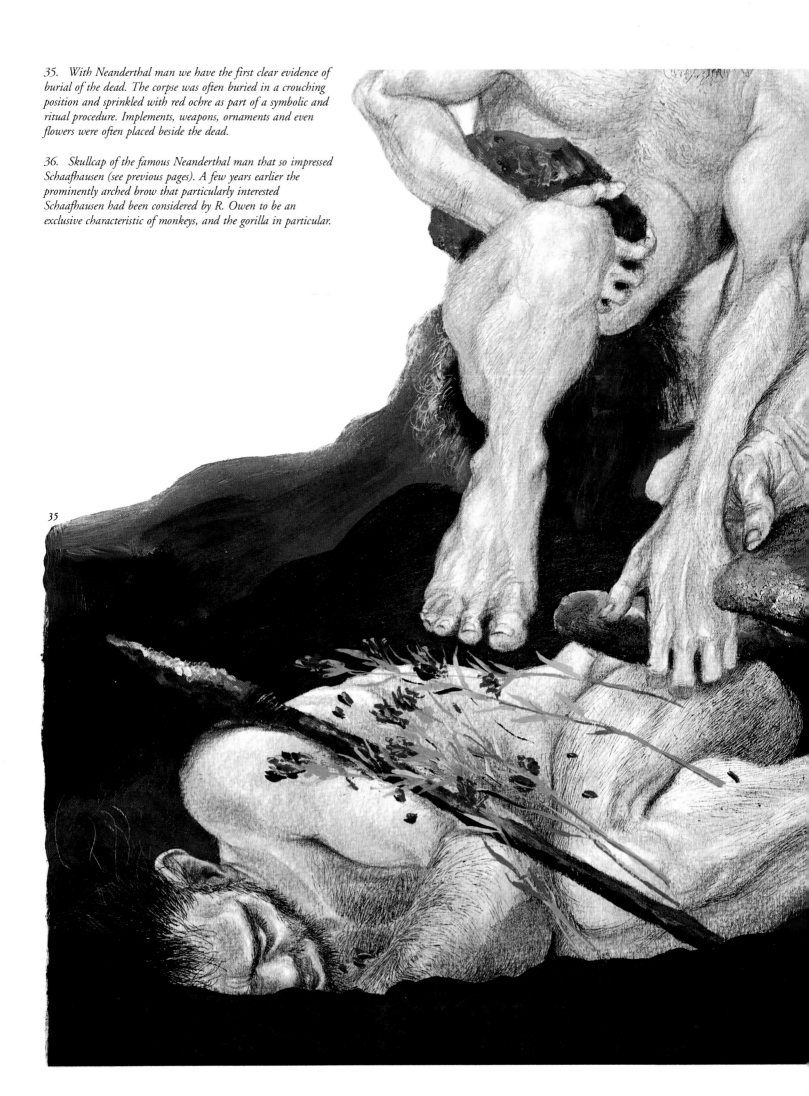

35

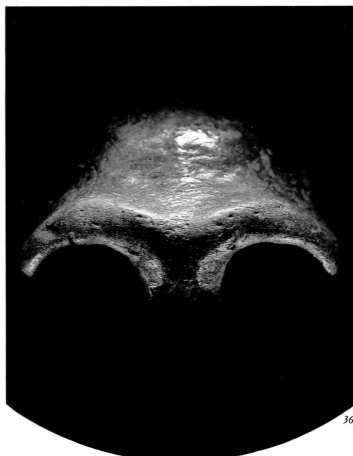

36

to become the norm during the Neolithic. The "new eyes" of the deceased were shells which in symbolic and religious terms stand for the ability to see in the afterlife.

The funerary practices of the Middle and Upper Paleolithic, repeated and preserved over a period of over eighty millennia in Europe, Asia and Africa, could not have been merely casual or fortuitous. The rites, actions and labor that the living devoted to the burial of their dead not only bear certain witness to feelings of respect and affection, but also demonstrate a belief in the afterlife: the placing of food, furnishings and skulls with eye sockets set with shells indicate the idea of postmortem continuity for the deceased. In his funerary practices, the Neanderthal *Homo sapiens,* like the *Homo sapiens sapiens* of the Upper Paleolithic, proved himself to be a *homo religiosus* concerned with life beyond death.

10 Franco-Cantabrian Art

The Art of the Upper Paleolithic

PREHISTORIC ART is divided into two categories according to the type of support the work is created on. Works executed on fixed supports, such as slabs of stone or caves, belong to the field of cave art also known as mural art. When the works are executed on movable supports, we talk of miniature art. Prehistoric art was created by the civilizations of hunters of the Upper Paleolithic and stretched from 34,000 to 8000 B.C. Franco-Cantabrian cave art was less extensive in space and time than miniature art, the latter beginning around 25,000-20,000 B.C. and ending approximately 10,000 B.C., at the same time as the Magdalenian civilization. It chiefly flourished in southeast France, in the Pyrenees, in Spain and the Asturias (Cantabrian Mountains), and to a lesser extent along the European coasts of the Mediterranean. Since there are particularly numerous traces of its existence in the shelters and caves of France and in the region of the Cantabrian Mountains, it is referred to as *Franco-Cantabrian* art. On the other hand, the art of the *Spanish Levant* designates the category of mural paintings that are not situated in caves, as those of the Franco-Cantabrian region are, but in rock shelters located in eastern Spain. Finally, the cave and shelter paintings and engravings of southern Italy, Sicily and the French Languedoc constitute the art of what Paolo Graziosi called the *Mediterranean* province. Within the sphere of Upper Paleolithic art, it is Franco-Cantabrian art that has been the main focus of scientific research, occupying a position of preeminence because of the sheer quality and quantity of well-preserved works.

The Styles of Paleolithic Art

André Leroi-Gourhan divided Paleolithic art into four styles. Style I (from 34,000 to 25,000 B.C.) comprises illegible graffiti, lines, engravings, and cup marks. These primitive works are examples of geometrical figurative art. In Style II (from 25,000 to 15,000 B.C.) we find rigid outlines of animals devoid of detailing. Style III, or the preclassical style, comprises works in which the artists reproduced the proportions of visual reality and the essential details, as in the case of Lascaux and Pech-Merle. Style IV, called the classical style, goes from the Middle Magdalenian to the end of the Paleolithic. This is the phase in which the art of the Upper Paleolithic reaches its highest point and the movements, proportions and forms are reproduced with realism. The works of Style IV are in their turn divided into three phases, the last two of which tend toward decadence. The first phase, on the other hand, embodies the greatest artistic perfection, with the paintings of Altamira, Niaux, Font-de-Gaume, Les Combarelles and Les Trois Frères. The most significant works of the prestigious Franco-Cantabrian art belong to Styles III and IV (A. Leroi-Gourhan, 1965).

The Civilizations that Produced Franco-Cantabrian Art

Chatelperronian civilization is named after the Fairies' Cave at Chatelperron in France, and belongs to a transition phase that took place between 34,000 and 30,000 B.C. It still comprises the work of Neanderthal man, but also introduces the first symbolic representations of Paleolithic art: engravings on bone and geometrical figures on slabs. The geographical area involved largely coincides with that of the future Franco-Cantabrian art.

Aurignacian civilization, named after Aurignac in the Haute Garonne (France), produced very varied and elaborate tools and an abundance of furnishing objects, thus indicating the flowering of symbolic thought as expressed in art. Portrayals of men and especially women are commonly found on rock formations, along with stylized representations of certain animals. This civilization stretched from the

37. Group of figures and symbols (selected from those painted one on top of the other) from Caverne du Volp, Ariège, France. A bison-man plays the bow, a musical instrument that is still found among hunter populations. In the center, a zoomorphic figure, half stag and half bison, follows a reindeer and is associated with three signs that include a female silhouette (from H. Breuil and H. Begouen, 1958).

37

Near East to the Atlantic during the period between 33,000 and 26,000 B.C., affording the first manifestation of Paleolithic art.

The *Gravettian civilization* produced art that represents an important phase in the development of Paleolithic art (from 27,000 to 19,000 B.C.). The name derives from La Gravette in Dordogne. This civilization spread across the whole of Europe and is divided into different artistic categories. During the eight millennia of its existence, Paleolithic art developed widely, producing engravings, paintings and sculpture.

Solutrean civilization is named after the Crot du Charnier excavations at Solutré-Pouilly on the Seine and Loire in France. It coincided with the period of the greatest perfection in stone cutting, at the beginning of Style III. The only areas involved were France (Massif Central, Pyrenees) and Cantabrian Spain. A few paintings of animals made from 20,000 to 18,000 B.C. still survive.

It was *Magdalenian civilization* that produced the highest expression of Paleolithic art (from 18,000 to 10,000 B.C.), with over one hundred fifty decorated caves used as sanctuaries, most of them in the Franco-Cantabrian area. This civilization is named after the great Madeleine rock shelter at Tursac in Dordogne (France). The execution of works of mural art on the part of the Magdalenians in the dark depths of the earth is unique in history.

The *Epipaleolithic civilization* began around 10,000 B.C. Animalistic art began to decline in France and Spain, and Paleolithic art soon came to an end.

Franco-Cantabrian Art

Strictly Magdalenian civilization was limited to the Franco-Cantabrian area. Its miniature art pieces were characterized by an abundance of forms and decorative motifs. Mural art was executed in the tunnels and inner rooms of the calcareous caves that were used as sanctuaries. Of the 150 or so caves discovered so far, the most beautiful are those of Le Gabillou, Lascaux, Les Combarelles, Font-de-Gaume, Rouffignac and Niaux in France, and Altamira, Monte Castillo, Ekain and Santimamiña in Spain. These express an extraordinary intensification of mural art intensified. As hunters of large animals, the Magdalenians were able to portray them in complete anatomical detail: horses, bison, deer, mammoth, rhinoceros, felines and goats, the odd reindeer, the occasional bird, sometimes even fish. Engravings, cup marks and numerous signs were also drawn on implements, arms and tools, as well as reproduced in cave paintings along with certain figures (animal ears, horns, eyes and nostrils) that became increasingly stylized as they developed. The inclusion of nonfigurative signs and representations, some of them highly complex, is typical of Magdalenian civilization and illustrates the way the ability to elaborate concepts and use writing developed in *Homo sapiens sapiens*.

The Paleolithic Sanctuaries

Paleolithic mural art is associated with sanctuaries made from decorated caves and grottos, most of them located in France and Spain and divided into two categories. The first includes the sanctuaries located at the entrance to the caves, relatively close to the light; the second includes the dark sanctuaries located at some depth. A. Leroi-Gourhan (1965) believes that the latter followed those located near the entrance, in view of the mass movement toward the back of the caves that took place during the Magdalenian period. Carved walls have been found in the sanctuaries near the light, whereas the deep walls and ceilings are decorated with paintings. These two types of sanctuary existed during the same period. The area that indicates the beginning of the sanctuary is often marked with engraved or painted points or lines that were perhaps intended as directions for the visitor, but that nevertheless have an undeniable symbolic meaning. The central compositions of paintings typically portray combinations of animals: bison-horse, ox-horse, bison-mammoth; but also bison-horse-mammoth, sometimes accompanied by an ibex, a stag, or a doe. For a whole century now, scholars of prehistory have been trying to penetrate the mystery of these sanctuaries and their iconographic and artistic wealth.

38. *Naturalistic animals and schematized human figures (according to Almagro). La Losilla, Albarracín, Teruel (Spain).*

39. *Honey-gathering scene (according to Hernandez Pacheco). La Arana, Bicorp, Valencia (Spain).*

40. *Man with bull mask, from Racó Molero e El Cingle de la Mola Remigia, Castellón (Spain).*

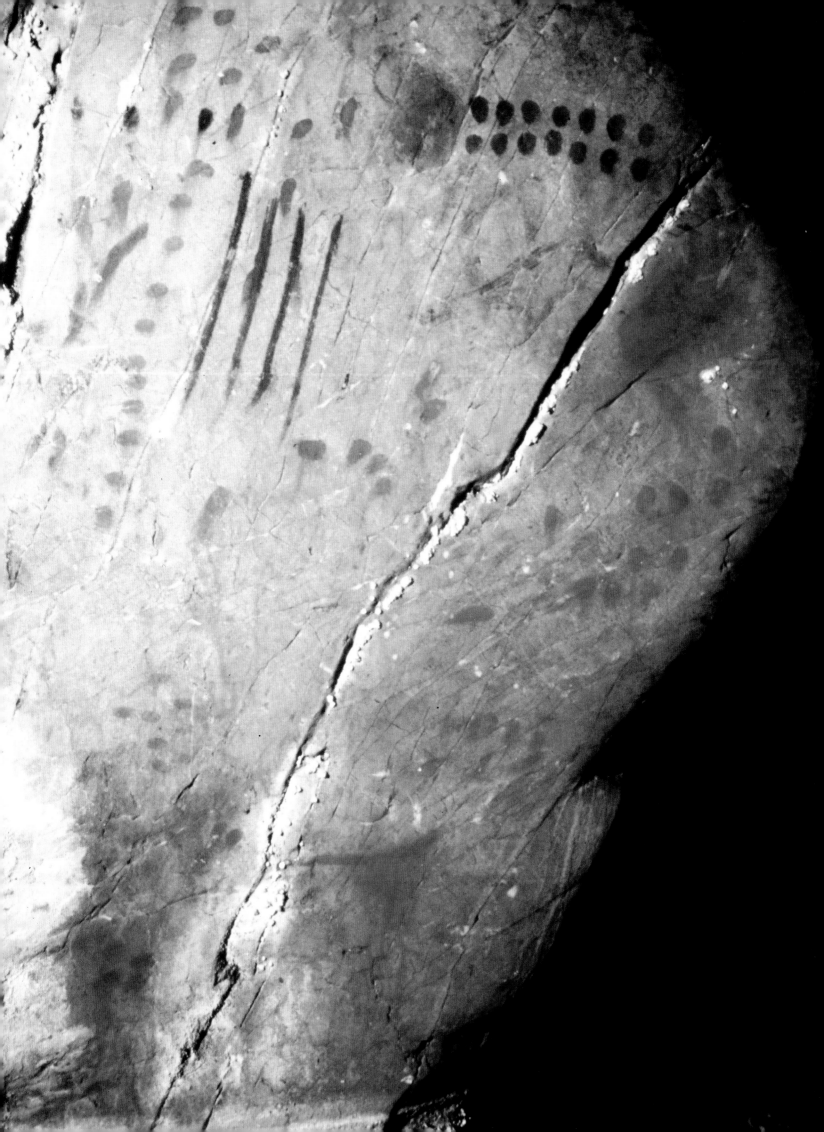

41

41. *Accumulation of signs on an unusually shaped rocky projection in the Niaux cave, Ariège, France. Some of the signs appear to have numerical value, whereas others seem intended to enhance the natural shape of the rock (courtesy of J. Clottes).*

42. *Three reindeer and a wild horse with magical signs of traps. Cave painting in ochre and mineral oxide colors in the Lascaux cave in Dordogne, France.*

11 The Religious Message of Mural Art

A Hermeneutic Approach

TO POSIT the problem of a message implies embracing hermeneutics, that is, the quest for meaning. The hermeneutics of cave art operates at two levels. *Descriptive* hermeneutics deals with the study of man *in situ* and tries to define the meaning that *Homo sapiens sapiens* of the Upper Paleolithic — Magdalenian man — attributed to the sanctuaries and their decoration; *normative* hermeneutics asks about the significance of this art for an understanding of humanity and of the human condition.

On the basis of the study of styles and their chronology, A. Leroi-Gourhan (1964 and 1965) has shown that "Paleolithic art was linked to the same symbolic foundation during the entire course of its development and followed a coherent evolutionary curve comparable to that of other known arts that lasted for a long period of time." This demonstration is of central importance for hermeneutics, since it introduces the problem of defining the message of this art, and in particular its religious message. Moreover, from the religious point of view it is also important to establish how long the decorated caves were used, since this allows us to evaluate the coherence of Magdalenian man's thought.

Earlier Explanations

One of the first explanations presupposed the principle of the gratuitousness of art, "art for art's sake." The artists of the Paleolithic were held to have behaved like children, amusing themselves by painting the animal figures that filled the environment in which they as hunters lived. This point of view excludes any quest for a message.

Another explanation derived from comparative ethnology as it was practiced at the beginning of the twentieth century. The point of departure was the *hunting magic* exercised by certain aboriginal tribes in Australia and elsewhere. The Magdalenians were believed to have painted bison, wild horses, aurochs, mammoth and deer in order to immobilize them during the hunt that was to take place the next day. Dressed as sorcerers, the artists would have mimed the hunt in the caves as a prelude to the real hunt. Such magic practiced by Paleolithic

hunters should thus be associated with the magic concerning the fertility of animals and women. H. Breuil has long advocated this hypothesis.

A number of authors have also referred to *totemism*. Within this perspective, the walls and ceilings of the caves were painted with totems of the Magdalenian clans: horse, bison, mammoth, and so on. The great cave frescoes were therefore not magical scenes but rather representations of the struggles and fights between the clans. Explanations of this sort are based on the evolutionist dogma of totemism and its conviction that all religions originate with the totem.

Finally there was reference to *shamanism* (see glossary), and to warriors who recovered the souls of the sick. According to this view, certain human representations, such as those of Lascaux, actually point more towards shamans than they do to sorcerers. As in the case of the totemism theory, we are again in the presence of a "religious" experience, in this case an experience of the hereafter.

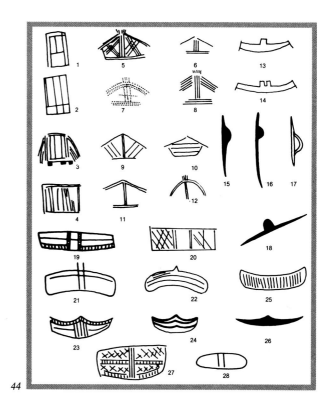

44. Geometrical signs in mural art. Paleolithic art incorporated numerous geometrical figures whose meaning is no longer clear. Nevertheless, their concentration in certain geographical areas and their arrangement within the overall decoration show that they had a definite meaning for Paleolithic man. The chart shows signs found in different regions. 1–4: quadrilaterals from the Périgord. 5–12: roof-shaped figures. 13 and 14: aviforms. 15–18: claviforms. 19–26: Cantabrian quadrilaterals and their derivatives. 27 and 28: Cantabrian quadrilaterals from Altamira (Spain).

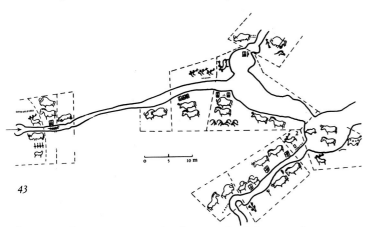

43. Map of Lascaux. A. Leroi-Gourhan considered this magnificent cave complex decorated by the Magdalenian artists to be a temple.

Founded on specific ideologies, these theories linked facts and evidence in a rigid schema of principles formulated a priori. They were not to go unchallenged. When studying Lascaux and Pech-Merle, A. Laming-Emperaire (1962) was struck by the frequent association of horse and bison. And A. Leroi-Gourhan regarded the hunting magic hypothesis as insufficient in that it set out from a secondary fact: the wounds visible on certain animals. Moreover, he felt that the symbolism of the fights of the shamans and the pregnant animals afforded too fragile a base for responsible hermeneutics.

A Systematic Study of the Evidence

These two authors set out from detailed examinations of the caves to compare the results of their respective observations and analyses. The outcome was substantial agreement over the main aspects of their views. A. Leroi-Gourhan counted the species represented in over sixty caves, noticing a systematic arrangement of figures whose spatial distribution and iconographic composition he was then also able to analyze. In the mural paintings the bison-horse association proved to be constant, with the horse, bison and aurochs portrayed in the same proportion. There are also bison-horse–mammoth compositions, and indeed other compositions made up of a larger number of elements, uniting in one scene all the species painted in the cave. These recapitulatory scenes are most often found at the back of the cave or in secluded places. We also find the bison-horse-antelope-deer group accompanied by twofold signs. In Leroi-Gourhan's view they embody a binary sexual symbolism, since the horse was a male sign and the bison a female one. A. Laming-Emperaire reverses the components of this sexual symbolism.

In numerous cases the area that marks the entrance, the passages, and the end of the caves is indicated by lines, points, marks and other signs. Now these signs and marks repeatedly appear in an orderly fashion in a great many central groups. On the basis of topographical statistics and stylistic chronology, A. Leroi-Gourhan suggests that these signs might also be symbols of a sexual nature, male and female. His interpretation would appear to be confirmed by the miniature art pieces. In fact these signs can also be seen on the statuettes carved in the rock or modeled in clay found at the cave entrance, on certain tools, and on small plates of stone and bone.

The cave itself had begun to become part of the symbolic composition. The figurative system developed according to the different shapes of the caves and the ethnic and cultural peculiarities. However, the conceptual framework behind this development was one and the same throughout the Franco-Cantabrian area and indeed in other parts of Europe. We are thus confronted with evidence that demonstrates the existence of cultural and symbolic traditions that differ from those of the Near East, the Sahara and South Africa. So the Franco-Cantabrian Paleolithic block — with the addition of the rest of Europe — constitutes a homogeneous reality that is distinctive within the Paleolithic period.

We thus have a key for interpreting the sanctuaries, their decoration, and the mural and miniature art of the Paleolithic. The essential features of this art are "the prevalence of the association of two animal species comprising a horse on the one hand and an ox on the other, the introduction of a third element variously associated with the basic pair (mammoth, antelope, deer), the eventual presence of felines and the rhinoceros. On this animalist structure, integrated into the natural shape of the cave, a second symbolic line was then sketched, this time inspired by man and expressed in the same positional relationships as those found among the animals, using complete representations of man and woman, or indeed, and more frequently, geometrical symbols" (A. Leroi-Gourhan, 1976, pp. 169-170).

A Symbolism that Expresses Religiosity

The works of A. Leroi-Gourhan and A. Laming-Emperaire mark a crucial turning point. They draw attention to the existence of com-

mon conceptual processes and thought structures among the peoples of the Upper Paleolithic that then continue for over twenty millennia by means of symbols reproduced in caves, in the rock shelters, and on certain objects throughout Paleolithic Europe and above all in the Franco-Cantabrian area. This symbolic thought is of remarkable complexity, and is expressed by means of an equally remarkable technique. *Homo sapiens sapiens* had reached a very high cultural and social level. But was this *Homo symbolicus* also a *homo religiosus*?

The available evidence shows that this man had a perception of the extraordinary in life. The study of the Paleolithic funeral practices with their characteristic use of red ochre, of food and object offerings, and of skull decoration with the insertion of shells in the eye sockets suggests the existence of a full-orbed emotional life and of belief in an afterlife (see no. 9). The funeral practices and the art of the Paleolithic are inseparable, since they are the products of the same men and the same society. This fact in itself suggests that we should look for the religious dimension of Paleolithic art.

Only the exterior representation of the Paleolithic has come down to us; we cannot know the oral context within which the symbolic grouping was coordinated. In his anthropological works, A. Leroi-Gourhan (1964) hypothesized a link between technique and language. In fact, language is connected with implements, since both indicate consciousness, intelligence and reflection. The graphism that begins with the Paleolithic represents a new stage in the development of man's intellectual capacity.

Graphism was accompanied by the development of the symbolic function, already active in *Homo erectus* (see no. 8), as the tool production indicates. This function is an essential property of man, first expressed in the production of implements and in technical development and reaching its richest and most advanced form in Paleolithic art. It presupposes aesthetic, psychic, and intellectual perception. Figurative art is inseparable from language; in Leroi-Gourhan's view, language derives from "the establishment of an intellectual union between phonation and writing." This union informed the symbolic grouping of the cave paintings and allows us to make an important advance in the discovery of their religious message. The symbols painted on the walls and roofs were meaningful insofar as they were part of a discourse that existed but could not be fossilized and thus passed down to us today. As A. Leroi-Gourhan points out, all that remains of this discourse are the mythograms (1988).

From Mythograms to Myths

Mircea Eliade argues that it is "plausible to state that a certain number of myths were familiar to the Paleolithic peoples, first of all the cosmogonic myths and the origin myths (origins of man, game, death, etc.)" (M. Eliade, 1979). Leroi-Gorhan speaks of mythograms as consisting of "complex arrangements whose figures would be organized in space and time such that they possessed some of the spatial and temporal properties of the myth." Unlike the pictograph, which is a figure or series of figures, the mythogram represents certain characters carrying out a mythological operation. Franco-Can-

45. Pages 40-41: Painted composition in black associating the bison and the horse, accompanied by a number of ideograms. The natural forms of the wall suggest a large face with two cavities for the eyes and a stalagmite for a nose. Santamamina Cave, Vizcaya (Spain).

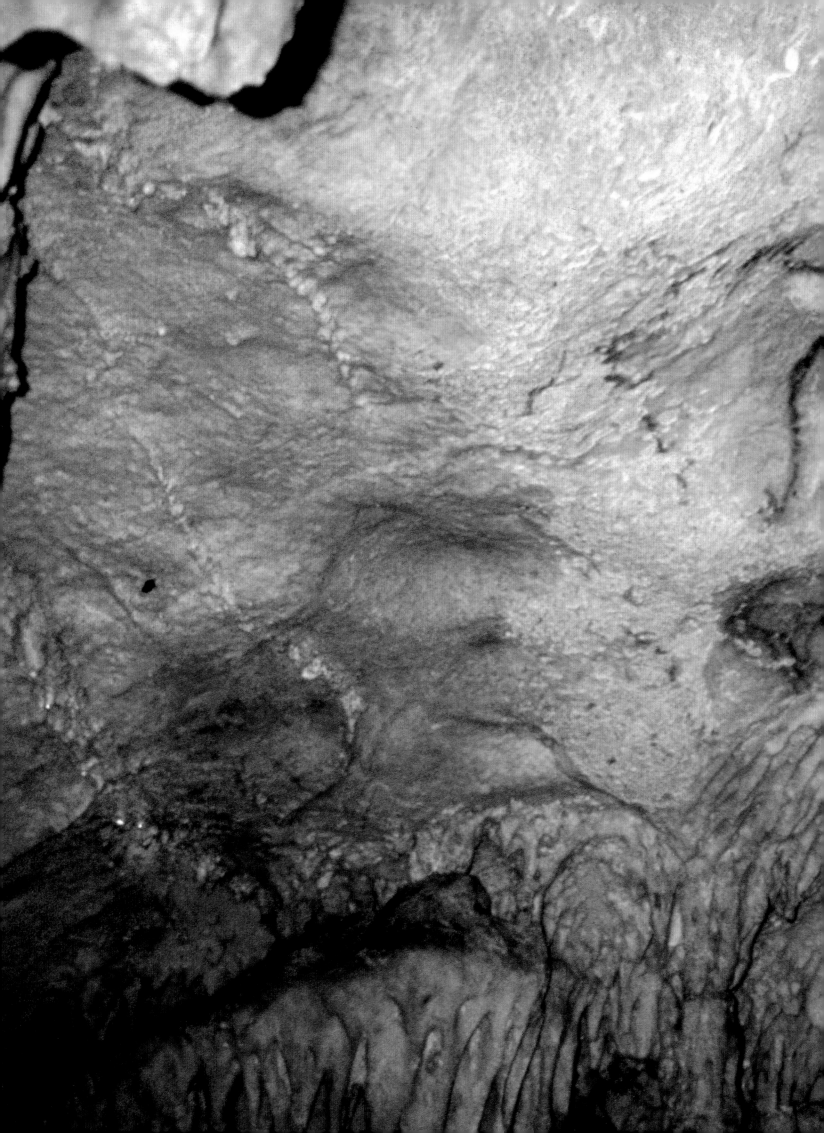

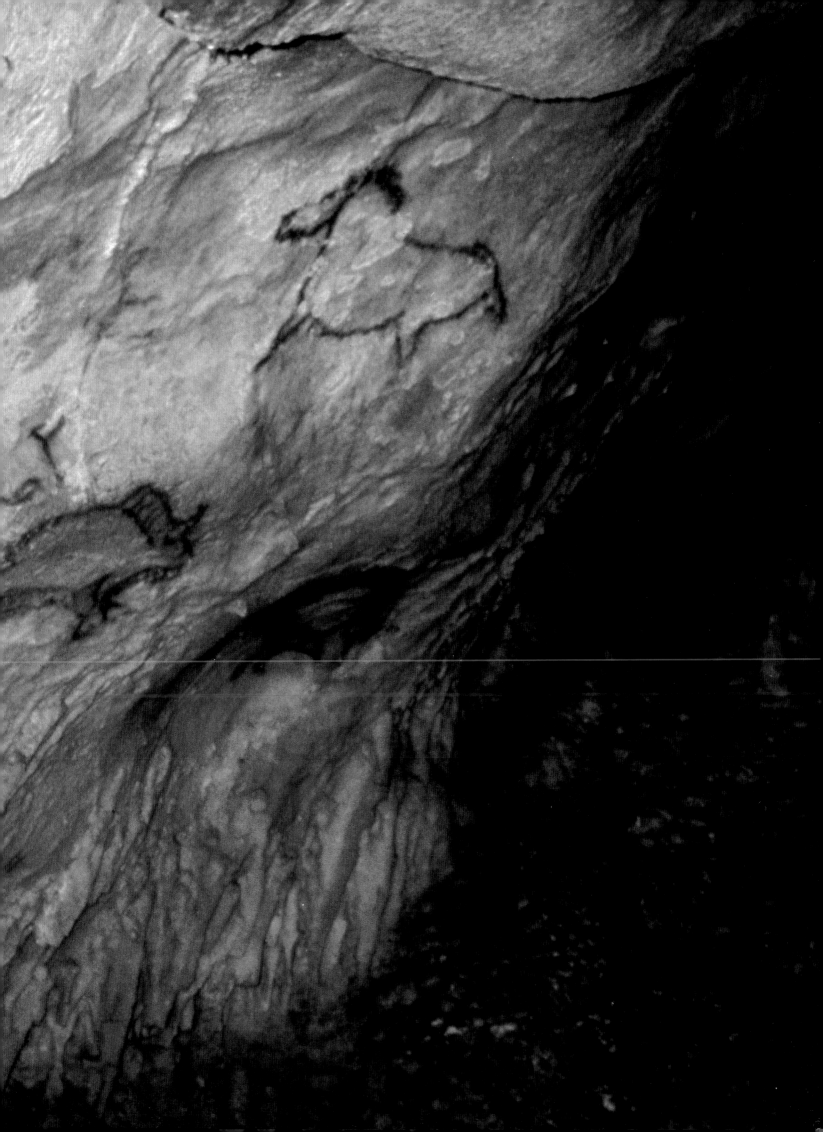

tabrian mural art possesses a wealth of mythograms: the arrangements and compositions are made up of characters — animals, men and women — that took on their authentic meaning only when animated by a discourse.

Through his conception of the mythogram, A. Leroi-Gourhan shows us how the roots of mythical thought stretch back into the Paleolithic. This second key to interpreting cave art suggests that we should take a fresh look at the various compositions in order to define the hypothesis relative to both the cosmogonic myths that reveal the creation of the world and to the origin myths that bear witness to changes in the cosmos and the various new situations that arise. Knowledge of these rites at the dawn of historical time in the Near and Middle East, in Egypt, and in the Mediterranean world has come down to us in written documents. If we set out from this first historical evidence and move backwards through history and the documents of the Neolithic, we should be able to employ comparative analysis in studying the mythograms of Paleolithic art. We will thus have a third interpretative key to the decorative art of the "cathedrals of prehistory."

A Tentative Synthesis of the Religious Message of Mural Art

The impressive evidence available to descriptive hermeneutics has been collected by specialists in prehistory and then studied, critically analyzed, and deciphered. The method applied for deciphering the religious method requires patience, comparative research and detailed examination of each cave and the various compositions. We now have the necessary tools for making decisive steps in the direction of our hermeneutical goals.

Paleolithic mural art is a religious art, typical of the sanctuaries located deep in the ground between the Atlantic and the Ural Mountains, above all in France and Spain. Its typical nature is what has given rise to the concept of "cave religion." The small plates that have the same symbolic structure as the caves are thought to be "portable sanctuaries."

This is clearly bipolar religious art, and this fact explains the dichotomy of the mural and the miniature art. This symbolic dichotomy is found everywhere, in the distribution of the animal figures no less than in the signs. It thus suggests the existence of a conception of the world informed by the complementary bipolar model whose basic structure consists of the male and the female essence. This is what emerges from the studies of A. Leroi-Gourhan, A. Laming-Emperaire and E. Anati. A cosmogonic vision of this sort was to have profound effects on man's later development.

The mythograms painted on the cave rocks and roofs bear witness to mythical tales, or indeed to foundation myths (G. Camps). These probably constitute the roots of the great cosmogonic myths and origin myths that appear around ten millennia later. Perhaps these mythograms acted as initiation aids for the young men of the Magdalenian clans; certainly the numerous footprints of young men in many of the caves would suggest that this might be the case. Surely the decorated vaults, connected by a rainbow to the compositions painted on the cave walls, suggest the celestial hierophanies to be found in the myths while the symbols of the rainbow and the bridge connote man's link with the hereafter. There are also myths concerning the sacred nature of the sky and celestial phenomena. Nor should we forget those pertaining to the origins of animals or those concerning animal and human fertility (M. Eliade).

Whereas descriptive hermeneutics leads us toward these different aspects of the sacred experienced by *Homo sapiens sapiens* during the Paleolithic, normative hermeneutics underlines the importance of this experience and its crucial role in the spiritual development of humanity. Cave art is a jewel in the artistic and religious heritage of mankind, and constitutes the environment in which modern man is born. Evidence of this birth can be seen in the achievement of the first great step in the direction of conceptual development, in a substantial advance in the formation of symbolic thought, in the emergence of a genuine religiousness based on the experience of the sacred, and in the formation of analytical, synthetic and communicative capacities with regard to the image of the world to which man belongs. Cave art constitutes the first evidence of man's ability to organize his world, to comprehend the cosmos, and to live the sacred experience within it.

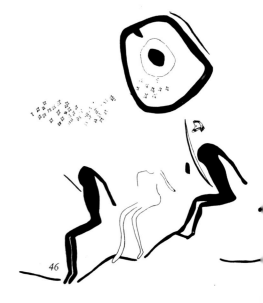

46. The rocks give us plentiful evidence of the religious and social function of sorcerers. These reproductions by L. Williams show sorcerers adorned with tree frogs and armed with sticks, dancing on a red line of supernatural energy. The energy they are harnessing is symbolized by the swarm of bees: the more-or-less square structure is possibly a hive. Cullen's Wood, Barkly East (South Africa).

12 The First Institutions

The Theories

LESS THAN a century ago ethnologists and sociologists described primitive societies using frameworks developed with reference to modern societies. Since then, scholars have come to realize that such schemes afford only limited indications of social life during the course of prehistory.

Homo erectus already possessed the requisites for making use of an articulated language. It is now thought that phonation structures had already been formed at least 400,000 years ago. The first signs of social life date back to this distant period; evidence of fire-making has been found, and this is an essential element for community life. Moreover, in 1966, on the slopes of Mount Boron at Terra Amata, near Nice, a seasonal hunters' camp was found. Constructing huts, making fire, cutting tools and hunting big game were the basis of associative life for *Homo erectus.* This was still the case in the culture of *Homo sapiens,* whose social life was cemented by articulated language. Is M. Mauss (*Essai sur le don,* 1925) right in claiming that gifts were the social contracts of primitive peoples? The archaeology of Paleolithic societies seems unable to verify this thesis. Nevertheless, it does supply us with certain rudimentary evidence concerning archaic social life, such as huts and caves with deposits of tools, worn animal bones, antlers and traces of fire.

Certain recent theories developed in America have tried to explain how such activities were organized: man would have been the specialist in hunting and supplying, whereas woman would have devoted herself to gathering the produce of the earth and bearing children. This argument has given rise to the theory of cooperation in dividing up responsibility for acquiring basic food resources, meat and vegetables (R. Lewin, 1984, 1991). A number of sociologists believe that this cooperation was the first element of stability in the union between man and woman.

The Facts

We have more evidence from the Upper Paleolithic. In the caves and rock shelters, in the camps and habitations on the plains and the border of the highlands, and in the winter refuges, explorers have found trampled charcoal, the frames of domes, the remains of dwelling structures, and areas indicating labor distribution, all of which prove the existence of organized social life. Examples of this sort have been found at the open-air excavation at Pincevent (Seine), inspected by Leroi-Gourhan from 1964 to 1985, and from the open-air archaeological site at Etiolles in Essonne (France). From the finds made in these two Magdalenian archaeological areas we can work out much about the daily life of the hunters and the organization of their activities according to a kind of hierarchy. These same models have also been found in other areas (J. Mohen, 1991). It is believed that the social structure of a hunter community would have comprised around thirty people at most, comparable to present-day hunter tribes.

One of the foremost specialists of the Upper Paeleolithic, Abbé Henri Breuil (1877-1961), insisted on the close connection between big game hunting and mural art. The knowledge of animals and the experience of hunting were essential to such artistic creation. At any rate, production of this art was of extraordinary importance in the life of the men of the Franco-Cantabrian Upper Paleolithic — a social and collective event that witnesses to both a common spiritual identity and to the existence of "a sort of institution" by which artists were selected and the most gifted were trained. H. Breuil claimed that various institutions would have been necessary to create cave art and handle initiation ceremonies for visitors to the caves (H. Breuil, 1952). Perhaps there were "schools" of artists and masters of ceremony whose task it was to initiate visitors.

Research currently tends to consider cave art as a reflection of Paleolithic society. However, such sociological interpretations should not be used as a new ideology. Recent works have shown that each cave has its own integrity within the cultural universe of the Upper Paleolithic. We can obtain some sense of communal life from a variety of indicators: the distribution of labor within the clans made up of hunters and gatherers; the training given to artists and artisans; the presence of functionaries responsible for organizing meetings and the initiation ceremonies through which the Magdalenians were introduced to their mythograms and the subsequent *Weltanschauung;* and an elementary family organization. At the end of the Paleolithic period the stage was set for a decisive development in the individual and social life of *Homo sapiens sapiens:* settlement.

47. *Pages 44-45: Artist's conception of a procession of young men taken into a decorated cave by the clan authorities to be prepared for an initiation rite. In A. Leroi-Gourhan's view, the importance attributed to these decorated caves is evident in the human energy and economic resources that the social group invested in ensuring that future generations of clan members enjoy their benefits.*

13 Hunting "Magic"

48. *Hunting scene with boleadoras. Reproduction of a cave painting by J. Schobinger in the Cueva de Las Manos Pintadas in Patagonia (Argentina).*

HENRI BREUIL collected prodigious documentation on cave art, basing his own hermeneutics on a theory of hunting magic and propitiation. There are indeed certain cave paintings, such as those at Lascaux, that show wounded animals. Moreover there are numerous images of the assegai, a sling made out of bone or antler that was used by the Magdalenian hunter as his principal weapon. The abundant evidence of animalist concerns in cave art, together with the importance of the hunter's weapons and the ethnological theories pertaining to present-day Arctic, Amazonian and Australian hunter tribes, led H. Breuil to interpret cave art in connection with magical and religious rites that are inseparable from both big game hunting and stalking and the natural reproduction of wildlife.

There was certainly no shortage of game, so the hunters' main concern was clearly its slaughter. Fruitful hunting expeditions called for the performance of particular rites: dances and ceremonies invoking (as primitive hunters do to this day) the "Great Spirit" governing the forces of nature (Breuil, 1952). There are some clear indications of propitiatory magic. In the Montespan cave in France, an expanse of wall several meters long has been riddled with assegai shots. Similar marks are to be found on the bodies of three horses engraved in the clay. There is also a statuette of an animal with its breast pierced by numerous assegai shots, and a recumbent bear with similar wounds. The Niaux cave offers further examples of the same sort.

H. Breuil attributed extraordinary importance to the "Great Sorcerer" engraved in the wall of the cave at Les Trois Frères in Ariège. In fact he made a famous drawing of it, with its stag's head replete with branched antlers, its owl's face, wolf's ears, chamois beard, fore-arms ending in bear's paws, and long horse's tail. Its genitals show that it is a human figure. H. Breuil does not hesitate to talk about ritual gestures and sacred rites. In his view, "the representations together embody the elements of a magical ritual aimed at multiplication or destruction." The hunters made effigies of the animal and then inflicted symbolic death on it by means of real wounds. Hence the bodies pierced with shots. Breuil claimed that the principal element in this ritual was mimicry. Hollow sticks and propelling implements would have represented at least part of the equipment commonly used for such sacred pantomimes. Moreover, certain details suggest that these performances were seasonal, linked to "the cyclical character of feasts and ceremonies." Such rites were intended to ensure the fertility of the animals and the success of the hunt.

In his interpretation of the religious practices of Leptolithic man, that is of the Magdalenian peoples who lived in the reindeer age, H. Breuil introduced one further element: masks. Inspired by the current initiation ceremonies in use among peoples without writing, he argued that such rites generate beliefs and myths related to the ancestor myths. Now, the fact that certain characters wear a mask is

49. *Copy by J. M. Orpen in 1873 of a cave painting showing sorcerers leading an animal. Two of the sorcerers wear a headdress with antelope ears and two carry aromatic herbs to soothe the animal. Sehonghong (Lesotho).*

50. *Famous reproduction by H. Breuil of the rock carving of a figure that is part man and part animal, known as the "Sorcerer." It was probably intended to represent a sorcerer disguised as an animal. Les Trois Frères cave, Ariège (France).*

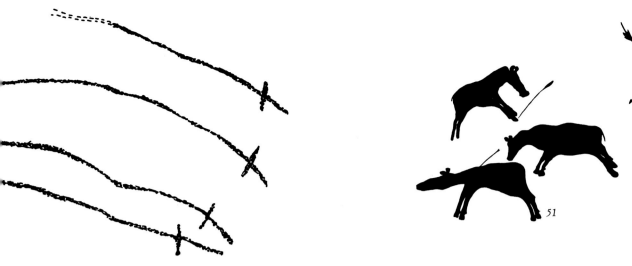

51

important because it draws attention to the duality of the mythical being. H. Breuil found a number of masked figures through which human features can just be discerned: the sorcerer from the Les Trois Frères cave, for example, or the dancer with the bear's head at Mas d'Azil, the small demons at Teyjat, and many other half-human, half-animal figures. The idea behind these ceremonies was evidently the participation of men from the Magdalenian clans in the power and life of the mythical ancestors. H. Breuil took this idea directly from the theory of participation developed by L. Lévy-Bruhl.

Although A. Leroi-Gourhan does not completely reject the idea of hunting magic, he nevertheless argues that it cannot alone explain the wealth of data derived from cave art. As he points out, the number of wounded animals is actually very low, less than ten percent. Moreover,

there is something ambiguous about the wounded creatures, as though they were meant to suggest female characteristics; the sling weapons, by contrast, clearly symbolize male characteristics. These observations lead us back to bipolar symbolism. If the presence of wounded animals is not enough to support the propitiatory magic hypothesis, then the idea of mating and fertility magic also appears to be fragile (A. Leroi-Gourhan, 1964, 1971). The views of the two scholars meet in their insistence on the mythical symbolism implicit in such compositions. In other words, even if the idea of hunting magic is not fully convincing, there is no denying the hunting myths and the myths pertaining to the origins of the game. The thought of the Magdalenian hunters was unquestionably related to the wealth of symbols concerning a mythical universe, the essence of which still eludes us.

51. *Reproduction by G. Prats of a cave painting of the Spanish Levant showing a horse-hunting scene.*

52. *Reproduction by L. Williams of an antelope-hunting scene. Though bleeding and moribund, the prey is so grand and majestic that it attests to the sacred nature of the hunting ritual. Barkly East (South Africa).*

52

53. *Cave painting at Tadrart Acacus (Lybia) showing a Paleolithic hunting scene in which men armed with bows and arrows attack a large ox with the help of hounds.*

53

54. *Artist's reconstruction of an alpine hunting scene. The men approach the stag with lances. The animal is large and appears to dominate, since beasts of prey were both feared and venerated.*

55. *Detail of a cave painting inside the Cueva de Las Manos Pintadas in Patagonia (Argentina). Pictographs and ideograms are often found together in cave art. This mixture of realism and conceptualization bears witness to a grasp of reality that is more than merely descriptive.*

54

55

14 The Religious Art of the Cave Age

DURING THE 1970s studies in prehistory made notable strides forward thanks to scholars such as A. Leroi-Gourhan, Y. Coppens, E. Anati, P. Graziosi and A. Beltran. It was thus that a group of specialists got together to coordinate research and study into cave art and to promote its preservation and appreciation. We now have a panorama of this heritage and have greatly progressed in interpreting the religious art of the caves.

Interpretative Keys

Various possible interpretations have now been added to that of H. Breuil, who drew attention to the importance of hunting magic and propitiatory rites. A. Leroi-Gourhan and A. Laming-Emperaire, who unfortunately died in an accident, threw light on the bipolarity of the figures and their significance, thereby revealing the formulation of dualistic concepts and a complex vision of society and the cosmos. Paleolithic figurative art should thus be seen as "an expression of concepts concerning the natural and supernatural organization (all one in Paleolithic thought) of the living world." This interpretation of cave art as a reflection of society has informed British and American social and cultural anthropology in its analysis of the society and "institutions" of the Upper Paleolithic. However, Leroi-Gouthan also suggested another interpretation. It is based on the mythograms visible among the great figurative compositions of the caves and aims at revealing to some extent the mysteries of the myths formulated by *Homo sapiens sapiens*. Finally there is E. Anati's conviction, based on his analysis of the diversity and wealth of symbols, that man's first formulation of concepts was actually in cave art, which implies the mental faculties of abstraction, synthesis and association.

The Sanctuaries

The first persons to celebrate animalist art were so astounded by their discoveries that their descriptions abounded in superlatives: the cave at Niaux was the "Versailles of Prehistory," and the Lascaux cave the "Sistine Chapel" of the Paleolithic. However, once the general tone cooled down, an important concept had been established: the caves were sanctuaries made in the depths of the earth. We are now able to see how the Cro-Magnon population relates to Magdalenian man. The Cro-Magnon *Homo sapiens* engraved and sculpted the first images in the shelters beneath the rocks, whereas the Magdalenians penetrated further into the darkness and mystery of the depths. Footprints, especially adolescent ones, and the mythograms of the vaults and walls suggest that there were initiatory meetings. This hypothesis is substantiated at Lascaux, where the number of youthful footprints is remarkably high.

The quantity and quality of the mythograms also suggest the existence of cosmogonic and origin myths which have been better defined by subsequent research. The union rather than the mating of animals has thus been seen as proof of the bipolar mythology thought to have characterized the reindeer age. The female statuettes known as "Aurignacian Venuses" that were found throughout Europe are thus held to be the earliest evidence of fertility cults and myths. Moreover, some scholars have interpreted the Magdalenian figures of masked men as "sorcerers" or shamans, indeed as possible masters of initiation ceremonies. The portrayal of circular dances may relate to initiatory practices, since traces of them can be seen among the hunter populations of present archaic populations.

Current research shows that the sanctuary was related to the culture of the surrounding population. This means that each sanctuary had an identity of its own and requires individual interpretation. For example, at Rouffignac a detailed study of the Serpent Ceiling has led C. Barrière (1979) to interpret the serpent as a symbol of evil and the mammoth as a symbol of life. The composition as a whole would thus be an illustration of the struggle of evil against life. In his study of the single-subject sanctuaries of Cantabrian rupestrian art, Fr. Jordà Cerdà (1979) came to conclusions that are encouraging for the study of the religiosity of the Magdalenian populations. He focused on the following subjects: portrayals of animals that seem to embody the appearance of the mythical animal; chapels seen as deliberate depositories for "sacred objects"; the clan symbolism in relation to celestial power; the hand viewed as a religious archetype of the rejection of hostile forces; and the cosmogonic myths.

Homo religiosus in the Upper Paleolithic

Interpretative keys can be used by specialists in this field for penetrating the mysteries of the sanctuaries and trying to understand the mythograms, the engravings on walls and implements, and the meaning of the female statuettes and of the compositions on the cave ceilings and walls.

Simultaneous use of the four different interpretative keys already described can help us identify certain aspects of the sacred experience and behavior of *Homo sapiens sapiens,* who created cave art. This man had a perception of kratophany and hierophany, albeit with some confusion. This suggests that his magical and religious behavior was inspired by a perception of transcendency. This perception on the part of *homo religiosus paleolithicus* is evident in the organization of the sanctuaries, in the cave compositions, and in the signs used in mural and miniature art. The representation of innumerable mythograms shows that this man's religiosity was built around the symbolic and mythical thought that also governed his behavior. He must thus have experienced initiation to these myths as a form of revelation of a "sacred story" of the cosmos and of man that showed him his place within the universe.

About 10,000 years ago, at the end of the Würm glaciation, Magdalenian cave art died out. The increase in the earth's temperature brought about the extinction of the large animal species that were familiar to the hunter-gatherers, and a period in human history came to an end.

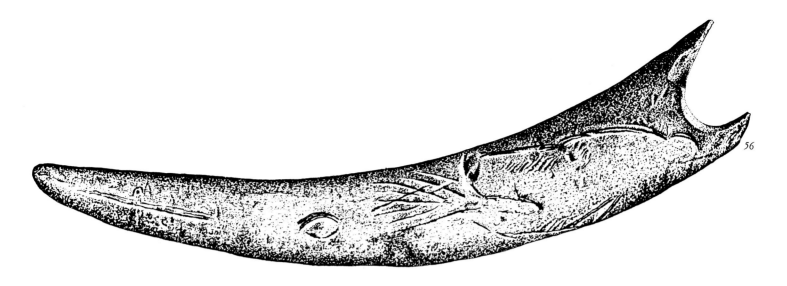

56. Decorated horn of the Magdalenian period, found in Ariège (France). Apart from the bear's head, there is also a linear and an almond-shaped sign, interpreted by E. Anati as male and female symbols.

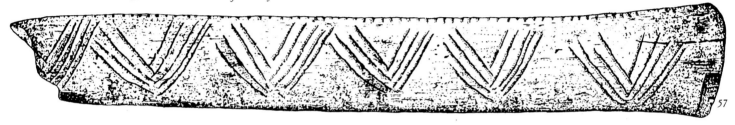

57. Part of an eagle bone carved with symmetrical motifs, found at Charente (France). This is a product of the Magdalenian period of the Upper Paleolithic. The eagle bone is completely hollow and is still used to this day as a wind instrument by certain populations of central Asia and New Guinea, where decorations representing sounds are common.

58. Schema drawn by A. Leroi-Gourhan of the cave sanctuary at Les Combarelles in Dordogne (France). The scholar shows how the paintings in the cave sanctuaries were arranged in a symbolic order according to different groups and associations of animals.

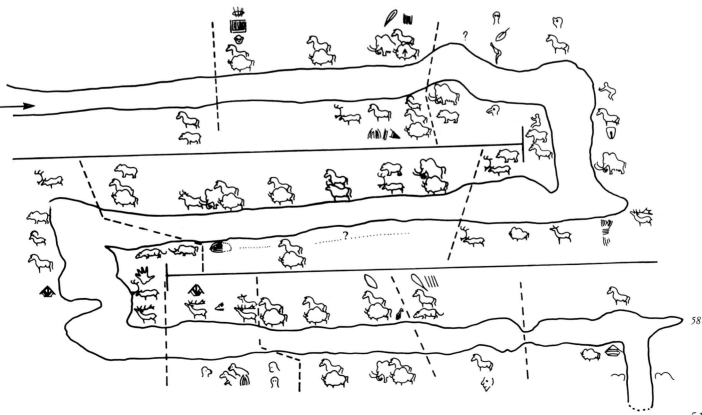

59

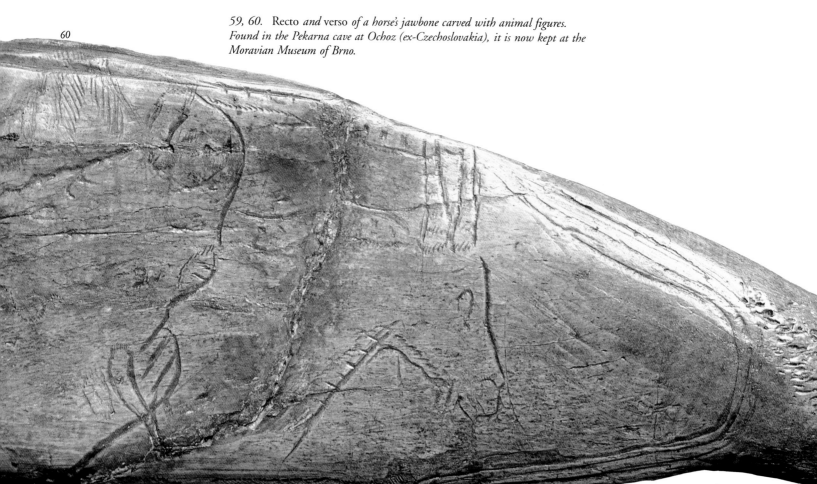

60

59, 60.   Recto *and* verso *of a horse's jawbone carved with animal figures.
Found in the Pekarna cave at Ochoz (ex-Czechoslovakia), it is now kept at the
Moravian Museum of Brno.*

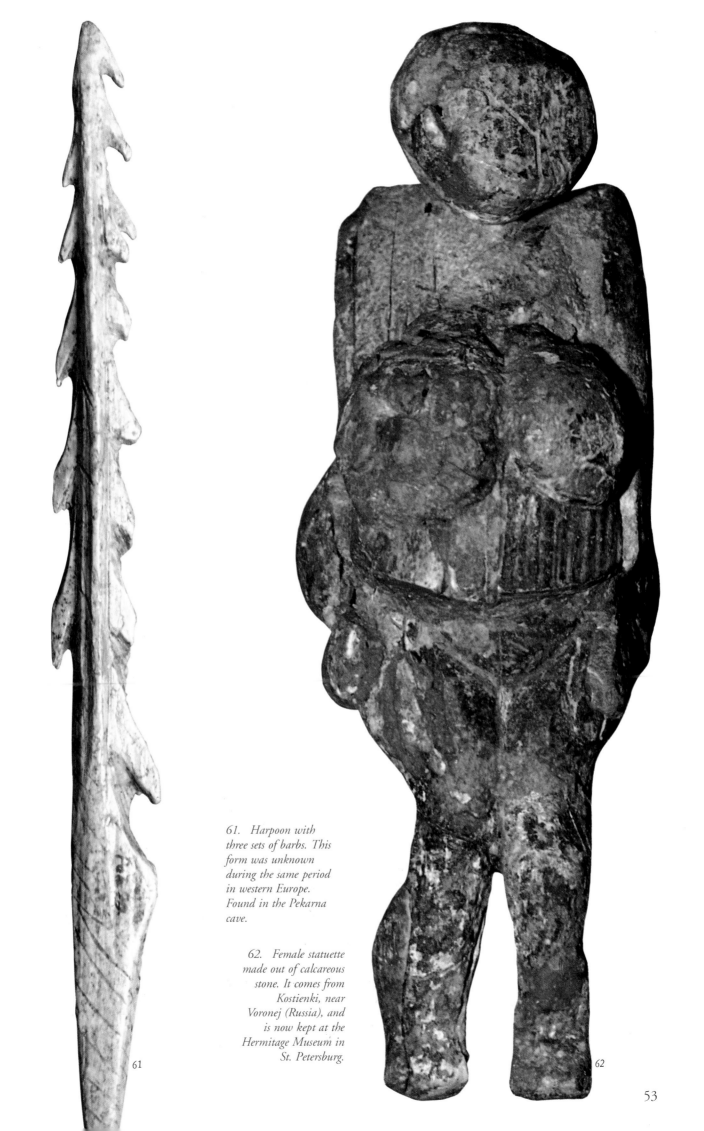

61. Harpoon with three sets of barbs. This form was unknown during the same period in western Europe. Found in the Pekarna cave.

62. Female statuette made out of calcareous stone. It comes from Kostienki, near Voronej (Russia), and is now kept at the Hermitage Museum in St. Petersburg.

61

62

15 The Funerary Rites of the Neolithic

THE WORD "Neolithic" has been used to refer to both the "New Stone" and the "Old Stone" Age. The concept has now been widened to designate a new stage in human life: from being a *hunter,* man becomes a *producer* of the animal and vegetable species. In passing from nomadism to settlement, he invents pottery, new ways of polishing materials, weaving, and the village in which the habitations are grouped together. The culture of the Neolithic originated in the Fertile Crescent of the Near East about 8000 B.C. and then spread around the Mediterranean. By the sixth millennium it had begun to penetrate the Balkans and during the fifth it expanded along the plains of the Danube, Mediterranean Africa and the Sahara. It reached central Asia in the fourth millennium. In recent decades scholars of prehistory have managed to define the various stages in the spread of the Neolithic. It is generally agreed that it came to an end with the birth of metallurgy. The Neolithic is not just a technical and economic stage in the growth of mankind but also a cultural and religious one.

The evidence on which we base our definitions of the behavior and mental situation of *homo religiosus* of the Neolithic comprises some outstandingly important funerary remains. They bear witness not only to man's desire to understand his natural environment and portray his own species, but also to his belief in life after death. In the Natufian period — a Syrian-Palestinian pre-Neolithic cultural stratum that lasted from 10,500 to 8200 B.C. — the dead were usually buried in dwellings, sometimes accompanied by ornaments. Necklaces, bracelets, suspenders, belts and headgear have been found in the graves of Mallaha and el-Wad, and even some miniature art pieces. The graves, arranged in a summary fashion, were sometimes lined with clay (Mallaha), and sometimes covered with stone slabs (Erq el-Ahmar). The skulls appear to have been treated with particular respect.

There are several skull deposits at Jericho dating back to the eighth millennium. They were arranged in a circle looking towards the center, or divided into three groups of three, also looking in the same direction. In the same period, before 7500 B.C., it was evidently common in Syria-Palestine to "separate the skulls from the skeletons for some particular purpose" (Cauvin, 1978, p. 128). The skulls discovered at Mureybet on the middle Euphrates date back to 7500 B.C. and were laid on the ground along the walls, each one on a specially positioned mound of red clay. They were thus visible for the inhabitants of the dwelling (Cauvin, ibid.). In Jericho skulls have been found with faces modeled on them in clay. The face is like a mask, with a painted surface and shells set into the eye sockets. Many such skulls were placed together. A similar situation is to be found at Ramad and Beisamun. Having drawn up an inventory of the Syrian-Palestinian funerary practices, J. Cauvin (1978, p. 35) argued that "Neolithic man of the seventh millennium tried to preserve the image of certain of his people after death so that they would be visible to the living community." This constitutes the beginning of "ancestor worship," which implies belief in life hereafter.

Scholars of prehistory have also noticed that in Syria-Palestine of the sixth and fifth millennia the interment ceremonies at Byblos, Ras Shamra, and Mount Judah were remarkably homogeneous. The presence of pottery in the burial sites bears witness to the practice of placing food offerings for the deceased in the graves ready for the next life. The vases used would seem to have been influenced by the Tell Halaf ceramics of northern Syria, a Mesopotamian influence that was widespread along the coast around 4500 B.C. Beside the individual graves there were also collective ones, such as the "house of the dead" at Byblos. This is a large central room containing thirty or so skeletons covered with various levels of earth, including red earth that had been taken there. There are also smaller cells adjacent to the main room with a skull deposit in one of them. In Cauvin's view (1972, p. 96), this building, "full of power made sacred by means of the red earth and the funerary deposits, would have exercised an evident attraction on the village."

Çatal Hüyük in Anatolia is the source of precious information concerning the relationship between habitations and burials because

63. *Spectacular scene of a funeral cult portrayed on rock at the end of the Paleolithic period (Zisab Gorge, Brandberg, Namibia). Archaeological evidence would seem to suggest that Neanderthal and Paleolithic man tended to separate the dwelling of the living from that of the dead. The dwellings of the dead may also have been ceremonial places. By contrast, in the Neolithic period the dwellings of the living and those of the dead tend to coincide.*

63

from the seventh and sixth millennia, the dead were interred beneath platforms in the houses and sanctuaries. The stripped bones were wrapped in mats and buried along with the personal effects (ornaments, weapons) and offerings. Some isolated skulls have also been found in the sanctuaries, along with painted bones. From the Middle Neolithic on, collective burial was common in Europe, first along the Atlantic coast and later elsewhere. Moreover, the practice of choosing a particular burial site also became more common.

Rites arise when practices are associated with beliefs. Funeral rites coincide with particular practices and reactions provoked by the death of other people. The fascinating examples presented here show that Neolithic man multiplied these rites, investing them with increasingly rich symbolism: the embellishment of the body in preparation for the afterlife; the special attention paid to the skull; the lifelike faces; the "eyes"; the proximity of the dead and the living. Such symbolism of life witnesses to a solid belief in the afterlife.

64. Reconstruction of two walls of one of the forty or so shrines at Çatal Hüyük (Turkey), with decorations reproducing ornamental motifs from textiles. These sanctuaries are similar in structure to the habitations (over a hundred of them), though larger and richly decorated with frescoes and carvings. The platform constitutes a characteristic element of the structure: a raised area set against the wall that acted as a bed, and a working area or a place of rest beneath which the dead could be buried. We do not know whether these shrines were permanently inhabited or by whom; such burials were common in both the shrines and the habitations.

64

65

65. Reproduction of paintings featuring a vulture in one of the shrines at Çatal Hüyük. These paintings were discovered by Mellaart, who believed they related to funeral rites. The vultures with their wings spread fly threateningly over headless beings, corpses perhaps; the bodies of the dead buried there, though anatomically intact, were found in positions similar to those of the painted figures.

66. Page 56: Interior of a large kiva *at Lowry Ruin, not far from Mesa Verde in Colorado, United States. The kiva were typical constructions of the Anasazi civilization that developed between the years 800 and 1200 in the southwest region of the United States. These circular underground rooms were part of the dwellings and were used for storage and for sacred events. They were domestic or group shrines in which meetings were held to transmit the origin myths that accounted for the link between life and death.*

67. Artist's conception of a shrine at Çatal Hüyük in Turkey. The platform beneath which the dead were buried is clearly visible. The clay heads and the horns indicate that this shrine was dedicated to the bull deity.

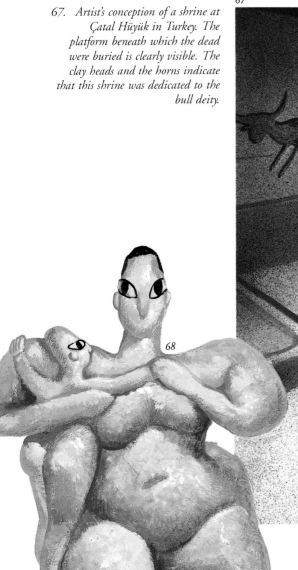

68. Reproduction of a terra-cotta female figurine with a child at her breast. It was found in the Hacilar excavations in Turkey (fourth millennium B.C.). The mother goddess, whom it probably represents, was an essential feature of Neolithic religious culture.

70. Reconstruction of a burial of the Yayoi period at the end of the Neolithic period and beginning of the Bronze Age in Japan (3rd century B.C.). The dead person was placed in an urn which was then buried beneath the house, as in China several millennia earlier, or under a dolmen.

69. Artist's conception of a burial scene in central-eastern Europe during the Neolithic period. The cemetery was shaped like the village and the tombs were built with slabs of stone. Gifts were laid beside the deceased.

16 Sacral Houses and Sanctuaries

IN THE NEAR EAST, the genesis of man's habitation or dwelling can be traced throughout the slowly spreading culture of the Neolithic. As early as 10,000 B.C., Natufian civilization gave rise to the first villages, which meant that settlement had begun. As the village of Mureybet on the Euphrates clearly reveals, from 8300 to 7600 B.C. habitations and the way they were grouped together were gradually undergoing architectural transformation. After the year 7600 B.C., with the population increase in Syria and Palestine, villages also began to grow in importance, thus giving rise to a new stage in their evolution.

Archaeologists working in the Konya plains of Anatolia have explored the major settlement of Çatal Hüyük, inhabited between 6250 and 5400 B.C., when the population migrated toward Haçilar and elsewhere. Apart from agriculture and crafts production, the city was also evidently a center of intense religious activity. In fact, 40 of the 139 houses were sacral, the first known sanctuaries. These contained painted frescoes, high relief sculptures, statuettes, and figurines, fifty of them portraying female figures. The iconography comprises two main symbols: a goddess, and a male figure resembling a bull or sometimes "a bearded man riding a bull, a surprising precursor of the Phoenician Hadad, the god of tempest and war" (J. Cauvin, 1987, p. 1478). The bull is often portrayed individually using small figures, especially bulls' heads modeled in clay. The two figures — the goddess and the bull — are oversized in relation to the other figures depicted. The sacral buildings embody various features similar to those of the sanctuaries, and their art, in J. Cauvin's view, shows that the sacred was perceived as belonging to a sphere above man. In other words, there was belief in a supreme divine entity represented by the goddess. Figurines of goddesses were also made in other archaeological areas of Anatolia, albeit in lesser quantities: Çukurkent, Erbaba, Suberde, Haçilar. Moreover in 1978 a vase was found at Arpachiyah in Iraq decorated with identical motifs: goddess and bull. This suggests that a certain religious unity prevailed in the Near East during the Neolithic.

The first village of Europe was Lepenski Vir. It certainly existed during the sixth millennium, at the very outset of the Neolithic, on the banks of the Danube, near the Transylvanian Alps in Serbia. It consists of 86 homogeneous buildings. In the center of the habitations, behind a large rectangular hearth, there is an altar, and also a sculpture made on a stone. Moreover, a highly evocative human face has also been carved into other stones. D. Srejovic, who explored this archaeological area, believes that this is a representation of the god of water. As at Çatal Hüyük, the funerary rites were related to these sacral houses: interment beneath or near the hearth, burial of children at the back of the house, and considerable use of red ochre. The houses were made sacred by both the presence of the dead and the image of the deity. All this leads us to the subject of the megalithic necropolises, which were characterized by similar features.

With the spread of Neolithic culture and the settlement of people in villages, a new attitude toward death gradually began to emerge. From 4500 to 2000 B.C., monumental collective burial sites characterized the western Neolithic. These were often grouped together in proper necropolises. Such were the first monuments of western and northern Europe. Traces of similar structures are also to be found in the Mediterranean countries, and later in northern Africa. The aim was to bring together in a single area all the deceased of the clan. These monuments are sacred places, or indeed sanctuaries, as the careful construction of the façade and interior layout show. The bodies placed in these collective tombs were accompanied by ornaments, funeral objects, pottery containing food offerings, and items of worship. The walls were decorated with engravings, relief carvings, and female figures. The image of the goddess protectress of the dead first makes its appearance in the third millenium. She was often portrayed as a face without a mouth, and also featured on stelae statues placed outside the necropolises of southern France, Spain, Brittany and Italy. At Capdenac-le-Haut in the Lot region of France there is a figure that bears some resemblance to the carved stones at Lepenski Vir, more than 2000 kilometers away.

There are remarkable megalithic monuments in the Maltese archipelago, built between the beginning of the Neolithic and 3500 B.C.

71. *Plan of a group of houses around the courtyard (c) at Çatal Hüyük: some of them are shrines (s).*

72. *A Çatal Hüyük dwelling showing the typical features: entrance from the roof with a ladder, raised hearth, ovens partially embedded in the wall, platforms.*

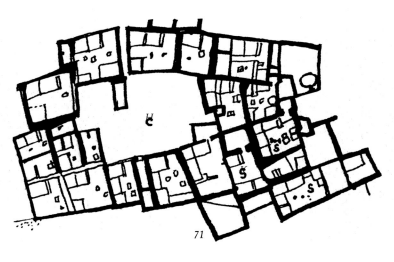

71

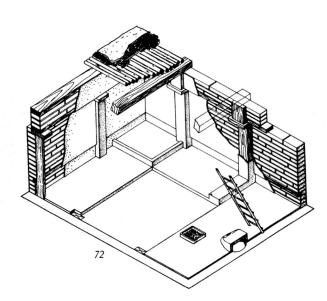

72

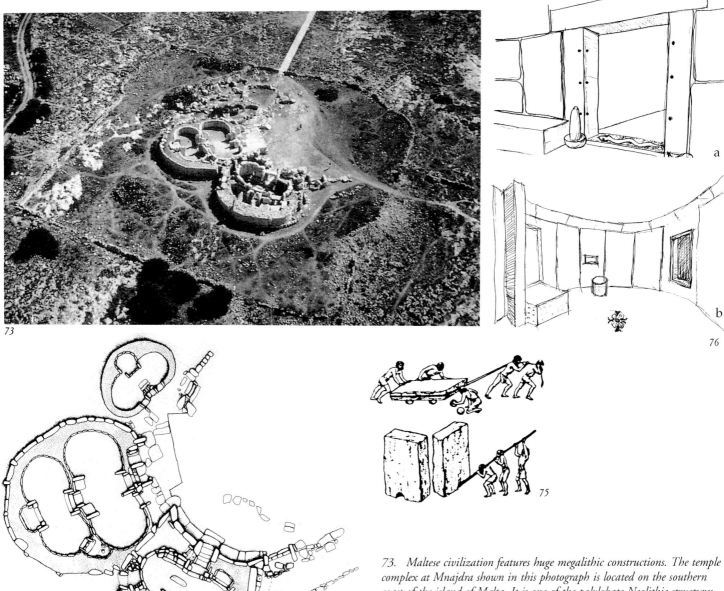

73

76

74

75

Numerous hypogea appear in the fourth millennium, including that of Hal Saflieni, a huge tomb containing thousands of bodies, but also a place of worship, as indicated by the statues of goddesses and variety of engravings and sculptures. During this period the construction of prestigious megalithic temples was also begun. These were built on a trilobate or polylobate ground plan and contained magnificent carved altars and statues, typically portraying goddesses. All this confirms one of the aspects of the religious practices of Neolithic man, the association of the deceased with a cult of the goddess.

73. *Maltese civilization features huge megalithic constructions. The temple complex at Mnajdra shown in this photograph is located on the southern coast of the island of Malta. It is one of the polylobate Neolithic structures there that seem to signify an entrance/exit to the promontories, like a territorial guardian. Three temples with a variety of rooms and stone furnishings have been identified at Mnajdra; there is also another unidentified structure. The religious ritual associated with this site is thought to have related to fishing.*

74. *Plan of the temple at Mnajdra drawn by Anati on the basis of aerial photos and surveys by J. D. Evans.*

75. *Round stones found in Malta were used for transporting the stone blocks used in building. They were then heaved into place with the help of levers fitted into notches chipped out of each block during the detachment and transport process.*

76. *a) Access portal at one of the temples of the Mnajdra complex. Note the meter-long snake-shaped fish at the foot of the jamb. It echoes the fish-shaped rock that emerges from the floor of the half-crescent. Beside the entrance there is a bowl with a cylindrical stone fit into it, a symbol related to fertility.*
   b) Room in one of the Mnajdra temples. Note the judas hole connecting it to another room. This may have been part of an oracular ritual, with another isolated room beyond containing an inset shrine and a repository suggesting secret rites, possibly of initiation.

78

79

80

77. Female figurine suckling a child. It dates to the fourth millennium B.C. and comes from Ur in Mesopotamia (Iraq).

78, 80. Artist's reconstruction of the plan of a Neolithic temple found at Sabatinivka in Moldavia and of a possible ritual scene that could have taken place inside. Note the presence of an oven and terra-cotta figurines and pottery. The statuettes and cult objects would have been fired in the temple.

79. Simplified artist's reconstruction of a Neolithic Moldavian village of the fourth millennium B.C. Note the prominent central position of the building dedicated to worship: the temple.

17 The Agrarian Myths

81. *Reproduction by E. Anati of carvings on a menhir statue in Valcamonica. Anati considers these Bronze Age (3200-2500 B.C.) menhir statues as expressions of a complex vision of the world. Here the sun disk can be identified at the top, with weapons, an ornament and animals in the center and a plowing scene below.*

81

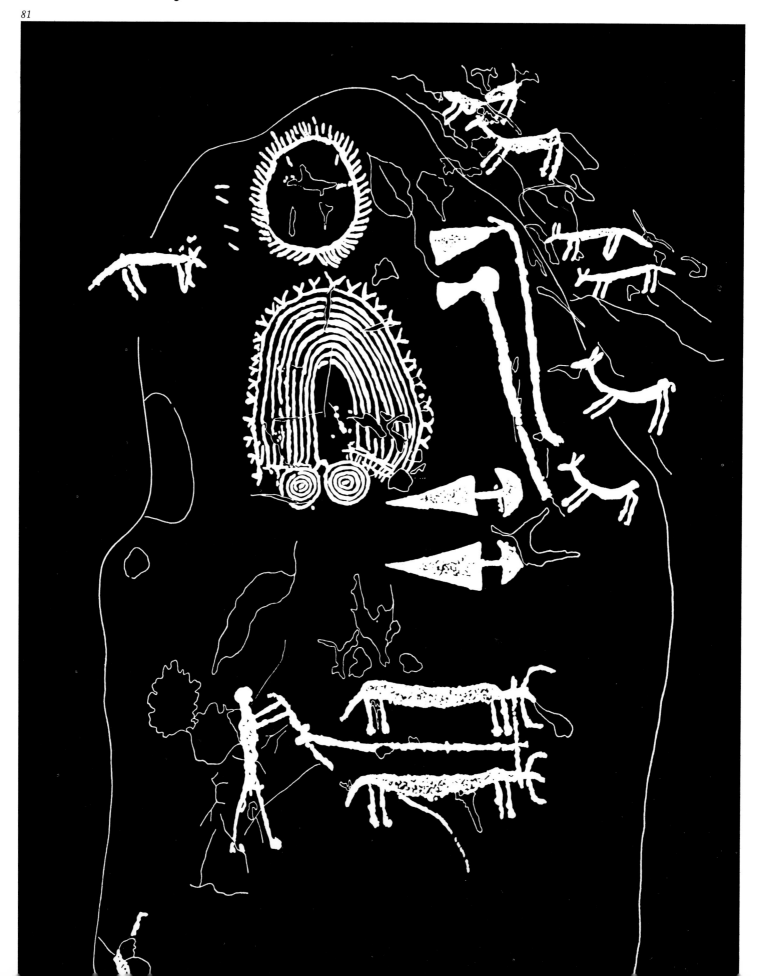

IN THE TENTH millennium in the Near East, man became the "gardener of the world." Natufian civilization began around 10,000 B.C., and lasted approximately two thousand years. The cultural area it covered reached from the Nile to the Euphrates at the outset of Neolithic civilization. Abandonment of caves and progressive settlement in villages built on sites where there had been no previous settlement characterized the Natufian period. (The impetus for the cave dwellers to leave their original shelter is thought to have been a rise in climatic temperature.)

The Natufian villages were built on the plains and at the foot of mountains (Aïn, Mallaha, Jericho), or along the banks of lakes or permanent water courses. The population relied for its survival on wild cereals, game from the forests, and fish. Abundant remains of fish and crustaceans have been found at Mureybat on the Euphrates and at Mallaha. Archaeological evidence shows that the first settlements allowed for a certain mobility in looking for food. Study of the pollens found around the Natufian villages has revealed the presence of large quantities of graminaceous plants, which indicate an early demographic increase (Mallaha, Mureybet, Cheik Hassan). Cereals could be grown once populations had settled and created villages (J. Cauvin, 1978). Numerous recent discoveries in Palestine, Syria and Israel show that settlement preceded agriculture: the domestication of animal species and crop cultivation were consequences of settlement. The earliest agriculture dates back to around 8000 B.C. This was the beginning of the eastern Neolithic.

The new food strategy had repercussions on the way man related to animals and plants. It brought about new concepts: field, plantation, sowing, the observation of growth and the seasons, harvesting, storage, labor. Such conceptual changes were also expressed in a new symbolism. The same can be said for raising livestock. With the evolution of technology, irrigation was introduced, new implements were developed (sickle blades, ground stone, hatchets, arrow heads), and the new art of making fire adopted. Man became a builder, breeder, and farmer, and this brought about a change in his ideas and attitudes toward life, labor, sustenance, and natural forces.

Animal domestication — of sheep, goats, pigs, dogs — was practiced from the Nile to the Euphrates. Rope, nets, boats and pottery also made their appearance. In producing his own food, man adapted his behavior and worked out a calender to regulate his seasonal tasks. In direct relation to the rhythms of vegetation, he discovered the mystery of birth, death, and rebirth. Observation of the sun, the moon and the stars fired the farmer's imagination, and his experience of cosmic time led him to conceive of time as circular and the cosmos as governed by cycles. Moreover, his religious appreciation of space is reflected in his dwelling, village and cultivated fields. The figurative art that developed between the ninth and the seventh millennium is indicative of a deep change in the psychic life of the individual and the community.

The roots of the great agrarian myths of the New East and the Mediterranean are embedded in the humus of the Neolithic period. Man has imagined and represented the deities as having female, male, and animal features. To penetrate the mystery of the growth of cereals, vegetation, and the rhythm of the seasons, the farmer created a sacred story of the birth of the cosmos, the animals, and vegetables. This sacred story is made of cosmogonic myths that explain the origins of the world, the mountains, the rivers, man and woman, and the animal and vegetable species. The various agrarian myths sacralize both woman as the giver of life and the male-female polarity implicit in the perceptions of the Paleolithic hunters and the mythical ancestor.

The agrarian myths developed the subject of the earth mother, the sacredness of life, and the periodic renewal of the cosmos thanks to the action of supernatural powers. The association of woman and bull in the iconographic symbolism of the Syrian-Palestinian Neolithic bears undeniable witness to the importance of the agrarian myths that we find in the European Neolithic from the sixth to the fourth millennium. There are two particularly fine examples of them: the thousands of figurines discovered by Marija Gimbutas in the Balkans, and the numerous stelae statues in the Alpine regions of the Valcamonica. In the engravings found in the latter location there is an evident social and religious tripartition into sky, war and agriculture that marks the end of the Neolithic.

82

82. *Reproduction of a cave carving of the early Neolithic at "Barranco" de Los Grajos in the Murcia region of the Spanish Levant. The archaeologist M. Gimbutas has interpreted it as a ritual fertility dance scene performed by men and women, with a huge phallus on the left.*

83

84

85

64

86

87

88

89

83. View of Lepenski Vir, from the Iron Gates of the Danube in Serbia. Remarkable archaeological discoveries were begun in 1965 on the lower terraces overlooking the river.

84, 85, 89. As these photographs illustrate, a population of hunter-gatherers who earlier lived in caves decided to build stable dwellings and temples in the open air. Plate 84 shows a shrine beneath the rock with two statues; plate 85 shows another shrine with sculptures; and plate 98 shows the foundations of a central building at Lepenski Vir 1 with an ellipsoidal altar and a rectangular hearth.

86, 87, 88. Three Lepenski Vir sculptures, the first large stone statues of European prehistory. According to D. Srejovic, who discovered Lepenski Vir, these sculptures — portraying figures that are part man and part fish — may relate to a conception of the world similar to that expressed many thousands of years later by the pre-Socratic philosophers of European civilization, such as Thales, Heraclitus and Anaximander. Water was held to be the origin of the world, of life and primordial creatures. Although they were not farmers, the men, artists, and priests of Lepenski Vir formed a society that was already culturally Neolithic.

18 Neolithic Goddess Worship

FEMALE STATUETTES with enlarged female attributes have come down to us from the Paleolithic. Often referred to by scholars of prehistory as the "Aurignacian Venuses," these fertility symbols were widespread in an area between Siberia and the Atlantic. However, they are small fare when compared with Franco-Cantabrian animalist art.

Shortly before 8000 B.C. and the earliest forms of agriculture, female figurines relatively similar to the Paleolithic Venuses appeared at Mureybet on the middle Euphrates. They far outnumbered the animal figures, thus evidencing the increasing importance of the human figure — especially the female form — in art. (J. Cauvin, 1987). The fertile woman and the symbolic depictions of the bull which typically accompany her actually precede the new agricultural fertility rather than being a consequence of it. This most recent discovery is of central importance for understanding Neolithic religion.

At Ramad in the Damascus region toward 6000 B.C., the female figurines began to feature some new characteristics. First and foremost, the occipital part of the head was elongated upwards and outwards. Moreover, the eyes "were made of clay disks carved into what is known as snake's eye shape" (Cauvin, 1978). This shape of eye was to gain widespread acceptance during the course of the sixth millennium: in Byblos, Munhata in Palestine, Hassuna in Mesopotamia and finally in Iran. There is no doubt that subject matter of this sort, which was constant in the Near East, presupposes certain thought processes and a specific symbolism. The new symbolism, with its particular attention to the head and eyes, was added to the typical imagery signifying female fertility (prominent breasts and a pregnant abdomen). In Cauvin's view, the artists wished to describe the female psyche.

Two thousand years later, female statuettes, frescoes and relief carvings abounded in the Anatolian city of Çatal Hüyük. Systematic study of this prodigious evidence has produced some astonishing fruits. The female depictions focus on a regal woman in labor, begetter of men and animals. Beside her, though subordinate, there is sometimes a bearded man riding a bull, and sometimes just a bull. Both goddess and bull are oversized in relation to the context. In Cauvin's view, the woman and bull symbols at Mureybet actually became two proper deities and, in contrast to features of the horizontal universe of Franco-Cantabrian art, they constitute the sacred perceived by man as transcendent: a goddess and a bull god. The goddess is the first deity with human features. In J. Cauvin's view, the "existence of a religion can be traced back to the Neolithic" (1987, p. 1479).

The female figurines found throughout the Near East from Damascus to Jericho and from Anatolia to Mesopotamia were also common in central Europe, along the Adriatic coast, and in Crete, Cyprus, Malta and Macedonia from the sixth millennium. They continued to spread from 6500 to 3500 B.C.: the Sesklo civilization in Greece; the Impresso in Italy; Karanova, Boian and Gumelnita in Bulgaria and Romania; Starcevo and Vinêa in Yugoslavia, Romania and Czechoslovakia; Lepenski Vir; Cucuteni in Romania; and Alföld, Lengyel and Tisza in Austria and Hungary. Thanks to the excavations and discoveries of Marija Gimbutas, evidence of this "Old Europe" comprises around 30,000 figurines from over 3000 Neolithic archaeological areas.

These figurines in bone, stone and clay are generally called "fertility goddesses." Their interpretation, including both the study of the ideograms and symbols that appear on them and comparative study of vase paintings and pottery, has led scholars to speak about a proper pantheon of the gods of "old Europe": bird goddesses, snake goddesses, vegetation goddesses, the great goddess of life, of death, of regeneration. As in the East, alongside each goddess there is a male deity.

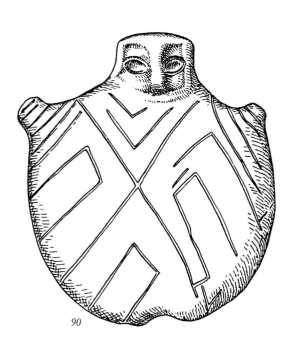

90

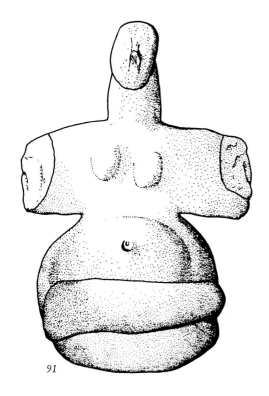

91

The masks, symbols and ideograms bear witness to the presence of rites, and hence to official goddess worship. The statuettes of worshipers and religious scenes are proof of this. Mythical symbolism of this sort shows that at the time of Çatal Hüyük a genuine Neolithic religion involving the worship of the goddess of life and fertility extended with all its rites throughout southeastern and central Europe. This was indeed the origin of the great pantheons of the Mediterranean and the East.

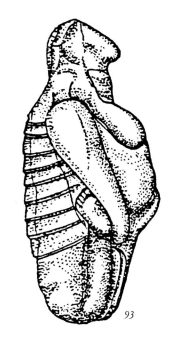

90. Bird goddess dating to around 5000 B.C., found in the Vinca area near Belgrade. A large X cuts the body up into four segments. Vinca culture is one of the several that flourished between the Dnieper and the Danube at the beginning of the Neolithic and of the spread of agriculture in the region. The bird goddesses had two opposing natures: on the one hand they dispensed life, well-being and food; on the other, as vultures or birds of the night, they dispensed death.

91. Marble statuette representing a snake goddess from an island in the Aegean. According to M. Gimbutas, the foremost expert in Mediterranean Neolithic deities, the snake is a fundamental image of vitality and continuity, the guardian of energy in the house and a symbol of family life.

92. Terra-cotta temple model from Porodim, Macedonia, with a goddess mask on the roof.

93, 94, 95. This bird goddess comes from Malta and is clearly a fertility symbol. In fact, the figure is visibly pregnant and the nine lines across her back represent the nine months of pregnancy. It was created toward the end of the fourth millennium B.C.

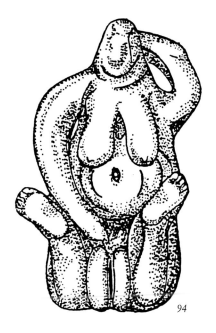

93

92

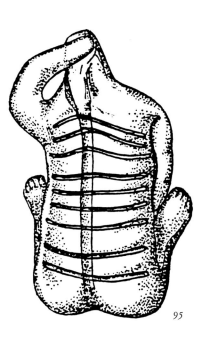

94

95

67

19 Petroglyphs, Menhirs and the Astral Cult

PAINTINGS AND carvings decorating the walls of caves or open-air rocks are to be found in all continents. They bear witness to a continuous tradition lasting from the Upper Paleolithic to the Bronze Age. The aim of this short chapter is to illustrate the cave art of the Neolithic period, that is, the petroglyphs and the decorations of the stelae statues.

There is a wealth of rock carving in Valcamonica in Italy, a narrow valley of Lombardy, north of Brescia. Shortly before 5000 B.C., the "Atlantic" climatic period began. It brought with it a population increase and the introduction of agriculture alongside the hunting and gathering typical of the early Valcamonica period, whose artists portrayed animals almost exclusively in their petroglyphs. In the Valcamonica periods I and II (5000-3000 B.C.), the symbolism of the petroglyphs underwent important artistic and ideological change. In addition to the numerous anthropomorphic figures in prayer-like poses with their arms raised skyward, there were increasing numbers of solar and heavenly symbols. Moreover, cup marks were frequently carved into the rock, suggesting rites of offering, or perhaps representations of constellations. The interest in the wild and domesticated animals that still populated the environment dissolved. Toward 3800 B.C., the beginning of period II A, a pair of oxen attached to a plow made its appearance. This period was particularly rich in praying figures, which were often portrayed in groups and accompanied by solar symbols.

96. Artist's conception of a decoration ceremony on block 1 at Cemmo in Valcamonica (Italy). The block was part of the megalithic complex (3200-2500 B.C.) of a sacred site. The animals and daggers were first scratched into the rock and then colored in.

96

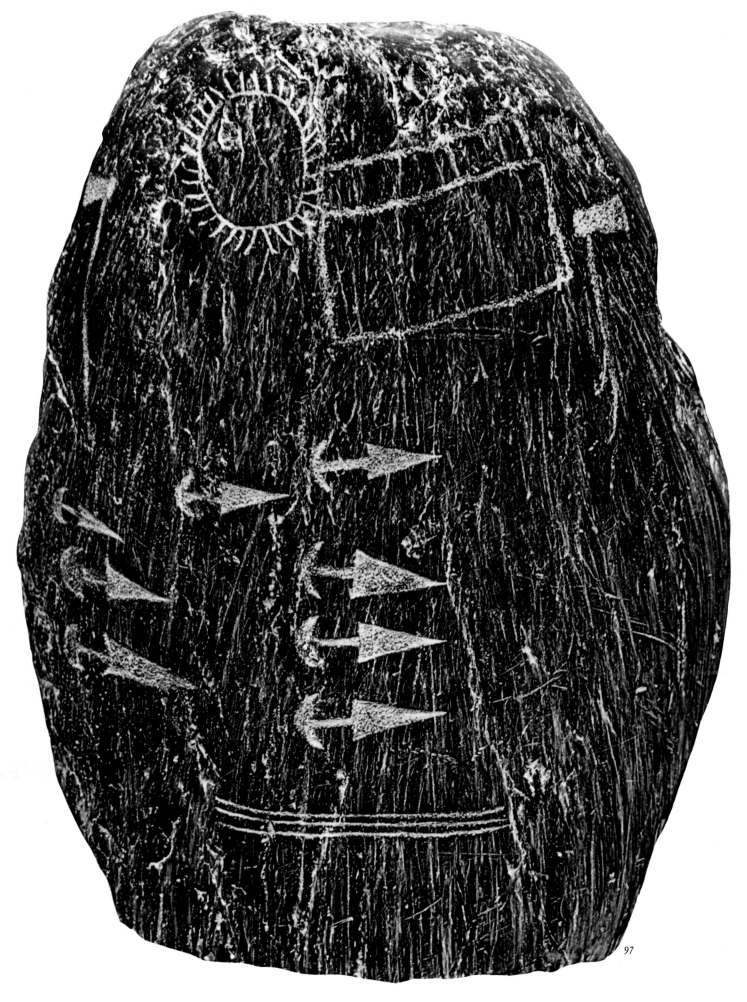

97

97. *This is one of the most important menhir statues of the alpine area of Italy. It was discovered in Valcamonica and dates back to 3200-2500 B.C. It is considered by E. Anati to be a classic example of the Camunian cosmogony in which the signs also relate to an anthropomorphic composition. There is the sun disk above, the earth represented by weapons flanked by two arm-like axes in the center, and below this a belt that is also the sign of water as a passage to the afterlife.*

98

It is noteworthy that the groups of praying figures were carved on rocky platforms located in the direction of the rising sun, toward which the figures raise their arms. Moreover, there were also idol-shaped engravings, some of them two meters tall. Such figures became more numerous during the course of the fourth millennium and would appear to correspond to the initial stage of the earliest stelae statues of the Lunigiana, of the Eveyron and the Tarn in southern France (E. Anati, 1978). During period II, the portrayals of "spades" became more frequent. Idols and other symbols were accompanied by solar disks. E. Anati (1978) has pointed out that the idols carved in rock should be compared with similar forms that were widespread in France, Italy and central Europe during the fourth millennium. Moreover, it is significant that the praying figures and the solar disk should be featured in the art of the Valcamonica in both of the Neolithic millennia, as though religious ideology were sustained by a central axis. For the historian of religion this would appear to indicate that sun worship was central to the religious beliefs of the Valcamonica peoples.

There is another aspect to cave art that should also be mentioned: the stelae statues of northern Italy (Alto Adige, Valcamonica, Valtellina, Val d'Aosta, Liguria), southern France, and Switzerland. Such monuments are of two different types: the stelae statues presenting

anthropomorphic figures, and the menhir statues or monoliths decorated with the same motifs as those found in the caves. E. Anati has pointed out that the location of some of these stelae statues in the Lunigiana area actually coincides with the sites of medieval churches (E. Anati, 1981). This suggests the permanent nature of the sacred. Indeed, some of the statues were mutilated and kept in the crypts of the Christian churches, while folk traditions have preserved the recollection of a pagan cult. The stelae statues were frequently found near a spring or a water course, or at the confluence of two streams (Pontevecchio). The remains of megalithic constructions have also been unearthed near some of these sites. Some of these anthropomorphic stelae are male, whereas others are female, suggesting that they are connected with funeral practices.

In the alpine area of Italy the decoration of these stelae statues is often divided into three bands: at the top, there are symbols including the great radial disk with two smaller disks beside it, standing for the sky, light, and heat (E. Anati, 1968); in the center, there are depictions of weapons; and below, symbols of fertility and wealth. Taken all together, they suggest a divine entity. However, such divisions into

99

70

three sections are less common outside the alpine region. The erection of these monuments began around the middle of the fourth millennium, and continued through to about 2500 B.C., when the Bronze Age was well underway. Scholars of prehistory have formulated various hypotheses concerning the meaning of these ritual stelae with their three bands of decoration. It is reasonable to suppose that the Indo-Europeans reached the alpine valleys around 3200 B.C. The presence in the Valcamonica area of solar symbolism with praying figures before the sun and a series of solar symbols suggests possible influences of the astral cult.

There is another Neolithic monument of considerable interest: the menhir, which appeared along the Atlantic coast starting in the fifth millennium. The Breton word *menhir* means a large single block of stone planted in the ground. In Brittany there are particularly spectacular rows of menhirs. However, the phenomenon is to be found throughout the world. They were built as ritual monuments, and related to the heavens and to astral worship. Apart from the menhirs at Locqmariaquer and Carnac in Brittany, those at Stonehenge near Salisbury in southern England have given rise to the greatest number of questions. Dating to the Neolithic period, this monument was twice enlarged during the course of the early Bronze Age. Since it is perfectly oriented toward the rising sun in the summer solstice, it is now generally thought to have been a sun temple.

From the Bronze Age forward, sun worship was to spread consistently through the West and the East. Certain Scandinavian carvings show the solar disk with rays ending in hands stretched out toward erect praying figures whose own hands are raised in adoration. Neolithic man expressed his particular predilection for celestial phenomena, and this tendency was to increase during the course of the Bronze Age. In fact, solar symbols were to multiply in both Scandinavian cave art and in the Mediterranean cultures. Funeral rites were also modified by an important innovation: the cremation of the body of the deceased with the aim of freeing the spiritual principle so that it could rise toward the heavens. In western and southern Europe, this new funeral practice related to astral worship was to indicate an important religious and cultural movement, the civilization of the urn fields.

100

99. Reproduction by Campbell Grant of a prehistoric cave painting by the Chumash Indians of the Santa Barbara region of California. In Grant's view, Chumash culture produced some of the most complex figurative works of North America, with fantastical double-ended zoomorphic and anthropomorphic figures. The multiple-contour (solar) circles are particularly noteworthy.

100. Graffiti, possibly representing sun worship, in Valcamonica (Italy), reproduced by E. Anati.

101. Scandinavian rock graffiti reproduced by Baltzer. As G. Camps has pointed out, the sun disk with rays that turn into hands is a Neolithic motif found also in Spain and Egypt.

101

102

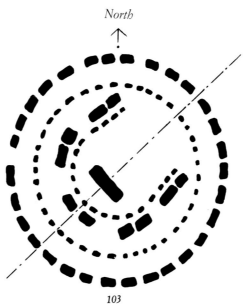

North

102.   Artist's conception of a hypothetical summer solstice in a place like Stonehenge (England). Priests and astronomers watch the sun rising in perfect alignment with the axis of the entrance to the megalithic temple.

103.   The plan shows the period of maximum expansion of the Stonehenge megalithic temple.

104.   These rich rock paintings are located in the Huashan site near the Zuojiang River in the Guangxi Province (China). They feature a great number of supplicants, their arms raised in the performance of a rite. Here and there are sun disks.

103

104

20 The Indus Civilization and Pre-Vedic Religion

SINCE 1922, excavations in the Indus valley have brought to light a prestigious Bronze Age civilization that flourished between 2500 and 1700 B.C. Archaeologists and historians have adopted various terms for it: Pre-Vedic, Indus, Mohenjodaran, Harappan. The civilization currently comprises around three hundred excavated archaeological areas in Pakistan and India. However, its fame owes largely to the two large and splendidly planned cities of Mohenjo-Daro, the ancient capital, and Harappa. Among the outstanding features of this civilization are its uniformity, its urban planning and innovative use of fired bricks for building, its advanced social organization, its prosperous agricultural economy, and its system of writing (that has yet to be deciphered, although specialists at Helsinki University and the Universities of Pakistan have some 3500 inscriptions to work with). The discovery in 1974 of the Mehrgarh archaeological area, together with earlier finds at Mundigak, indicate that this civilization was the culmination of an earlier Neolithic culture that must have originated around 7000 B.C. The Indus civilizations are currently believed to be related to those of the Euphrates. But what brought about their fall around the year 1700 B.C.? Was it war, Indo-European invasion, or a natural catastrophe? This last hypothesis is currently thought to be the most likely.

The study of the behavior of *homo religiosus* is greatly aided by the evidence found at Mohenjo-Daro and other archaeological sites. First and foremost there are thousands of small seals used for sealing and preserving objects and placing them under the protection of the deity. There is also a decorative repertory of pottery, female and male figurines, religious scenes, animals, skeletons and tombs. The seals are examples of superb craftsmanship. Made out of soapstone, they were carved into rectangles or squares, polished with an abrasive, and then engraved with a figure and an inscription.

The main character is the goddess, who is found on various seals as well as being represented by numerous terra-cotta female figurines. There is a remarkable ritual scene portrayed on one Mohenjo-Daro

seal: on her head the goddess wears a two-horned crown to symbolize her majesty and power; prostrate before her, a "priestess" holds out her arm in offering or prayer; behind her there is a goat with a man's head, which might be a symbolic reference to procreative fertility; below this

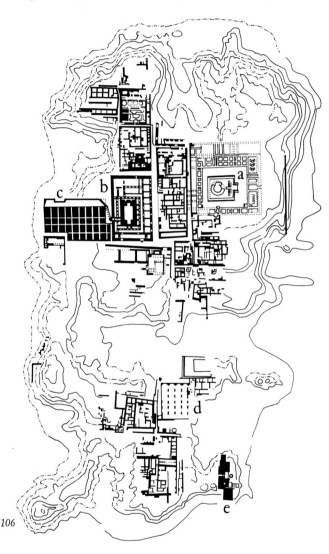

106

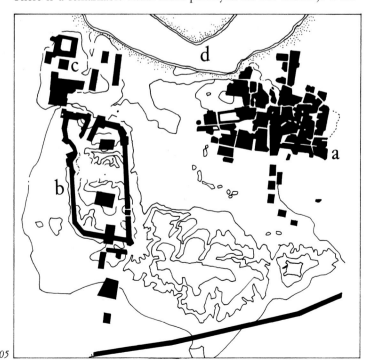

105

105. *Simplified map of the city of Harappa, in present-day Pakistan. a) Modern settlement; b) ancient citadel; c) ancient grain stores for preserving the cereals essential to a complex collective existence.*

106. *Plan of the citadel of Mohenjo-Daro (Pakistan). The buildings date back to a period between 2500 and 2100 B.C. a) Stupa built around 200 A.D. by the nomadic Kushan people who had become Buddhist. The presence of this structure makes excavations in this sector of the citadel difficult. b) Baths; the size of the pools suggests that they were used for ritual as well as hygienic functions; c) granaries; d) assembly halls; e) fortifications. The entrance to each large building was shaded by trees. These together with the network of canals must have created an impressive garden city.*

74

107. *Reproductions of animal figures and sign writing found on seals. Animals were frequently portrayed and thus probably had a sacred meaning. The sign writing has not yet been deciphered.*

there is a band of seven young women in short skirts. The theophany of the Great Goddess is inscribed in a *pipal,* the red-fleshed fig that served as a symbol of fertility. This same ritual scene appears on other seals, indicating that there was a religion common to the Indus peoples.

There are other seals decorated with a three-faced god sitting in the yoga position with a horned crown on his head. Ibex pass before his throne and he is surrounded by a tiger, an elephant, a rhinoceros and a buffalo. The horns symbolize power, the crown is the sign of the sun, the throne indicates majesty, all of which features are also to be found in Babylonian art. This is the god of animals; possibly a prototype of Shiva, the creator, lord of the beasts and prince of yoga.

The Great Goddess and the Great God bring to mind the Mureybet symbolism and the characters found at Çatal Hüyük. The context is that of a fertility religion and a richly illustrated cosmogonic myth. The seals and statuettes recall the Neolithic figurines of central Europe, and could represent secondary deities. The seven young women might well be a ritual symbolic expression of the cult of the Great Goddess, creator of life, protector of birth and infancy. Indeed, they are arguably symbols of family sanctuaries that India has preserved in the worship of the seven goddesses. This type of context recalls the numerous functions carried out by the Great Goddess from Mureybet to the end of the Neolithic in the Near East and in eastern Europe. The Mohenjo-Daro goddess is associated with the worship of the sacred tree, a symbol of fertility, procreation and life. The discovery of a sacerdotal figure suggests the existence of religious activity.

These hypotheses were formulated on the basis of the rich symbolism common to Asia and Europe during the Neolithic period. Clearly they can only be verified once the writing has been deciphered. The religious fabric of thought, rites and cults must have been interwoven with a rich mythology. The cemetery found at Harappa in 1937 contained tombs of unusual sizes that were rich in pottery, the remains of offerings, ornaments, pearls, and mirrors which all indicate Harappan belief in the afterlife.

108. Soapstone seal with the figure of a unicorn and primitive writing that has not yet been deciphered.

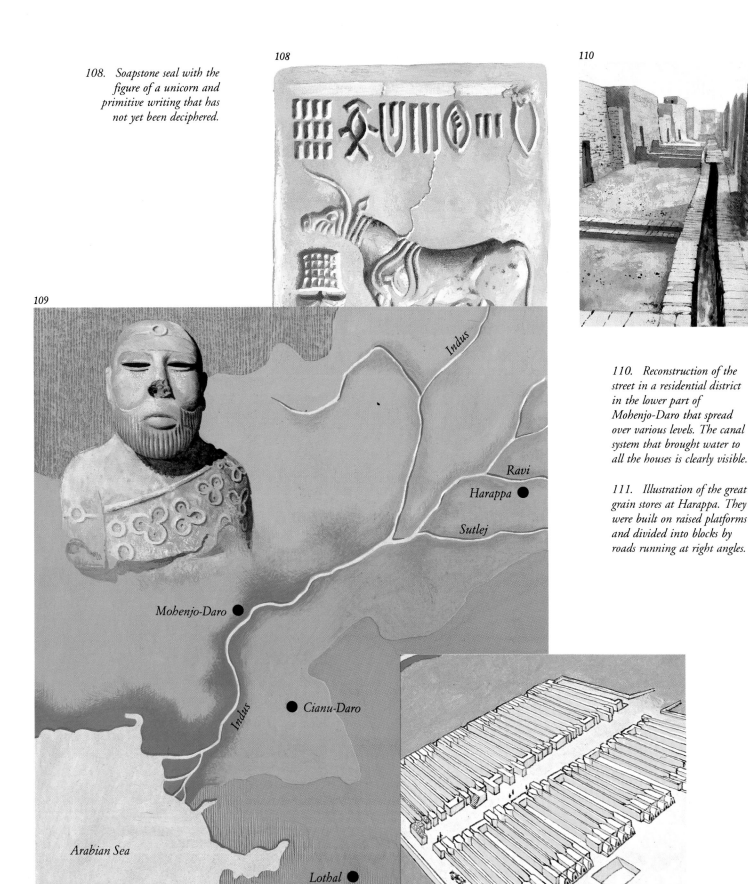

109

110. Reconstruction of the street in a residential district in the lower part of Mohenjo-Daro that spread over various levels. The canal system that brought water to all the houses is clearly visible.

111. Illustration of the great grain stores at Harappa. They were built on raised platforms and divided into blocks by roads running at right angles.

Indus

Ravi

Harappa ●

Sutlej

Mohenjo-Daro ●

Indus

● *Cianu-Daro*

Arabian Sea

Lothal ●

111

109. Illustration of the area of expansion of the Indus civilization with the principal sites, most of which are located in present-day Pakistan. The red area corresponds to present-day India and the striped areas at the top to Afghanistan. The figure of a priest-king that dominates the map is taken from one of the rare sculptures found in these excavations. It came from Mohenjo-Daro.

115. Hypothetical reconstruction of the city of Mohenjo-Daro at the height of its prosperity, toward 2500 B.C. In the foreground is the citadel with the grain stores. Some of the houses are remarkably large. The laborers lived in two-room dwellings in the lower part of the city. The urban planning and waterways were remarkably modern in concept.

112. Bronze statuette found at Mohenjo-Daro, probably portraying a sacred dancer.

113. Soapstone seal of great beauty featuring a horned animal. Found at Mohenjo-Daro.

114

114. Famous seal featuring a ritual. Above, a goddess with a headdress and numerous bracelets is surrounded by the branches of a sacred red-sapped fig tree. Before her there is a prostrate praying figure making an offering, followed by a goat with a human head. In the lower portion of the seal there are seven female figures (the south of India has seven goddesses) with long braids and short skirts who make up a religious procession.

112

113

115

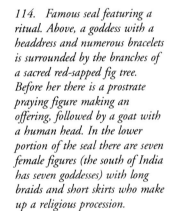

116

116. Ground floor of an average dwelling at Mohenjo-Daro. Note the vestibule and the small porter's lodge. The central courtyard was paved in brick, beneath which were terra-cotta drainpipes for the waste-water from a shower and other conveniences on the first floor. Small service rooms overlooked the kitchen. The master's apartments would have been on the first floor.

21 Settlement, Culture and Religiosity

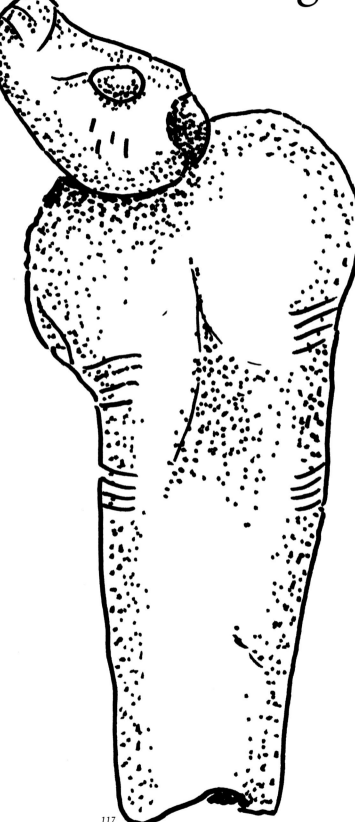

117. Illustration of a bone implement handle decorated with an animal's head. Animals were an essential subject for the artists of the Natufian civilization.

IN THE NEAR EAST, *Homo sapiens sapiens* made sudden remarkable progress, thus taking a decisive step towards modern humanity. This event took place on three levels: settlement, culture, and religiosity.

Settlement

Settlement is a progressive process by means of which dwellings are built by human communities in a particular place. These communities are contained by the resources of a stable natural environment, thus giving rise to the agricultural village that was to become the basis of the future urban civilization (J. Cauvin, 1978, p. 2). For settled populations, this implied grouping together for shelter, food, equipment and growth. Necessary conditions were a favorable environment and an appropriate climatic, botanical and zoological context for the group's sustenance.

Following Gordon Childe, archaeologists and scholars of prehistory have argued that food requirements explain the settlement patterns and cultural and social changes of these groups. However, evidence derived from recent excavations in Syria, Palestine and Lebanon has led Jacques Cauvin to argue that such sustenance could not have been produced in those areas before the eighth millennium. The discoveries at Aïn Mallaha in Israel reveal that these villages actually existed before sustenance was produced there, which means that all evidence pertaining to the tenth and ninth millennia, the outset of the Natufian period and the time when Paleolithic man "left the caves" calls for in-depth critical review. The village of Aïn Mallaha would appear to have maintained a hunter-gatherer economy, and the heavy materials found there exclude any form of the seasonal transport practiced elsewhere by semi-nomadic populations. Moreover, in certain Natufian villages such as Mureybet, Abu Hureyra and Mallaha, there is archaeological and ecological evidence of fishing and the gathering of wild cereals that grew abundantly in the surrounding areas: mountain wheat, wild spelt and barley, lentils and tare. Ecological analyses confirm the outcome of archaeological research: the first Natufian villages of the ninth millennium practiced residential and domestic settlement without practicing agriculture, since their inhabitants lived off the natural resources of the environment: harvesting cereals, fishing and hunting mountain game. Settlement thus preceded agriculture. Agriculture first appeared in the pre-agricultural Natufian villages of the Jordan (Jericho), the Euphrates (Mureybet), and the Damascus oasis (Tell Aswad) during the eighth millennium.

Culture

In his studies of villages and pre-Neolithic society, Jacques Cauvin has tried to identify the human motivations behind the creation of agriculture, the domestication of wild animals, and the invention of new technologies. In analyzing the architectural evolution of the dwellings he became aware of a progressive expansion of the villages from 10,000 to 6000 B.C. This in turn meant that the population must have grown in concentration. However, by means of a careful examination of the production of sustenance it is possible to evaluate the food resources of the populations. Now, the humidity of the climate began to increase around 8000 B.C., which meant that the surrounding steppes became extremely rich in graminaceous plants, thus favoring the natural proliferation of wild cereals. So the agriculture that was invented in this period cannot have been the direct result of a food requirements as such. Nor can it be convincingly claimed to be a case of adapting to the external environment. Indeed, the cause should be sought within pre-Neolithic society: the need for maintaining the balance within a society stressed by population increase. The appearance of agriculture would appear to be the solution to this problem in that cultivated fields became a place for simultaneous collective labor.

With the spread of rectangular houses and cereal farming, these villages also witnessed the dawn of animal husbandry and the first

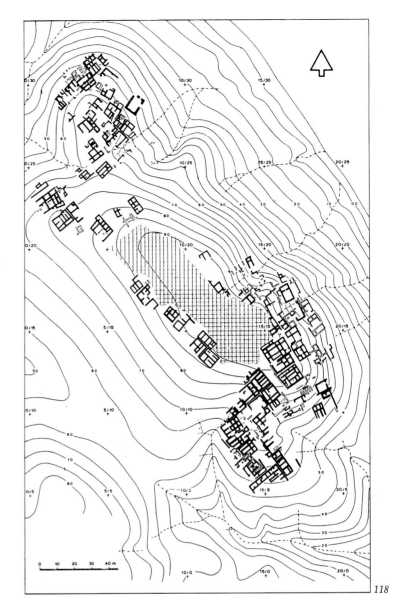

118

118. Plan of the Neolithic village of Buqras, on the right bank of the Euphrates, near modern Dei ez-Zor (Syria). It belongs to the last stage of the process of village expansion that attests to man's cultural evolution. Note the rectangular houses with doorways between the main rooms and smaller noncommunicating spaces used for storage. A fresco with depictions of ostriches and numerous animal and human figurines bears witness to the cultural level achieved.

119, 120. In 1973 and 1974, a group of archaeologists from the University of California led by M. Gimbutas discovered a Neolithic village in Thessaly, Achilleion, inhabited from the middle of the seventh to the middle of the sixth millennium B.C. The discovery of two hundred or so statuettes suggests that the religion centered around female deities. Many of these items were found with ritual vases on altars in temples such as the

one whose ground plan is indicated on the left. To the right there is a reconstruction of courtyards used for religious purposes: 1) oven; 2) stone bench; 3) sloping platform with holes for fire; 4) circular fireplace. These activities came under the aegis of a goddess who was portrayed as pregnant in the figurines found at the site.

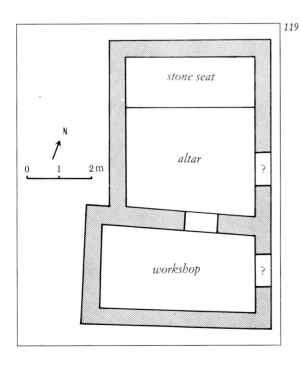

119

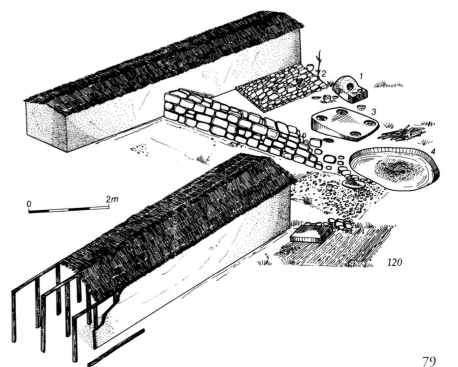

120

121. *Artist's conception of a dwelling from the eighth millennium* B.C. *found in the village of Mureybet in Syria. It has a circular plan with a six-meter diameter and a fairly elaborate interior spatial arrangement with low walls separating the hearth area from the sleeping and storage areas. The complex load-bearing structure is in wood, and the roof and walls in a mixture of clay, pebbles and straw. Just outside the dwelling there would have been a permanent flock of sheep and goats, with the the male tethered to a pole to stop the females from straying. Husbandry had begun.*

122. Drawing of one of the first terra-cotta figurines discovered at Mureybet. It would have been made just before the earliest days of farming. The wide hips and the arms on the stomach clearly indicate that it was a fertility symbol.

123. Hedgehog-shaped vase in alabaster found at Buqras.

124. Drawing reproducing the recto and verso of a mask of the goddess of maternity. Masks of this sort have been found in the courtyards of Achilleion, where the goddess was the guardian of the domestic activities that took place there.

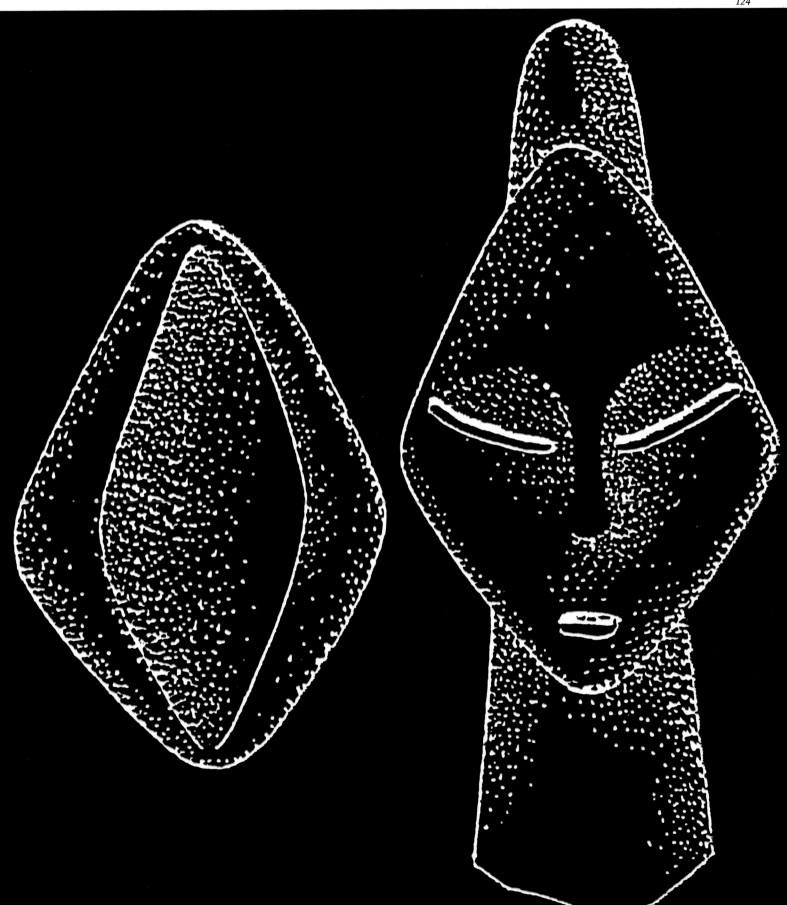

examples of irrigation, along with the social organization that the latter implies. Moreover there was also technological evolution: stone polishing, pottery and the fashioning of new implements. Such progress is always, at base, a cultural phenomenon. Pottery, which is the outcome of familiarity with the properties of clay and mastery of fire, was at first used to make figurines of goddesses and receptacles. Polished stone and pottery both appeared first in an ornamental or religious context; in other words, they were more symbolic than utilitarian in value. Indeed, all the innovations and inventions of the early Neolithic bear witness to the profound mental changes that man was undergoing.

Religiosity

The "birth of the gods" came about at the end of the Natufian period, just before agriculture was invented. The art of the Franco-Cantabrian hunters was essentially animalist. However, the human figure was also occasionally included, such as the Aurignacian Venuses of the Paleolithic. Anthropomorphic figures were scarce during the Natufian period, and only began to appear more frequently during the eighth millennium. This was especially so in the Euphrates region, where female figurines became increasingly common from around 8000 B.C. The established shape and positions of these figurines were symbolic, and thus indicative of a certain way of thinking. Following his systematic study of them, J. Cauvin readily claims that the figure portrayed at the beginning of the eighth millennium was the "Great Eastern Goddess." At Mureybet she appeared within the sphere of a settled village still unacquainted with agriculture. Therefore her appearance could not have symbolized an idea of agricultural fertility (this was to come later), but rather a new sense of the divine. Around 7000 B.C., the goddess was sometimes accompanied by a second human figure, this time male. But it was not until the sixth millennium at Çatal Hüyük that this deity became part of the Neolithic pantheon.

Animalist art predominated among the Natufian hunters. Ox skulls dating back to the year 8200 B.C. were used at Mureybet to create seating, although the animal was still not used for food. Half a millennium was to pass before beef was eaten (toward 7700 B.C.), which suggests that very early on the bull played a role in the religious ideology of the inhabitants of Mureybet. Well before it was ever captured, this creature captivated man's psyche and won a place in his conception of the sacred. Such was the beginning of bull worship, a cult that was to spread throughout the Near East.

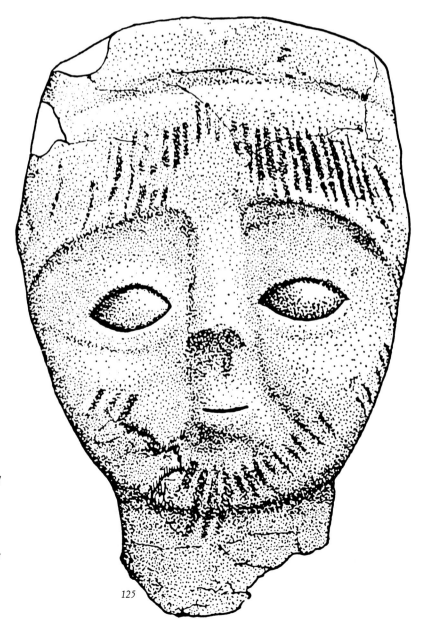

125. Face of a clay statue with shells for eyes and red paint, found at Jericho. The archaeologist E. Anati argues that Neolithic culture in Palestine derived from Natufian culture. A fortified city was built at Jericho long before the discovery of pottery and systematic agriculture.

125

22 Vestiges without Writing: The Message of Prehistoric Evidence

DURING THE past fifty years, archaeology, paleoanthropology, paleontology and palynology have yielded an enormous amount of new evidence concerning the origins of man and the culture and civilization of the Paleolithic and Neolithic (F. Facchini, 1990). Such evidence drawn from the ground lacks any system of writing. Nevertheless, a number of paleoanthropologists (Y. Coppens, 1982) believe that *Homo erectus,* who was already shaping symbolic objects, actually made use of a language. This language has not come down to us because it could not be fossilized, yet the evidence is far from mute once its message has been deciphered.

First of all it tells us that man was the creator of the culture that began with the double-sided cutting of tools and the choice of colors (F. Facchini, 1990). Man's intelligence, his capacity for observation, and his imagination allowed him to represent the world, and to represent it through art. By the same token, he was also able to multiply his efforts in the ceaseless creation of tools better suited to the demands of his existence, to master matter in order to create his own habitat and satisfy his needs, to dominate nature and to achieve artistic masterpieces such as the unsurpassed Franco-Cantabrian cave paintings. From *Homo erectus* to *homo neolithicus,* this extraordinary passage of one and a half million years of culture shows that man already embodied a *ratio seminalis* — an innate and constant organizational principle that ensured the harmony of the fundamental stages of a process of permanent growth. Moreover, the course of this development also reveals the symbol as the characteristic trait of *Homo sapiens.*

One hundred millennia separate Qafzeh man from the megalithic necropolises; we have, from this period, the vestiges of funeral rites that show how the living cared for the dead. The message these rites embody is highly charged but easily understood, and allows us to recognize *homo religiosus* of the Paleolithic. The offerings placed in the tombs, the respectful treatment given to skulls, the act of placing the corpse on a bed of flowers (at Shanidar), the position of the body, the concern for the protection of the deceased, the symbolic character of the ornaments, the frequent use of red ochre, the depositing of objects to be used in the afterlife, the shells set into the eye sockets: these all bear witness to man's firm belief in life after death. This belief proves to be universal. In the Neolithic, the modeled skulls of Syria and Palestine, the sanctuaries with tombs at Çatal Hüyük and Lepenski Vir, and the megalithic necropolises with the presence of a goddess and protector are all unequivocal signs of a belief in a life after death.

The Franco-Cantabrian hunters created magnificent animalist art that bespeaks highly developed imagination, exceptional artistic abilities and well-developed mythical thought. The latter proves that *homo religiosus* had reached a stage in which he could conceive of the essential elements of a cosmogony and a sacred story of the origins. In the Near East, between the ninth and eighth millennia, man made his first timid attempts at human portrayal. These were little more than tentative sketches in the Paleolithic, but they soon multiplied and spread, so that tens of thousands of female figurines representing the Great Goddess, mother of mankind and animals, were soon to be made from the Euphrates to the Nile, from Anatolia to the Balkans

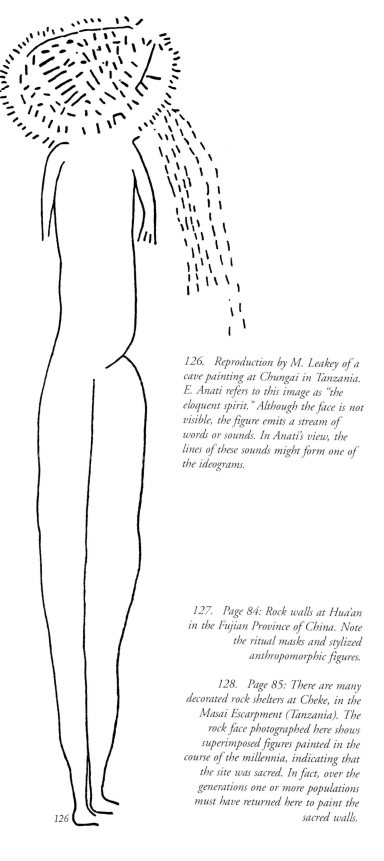

126. Reproduction by M. Leakey of a cave painting at Chungai in Tanzania. E. Anati refers to this image as "the eloquent spirit." Although the face is not visible, the figure emits a stream of words or sounds. In Anati's view, the lines of these sounds might form one of the ideograms.

127. Page 84: Rock walls at Hua'an in the Fujian Province of China. Note the ritual masks and stylized anthropomorphic figures.

128. Page 85: There are many decorated rock shelters at Cheke, in the Masai Escarpment (Tanzania). The rock face photographed here shows superimposed figures painted in the course of the millennia, indicating that the site was sacred. In fact, over the generations one or more populations must have returned here to paint the sacred walls.

126

and the Danube. The deity thus portrayed in human form implies a religious idea that is rich in itself and in its consequences: man represents the deity in his own image, and in conceiving her as transcendent posits himself as a being created in the divine image.

Alongside these female figurines there were also occasional male representations of the deity. Far fewer in number, they began to appear around 8000 B.C., when the earliest forms of agriculture were starting to develop and religious symbolism was undergoing considerable change. *Homo religiosus* perceived a new structure of the sacred that was to inspire Neolithic religion. But religiosity itself dates to the Paleolithic. Religion arises when man personifies the deity as a transcendent being. In the course of the Neolithic, the thousands of praying figures grouped together on the rocks of the Valcamonica constitute the first images of prayer meetings to have come down to us. At the start of the Neolithic, *homo religiosus* conceived the divine not only in the guise of a transcendent human figure, but also as the author of life. This is the meaning of the message of the Great Goddess. It would certainly seem that the religion of the first farmers was matriarchal.

The mythograms of the caves embody the first signs revealing a sacred story of origins. During the Neolithic, this religious memory became part of a complex of cosmogonic myths, of myths pertaining to the origins of animals, vegetables and man himself, and of eschatalogical myths, some of which refer to a flood. Mircea Eliade (1979) has drawn a fascinating picture of the mythographic activity of *homo religiosus* in the Neolithic; and Jacques Cauvin (1986) has proposed a most appealing scientific hypothesis: the first chapters of the Bible (Genesis 2–4) that tell of the departure from Eden and the killing of Abel are no mere myth with spiritual and moral meaning, but rather the account of a true story based on the memory of Near Eastern man.

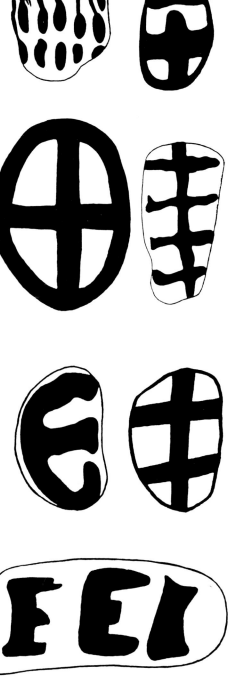

129. *Reproduction of the Mas d'Azil pebbles from Ariège in the French Pyrenees. They are products of the Mesolithic period. When they were discovered inside a cave in 1887, these river pebbles were thought to be part of a primitive alphabet. In fact, comparisons with similar phenomena found from the Alps to Australia led H. Obermaier to a more realistic interpretation: the pebbles were the "stones of the soul." In other words, they represented the ancestors in an animistic cult. Clan members could keep such stones in their own dwellings.*

129

130

130. *The outline of a hand with an ideogram in the center, cut into the rock in the Yinshan Province (Chinese Inner Mongolia). The reproduction was made by Chen Zhao Fu, a specialist in prehistoric cave art. These graffiti date to the Mongol period in China, bearing witness to the way two cultures could overlap: on the one hand a culture without writing that was limited to signs like the handprint, on the other, a culture with writing.*

23 The Religion of Sumero-Babylonian Man

TOWARD 8000 B.C., man created the first images of the deity at Mureybet on the Euphrates. Around 3000 B.C. in the southern part of Mesopotamia, the Sumerians developed cuneiform writing. This brilliant invention gave rise to a remarkable cultural and religious explosion to which five hundred or so intelligible documents currently bear witness (J. Bottéro, 1987). Cuneiform writing was man's first written language. It bespeaks major mental progress and allows us to penetrate the thoughts of Mesopotamian *homo religiosus*.

The Sumerians reached Mesopotamia during the fourth millennium and immediately exercised a strong influence on the peoples of that region thanks to the construction of the great city-states of Nippur, Eridu, Uruk, Lagash, Ur and Mari (G. Roux, 1985). The Accadians, who were Semites of Western origin, mixed with the Sumerians and adopted their writing, art and culture. Moreover, the two religions also interwove. We can thus talk about a Mesopotamian religion that was initially expressed in Sumerian and Accadian documents, and later, after 2000 B.C., in those of Babylon as well.

After the eighth millennium, *homo religiosus* of the Near East began to conceive of the divine as personal and transcendent, and to portray this by means of growing numbers of human figures. This tradition continued and consolidated with Sumer, Accad and Babylon. The Sumerian word for the divine being is *dingir*, the Accadian word *ilu*. We do not know the etymology of these words, but their meaning is clarified by the presence of a roughly drawn star. This ideogram precedes the name of the deity, thus signifying the divine presence above, in the sky. So the divine world is conceived as a celestial world, and life on earth a reflection of the heavens. In this way astrology becomes a religious science that relates man's destiny to the will of the gods and goddesses. The divine is divided into numerous personalities who govern the four great spheres of the cosmos, the stars, nature and the city-states. The foremost national god was to be Marduk of Babylon.

In continuing the traditions of the Early Neolithic and Neolithic, the Sumerians and Semites portrayed their deities with human features and invested them with characteristic light and splendor. Sometimes this light radiated outwards, a luminous gleam around the head of the divine statue, the halo that we find in India, in Iran, and in the West. Perceived by the faithful, this radiance highlighted the divine attire and the inside of temples and sanctuaries. The ritual crowning of the statues of gods and goddesses was of consummate significance in that it invested them with supernatural power (E. Cassin, 1968). The texts of the epics and prayers show that Mesopotamian *homo religiosus* perceived the true dimensions of the sacred: the transcendency of the gods, the sacred architecture of the temples, the sacred art of the statues, and the breadth of rituals related to light, fire, and the mediation of the priests.

The wealth of documentation in the cuneiform tablets reveals poems and myths telling of the genesis of the gods, the cosmos, and mankind. This first sacred story constitutes a collection of memories of the East, and as such acted as an archive for the compilers of the biblical traditions. It comprises various versions of the creation of humanity and the flood. According to some myths, man was created by the gods so that he could take on all unpleasant, oppressive tasks, make plants abound, pile up grain, and organize feasts to honor the deities. The human condition is thus totally subordinated to the gods, who demand service and establish the destiny of each individual by

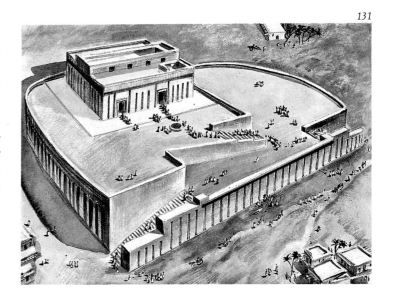

131

131. *In the fourth millennium* B.C., *just before development of the great Sumerian period, what is known as Uruk culture spread through Mesopotamia. During this age the first cities arose with complex central buildings raised up on huge elevations by means of a system of terraces. These were both seats of government and places of worship. They can be considered the prototype of the Sumerian temple.*

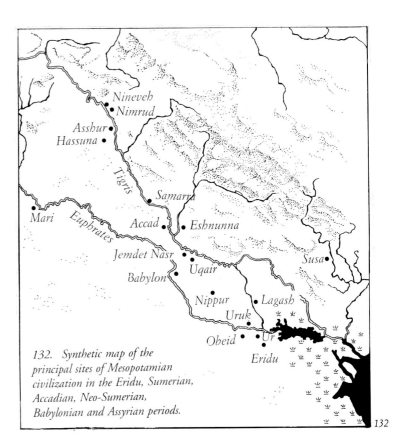

132. *Synthetic map of the principal sites of Mesopotamian civilization in the Eridu, Sumerian, Accadian, Neo-Sumerian, Babylonian and Assyrian periods.*

132

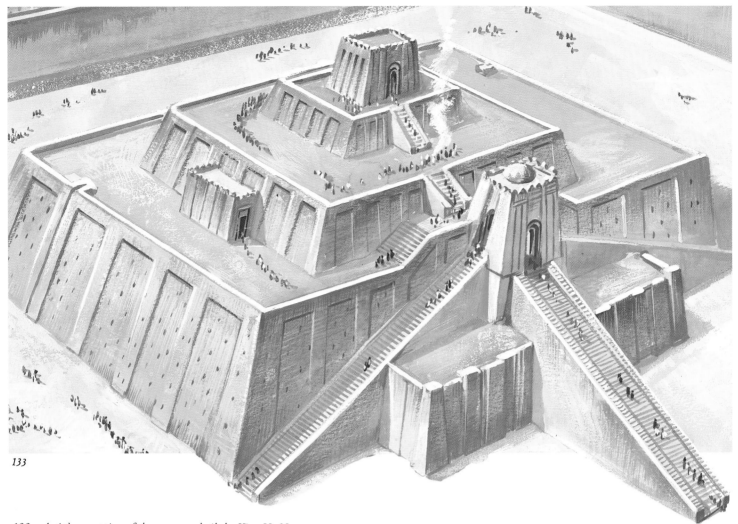

133

133. *Artist's conception of the* ziggurat *built by King Ur-Nammu toward 2100 B.C. It symbolizes the Sumerian renaissance. The ziggurat is preeminently a building devoted to worship. With its complex system of elevations, it was also suitable for astronomical studies.*

134. *The photo shows that only two terraced levels have remained out of the original four of the* ziggurat *at Ur.*

134

135. Many statuettes were found in the Sumerian temples; they probably served as votive offerings. This delicate portrayal of a man and a woman holding hands expresses a human and religious feeling that seems to contrast with the imposing monumentality of the ziggurat.

135

means of precepts and decrees (the *me*). Man is obliged to recognize these divine orders and to carry them out in complete submission. This aspect reveals a note of pessimism and draws attention to the fundamental importance of divination. Subject to divine decrees, man's life unfolds in a straight line and ends with death and the introduction to the realm of Nergal, where he becomes a mere shadow. Convinced of the existence of divine tablets that reveal destiny, the Mesopotamians believed that fate could be expressed by natural phenomena. This explains the extremely complicated structure of their religious and prophetic science (J. Bottéro, 1989).

Anu, the supreme god, is the guarantor of primordial sovereignty and makes it descend from the sky to the earth, where it can benefit mankind. The Sumerian king, called *ensi,* the vicar-prince, is chosen when the god looks upon him. Then, to show benevolence and to prepare the investiture, he pronounces his name out loud. Ordained king and priest, he worships daily by means of blood sacrifices and offerings. Apart from the monthly feasts of the new moon and those pertaining to each temple, Mesopotamia also celebrated the feast of *akitu* to mark the beginning of the new year and the renewal of life. These celebrations were extraordinarily rich. Each god lived in his own temple, which was located on a terrace and continually rebuilt on the same sacred site. However, the gods also inhabited the heavens, where priests would go fetch them for the feasts. This they did by climbing up the *ziggurat,* or sacred towers built on ascending levels connected by stairways leading up to the heavenly vault. We have plenty of evidence attesting the regal, priestly, and popular piety characteristic of Mesopotamian civilization.

The inhabitants of the Tigris and Euphrates valleys must have been impressed by the heavenly vault and the brightness of the stars. Likewise, they would have been sensitive to the sacred and aware of the existence of a divine world. Thus Mesopotamian religion was rooted in fertile ground and could embody the first detailed contemplation of the divine and the genesis of the gods. It therefore represents man's first known coherent attempt at attuning his behavior to the divine decrees.

136. *The Assyrians inherited the Mesopotamian tradition and founded a state religion in which the king is the supreme priest. However, before the deity, he adopts a humble kneeling position in recognition of that which is incommensurably greater. There are many portrayals of scenes such as this. On this stone altar of the 13th century* B.C., *King Takulti Ninurta kneels before an altar on which the invisible god is symbolized by a flame.*

24 The Religious Message of Pharaonic Egypt

RELIGION WAS the humus that nourished the roots of Egyptian civilization as a whole: art, literature, science, medicine, architecture, astronomy, geography, linguistics, politics, administration, and law (S. Morenz, 1960). For a long time Egyptologists believed that the Egyptian miracle came about like a sudden explosion at the beginning of the third millennium, once the country had been unified and hieroglyphic writing invented. However, archaeologists have unearthed considerable evidence from the Neolithic period showing that there was an archaic cult of the goddess of life parallel to those of the East (E. Baumgartel, 1948, 1960).

The inhabitants of Egypt never ceased to marvel as they contemplated nature: the sunrise every morning; the wondrous regularity of the annual flooding of the Nile and its valley; an abundance of water and rich silt that ensured plentiful harvests; dark earth covered by luxuriant vegetation beneath an ever bright sky. Egyptians used the words *tep zepi,* "the first time," to indicate original creation. And this was perceived as a period in which the earth, light, and man were born, and chaos was turned into cosmos.

Theologians started trying to explain this mystery as far back as the third millennium. At Heliopolis the reference was to Atum-Re, the sun god who created a primordial hill. Each Egyptian sanctuary was then considered a symbolic copy of this hill, which was later reproduced in the pyramid and obelisk with its *piramidion.* The theologians of Hermopolis introduced an entire system of cosmogonic symbolism: original hill, island of fire — an allusion to the sun — world egg, god in a lotus flower. At Memphis, the capital of the first dynasty, the

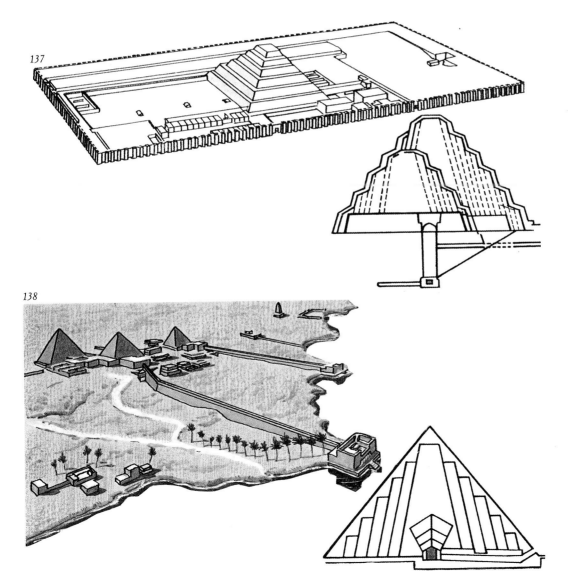

137

138

137. Plan of the Saqqara site of the 3rd Dynasty, Memphis (Egypt). These architectural complexes comprised the pyramid tomb of the pharaohs — in this case Djoser (2649-2575 B.C.) — one or more temples and the secondary buildings. In Egypt and elsewhere, religious monuments often expressed both utilitarian functions and a symbolic construct. The step pyramid shown here helped the pharaoh in his skyward ascent toward the sun. The section shows the same pyramid with the mummy chamber.

138. Abu Sir complex of the 5th Dynasty with the pyramids of the pharaohs Sahre (2458-2446 B.C.), Neferikare (2446-2426 B.C.) and Neuserre (2416-2393 B.C.). The section is that of the Neferikare pyramid. One of the temples belonging to this complex is considered a copy of that of Heliopolis, indicating how widespread sun worship had become.

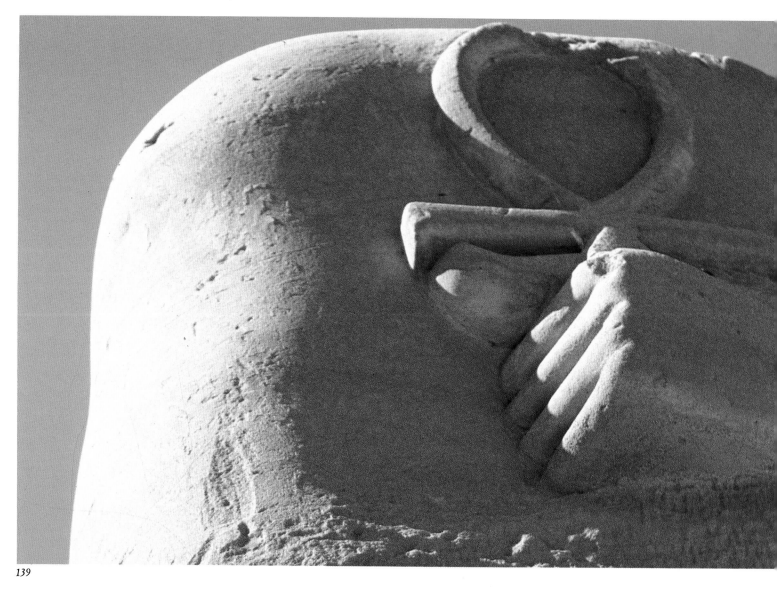

139

140

141

139. *Karnak. Temple of the god Amon (meaning "hidden"), 8th Dynasty. The hands of this large statue clasp the* ankh, *or sign of life. Life is a theme that runs through Egyptian belief in the afterlife.*

140. *The falcon god Horus, god of the sun and sky. He was worshiped in pre-dynastic times, and was then believed to be incarnated in the pharaoh, who became the living Horus, as his earliest appellative "the name of Horus" indicates. Here he is shown with the* ankh *in his hand.*

141. *Another image of Horus making a protective gesture toward the pharaoh. From the Nefertari rupestrian temple at Abu Simbel (Egypt).*

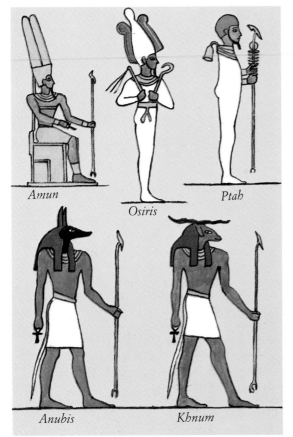

142

Amun

Osiris

Ptah

Horus

Thoth

Anubis

Khnum

Hathor

Isis

142. Some of the most important Egyptian deities. The deities were numerous and often overlapped: Amon, hiddenness, savior of believers; Osiris, god of the dead and life in the netherworld; Ptah, creator of the world through the word; Horus, god of the sky; Thoth, messenger and god of wisdom; Anubis, deity of the necropolises; Khnum, the creator god who shaped human beings on a potter's wheel; Hathor, goddess of love; Isis, incarnation of the throne.

prime mover was believed to be Ptah, the god who creates with his own heart and tongue, thus bringing about the visible and invisible universe, living creatures, justice and art. Ptah also created the gods, assigning to each his place in the country and cosmos.

Egyptologists have counted 753 deities: local divine lords, cosmic gods and goddesses, gods of the sages. All possess a power that Egyptians tried to express by means of images, symbols and signs, which accounts for the apparent strangeness of these representations. The notion of power was conveyed in written form by the sign of the regal scepter. The deities were represented and impersonated by figures holding power, and this gives the Egyptian pantheon its curious aspect: human body, animal, human body and animal head. The Egyptians considered their gods as personal beings, giving them names that express some of their salient characteristics: Amon = the hidden; Neith = the terrible; Thoth = the messenger. During the whole course of its history Egypt maintained a twofold theological system: contemplation of the divine coexisted with the practice of a polytheistic cult.

The wonder of creation led the Egyptians to consider the mystery of life and its sacred character, for this was the preeminently divine work. Protected by the gods, the mystery of life was represented by the symbol *ankh,* a sign that appeared in prehistory and was later adopted by the Coptic Christians (J. Ries, 1986). This sign of life was carved on the temple walls, on funeral stelae, on statues. The gods and goddesses offer it to the king, and place it under the nostrils of the deceased to make him breathe the air of eternity. The same sign usually appears in the pharaoh's hand. At El Amarna, Amenhotep IV (1375-1357 B.C.), who changed his name to Akhenaton, worshiper of Aton, stood with Queen Nefertiti before the sun disk to offer it the goddess Maat, the symbol of truth and justice. By way of a reply the sun god made the sign of life descend upon the royal couple. The symbolism of this scene is fascinating, in that it embodies a complete sector of regal theology. The god Aton is the creator of life; the royal couple is responsible for his upkeep and permanence

Human life requires a body, a heart, a mind. In contemplating the mystery of man the Egyptians formulated the theory of the union of the vital forces. *Ka,* symbolized by two arms raised skyward with open hands, is the divine breath that sustains man's being, the principle of his personality, the divine and living part of him. *Ba* or *bai* is individual conscience, the basis of responsibility. *Akh* is the immortal

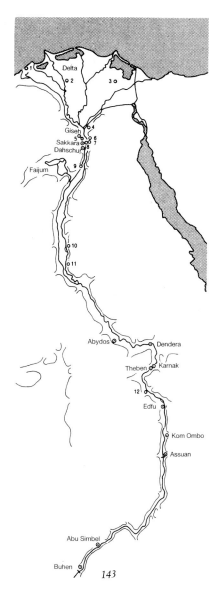

143. Map of pharaonic Egypt: 1. Alexandria; 2. Sais; 3. Tanis; 4. Heliopolis; 5. Abu Sir; 6. Tura; 7. Heluan; 8. Memphis; 9. Meidum; 10. Beni Hasan; 11. El Amarna; 12. Esna.

144. Scenes inspired by the Book of the Dead. In the top left corner: the sun barque with the god Horus. In the upper band: the dead man in judgment before Horus, Osiris and the council of the gods. In the large scene, the ceremony of weighing the soul. From the left: the dead man led by the god Anubis to be weighed; Anubis performs the weighing by placing on one side of the scales a vase symbolizing the heart or actions of the dead man; a feather on the other side represents Maat, justice and truth. Below the scales there is a monster waiting to devour the wicked souls. The scribe god Thoth records the outcome. Souls that are recognized as just are led to the duat, or afterlife.

145. *The ruins of the city of Akhethaton are located about 300 kilometers from Cairo, at Tell El Amarna in a plain near the Nile. Akhenaton intended this city as the new capital, marking out its boundaries with great sculpted stelae. This is a drawing of the relief carvings in the lunette of one of these stelae. It shows a royal family worshiping the sun disk, the god Aton, whose rays end in hands that transmit the* ankh, *or sign of life.*

principle that is rejoined with man after death. United with the body, *zet,* these three elements are what makes man live until the moment in which death occasions the disjunction of their harmony. An eternal body is reconstituted by embalming the body and thus keeping the heart intact. Symbolic representation is made of the mouth, nostrils, eyes and ears, and the Book of the Dead is placed on the heart to guide the deceased in his future life among the immortals in the kingdom of the god Osiris or on the barque of the god Re. Belief in the afterlife is a constant feature of Egyptian religion.

The Egyptians were preoccupied with the maintenance of creation and life. The pharaoh acted as their guardian: he is Horus, Lord of the Two Lands, son of Re, successor to Osiris. Through the double coronation ceremony he becomes a priest like Osiris. His government is a divine task; his throne represents the original hill. He builds temples, the houses of the gods, and ensures daily worship by means of appointed priests. In every temple the *naos* is the preeminently secret and sacred place, the residence of the statue of the god, the cell of divine mystery where the eternity of life is renewed daily through worship. Each temple is the reproduction of the primordial hill. The people can never enter it, but must wait outside until the priests bring out the statue of the god or goddess in preparation for a solemn procession by boat to the Nile.

Maat is the state of creation, of nature, of Egypt as established by the creator gods. It is also the right, order, justice and truth that are guaranteed by the Pharaoh. As a divine gift personified by a goddess, it constitutes the fundamental rule of human life. It is truth in words, justice in action and rectitude in thought. Egyptian religion is not a revealed religion or a religion of the book, but rather an expression of the sacred as man experiences it in his wonder at creation and the splendor of the heavens. Man is thus characterized by his sense of the divine and his love for life. The message of this religion was to exercise a profound influence on the thought of the Mediterranean peoples.

25 China, Dao and Yin/Yang

AGRICULTURE AND SETTLEMENT in villages in China began in the sixth millennium, when people started to polish stones and fire pottery. The tombs of this Neolithic civilization have revealed terracotta pottery and remains of food, which bear witness to belief in an afterlife. There is plenty of evidence from the Shang Dynasty (from 1751 to 1028 B.C.) in the Bronze Age attesting the existence in that period of a twofold religion: the cult of Shang Ti, god of the heavens and lord of above, who governed the cosmic rhythms and the phenomena of nature; and ancestor worship, particularly developed

146

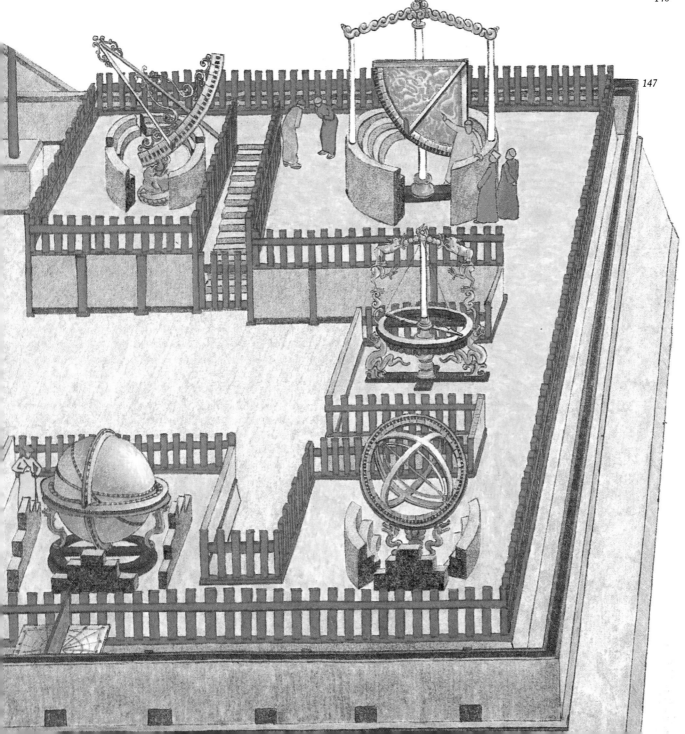

147

146. Symbol of the Yin and Yang that make up the Dao. Yin and Yang are the contrary and complementary principles on which the dynamics and harmony of the universe and mankind are based.

147. C. Larre has written that "Daoist cosmology represents the origins of individuals in their complete dependence on sky and earth, which are revered as authentic progenitors." For the Chinese, observation of the sky is deeply rooted in tradition. In the 13th century, during the Mongol period, the famous Beijing Observatory was built. One of its large terraces is reproduced in this picture. The instruments now installed there date from the last Qing Dynasty.

148

149. *This photo shows part of the sacred path in the Wudangshan mountain in Hubei Province. A temple can be seen right above the south precipice. To reach it the pilgrim has to go around the mountain and through the south gate that gives access to the sky.*

149

148. *J. Lagerwey has written that "in China the mountains have never lost their sacred aura, their role as a microcosm of the great all." Although each mountain is considered sacred, there are actually five great Daoist peaks. On Mount Huashan in Shaanxi Province (East Peak), as on the other sacred mountains, there is a path that reproduces the five peaks: North, South, East, West, Center. The photo shows a terrace at the exit of the southern celestial gate where the pilgrim can send a message to the sky.*

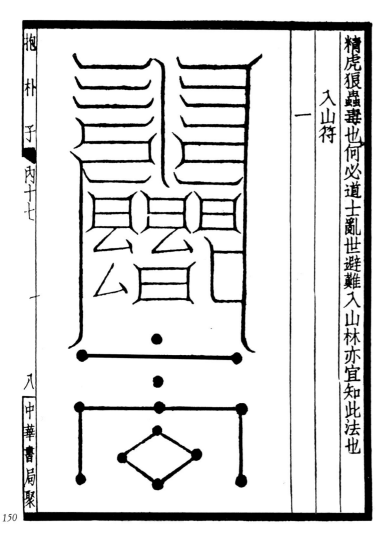

抱朴子內十七

入山符

一

八 中華書局聚

精虎狼蟲毒也何必道士亂世避難入山林亦宜知此法也

150

150. Fourth-century symbol used by the hermit for "entering" the mountain. At the time, whoever climbed a mountain could meet with danger, so the hermits had to choose propitious days and take with them protective symbols such as the one reproduced here.

151

151. The Chinese characters signifying "primordial breath," the vital energy expressed by the clouds that issue from the mountain.

152

152. The Chinese character signifying "cave" is composed of an element indicating water and another that suggests spatial volume.

around the king and the dynasty. In 1028 B.C. the last Shang monarch was overthrown by the Zhou prince, who proclaimed the doctrine of the "Mandate of Heaven" and began what was to be a long dynasty (from 1028 to 256 B.C.). The texts mention the celestial god Tian (sky) or Shang Ti, a personal, anthropomorphic deity that resides in the center of the heavens as the all-seeing and all-knowing protector of the dynasty. Ancestor worship was also practiced at the time.

Both texts and myths tell us about this ancient period, when the Chinese would raise their eyes to the heavens and admire the celestial order while speculating about the nature of the cosmos and man's place within it. To help man conform to the universe, special symbols and rituals were invented (Ch. Zheng, 1989). These rites were perceived as containing the secret of universal harmony and were essential to the workings of the eternal triad "Heaven, Earth, Man" that was to shape the entire course of Chinese thought. The universe was conceived as an immense organism whose origins and causes should not be sought.

This original conception of the sacred is based on the alternation and complementarity of the two poles, *Yin* and *Yang.* "In their alternation these correlative contrary principles weave the future," and feature in the philosophical texts of the fourth century B.C. (N. Vandier, 1965). Yin/Yang is the dual principle on which everything is based, the symbol of recurrence and the everlasting system of reference for the law of the universe. It is also the contrast of shadow (Yin) and light (Yang). The shadowed side that contrasts with the side of the sun constitutes the static aspect of Yin/Yang. Its dynamic character is brought about when the shadow Yin takes the place of the light Yang. This symbolism of polarity and alternation was frequently illustrated in the iconography of the Shang Dynasty (1751-1028 B.C.). It represents the totality of both cosmic and human order. Yin/Yang are inseparable. Yet they are merely aspects of *Dao,* which is the principle of unity and a mysterious Absolute.

The ancient myths refer to the paradisal nature of the primordial age, when heaven and earth were close. Their separation was due to a ritual error, which explains the Chinese nostalgia for the origins and the desire to reestablish the original unity/totality *(Hundun).* Laozi, a sage who was faithful to the ancestor cult and to traditional rites, referred to the archaic myths in founding an ethics of virtue. He was probably a contemporary of Confucius (551-470 B.C.), and in his *Daodejing,* or Book of the Way and Virtue, placed above everything else the Dao: the absolute, ineffable, primordial totality that is alive and life-giving, born before heaven and earth. Dao is the art of making heaven and earth communicate. It is an immanent principle of universal order.

Daoism developed over a long period of time and constitutes an attitude toward life (Cl. Larre, 1977). Founded on the principle of Dao, of Yin/Yang, and influenced by a complex stratification of ancient Chinese rites, Daoism is a way of life that embodies philosophy, ethics and religiosity. At the beginning of our era a new form appeared, a Daoist religion of salvation that promised to lead the faithful to immortality. The Daoist adept, the *Daoshi,* believes in the presence of divinity and life-bearing spirits within the human body. This religion has its own schools, temples, priests, cultic rites and customs. Its followers try to communicate with heaven, to spiritualize their bodies in order to unite with the Dao, or supreme deity. Through meditation they strive to attain wisdom. The main objective of religious Daoism is the search for longevity and immortality.

26 Indo-European Religions and the Religions of India

DURING THE COURSE of the third millennium, groups of conquerers moved across from the Indus to the Atlantic. At the outset they shared the same language, possessed a certain cultural and spiritual unity, and had similar social structures. The heirs of these colonizers are called Indo-Europeans and consist of the Italo-Celtic, Indo-Iranian, Germano-Scandinavian, Helenic, Anatolian, Slav and Caucasian peoples. To refer to their deity they used the word *deiwo,* which indicates a personal and luminous being. This word derives from the root *dei-,* "to shine, to give out light," and is the root of the words for "sky" and "day." Thus the religion of the archaic Indo-Europeans would have been a celestial religion with the heavens as the central element. Georges Dumézil has shown that Indo-European society comprised three aspects: the sacred, war, and fertility. Each of these was represented by men with well-definied duties: priests, warriors, and farmers.

Their thought concerning the gods was likewise expressed in a tripartite theology: sovereign gods, war gods, and fertility gods (Dumézil, 1958).

The Indo-European religious tradition developed largely in India. Here the ancient oral heritage was compiled in the four Veda at the beginning of the millennium preceding the Christian era. The Veda bear witness to the 33 deities governing three different categories of functions. The Vedic gods Varuna and Mitra rule the cosmic order and exercise spiritual sovereignty. They are the celestial deities. Varuna is the guardian of the *rita,* the "organization" of the cosmos, while Mitra is the god of the contract, of human organization. These two gods are joined and complementary. Varuna rules over the night, whereas Mitra has responsibility for the sun and the day. Vishnu is the immanent god, the power that brought the cosmos into being. He is the symbol of eternal life, whereas Shiva is the time that allows the universe to exist and the potential destroyer of this universe. As the creator god, Shiva brings one world to an end so that he can create another. He is the god of cyclical time and eternal return. Such concepts have left a profound mark on India.

Central to the dynamics of this mythology is the god Agni, who is fire, the messenger of the gods — heavenly fire, sacrificial fire, the fire of the hearth. Since he is the messenger, he acts as the link between the gods and men. Indo-European *homo religiosus* was moved by the fire of heaven that descended on earth. In inheriting this idea, the Brahmins of India saw sacrifice as a cosmogonic principle. Thus in the hymn to *Purusha* (Rig-Veda X, 90), the origin of the cosmos is attributed to the sacrifice of *Purusha,* primordial man. Founded on the

153

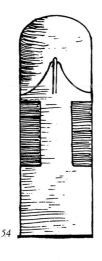

154

153, 154, 155. In the Encyclopedia of Religion *edited by M. Eliade, S. Kramrish lists Vishnu, Shiva and Devi as the fundamental and most frequently represented deities.*

Left: Vishnu Trvikrama, stone sculpture, Bengal. During his fifth incarnation Vishnu spanned the cosmos in three strides and conquered the demon Bali. Center: image of the principal object of the Shiva cult, a linga, which in Sanskrit means a sign or phallus. The linga symbolizes biological, psychological and cosmic creativity. Right: Devi, the great goddess who represents the creative principle, is venerated as a female principle. She is usually portrayed as Durga, who shows her power in conquering the buffalo demon, as illustrated in this stone carving from Bhubeneswar, Orissa (India).

155

156.   *Large sculpture of Shiva-Mehesvara (Three-Headed Shiva), located in front of the back wall of the main hall of the rock temple at Elefanta (India), 6th century* A.D. *Although the earliest Veda used only the adjective "friendly" or "benevolent" and not the actual name Shiva, the post-Vedic world considers Shiva to be the most important divine figure alongside Vishnu.*

156

157.   *The front corridor flanked by massive columns in the rock temple at Badami (India), 6th century* A.D.

belief in the identity between heavenly fire (the sun, lightning) and earthly fire, the religious symbolism of fire penetrated the whole of Hindu ritual life. Sacrifice is fundamental to Indian society and is celebrated by means of three types of fire: *garhapatya,* the fire of the master of the house that sustains the sacrifice; *ahavaniya,* whose flames carry the gifts of men to the gods; and *dakshinagni,* the fire that keeps watch against the enemy. These three fires situate Indian society in relation to the gods. (The origins of Rome also bear witness to a tripartite theological and social structure, and here too the three fires were held to be of great importance [Dumézil, 1966]). Each fire is part of the social fabric and represents a sacred space. Thus every morning and evening the master of the house must kindle the flame smoldering beneath the ashes: this is the *agnihotra,* through which Agni is united anew with the family of the gods.

The Brahmana, or Ritual Treatises, were compiled during the eighth century B.C., when the mystique of sacrifice and immortality obtained through sacrifice introduced the idea of a creator god. This was Prajapati, the lord of all creatures and the first priest. Within this theology and the relevant rites, sacrifice becomes the central element of the religion of Brahmanic India. Its purpose is to reconstruct the cosmos worn out by the effects of cyclical change. Sacrifice is what keeps the cosmos alive. Prajapati is both the creator and the sacrifice. However he is also the year, symbolized by the altar, since it is thanks to sacrifice that he guarantees the succession of the seasons, human

and animal fertility, and that of the land. The mystique of sacrifice implies the birth and preservation of life and the promise of immortality, and lies behind the Indian custom of cremating the dead.

In the sixth century B.C., the Vedic Upanishad constituted the last stage of the *shruti* or "revelation." This eternal truth was originally heard by the mythical rishis who witnessed the proclamation of the Veda. In the Upanishad texts philosophical speculation takes the place of rituals, and sacrifice becomes a contemplative operation. The *Brahman* is the Absolute, the hypostasis of the Veda and the values of Indian society. The human correlative of this Absolute is the *atman,* the immortal principle in man that must free itself of the body in order to achieve perfect identity with the *Brahman.* Man's salvation, or *mokhsha,* no longer depends on the sacrificial rites of fire, but on the inner fire of mystical exaltation and knowledge. The fruit of men's actions, or *karman,* ensures that every good deed brings the individual closer to release through the redemption of *samsara,* the perpetual reincarnation.

Toward the fourth century B.C., following upon the impact of Buddhism, the *bhakti* religion developed with its devotion and popular piety surrounding the gods Shiva, Vishnu and Krishna. The founding text was the Bhagavad Gita, or "Song of the Blessed One," and it gave rise to the spread of the "revelation" of Krishna, the representation of the deities, the flowering of art, and the construction of temples where the faithful could make offerings to the deities of their choice.

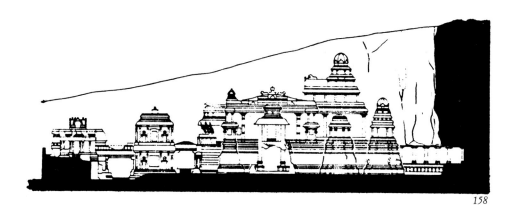

158

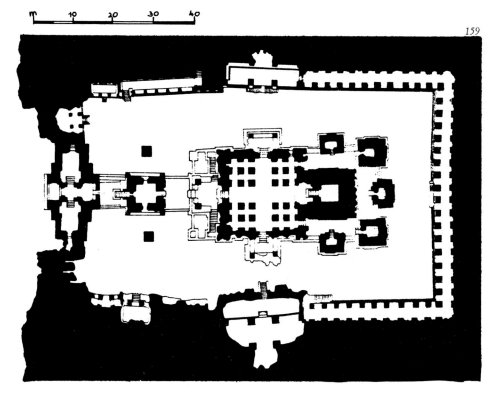

159

158, 159. The rupestrian sanctuary at Ellora, 180 kilometers northeast of Bombay, is the biggest, most richly adorned temple structure hewn out of rock of the whole of India. The Kaila granite mountain is the mythical dwelling of Shiva, so it was decided to carve a temple out of the rock; Shiva's dwelling had to be the rock of that same mountain. Ellora was begun in the 8th century A.D. and finished around the middle of the 9th century. Elevation (above) and plan (below) of Ellora. Black indicates the rock, and white the wall of rock that has been dug away.

27 The Message of Zoroaster

AFTER THE END of the second millennium B.C., certain Indo-European populations occupied ancient Iran. We have considerable evidence showing that the deity there was tripartite, while society, which was feudal and largely agricultural, comprised three different classes. Zoroaster was a priest and prophet who lived in the northeast of the country at the beginning of the first millennium B.C. Opposed to the sacrifice of oxen, he started a reform of the ancient religion, abolished the sacrificial cult and replaced it with spiritual offering, maintaining the fire as the symbol of truth. He presented his doctrine as a revelation received from the supreme god Ahura Mazda. Seventeen hymns of this doctrine have come down to us. They are called the *Gatha,* and were added to the *Yasna,* or collection of priestly and religious writings, by the compilers of the *Avesta,* the sacred book of Iran.

From the ancient Aryan tradition Zoroaster took the notion of a personal god, a being of light. Likewise he adopted the idea of the three divine functions: the sacred, war and fertility. The god he envisaged resides in light, with the sky as his robes. This is Ahura Mazda, the Wise Lord, who knows and sees everything. He is surrounded by six archangels who together embody the three Indo-European divine functions, albeit in a totally spiritualized context. Mazdaism, the religion that arose after the death of the prophet, called them *Amesha Spenta,* Immortal Benefactors. *Vohu Manah,* Righteous Thought, and *Asha,* Justice, are the bestowers of the sacred. They resemble a glowing fire, taking part in creation and helping Ahura Mazda to govern the world and enlighten mankind. *Kshathra,* the Empire, fights a mystical battle against evil and falsehood and helps Ahura Mazda to found his reign. *Armaiti,* or Devotion, puts all energy into serving the faithful. *Haurvatat,* Salvation, and *Ameretat,* Immortality, are the reward of the pious man.

In dealing with the problem of good and evil, truth and falsehood, Zoroaster posits on the one hand *Spenta Mainyam,* the Good Spirit that is inseparable from Ahura Mazda, and on the other *Ahra Mainyu,* the Evil Spirit, surrounded by daeva, demons. Thus man has to choose between good and evil, between the author of life and inspirer of human actions, and the enemy of truth, the deceiver and destroyer of order and happiness. The choice is a command of the Wise Lord. The two precepts are the conservation of life and the struggle against evil. Good deeds constitute praise to Ahura Mazda and bring long life as their reward. Falsehood and wickedness will receive the punishment they merit. Thus there are two kinds of men, the faithful and the perverse.

Zoroaster abolished cyclical time, bringing about a transformation of the world *(frashokereti)* and the human condition. His theology was new in the sense that it was based on the Wise Lord and exalted truth and emphasized wisdom and knowledge. The prophetism of the *Gatha* also speaks for the importance attributed to worship by means of hymn singing. Zoroaster can be seen as part of the prophetic movement that brought relief to mankind during the first millennium B.C., inaugurating important change.

160. *Image of the Supreme God, Ahura Mazda, with the winged wheel symbolizing the sky.*

160

161. *Above: Illustration of a building near the royal tombs at Naqsh-I-Rustam, to the southeast of Susa, not far from Persepolis. The edifice is widely believed to have been a fire temple (6th-5th century B.C.). Below: a fire altar at the same site but dating to a later period (3rd century A.D.). The standing figure is modeled on a gold plaque of the 6th century B.C. showing a priest celebrating the fire cult.*

161

162

162. *Palace of King Darius at Persepolis. Shown here are archaeological remains on the east side of the steps, completely covered with relief carvings, that led up to the great audience hall. On either side of the guards portrayed in the foreground there are sculpted images of a lion defeating a bull, symbolizing the triumph of good over evil, one of the central themes of Zoroastrianism.*

105

28 God Revealed and the Monotheistic Religions

The Religion of Israel

IN TRACING the course of history we have seen how man has sought God. In the third millennium B.C., *homo religiosus* of Mesopotamia multiplied the divine images and gave his gods a human face. The texts show that man became attached to his "own" gods, who accompanied him on his way and gave him commands to be carried out. At the beginning of the second millennium B.C., an event of extraordinary historical importance took place in Mesopotamia: God appeared to Abraham and chose him to be the founder of the people of Israel (H. Cazelles, 1989). Abraham was promised numerous posterity, and following this divine election felt close to his own God who walked beside him, and accepted the ties of total faith. Once this God had become part of history, he was thought of as the "God of Abraham, of Isaac and of Jacob." The patriarchs actually identified him with this name. History thus became a holy story related to a book, the Bible, the sacred book of Israel.

A few centuries later the theophany of the burning bush brought about an important change in the religion of Israel. God appeared in a fire to Moses, who had escaped from Egypt, saying: "I am the God of your father, the God of Abraham, the God of Isaac, and the God of Jacob" (Exodus 3:6). In the course of this theophany, the personal God of Abraham and the patriarchs revealed his own name, Yahweh: "I will be with you" (Ex. 3:12); "I am that I am" (Ex. 3:14). God revealed this name to Moses as a guarantee of his presence with the people of Israel. Apart from giving him this sign, he also added that the land on which Moses stood was holy. The Bible then relates a series of events that are presented as established by Yahweh: the missions of Moses in Egypt, the exodus of Israel, the journey to the promised land, and the theophany on Sinai, Yahweh's covenant with his people. The God of the patriarchs thus became the covenant God, who called Israel "my people." In the theophany of the desert Yahweh appears as the Lord of nature (rain, the smoking mountain) and as the God who cures the sick. On the mountain the God of the covenant, the national God of Israel, reveals his law and his commandments to his people. The essence of the revelation is summarized in the Ten Commandments. Hebrew tradition assigns priority to the Law *(Torah)* of Moses as the definitive foundation of the religion and social life of the people of Israel.

Worship of Yahweh specifically rejected pagan sacrifice, idols and

163.

163. The word temple *(from the Greek* témenos, *sacred enclosure) designates the emblematic location of the theophany of the divine. The temple of Jerusalem was first erected on a hill by Solomon in 965 B.C. and contained the Ark of the Covenant containing the Tables of the Law. The Ark had been a preeminently sacred object since the time of Moses, a symbol of the presence of the invisible God among his people. Thus the temple embodies absolute value for the people of Israel. This depiction shows the temple of Jerusalem as it was rebuilt by Herod the Great (from 20-19 to 10-9 B.C.). The basis of this reconstruction is the description by Flavius Josephus and in the Middot Treatise (Measurements of the Temple) in the Mishnah.*

agrarian rituals. Faith became the new statute of *homo religiosus*. Surrounded by the cosmic hierophanies, the faithful perceived the theophany of Yahweh and the sacredness of the "Divine Person," the living God as revealed in the histories, to the extent that the story itself became a theophany. Yahweh disapproved of any representation that tried to identify him with a created being, with any kind of human likeness, or with the sun, the moon or the stars (Deuteronomy 4:16-19). The power of Yahweh, creator of the heavens and the earth, of light and men, is chanted in the Psalms, where the theme of Genesis (9:4) reappears. Yahweh made man in his own image. Worship of the one God was celebrated in the only temple built on Mount Zion.

As messengers of the God of the covenant, the prophets helped the faithful to deepen their understanding of the faith. In the ninth century B.C., Elijah arose as the intransigent defender of Yahweh before the Syrian cults. Toward 740 B.C., Elijah had a magnificent vision in the temple that led him to proclaim the holiness of Yahweh seated majestically on his high throne (6:1). In a lapidary formula he then distinguished the holiness of the God of Israel from that celebrated by the pagan religions. The law of holiness (Leviticus, ch. 17–26) demanded a special statute: ordained priesthood, offerings, consecrated Sabbaths and feasts and a holy people reflecting the image of the holiness of Yahweh. The laws of morality and justice were proclaimed in the name of the holiness of God. It was Yahweh himself who gave his people the law of holiness, and the wisdom to complete their education. The Psalms echo the faith, the holiness and wisdom of the faithful.

Mention is already made in Genesis (49:8-12) of a sovereign whom all people will one day obey: this is the root of the expectation of a messianic king. In Deuteronomy (18:15-22) Moses announces that God will bring to his people a prophet who resembles him. This text prepares the way for prophecies of the Messiah in Israel. Isaiah speaks of the "servant of Yahweh" and the birth of Immanuel, who through his own suffering will prepare the coming of the universal kingdom of God (Isaiah 7:14). The new world will be ruled by a king who will govern in the name of Yahweh. He will be "the Lord's anointed." The title "Son of Man" is introduced in Daniel (7:13) in reference to a celestial being who will receive his power over the people from God. This is a statement of the definitive kingdom of God and the preparation in Israel for the appearance of the messianic king. The Essenes of Qumran thus began to await the arrival of a real priestly Messiah, the son of David.

164. Mosaic floor of the synagogue at Beit Alfa in Palestine (518-527 A.D.). At the top is the Ark of the Covenant and the seven-branched candlestick or menorah, *symbol of the Hebrew religion. Below the sacrifice of Isaac is depicted, in the center a zodiac.*

165. Reproduction of a wall painting illustrating the prophet Ezekiel's vision of the resurrection of the dead. It is part of the complex cycle of mural paintings in the synagogue at Dura Europos on the Euphrates in Syria, one of the oldest extant synagogues.

164

165

Jesus Christ and the Christian Religion

166. Christ and the Samaritan woman at Jacob's well, from a painting in the late 4th-century catacombs found in 1955 beneath the Via Latina in Rome. The same subject had already been illustrated in other very early catacombs: water is replete with symbolism referring to life and death and also evokes the baptism, sign of the new Christian birth.

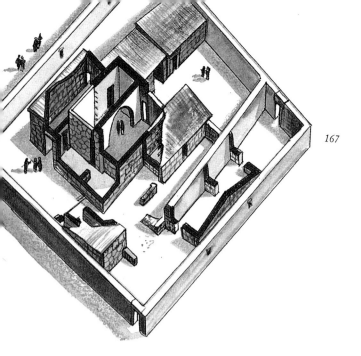

167

Jesus and His Message

The origins of Christianity must necessarily be referred to Jesus of Nazareth, the founder of this religion. For the latter-day historian the evidence shows that the Christian movement began in Palestine, which implies the historical existence of Jesus as described in the Gospels. A number of recent discoveries seem to confirm the convictions of certain exegetes who argue that the first texts, including that of Saint Mark, were compiled around the middle of the first century. Historically speaking, the entire gospel tradition revolves around events experienced by the twelve apostles whom Jesus brought together so that he could send them out to preach. In fact, what we know about the fundamental message of Christianity is rooted in their testimony (Ch. Perrot, 1979).

According to the Synoptic Gospels, the messianic message was reiterated at the start of Jesus' public life. After recording the baptism of Jesus by John the Baptist, Mark writes (1:10): "And just as he was coming up out of the water, he saw the heavens torn apart and the Spirit descending like a dove on him." The prophetic and christological dimension of this text is evident. Moreover, it is confirmed by the title "Son of God" which Jesus claimed (Matthew 10:32; Luke 22:29). When first preaching, he announced the coming of the kingdom of God, saying that it was near at hand (Mark 1:15). He also declared that the prophecies were shortly to be fulfilled (Luke 4:18-21). Thus the disciples understood that Jesus was both the prophet announcing the kingdom of God and the Messiah. They saw his coming as ushering in the kingdom of heaven.

Christ's parables constitute the primitive form of the announcement of the kingdom of God, the presence of which was then proven by his miracles. Parables and miracles are interrelated: Jesus himself spoke of the miracles as signs of the kingdom (Matthew 11:5), expli-

citly linking the imminent coming of the kingdom of God to his own thaumaturgical deeds (Matthew 12:28; Luke 11:20). The miracles gave witness to the transformation of the present world. Jesus opened up the way to salvation; even before his resurrection, his apostles recognized him as the Son of God.

Ties of paternity and filiation express the relationship between Jesus and God. Jesus speaks of God as his Father both explicitly and insistently. But other passages are also noteworthy. The account of the transfiguration occupies a central part of St. Mark's Gospel (9:2-10), just after the confession of Peter at Caesarea. After close exegetical examination, the account of the transfiguration appears as a testimony to the astonishment of Peter, James and John, who witnessed the revelation of Jesus' divine filiation ("This is my beloved Son") and understood that the event was in some sense a replication of what had taken place on Mount Sinai.

Jesus' death left his disciples in a state of complete dejection. However, a few days later they were insisting on his resurrection. The Easter experience of the apostles and disciples is what gave rise to this proclamation, the conviction that they had encountered afresh the same Jesus and Son of God that they had followed before the events leading up to the Passion and his death. The resurrection of Jesus is what gives the apostles' faith in God its objective and energy.

Church and Christian Doctrine

THE Acts of the Apostles offers a coherent picture of the first thirty years of the spread of the Christian community in the Hebrew and Hellenic world. The epistles of St. Paul are the founding documents of a theology, Christology, and ecclesiology that were to be further developed by the fathers of the Greek, Latin, and oriental churches. The risen Christ, author of human salvation, is central to the doctrine of St. Paul. He is the Lord, the new Adam who renews mankind and makes of the Christian a new man. Baptism is the door leading into the Church, while the eucharist ensures the presence of Christ in the ecclesiastical communities and the growth of the body of Christ, that is, the Church. Christ's resurrection is the pledge of the resurrection of all Christians. The Christian inherits the divine life of the Father by means of the Son and through the Spirit. The whole of his life should bear witness to this.

In the course of the four centuries separating the Acts of the Apostles from Saint Augustine's *City of God,* the Christian Church spread to the East and to the West. Although it claimed to be the *verus Israel* and heir to what the covenant and prophecies had promised, it nevertheless explicitly distanced itself from the Torah and the Jewish rites. Thus a new religious art of Christianity arose in contrast to that of the synagogue. Faced with the opposition and clashes with the heathen, the apologists defended the doctrines and practices of the Christians and criticized all idolatry. However, the Greek fathers of the Church did not deny the value of Platonic and Stoic thought. Alexandria was where Christian faith and the culture of antiquity met. In the golden age of the fathers of the Church, Lactantius laid the grounds for Christian humanism, while Eusebius of Caesarea compiled the first collection of memories of events following the life of Christ. Surrounded by theological discussions that became opportunities for insisting on the dogmas of the Christian faith, Saint Augustine developed his *De civitate Dei,* a story of salvation that is also a theology of culture and history.

Jesus celebrated the Last Supper with the apostles in Jerusalem before the Passion, telling them to perpetuate the rite. Christian worship is founded on this event, reenacting the eucharist and the recalling of Christ's resurrection, which the first Christian generation established as having taken place on Sunday, the day of the Lord, immediately after the Sabbath. When other doctrines clashed with the apostolic tradition, in the second century certain synods of bishops made pronouncements on Christian doctrinal orthodoxy. After Constantine's recognition of Christianity, a series of great ecumenical councils of the East and West were held: at Nicaea in 325 to define the doctrine of the trinity in opposition to Arius; at Constantinople in 381, to define the creed of the Christian faith (Nicene Creed); at Ephesus in 431, to affirm Mary as *Theotokos* or "Mother of God"; at Chalcedon in 451, to define the Christological dogma of "Jesus the true God and true Man." These four councils laid the definitive foundations for the faith of the Christian Church.

168. Copy of a fresco painted toward the end of the 2nd century in the cubiculi *of the San Callisto cemetery in Rome. The subject is a fish and a basket full of bread. Such eucharistic symbology was used in many sepulchral monuments of early Christianity. Indeed, "breaking the bread" is the most important Christian rite, and the fish is a symbol of Christ himself.*

168

169. Print showing the interior of St. Peter's Basilica in Rome before its reconstruction. As H. P. L'Orange has pointed out, in the Christian basilica everything is subservient to the interior, where the light is

the favored element and the highest part of the building appears to radiate luminosity that contrasts with the half-light beneath and the dimmer areas in the side aisles.

169

Islam, Religion and Community

THE BIRTH OF ISLAM, the third religion which claims Abrahamic origins, is related to the two Arabian cities of Mecca amd Medina, and to the prophet Muhammad of the Hashimite tribe. A seeker of God *(hanif)* and merchant, he had encountered some Jews and Christians, and around 610-612 had a vision on Mount Hira near Mecca (Koran 53 and 96). Conscious of his prophetic mission, he propounded teachings which constitute the basis of the message of Islam: the power and goodness of the only God; man's need to return to God in preparation for judgment; man's answer expressed in gratitude and worship; faith and prayer; the protection of orphans and the poor. Mecca was a polytheistic plutocracy whose citizens were opposed to Muhammad's teaching, so on July 16, 622 he left the city *(hidjra,* Hegira) to seek refuge in the Yathrib oasis (Medina), where he founded Islam, religion and community *(umma).* In 624 he ordered

170. Three images that capture fundamental moments of the Islamic religion: in the center, the name of Allah, the one God, an object of worship with a number of different calligraphic transcriptions; left, reading the Koran; right, the characteristic prostration of Islamic prayer.

171. Copy of a Turkish manuscript showing an imaginary view of the ka'aba, *the small cubic edifice at the center of the sacred enclosure of Mecca. Attached to the eastern wall of this building is a black stone that is worshiped during the Islamic pilgrimage.*

170

172. Plan of the transformation of the prophet's house in Medina into a mosque. According to Islam, Medina is the foremost of cities because it offered Muhammad hospitality. The house was turned into a mosque during the Umayyad age, 8th century A.D.

172

173. Page of a Turkish codex kept at the Museum of Turkish Art in Istanbul. It illustrates a meeting between Muhammad and a monotheist shepherd.

171

his followers to say their prayers facing Mecca *(Qibla),* which he conquered on January 1, 630. He died on returning from a pilgrimage to Mecca in 632, so it was his successors (the caliphs) who gave Islam its definitive form: Abu Bakr (632-634) organized the first military conquests; Omar (634-644) continued the military expansion and created the first institutions; Othman (644-656) of the Umayyadi tribe created a proper feudal system and compiled the Koran, the sacred book of Islam; Ali (656-661), the prophet's son-in-law and head of prayer at Medina, rebelled against the Umayyadi, left Arabia, and settled at Al Kufah. His followers were to be the first Shiites.

For the historian of religions, the Koran is the diary of Muhammad, the reformer and founder of Islam; for Muslims, on the other hand, it is the word of God revealed to the prophet, proclaimed by the latter and received in the memory of the faithful. The Koran recognizes the validity of the Torah and the Gospels, the two earlier revelations. The *Sunnah* is the body of traditional Muslim law and is essential to the life of the faithful. The *Hadith* are the oral precepts derived from the prophet, and as such bear wide-ranging witness to the development of Islam. Based on the *Fiqh,* or Muslim law that applies the precepts of the Koran and the *Sunna* to everyday life, the *Sharia* indicates the way to be followed: it is considered the expression of the divine law that makes one a true Muslim. In fact it makes daily life sacred, giving it unity and making it comply with the will of Allah. Islamic theology, or *kalam,* deals with the value of actions, the relationship between faith and works, and the question of human freedom subject to divine law.

The Islamic religion is strictly monotheistic: Allah is the one God, creator, judge and rewarder. His reign is universal (Koran, 112). However, he is also merciful, lenient and clement toward his followers. He is the Totally Other, unique, one, transcendent; although known through the signs of his creation he remains inaccessible. Prophecy and revelation are closely related, since the prophets are *nabi,* or messengers of God, and *rasul,* his ambassadors. The Koran has words of praise for Noah, the first messenger sent to man, and Abraham, the first advocate of faith in the Only One, founder of Hanifism, restorer of the *Kaaba* in Mecca and inspirer of the *shahada;* for Moses, who freed the enslaved people of Egypt (the Passover lamb is not mentioned); and for Jesus, the prophet and virginally conceived son of Mary, the Messiah, the holder of the Gospels, *rasul* and *nabi.* Islam is centered on the Koran, revealed to man through Muhammad, who was entrusted with the task of passing down the definitive message begun at the time of the Adamic pact. For the Muslim, Muhammad is *nabi,* the prophet who announces the message, *rasul,* the leader who must organize the community *(umma),* and *nadir,* the last ambassador of God. One of the tenets of Islam insists on God's judgment after death, on the final resurrection (Koran, 75), and on the last judgment followed by reward (paradise) or punishment (hell).

There is no priesthood in Islam: the cult consists of individual and community prayer. The life of the Muslim is based on five principles. The *shahada* is the testimony made to the one God and to the prophet by means of the word. Ritual prayer *(salat)* five times a day is an expression of monotheistic faith and therefore constitutes the divine service of the faithful. The daily performance of such prayers in the mosque is the community's way of worshiping. From the outset, Muhammad showed concern for the poor and for orphans. Thus legal charity *(zakat)* together with free charity *(sadaqa)* has real salvific value. The fourth principle involves the fast of *ramadan,* the month of revelation. This is conceived as a time of renewed awareness on the part of the Muslim and the whole community. Finally there is the pilgrimage to Mecca, an authentic return to the source which removes all sin and makes of the pilgrim a model and special witness of the benediction of Allah.

174. A remarkably elegant page from one of the earliest Koranic manuscripts in the Kufic literary alphabet. 9th century, Abbassid period.

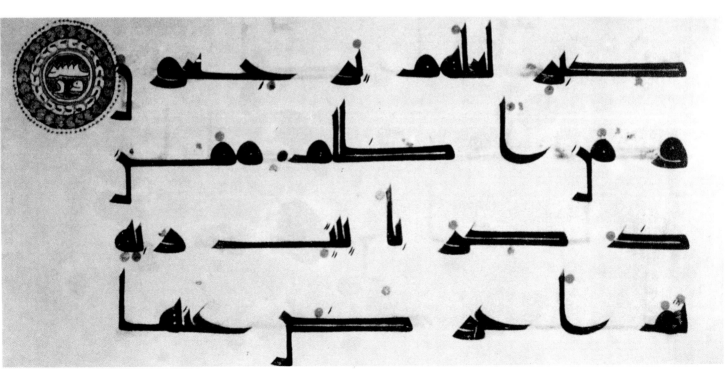

174

PART THREE
Religious Man: Behavior and Interpretation

29 A Short Discourse on Method

SO FAR WE have traced man's development from his first appearance to the moment in which he perceived a revelation of God. In so doing we have examined a number of the important facts, vestiges that have come down to us in the course of numerous millennia. Such evidence is clearly the product of man, and thus calls for interpretation. In other words, thanks to the undeniable evidence of human history we can inquire into the reasons behind man's behavior and what motivated his signs and deeds.

History of Religions and Anthropology of the Sacred

The published work of Mircea Eliade models three distinct procedures used by the historian of religions (D. Allen, 1982). The first concerns history in the strict sense and involves using all the resources of heuristics. This means subjecting all the available evidence to individual critical analysis, so that each is treated according to its specific characteristics.

Religious evidence should be examined as such, and within the context of a particular religious phenomenon. The phenomenologist names and classifies the documents (sacrifice, prayer, offering, etc.) in order to understand their essence and structures. This implies taking into account the historical and cultural conditioning of each item as well as the traces of man's behavior in experiencing the sacred. Phenomenology is the second approach.

However, the phenomenologist's task also leads to a third procedure that examines events and phenomena as significants and tries to interpret them. This approach makes the meaning of these events explicit. The science of interpretion thus conceived is called hermeneutics.

The hermeneutic approach projects the historian toward the person who actually created the evidence in hand. Hermeneutics therefore requires the involvement of the religious anthropologist, whose task it is to examine man in his role as creator and user of sacred symbolism. Religious anthropology was only established relatively recently. It is part of the anthropology of symbolic systems whose workings have been studied by C. G. Jung, H. Corbin, G. Dumézil, M. Eliade, A. Leroi-Gourhan and G. Durand (J. Ries, 1989).

Comparative Research

Both phenomenology and hermeneutics have made use of comparative research in dealing with religious facts. The first attempts at applying the comparative method date back to the Hellenic age, when the Eastern religions met those of the Mediterranean world. Having set out from the discovery of an important religious complex, comparative research has developed enormously during the course of the nineteenth and twentieth centuries (H. Pinard de La Boullaye, 1929). Thanks to the work of M. Eliade and G. Dumézil, the historical comparative method has opened up new vistas of understanding.

G. Dumézil, who limited his research to the religion of the Indo-European peoples, made several fundamental observations: on the one hand there are remarkable correspondences between the elements that make up the vocabulary of the sacred; and on the other, homologous data are also to be found within the socioreligious field. Taken together, these facts point to a heritage characterized by three functions: sovereignty, war and fertility. By means of genetic comparisons, Dumézil has tried to obtain "as precise as possible an image of a particular system whose survival largely depends on a certain number of historically attested systems" (Dumézil, 1943, p. 29). This method defines a framework based on the attested systems and then projects it onto prehistory in order to throw light onto the more obscure ages of human origins. This genetic comparison has allowed Dumézil to establish the structures of the religious thought and social conceptions of the Indo-Europeans.

Mircea Eliade extended and adapted this method to the whole of the history of religions and at the same time used it with the typological approach that aims at defining the basic elements of religions (symbol, myth, rite) and the historical and cultural processes of their growth in the course of time. In his studies of religious events he examined man's behavior and the meaning of his actions, deeds, symbols, myths, and rites. This approach is both phenomenological and hermeneutic, and has brought to light certain constant features of the human spirit and of man's consciousness. Eliade calls them archetypes since they are to be found everywhere, albeit in different forms. He thus set out from religious events to inquire into the fundamental connections and correspondences that could reveal the guidelines of behavior, the thought structures, the symbolic logic and the mental universe of *homo religiosus*.

Our study of the historical behavior and evidence that bear witness to *homo religiosus* is based on this twofold comparative approach.

30 The Sacred Experience

A Universal Experience

IN REACTION to the sociological theories that recognized the universality of the sacred but identified sacred with mana (see chap. 5), Rudolf Otto adopted three strategies in his approach to the subject: intuition as knowledge of the religious phenomenon; faith as experience of the mystery; and the religious heritage as a historical basis. In his view the only way to explain the sacred is by means of real experience (Otto, 1917). The process through which man apprehends the "divine" or mysterious consists of four stages: first there is the awareness of being a created being, then a sort of terror *(tremendum)*, followed by the sensation of beholding a mystery, and finally the fascination of the discovery *(fascinans)*. The sacred consists of three aspects. First and foremost it is the intimate living principle of all religions: the "noumenous." However, it is also a value in itself and a

175. Reproduction of a statuette of the second millennium B.C., now at the Louvre. It is known as the Worshiper *of Larsa, a Babylonian city to the south of the Euphrates. The genuflection signifies a position of dependency with respect to the deity.*

176. Culture of Lavinium, expression of the religiosity of the populatin of Latium before the Roman age. Terra-cotta statuette of a person offering a gift to a deity.

177. Cave graffiti on the Naquane Rock in Valcamonica (Italy). Series of "praying men" of the Neolithic period of Camunian civilization — a veritable prayer meeeting.

175

176

177

value for man: the *sanctum* or sacred. Finally, as an a priori category and primary datum, the sacred constitutes a special faculty through which the divine can be apprehended. It is at the origin of interior religion and God's revelation in history; it is basic to the various religions of humanity.

Mircea Eliade returned to this analysis and developed the subject of the universality of the sacred in human experience. He considered the sacred as the basis of all religious experience and as the central element of the history of religions (Eliade, 1965). In his view, the sacred manifests itself as a power that is totally different from that of the natural order. He uses the word hierophany to refer to this manifestation, which takes place through objects or persons of our visible world. Each hierophany is made up of three elements: a visible reality that is mysterious and divine; a natural object or being that acts as a mediator; a sacral dimension produced by the manifestation of transcendence through a contingent reality. *Homo religiosus* is the man who claims to witness hierophanies and lives the sacred experience.

A Phenomenon Related to Culture and Beliefs

The sacred is not an invention of historians of religion but is rather the object of their inquiries. Recent research shows that the terminology of the sacred was created within the great cultures when man needed to describe the specific experience that he witnessed. Analysis of the resulting discourse reveals that he felt the presence of a mysterious but efficacious power that determined his behavior. The abundance of evidence regarding the vocabulary of the sacred and the convergence of meanings in different cultures constitutes a remarkable, almost inexhaustible dossier (J. Ries, 1978-86).

Dating back to the origins of Rome, the *Lapis Niger* discovered in

178. *Copy made by Chen Zhao Fu of a cave painting at Huashan in Guangxi Province (China). It illustrates a ritual dance before two dogs that were probably considered sacred. The position of the figures is typical of the praying men with their arms raised.*

Rome in 1899 bears the word *sakros* that expresses a form of thought and behavior found in the entire area touched by Indo-European migrations (J. Ries, 1982). The root *sak-* is the source of terminology concerning the sacred and forms the Latin verb *sancire*, meaning "to confer validity, reality, to make something become real" (H. Fugier, 1963). Thus the sacred determines the basis of the real and concerns the fundamental structure of beings and things. This conception, found among the Hittites in India, Iran, and in Germany, underwent considerable development in Greek thought.

At Sumer the sacred appears as inseparable from the cosmogony. In the Babylonian world and among the Western Semites the sacred is always to be found in a religious context. This implies bringing man closer to the deity, to whom he bears his offerings or consecrates himself. In Egypt, from the earliest constructions men showed their desire to transcribe the divine on stone, thus contrasting the precariousness of the things of this world. The sacred persists, always present, during the passage of three millenia.

The nature of the sacred changes in the three great monotheistic religions because man finds himself before a single, personal and transcendent God who no longer speaks through oracles but reveals himself directly to man and demands faith from his followers. This notion of the sacred is accompanied by a notion of personal holiness, appropriate human behavior. Thus the experience of the sacred undergoes substantial change. That which is deemed "sacred" in the Bible is very different from Canaanite sacredness. Yahweh has left his mark on the story of the patriarchs, the exodus, the covenant, the prophetic movement, and worship. In Islam, where religion, culture and community come together, the origins of the sacred are to be found in Allah, whose will shapes the whole of the Muslim's life.

For Christians, the sacred is identified with the living God made present through Jesus Christ. The messianic interpretation of the sacred leads humanity toward salvation and creation to its fulfillment: the sacred and holiness are thus inseparable. Founded on the doctrine and terminology of the New Testament, the messianic sacred has four aspects: Jesus Christ the mediator; the sacredness of the sacramental signs; the sacred teachings; and the sanctification of daily life.

178

31 Symbols and Symbolic Language

Symbols and the Imaginary

SIGNS AND SYMBOLS are two essential elements of man's imaginary sphere. G. Durand (1992) has defined this sphere as "the set of images and relationships between images that make up the thought store of *Homo sapiens*." A sign is a reality that has a consistency of its own but nevertheless refers to another reality by way of a convention or a natural and intrinsic relationship: smoke is the sign of fire. All signs are a means of communication between persons.

Symbols are signs. For the Greeks, *symbolon* designated an object cut into two parts that were kept by two different people and used as a means of recognizing whoever possessed them: identity, guarantee, pledge, testimony, covenant. The symbol is a sign that refers to an invisible reality, thus creating contact between man and this reality by means of the intellectual passage from the visible to the invisible. The symbol brings about an opening that goes beyond immediate space and time. It is an initiation to the invisible, and thus possesses a signifying structure that leads to what is signified. The signifying structure belongs to the visible world: tree, sky, sun. Each symbol has a visible base, an identifiable aspect. What is signified is the invisible and unknown part whose content man must discover.

Gilbert Durand (1992) has drawn attention to the role of anthropological development in symbolization. The point of departure for this development was the perception of impulses deriving from the cosmos and the entire natural environment which in their turn were affected by the subjective activity of the human psyche. Between these two poles an incessant exchange was established that drove the creative imagination. This anthropological development — with its subjective thrust on the one hand and the objective external influences on the other — is specific to man. It acounts for G. Durand's claim that "the symbol is the identity card of *Homo sapiens*." The universe of the symbol is the exclusive prerogative of man.

Functions of the Symbol

Recent studies by G. Bachelard, C. G. Jung, G. Durand, M. Eliade, P. Ricoeur and J. Vidal have defined the functions of the symbol. The starting point is the symbolic system made up of all the possible human actions and the primeval universal images (sky, sun, and so on). The images derived from objects awaken man's consciousness, introducing an element of unity that generates a dynamic reaction. Man becomes a creator. Culture itself and all the cultures of the world

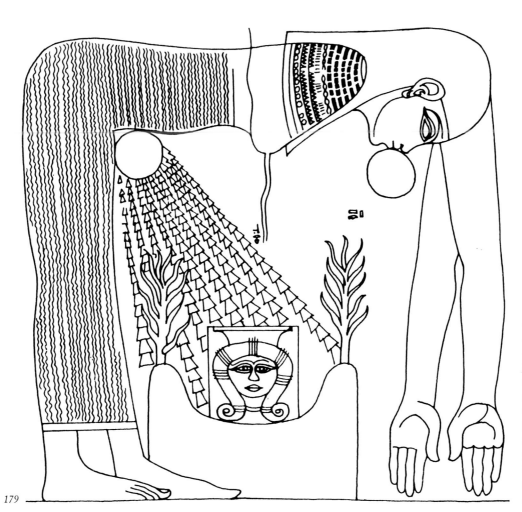

179

179. Copy of a decoration inside the temple at Dendera in Egypt. The figure forming an arch with its body symbolized the vault of heaven for the ancient Egyptians. The goddess of the sky gives birth each morning to the sun that in this illustration illuminates the temple dedicated to Hathor.

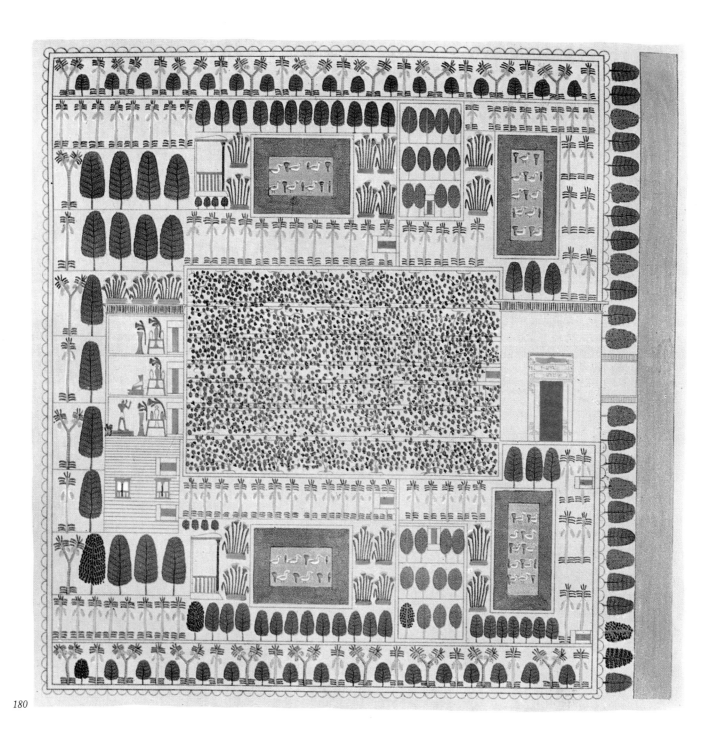

180

180. In the Egypt of the New Kingdom, around 3500 years ago, a
dignitary had a fresco painted in his future tomb at Thebes showing a
garden invested with particular values. The result is a symbolic prototype of
a garden: an orderly arrangement of water and plants that stood for the
original harmony of all that lives and allows man to live, in contrast to the
disorder to which nature itself would otherwise succumb.

181. The most famous monolith of Aztec civilization, the Sun Stone, now
at the National Museum of Anthropology, Mexico City. The relief carving
represents the Aztec calender. The face in the center combines features of
Tonatiuh, god of the sun, and Tlatecubtli, the monster-god of the earth.
Aztec civilization lived in fear of the disappearance of the sun that brought
life to earth. To ward off so dreadful an event no sacrifice was too great: not
even that of their finest sons.

181

are creations whose roots are embedded in man's symbolic imagination. The creativity (artistic, poetic, literary, architectural) of the human mind is based on this *biological* function of symbols.

Symbols also play an essential role in the workings of man's *psychic life*. They establish a relationship between consciousness and the particularly rich field of the subconscious that is only accessible by means of symbols. Symbols then give consciousness the power to govern the energies of the unconscious and to penetrate down to the very roots of the primordial universal images known as archetypes. Essential to the vitality of *Homo sapiens,* the archetypes are to human consciousness what roots are to plants and trees.

A third function has been described by J. Vidal (1990): symbols offer consciousness the possibility of alliance with the energies of what he termed the "surconscience," thanks to the opening toward the archetype of the divine. For man this is the discovery of the existence of transcendency, of the Totally Other with which he can create an alliance. Experience of the sacred is precisely this: man's perception of himself as a unifying factor, an agent of alliance between sky and earth. In other words, the symbol is essential to man in his experience of the sacred.

Homo religiosus and Symbolic Language

Thanks to the anthropological development that produces an incessant exchange at the imaginary level between man's psychic life and the external impulses deriving from the cosmos, *Homo sapiens* continues to grow. This is the secret of man's growth in the course of history. The world communicates with him through symbols, revealing aspects of reality that are not in themselves evident. This observation can help us clarify the role of symbolic language in the experience of the sacred.

Every hierophany or manifestation of the sacred embodies an invisible element, a mediator through which the invisible makes itself manifest, and a sacral dimension. Such are the three inseparable elements that make up the hierophany. The mediator may be a stone, a tree, a mountain, a cave, a river, or a man (prophet, priest, shaman). Whatever its form, the mediator constitutes the visible part of the symbol, and the means through which the epiphany of the invisible, the revelation, takes place. In symbolic languages the role of the mediator is of crucial importance. An eloquent example of symbolic language as a language of revelation is to be found in the biblical Apocalypse (21:9-27), in the description of the future Jerusalem. The text abounds in references to gem stones to signify the transformed quality of the new creation. It is an intense message: light, freedom, fulfillment and plenty. Great value is attached to the symbol of the sacred mountain in all religions, especially in the biblical revelation, where mountains were often the site of the theophanies (Sinai, Carmel, Horeb, Zion).

In a fascinating study of the symbolic function of a series of hierophanies, Eliade focuses on their language and message for *homo religiosus.* He examines sun worship and the mystics of the moon, the symbolism of water, sacred stones, symbols of fertility, of the renewal of vegetation, of sacred space and time (Eliade, 1986, p. 42-422). The whole inquiry, which is central to his *Treatise,* led him to declare that he believed the authentic structure and function of symbols, as extensions of hierophanies and as autonomous forms of revelation, to be basic factors in the comprehension of experience of the sacred. The various hierophanies are simply punctual manifestations, whereas heavenly, lunar and aquatic symbolisms are autonomous systems through which we perceive an authentic revelation based on intrinsic coherence.

182. Example of an origin myth taken from the Codex Boturini, *a post-Columbian Aztec codex. It reads from left to right. A population leaves the native city of Aztlan on an island in the center of a lake. The migration tracks begin in the year "1 knife" (year 1). They encounter the god of war, Huitzilopochtli, in a cave in the curving mountain. There are eight tribes, led by four* teomamaque, *religious chiefs bearing the symbols of the gods. They build a temple to the god of war, but the tree above it splits in two, which is a bad omen. Six weeping figures ask the image of the god for advice. Following the divine will, the head of the Aztec tribe separates from the others and the Aztecs continue their peregrination, still guided by* teomamaque. *Finally they reach their destination, a new island in a lake.*

182

32 The Myth as an Explanation of the Origins

Myth and Mythography

IN THE eighth century B.C. Homer *(The Iliad* and *The Odyssey)* and Hesiod *(Theogony, Works and Days)* supplied the first Greek mythological documents describing the birth of the gods and the way they brought about the birth of the cosmos. Two centuries later the Ionian philosophers (Thales and Heraclitus) severely criticized this theogony and cosmogony, claiming that at the beginning there was, rather, a principle: for Heraclitus of Ephesus, this was the Logos, a divine formula. Plato (428-347) collected the criticisms of popular myths together in a system, but in his turn also created philosophical myths in order to offer people images of the truth. In the third century B.C. Euhemeros secularized the myths, considering them to be legendary tales relating to certain historical characters and real events. This theory was then adopted by the Christian apologists and the fathers of the Church who wished to prove the inconsistency of the pagan gods. Neoplatonic thought was to react strongly to such efforts. For Plutarch, Maximus of Tyre, Plotinus and Porphyry, the myth was an image that reflects the truth, preserving its truth and at the same time initiating man to the divine secrets *(Pépin, 1976).*

Following the long centuries of the Middle Ages, when myths became faint memories (Seznec, 1980), the Renaissance returned to the documents of the ancient world and compared them with the stories of origins as told in the Bible. This comparative effort continued during the Enlightenment. However, in his *Scienza nuova* (1725), G. B. Vico considered myths as a means of understanding ancient cultures, civilizations and religions. Through myths he worked out the ages of mankind (infancy, adolescence, adulthood), and in them he discovered a symbolism that reflects eternal truths. During the course of the nineteenth century, a succession of discoveries made it possible to put together the great mythographic repertories of different peoples that were to be completed in the twentieth century. The hermeneutics of myths, begun by Vico, continued to develop later. During the Romantic age the goal was to discover a language common to all mankind. The Romantics saw this symbolic language as an expression of truths and as a possible vehicle for a message. Schelling (1945) insisted on the prophetic content of myths, considering them to be part of the revelation that illuminates mankind. In the mythographic studies of the twentieth century, history, phenomenology, and hermeneutics have cut innumerable furrows into a field that has been farmed for the last three thousand years. There are scholars who have focused on the definition of a language — Cl. Lévi-Strauss, for example — and other hermeneuticists who have proposed various interpretations on the basis of plentiful evidence, thus throwing new light on the message of myths. M. Eliade, along with G. Dumézil and P. Ricoeur, have made crucial contributions to the interpretation of myths (H. Limet and J. Ries, 1983).

The Nature and Function of the Myth

M. Eliade began his studies using a twofold historical procedure: he first examined the living myths of present-day populations; he then considered the myths of peoples that have had an important role in history — Greece, Egypt, Near East, India — but whose myths have since been transformed and enriched. Lastly, together with P. Ricoeur, he tried to penetrate these myths and with the help of phenomenological and interpretative research, to discover their meaning.

Myths refer to events that took place at the beginning, at the primordial and fabulous time of origins. In so doing, they explain the genesis of realities that exist in the world: the cosmos, man, plants, animals, life. In telling of the actions of supernatural beings, they describe the irruption of the sacred in the world. Indeed, a myth is "a

183. Pages 124-5: Cave painting near Laura on the York Peninsula (Australia). The great series of images regards what archaeologists have called the "Dreamtime." The paintings are the work of a hunter-gatherer population. The Dreamtime was the original age, and the painting evokes the myth. There are various overlapping vegetable, animal, and anthropomorphic figures.

sacred story of a people" whose structure depends on a system of symbols. In this sense it is a significant structure (Eliade, 1974).

Thanks to myths man can place himself within the cosmos. However, these myths are also models for him, guidelines for behavior that shape human action. In revealing the existence and activities of supernatural beings, of primordial ancestors, the myth establishes what behavior is in keeping with these models. Man must repeat the intial act, since this is an archetype, and in so doing will be projected back into primordial time. In this way profane time is replaced by the sacred time of the origins.

It is myths which permit human action to achieve the experience of the sacred. Their role is to awaken and maintain the awareness of a world different from that of everyday life. This presupposes the crucially important ceremony of initiation, and thereby the knowledge that makes the experience of the primordial event possible.

Myth and Origins

The *cosmogonic* myths constitute the sacred history of different peoples, a coherent story revealing the drama of the creation of the cosmos and man and the principles that sustain the cosmic process and human existence. Through the cosmogonic myths, archaic man adopted in his own terms a history of the origins that was rich in symbolism. Thanks to these myths, we are now able to understand the structure of the cultural and religious life of archaic peoples.

The *origin* myths narrate and justify a new situation that constitutes a change in the created world. They comprise genealogies, healing myths, the myths concerning the origins of medicines and medical sciences, but also the myths about the birth of institutions and societies. These myths also include those concerning changes in the human condition, the solar and astral mythologies, the myths about the origins of death, about vegetation and fertility.

The myths about the *renewal of the world* were important in the early stages of the Near East, in Indo-European thought, and in numerous traditional societies. These myths revolve around the movement of the seasons, the new year, the enthronement of the king, the scapegoat and initiation. They constitute interpretative keys to the cave paintings and rock carvings.

The numerous *eschatological* myths refer to cosmic catastrophes: floods, earthquakes, landslides, the destruction of the world. However, they often end with the image of a new creation.

The Myth and Its Message

To understand the place and role of the message of a myth it is necessary to observe the symbolic structure of the myth itself and to be aware of the importance of initiation in the different cultures.

The myth is a symbolic expression by means of which man interprets the relationship between present time and the time of origins. By means of the mythical tale, man perceives primordial time as a golden age during which chaos became cosmos. In such time supernatural beings brought about creation, and the clans and their institutions were born. Initiation is what allows contact with this most sacred of times. This message of the sacred story is the basis of man's belief in the deity.

A second aspect of the message of the myth concerns the possibility and necessity of embracing the golden age. For only thus is one able to imbue life with stable order, direction, meaning and efficacy. The ritual celebration of myth gives man the opportunity to fulfill his longing and reach out to the time of the origins.

A third aspect of the mythical message is the way it determines behavior in one's daily life by supplying models to be imitated. Human actions naturally refer to archetypes, since this gives them coherence, meaning and efficacy. In Vedic India, the priests and those who offered sacrifice were enabled, by means of the sacrifice, to free themselves from profane time and return to the golden age, thereby attaining immortality. In pharaonic Egypt, the myth of Osiris determined the passage from death to life in the netherworld thanks to the rite of embalming that ensured bodily immortality. The agrarian myths and feasts of the New Year invested nature and vegetation with new life, thus acting as the source of fertility and abundance.

184. Illustrations of a theory of twins, quoted by Campbell Grant in his study of North American cave art. A large number of similar figures have been found along the middle reaches of the Columbia River. They are probably mythical beings, like the twins revered by the Navajos. Images of twins are a very ancient expression of mythical and ritual systems to be found in various parts of the world where bipartition, polarity, and dichotomies tend to become the meeting of opposites, tension, and symbiosis to explain the cosmic rhythms and the contrasting aspects of reality.

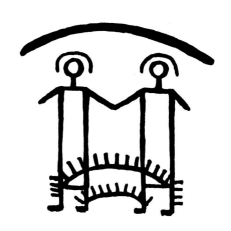

·184

33 Rites in the Life of *homo religiosus*

Ritual and the Human Condition

"RITE" is an archaic Indo-European word that has been preserved among Indo-Iranian and Italo-Celtic peoples thanks to the presence of sacerdotal colleges responsible for the upkeep of rituals and celebrations. In the Rig-Veda (X, 124, 5) the word refers to the immanent order of the cosmos. This is the *dharma*, the fundamental law inherent in nature. Hence the meaning of *ritu*, which indicates the tasks to be undertaken in each season, in relation to the *dharma*.

Based on the cosmic order perceived by archaic man, this interpretation also gave rise to religious and moral values: necessity, rectitude, truth. In India the word *ritavya* designates the bricks of the altar of the sacrificial fire that symbolizes the year, but also the creative power by means of which he who makes the sacrifice "ascends" to the heavens.

Rites concern the human condition (J. Cazeneuve, 1958), and as such serve to conjoin man, culture, society, and religion. Moreover, they also relate to symbols, myths, and the sacred. This being so, ethnology, anthropology, sociology, philosophy and theology have all identified meanings pertaining to particular aspects of the rite. The history of religions tries to circumscribe and synthesize these elements in order to understand the ritual phenomenon in itself and in the way it relates to man and his interpersonal behavior within society.

Rites, Archetypes and Sacred Experience

C. G. Jung used the word archetype as a synonym for *Urbilder* and *Motive* — primordial images and vital forces that make up the content of the collective unconscious. By means of a symbolic language, these primordial images known as archetypes communicate facts about the life of archaic humanity.

Following Eliade's example, in our use of the word archetype we

185

185. *Hypothetical reconstruction of a sacrifice before the funerary chapel of a rich dignitary of pharaonic Egypt. Food was a propitiatory offering for the well-being of the deceased in the netherworld.*

186. *Detail of the floor of the synagogue at Beit Alfa' (Palestine) showing the sacrifice of Isaac that God called Abraham to perform as a sign of his unconditional faith. God then intervened to prevent Isaac's death. Among the Canaanites, where Abraham lived, human sacrifice was sometimes performed in moments of particular social gravity. The biblical account fits into this context, but the God of Abraham stays the father's arm and shows his approval of the patriarch's faith.*

186

188

187.   *Remains of a sacrificial altar of the Punic civilization, located on the small island of Mozia off the far eastern coast of Sicily. The altar was part of a sanctuary. The Punic people (Carthaginians) founded various cities and trading centers in the western Mediterranean and there built religious centers of great importance.*

188.   *This funerary stele also comes from Mozia. It was located in a* tofet *to the northwest of the residential district. For the Punic people, a* tofet *was a "sacred enclosure" — we would call it a temple — often erected on a hill. Here the priests carried out their principal religious function, sacrifice. In the* tofets *numerous funerary stelae have been found with portrayals of the dead (as in this case) or the deities or sacred symbols.*

are also referring to a "primordial model." In defining the archetype, Eliade did not turn to psychology based on the collective unconscious, but rather focused on the religions of the early Near East, the first religions that have come down to us in written documents. He observed that in Mesopotamia the river Tigris had the star Anunit as its counterpart or model. In Egypt, the denomination of the 42 nomes — the archaic territorial organization through which the Nile flood waters were distributed — derived from the heavenly fields. In Iran, in Zurvanist tradition, each earthly phenomenon corresponded to a celestial reality. The cities of Nineveh and Asshur both had celestial models. The idea of a corresponding cosmic double that gives sacrifice its efficacy is also to be found in the Vedic tradition. The temple of Jerusalem was built according to a plan that came from the sky (Exodus 25:1-9). So religious man of these Eastern cultures looked to the sky for a model and a framework that would guide him both in his relationship with the heavens and in his work as a builder of cities and temples. By means of the heavenly archetype *homo religiosus* was aware of entering into relationship with transcendency (Eliade, 1981).

Before dedicating the newly built temple to the cult of the deity, the king of Babylon and Egypt would consecrate the building with the assistance of priests. The rituals that have come down to us show that ritual words and actions were used to create a perfect correspondence with the archetype. Thus the building could be separated from its profane use and imbued with efficacy and a new dimension owing to its relationship with the heavenly archetype. In addition to these consecration rites there were also rites pertaining to the king's investiture, such that he became the earthly representative of the deity.

There is a second archetypal component in ancient religions that is revealed in the symbolism of the center: cosmic mountain, tree of life, center of the world, sacred space. In the rites relative to the symbolism of the center the cosmic tree is the archetype of all sacred trees. It allows man to ascend to the sky.

A third component is to be found in the divine model that man should imitate. In Egypt the priests reproduced the actions of Thoth, the god who created the world with his tongue, and natural life was related to the primordial action of the god Osiris. In Babylon the feast of *akitu* celebrated the new year and prepared the renewal of vegetation. In both these cultures an impressive series of fertility rites connected the growth of vegetation to divine power (Eliade, 1975).

This brief excursus is based on the abundant documentary evidence concerning the early religions of the Near East whose rites have come down to us on tablets and in inscriptions. Its aim is to show how rites were a form of hierophany for the people of the first great civilizations. By means of rites men experienced the sacred in relation to the divine world. The rite was thus the mediating element of the hierophany. Thanks to the words and actions of the priests, the consecration rites established a relationship between man and the deities. Through these rites, human actions were invested with power and efficacy deriving from the gods.

The Nature and Function of Religious Rites

Various works are available that deal with the typology of rites, so we need not focus on the question here. E. Durkheim and M. Mauss constructed their typology from the point of view of the relationship between individual and society; M. Weber opted for the perspective of the meaning actually experienced; J. Wach chose a framework related to the religious experience of the social group; Cl. Lévi-Strauss preferred to focus on the structuralist aspect of the language by means of which past and present could be connected.

As far as the difference between religious and magical rites is concerned, it is worth noting that magic is characterized by a desire for ascendancy by means of particular cosmic powers, whereas religion is oriented toward transcendency. Religious rites operate within the context of hierophanies, whereas magical rites turn to powers that are not related to the sacred (kratophany) (J. Cazeneuve, 1971).

The present study confines itself to analyzing rites in the existential experience of *homo religiosus* as he leans toward hierophany. Within this perspective the rite should be seen as a symbolic expression through which man seeks vital contact with transcendent reality, with the divine, with God. It is made up of technique and a system of symbols, both of which are used to achieve an effective vital experience of the sacred. The rite is a set of gestures and actions accompanied by an explicit or implicit verbal language that together lead toward ontological reality. In other words, it is a path leading from significant structure to inner being. When *Homo sapiens* and *religiosus* carries out a rite, it becomes the palpable expression of belief.

The first rites of which we have archaeological evidence are the funeral rites of Qafzeh and Neanderthal man, followed by those of the Upper Paleolithic and the Neolithic. The offerings placed in the graves, the red ochre on the corpses, the arrangement of the tombs, the shells set into the eye sockets, and the special treatment of skulls are evidence of belief in an afterlife.

In various Franco-Cantabrian caves such as those at Lascaux and

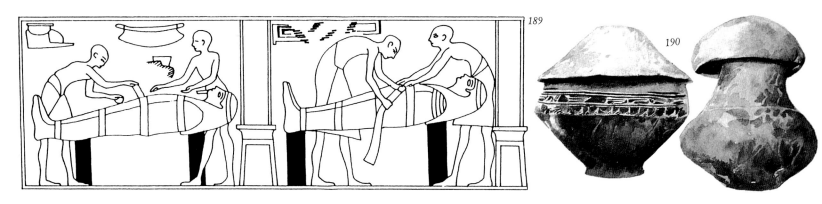

189. *Illustration of some of the stages of bandaging an Egyptian mummy. The operation called for several hundred meters of fine material.*

190. *Reconstruction of two funerary urns made in Germany during the Bronze Age (1000-700 B.C.). They were used for burying the ashes of the dead. For Europe this was the beginning of a new ritual that was soon to become very widespread.*

191. *Mosaic in the vault of the Ariani Baptistry in Ravenna (Italy). It illustrates the baptism of Christ in the center, surrounded by apostles and the cross. Christ affirmed the necessity of a rebirth by water and the Spirit. This is why he himself was baptized with water. His death was also termed a baptism: an expiatory death that Christ submitted to for the sins of mankind so that man in turn could receive the Spirit through baptism. Ritual purification with water was characteristic of many civilizations.*

Rouffignac, adolescent footprints have been found that suggest the performance of initiation ceremonies. The mythograms of the wall paintings would seem to corroborate this interpretation and indicate that initiation myths date back to the very distant past (J. Ries, 1989).

In the Neolithic period, the praying men of the Valcamonica with their hands raised skyward bear eloquent witness to *prayer rites* that we also find in elegant terms in the Sumerian world — in the clasped hands and the hand raised to the mouth in the praying figure at Larsa and in those found at Ur III (Limet and Ries, 1980). From the third millennium, the Egyptian and Mesopotamian temples were used for *consecration rites*. These expressed special relationships between men

and the gods and therefore took pride of place in the great religions. The *sacrificial rites* were contemporary with the construction of the temples, sanctuaries, and altars. By sacrificing an object, a living being or an animal, *homo religiosus* established or reestablished his ties with the deity.

Rites are repetitive for the very reason that they relate to the rhythms of nature and life, and indeed culture and society. They afford communion with the various aspects of the divine, and through the celebration of the myths bring about a primordial event. Within society the rite is a principle of coherence. Even if it is carried out in solitude, it relates to a community.

191

192. Human skull found in Tomb 7 at Monte Alban, near Oaxaca (Mexico). The Mixtecs (9th-15th century A.D.) had a particular cult of the dead: they not only buried them in frescoed funerary chambers enriched with gifts, but also decorated their bodies. This involved stripping off the flesh and preserving them so that they could be turned into precious statues. This skull was covered with a mosaic of turquoise, a stone much valued in the pre-Columbian world. Shells were used for the nose and eyes, recalling the early Neolithic practices of the first settled populations of the Middle East.

192

193

132

34 The Structures of Religious Behavior

SO FAR we have looked at the religious facts (the hierophanies) preserved from Paleolithic times through to the great monotheistic religions and man's behavior in the sacred experience expressed through myths, symbols and rites. At this point we should therefore focus on the structures of behavior of *homo religiosus,* that is, of *Homo sapiens* in his experience of the sacred. In so doing, we will also be dealing with the question of the validity and aims of religious anthropology.

Religious anthropology studies man as the creator and user of sacred symbolism and as the keeper of religious beliefs that guide his life and behavior. Apart from the religious anthropology that is specific to a particular religion (Hindu, Buddhist, Jewish, Muslim, Christian) there is also an anthropology that focuses on *homo religiosus* and his behavior in the course of sacred experience (J. Ries, ed., 1989). Durkheim and Mauss were convinced that the sacred was an exclusively social phenomenon, whereas R. Otto later developed the idea that experience of the sacred could be interpreted as a human experience of the transcendent, of the "noumenous," of the divine. Since then the works of Eliade and Dumézil have drawn attention to the important role of culture in the life of *homo religiosus,* who necessarily related to a group and a society. *Homo sapiens,* and therefore *homo religiosus,* did not live isolated from his cultural environment: he was a creator of culture and his historical appearance took place in an environment characterized by cultural traditions.

At this point there is a question that calls for an answer: what are the structures that enable man to live the sacred experience by means of symbols, myths, and rites?

Image, Symbol and Creativity

In *Sacré, symbole et créativité,* J. Vidal (1992) examines in detail the dynamics of the symbol in man's psychic life and its role in religious experience. Symbolic experience begins with images taken from external objects such as the sky, the stars, the moon, water, a tree, a stone, and so on. "The symbol does not work on objects but on images" (Eliade, 1979, 1981). The passage from object to image takes place precisely when the symbolic experience begins. Bachelard has shown that thanks to the image the symbol adopts a life-bearing role. In fact, the image introduces unity and totality as well as agility and dynamism. By contrast, the object communicates fixity and coldness: hence the weakness of positivism with its methodological exclusion of image and symbol as a means of knowledge.

By embracing the dynamics of unity (center) and totality (expansion), images stir the consciousness, arousing impulses and creating contact with primordial images and archetypes. In other words, they awaken the primordial impulses present in the individual and collective consciousness. Through its activity the symbol generates psychic forces, creating a link between the conscious and the subconscious mind. This means that the consciousness is fired to discover the primordial images from which it began. In Eliade's view, the archetype confers efficacy on human action, establishing a relationship between the interior and exterior worlds. This is how man's creative sense is born.

Man's Imaginary Sphere and Anthropological Development

G. Durand defines the imaginary sphere as "the set of images and relationships between images that make up the thought store of *Homo sapiens.*" There is an organizational dynamism in the imaginary sphere that gives the representations their homogeneity. G. Bachelard has shown that "the fundamental objectives of the imagination are based on the trend set by man's principal actions relating to his natural environment." This is a reversible trend, however, since man is also shaped by the environment in which he lives. Durand has thus argued that in analyzing symbols and the way they work we should also take into account this two-way *anthropological development:* an incessant imaginary exchange of subjective impulses that assimilate human psychic life and objective impulses deriving from the cosmic and social environment. The human imaginary sphere is therefore shaped by two factors: on the one hand, psychic life and its imperatives that assimilate the representation of the object; and on the other, the reactions of the objective environment that influence man's psychic life. This ceaseless anthropological trend is essential to explanations of the personal growth of *homo religiosus.*

Heritage and Initiation

On the one hand we thus have the "image and symbol" complex, whereas on the other there is the "anthropological trend" as it works in the imaginary sphere of *Homo sapiens.* To these two structures we now need to add a third that can explain the growth of *homo religiosus* in the course of history, from the Paleolithic to the great monotheistic religions. This is the initiation tradition that gives access to the cultural and religious heritage created in the course of the previous millennia and preserved in the collective memory. At this point the concept of "heritage" emphasized by G. Dumézil proves to be of fundamental importance.

Initiation reveals sacred things, symbols, and truths to the neophyte, giving him knowledge of the deeper meaning of his origins, the group that he is part of, his relationship with others and with the Totally Other or deity. Initiation is thus a revelation of the fundamental truth that makes up the structure of his existence and directs his experience of the sacred. Through this revelation he will partake of a heritage and wisdom derived from the ancestors and passed on through the community memory. It is a heritage that can transmit myths, symbols and rites, beliefs, ideas and representations, sacred writings, temples and sanctuaries. Both a religious and a cultural heritage, it offers *homo religiosus* accumulated capital that he can increase, a store of images and symbols that can also be used for living new experiences of the sacred. The initiation tradition is a social, cultural, and religious structure that is essential to the growth of *homo religiosus* and *humanitas religiosa.*

35 The Oral Tradition Religions Today

194

IN THE course of the nineteenth and twentieth centuries, Western interest in what were once known as "primitive" religions has grown enormously. These religions of cultures based on the oral tradition, as they are now defined, clearly presented no written evidence, so scholars turned to colonial records and the accounts of missionaries and other observers for information. Despite different ideological guidelines, anthropologists, ethnologists, and historians were all intent on discovering the origin of religion. Most of these specialists believed contemporary "primitive" peoples to be in a stage of development similar to that of the earliest cultures (E. Evans-Pritchard, 1971). However, the various studies undertaken on this basis proved to be misguided and one by one were abandoned (U. Bianchi, 1963).

Following a pause that lasted a few decades, these religions have

194. A moment in a corroboree of Australian aboriginals. This event is generally seen as a medley of dances, rhythms and singing that unites the group. There are also secret women's corroborees that can only be attended by girls who have reached sexual maturity. The social character of the ritual is probably accompanied by a deeper symbolic meaning.

become the object of renewed interest, albeit from a substantially different standpoint. The cultures in question are largely those of black Africa, Oceania, the Arctic regions, the North and South American Indians, and the Altai peoples of Siberia. These populations are no longer seen as *Naturvölker* since the studies now focus on their vitality and historical continuum. Anthropologists of the caliber of

135

195. Bark painting done in the 1950s by a population of aboriginal hunters from Arnhem Land in the far north of Australia. It refers to a Dreamtime myth. E. Anati has described it as follows: "A couple of Mimi spirits wander through the forest (the leaves) looking for food (small bags hanging from their shoulders). They have the necessary implements: a stone axe, a stick for digging out roots and a dart with a dart-thrower."

196. Detail of an alusi figure in wood, by an Ibo sculptor, Nigeria. The Ibos represent their main deities in groups of sculptures structured according to the family model: husband, wife, son, future heir, and so on. These guardian deities were once thought to be ancestors. They are called alusi and are kept inside enclosures or on altars that are dedicated to them. As a sign of devotion, during the ceremonies they are painted with earth and pigments and are even dressed by the women.

M. Griaule, E. Evans-Pritchard, and R. Lienhardt and historians of religions such as M. Eliade have identified certain essential phenomena of the religious life of these peoples: myths, symbols, rites, initiation. These populations consider the whole of their human creativity as religious (Eliade, 1979).

Myths and Their Revival

Today's traditional societies transmit living myths that supply "models for human behavior and give man's existence direction." In his famous tetralogy, Cl. Lévi-Strauss analyzed approximately eight hundred myths of the American Indians (Lévi-Strauss, 1964, p. 71). Having explained their passage from nature to culture through the discovery of fire, culinary and farming techniques, and ornament (vol. 1), he tried to demonstrate the convertibility of alimentary, astronomical, and sociological codes (vol. 2). Next he dealt with the question of social ethics (vol. 3), and lastly with the opposition between nature and culture (vol. 4). In his view, these myths tell us nothing about the order and nature of the real world, or about the origins of man and his destiny. However, their structure does reveal the unity and coherence of things, integrating man with nature, but without producing any religious message. By reducing the myth to the status of a language, Lévi-Strauss's structuralism does little more than define its syntax.

For the men of traditional societies, the myth is a language that bears a message full of meaning. M. Eliade devoted considerable effort to the living myths of contemporary traditional peoples, thus providing us with an interpretative framework for their religiosity (Eliade, 1974). The myths refer to a sacred story of primordial times, relating how supernatural beings and ancestors created or re-created the world. For traditional man, this revelation has many consequences since it transmits meaningful models of all human activities: those related to food, work, education, marriage, art, and wisdom. Man as he is today is thus the result of this creation of the origins. If the creation and its concomitant situation is to be preserved, then the myth must periodically be revived and time regenerated. This recreation of the cosmogony of the world brings about a return to the golden age. Such, in a nutshell, is the message of the myths.

To effect this return a revival of the myths is necessary, and this implies the existence of particular feasts and a precise calender of celebrations. Each feast is essentially a commemoration of divine actions, since the supernatural beings and the mythical ancestors should never be forgotten. However, the feast is also a celebration that allows the tribe to relive the primordial events, to reach the golden age, to recover and imitate the exemplary actions of the gods. The feast thus regenerates its own powers in order to fuel the activities of daily life. Revelation, feast, memory and revival relate to both the origins on the one hand and to daily life on the other. Myths are the

197

197. The art of the Indian peoples of the northwest coast of Canada has developed enormously in the last decades. Although these populations are now integrated into modern life, they have maintained their traditional visual culture. This Haida design comes from a silver ornament made by the artist and sculptor Bill Reid, who also works with the Museum of Anthropology in Vancouver. The title of the work is The Woman in the Moon *(1954). The subject relates closely to that of the origin myths. In 1980 Reid made a wooden sculpture to occupy a room of its own in the Museum:* Raven and the First Men. *The raven is the bird of origins, and sits on the egg from which the first men are hatching.*

138

religious framework of traditional societies, of their institutions, and of the daily activity of the men and women who belong to them.

Oral Tradition and Initiation

The initiation of adolescents plays an important role in cultures based on the oral tradition. Universally attested, initiation acts as the matrix of society in that it shapes culture, supports religion, and promotes the perfecting of *homo religiosus*. Initiation rites call for the preparation of a sacred site in which the supernatural beings can re-create the world. This chosen space makes it possible to communicate with the transcendent world. Initiation takes place within a sacred time, and this provides access to the time of origins that the neophyte can attain by means of the rites: sacred time and place are two prerequisites of initiation.

Initiation begins with a break from the life of childhood, typically involving a sacred enclosure, brushwood, separation from the mother, isolation in a wood. Next there are initiation trials: dances, sleep deprivation, hunger, thirst, flame throwing, purification rites; in Africa and Oceania there is circumcision; in Australia, the shrieks produced by instruments called bull-roarers that are held to echo the voice of the Supreme Being. Finally there is the tradition of the myths, by means of which the neophyte is introduced into his community (Eliade, 1979). Since this tradition gives access to the mysteries and is therefore a revelation, it may be drawn out over a space of several years.

The Supreme Being

A major research project carried out at the beginning of the twentieth century by W. Schmidt and a team of ethnologists among the Australian aboriginals provided evidence of tribal belief in the existence of a Supreme Being. Further work directed by Schmidt and undertaken by Koppers, Schebesta, Gusinde, and others drew attention to parallel beliefs among the African Pygmies, the Bushmen, the peoples of Tierra del Fuego, and the Arctic and North American populations. Numerous ethnologists and historians of religion have agreed with the claims made by these scholars (W. Schmidt, 1912-1954).

As a result of the debate between Pettazzoni and Eliade, we now have a better understanding of this belief in a Supreme Being that "is always a primordial character and creator" (Eliade, 1979). Primordiality and creativity are characteristic features of mythical thought. Moreover, current research and the analysis of myths, rites, and traditional symbolism as a whole tend to confirm such beliefs. In Africa the Supreme Being is the creator and lord of the cosmos. According to several myths, he once lived among men, but later moved away (D. Zahan, 1976). The mythical traditions of South America tell of an omniscient Supreme Being, an all-powerful, benevolent creator and lord of the universe (E. Schaden, 1976). The Supreme God of the American Indians occupied the highest position in the hierarchy, whence he could control human activity. Associated with the sky, he was invisible, a fact which confirms his transcendency.

198

198. *Design made with a carved stone stamp by the Inuit people near Baker Lake in the Northwest Territories of Canada. It shows an Inuit shaman taking flight accompanied by his guardian hosts. In the culture of the North American Indians, the guardian spirits bring blessing to their human partners.*

199.   Contemporary aboriginal burials on Melville Island, in the Arafura
Sea to the far north of Australia. The presence of the cross and the
acceptance of Christianity do not imply rejection of traditional rituals.

200.   Ayers Rock in the center of Australia. Considered the largest
monolith in the world, it is not difficult to understand why it has always
embodied sacred values for the indigenous population.

201.   A view of the Olga Mountains with Ayers Rock in the background.
It seems even more imposing when seen from a slightly higher position.

36 *Homo habilis* and *symbolicus*

Creative Imagination, Implements, and Their Message

The Recent Discovery of *Homo habilis*

EXCAVATIONS BEGUN in 1959 at Olduvai in Tanzania and to the east of Lake Turkana in Kenya brought to light skull remains dating back two million years. In 1964 L. Leakey, Ph. Tobias and J. Napier adopted the term *Homo habilis* to designate man of that period in view of his evident ability as a maker of tools — specifically choppers made from pebbles cut on one side, and chopping tools that were worked on both sides (F. Facchini, 1990). These discoveries have led certain paleoanthropologists to consider East Africa as the cradle of humanity. Moreover, further research has recently encouraged Ph. V. Tobias to formulate a hypothesis that the skulls of *Homo habilis* of the Broca and Wernicke areas indicate a capacity for articulated language (Tobias, 1992).

The archaeological remains found in Africa in the course of the past thirty years comprise carved flints (including numerous choppers), pebbles used as hunting weapons and strikers, recycled animal bones, hut structures that acted as habitations, and remains of work areas. Paleoanthropologists identify in *Homo habilis* the physical, cultural, and social characteristics that were to constitute the basis of the development of *Homo sapiens*. This in its turn implies that there was a network of consciously experienced relationships with respect to family, group, and territory. It is thus clear that *Homo habilis* had made a substantial stride beyond his predecessor, the Australopithecine. *Homo habilis* was a new man.

Homo habilis has left us various traces of the earliest human culture: industry, technology, dwelling structures, a hunter-gatherer economy, objects, and tools. Called Olduvaian after the name of the place where the richest remains were found, this culture dates back over two million years. It is the oldest human culture and bears witness to the psychic activity of *Homo habilis:* the ability to plan, to organize work and hunting, to observe the surrounding environment, nature, vegetable, and animal resources. In Tobias's view, "*Homo habilis* was the principal representative of hominid evolution for a span of one million years." Moreover, his discovery provides the missing link between the Australopithecines and *Homo erectus*.

Homo habilis and Tools

Pebble culture tells us a lot about *Homo habilis:* the types of implements he used and the food that he consumed daily, the natural environment and the kind of life he led. It also provides the first example of the use of an intermediary object between hand and natural object: the tool. Tools presuppose manual grasp, and thereby the existence of a biped whose hands were free. In the culture of *Homo habilis* the hand is no longer in itself a tool, as it is in the animal world, but rather what activates the tool and gradually improves its application. Human progress is greatly enhanced with the development of the tool, since the techniques implicit in its application call for conceptual mediation, the idea, the design. To shape a chopper man had first to work out an image of the finished object, which meant choosing a particular pebble that could be chipped on both sides. Next he had to have an idea of all the operations necessary for achieving his design. *Homo habilis* was evidently not only a technical inventor fired by a sense of initiative, but also a being endowed with human intelligence and imagination. There were two factors at play: on the one hand the intellectual faculties implicit in grasping the relationship between the stages of the job and the objects themselves; and on the other, the symbolic imagination that allowed him to project a design on objec-

202. *Petroglyph of the Mississippi culture (700-1600 A.D.), upper Mississippi, Minnesota (United States). It is painted in red and represents a bilobate arrow (short arrow flanked by two circles). In Campbell Grant's view, it was an important ceremonial symbol.*

tive reality (A. Leroi-Gourhan, 1964). The two factors that made the appearance of *Homo habilis* possible were the freeing of the hand and the contemporaneous growth of intellectual reflection. Together these factors made him a creator.

The Birth of *homo symbolicus*

Homo habilis possessed the techniques necessary for acquiring, making and consuming. He was able to conceive of expressive symbols and translate them into action, sounds, and the creation of objects. The upright position was an essential condition for physical evolution and the freeing of the hands. Moreover, it also offered vision of the horizon and the surrounding environment, which in its turn led to discovery. Although necessary, however, this condition was not in itself sufficient. A new psychic element was also required, a consciousness that was both symbolic and creative.

We have archaeological evidence to show that *Homo habilis* possessed such consciousness. Cutting pebbles implied experimentation, imagination and the choice of materials and shapes. In Olduvaian culture the areas devoted to stone cutting have supplied us with a wealth of evidence proving that the pebble cutters, in selecting their materials, took into account solidity, quality, and color. Everything that failed to satisfy such requirements was discarded. Chipping bifacial choppers indicates a search for symmetry and particular aesthetic qualities. Hunting implies working out collective strategies, and there are remains of meals showing that big game hunting was a common activity. The organization of space is another sign of the symbolic consciousness. The huts were structured in three different sections: living area, space reserved for cutting up meat, and the tool-making area. Yves Coppens has argued that this period is of crucial importance because mobility and intellectual reflection made it possible for "man to extend his territory and gain awareness of his knowledge for the first time in the entire history of Life" (Y. Coppens, 1987).

The prodigious discoveries made in the Rift Valley in Africa give us no explicit clues to the religiosity of *Homo habilis*. However, in revealing what he created, they certainly prove that he was a *homo symbolicus*. Olduvaian culture thus establishes a fact that has remarkable consequences for paleoanthropology, for anthropology, and for the history of religions: *homo symbolicus* was born two million years ago.

203. Drawing by Chen Zhao Fu of cave graffiti at Lianyungang in Yangzhou Province (China). According to the author they are a cluster of symbols: series of dots, lines, circles, radiating circles, concentric circles, and ideograms.

204. Page 144, above: Chipped point of the Levallois variety used by Neanderthal man nearly one hundred thousand years ago. This is an example of refined Mousterian industry. However, bifacial flints had already been used a million years earlier, when man discovered the symmetry that various paleoanthropologists have interpreted as the association of a symbolic meaning with a utilitarian objective.

143

205. *The mouth of a decorated cave in the Masai Escarpment, Tanzania. The fact that this and many other caves had decorated walls shows that in his artistic and ritual activity prehistoric man expressed his faith in the sacred nature of caves and the way they relate to the afterlife.*

206. *Symbolic rock graffiti at Gua Badak in Malaysia. The cave walls are in colored veined marble. The exploitation of the marble at the end of the 1980s destroyed many of the decorations. The meaning of the abstract designs photographed here is still not clear. They belong to a complex symbology that was part of the cultural heritage of the Malay Negritos, a hunter-gatherer population. (In 1928 the anthropologist Ivor Evans suggested that the many abstract designs might be reproductions of the mats on which the ancestors slept). This is truly remarkable artistry on the part of* Homo symbolicus.

205

206 ▷

37 *Homo erectus, homo sapiens,* and Symbolism of the Vault of Heaven

From *erectus* to *sapiens*

PALEOANTHROPOLOGISTS use the term *Homo erectus* to refer to the human species that appeared in East Africa, to the east of Lake Turkana, 1.6 million years ago. This species came after *Homo habilis,* populated the Ancient World (Asia, China, Africa, Europe), and disappeared around 150,000 B.C. (F. Facchini, 1990). The most important traces of *Homo erectus* in Asia have been discovered at Zhoukoudian in China and in Java. They prove that his brain size had grown from 800 cubic centimeters to 1250 cubic centimeters and that he lived by hunting and gathering wild vegetables. His camps were open to the sky and he preferred to settle along water courses, as close as possible to rock formations. He had developed a certain ability in fashioning stone and used fire for cooking his food. The earliest traces of fire were found at Zhoukoudian, in the Near East, and in Europe; the latter date to 450,000 B.C. The invention of fire was an act of genius that allowed man to make an important step forward in family and social relationships. Not only is fire the first source of energy that man managed to dominate; it is also a sign of religiosity, to the extent that certain paleoanthropologists mention evidence of fire rites (C. Perlès, 1977). Considerable expansion of the stone industry would seem to suggest the existence of a language by means of which such techniques could be transmitted. The discovery of a number of skulls mutilated at the base also indicates that there were rituals attesting belief in the afterlife. Apart from the fire rites, the funeral rites constitute the only evidence that we have at present of the religiosity of *Homo erectus.*

By means of a very slow morphological evolution, *Homo erectus* turned into *Homo sapiens* (R. Vandermeersch, 1988). His earliest representatives probably lived around 300,000 B.C. Then, about 80,000 B.C., a subspecies of *Homo sapiens* developed in Europe. This was Neanderthal man, who disappeared about 35,000 B.C. and was succeeded by *Homo sapiens sapiens,* whose origins date back very far into the past and outside Europe. The origins of present-day world populations actually derive from the many diversifications of *Homo sapiens sapiens.* We know quite a lot about Neanderthal man thanks to the discovery of many graves that bear witness to a highly developed cultural and religious level. The earliest tombs located at Qafzeh in Palestine (90,000 B.C.) are the work of *Homo sapiens,* which means that they have nothing to do with Neanderthal man. Funerary religiosity underwent rapid development from the Qafzeh period, indicating that the religious consciousness of *Homo sapiens* was growing.

Traces of Religiosity

We have considerable evidence of the culture of *Homo erectus* and *Homo sapiens,* most of it in the shape of implements. A. Leroi-Gourhan (1964) has drawn attention to the link between technique and language and has argued that language is a contributing factor of hominization rather than the result of it, since language and tools are expressions of the same symbolic faculty characteristic of man. We have seen that the symbolic faculty was already in use by *Homo habilis.*

Thus Y. Coppens (1983) has suggested that archaic man could already avail himself of language. In any case his tools and culture show that his symbolic faculty was remarkably developed. In the view of Professor Coppens, "this is already Man, with all his functional and behavioral characteristics" (1984, p. 120). Setting out from A. Leroi-Gourhan's studies of language, implements and symbols in man from the Lower Paleolithic on, J. Molino (1988, p. 147) has claimed that "symbolization is an essential property of the human species, as real as the functions of nutrition or reproduction." The entire work of G. Durand also proceeds in this direction.

In Eliade's view "it is inconceivable that the implements were not invested with sacral value" (Eliade, 1979, p. 16). As an example the author considered the role of implements in religious life and in the mythology of today's hunter-gatherer populations. He also looked at the mythologies built around the image of the lances thrust into the heavenly vault to allow access to the skies, arguing that the obscurity of prehistoric evidence should not lead us to "relinquish the reconstruction of an enormous part of the history of the human mind."

In the end the message of implements and traces of fire rites and funeral rites makes it clear that the passage from *Homo habilis* to *Homo erectus* and *Homo sapiens* entails a sacred experience.

The Vault of Heaven

The term *Homo erectus* created by paleoanthropologists actually has nothing to do with the upright position, since *Homo habilis* already possessed this characteristic. The designation derives from the late nineteenth-century discovery in Java of human fossils belonging to what the paleoanthropologists of the time called *Pithecanthropus erectus.* In those days nothing was known about the Australopithecenes or indeed *Homo habilis.* The Australopithecines were hominids that appeared three and a half million years ago. A famous specimen found recently is Lucy. The Australopithecines were bipeds who were certainly familiar with the upright position. However, the exact relationship between the three or four Australopithecine specimens known and the *Homo* species has still not been fully established (F. Facchini, 1990).

The historian of religions is not interested in the Australopithecines, who disappeared without leaving traces of culture. Instead he focuses on the study of *Homo,* the earliest example of which is the *Homo habilis* found at Olduvai in Tanzania in 1959. This man is remarkable for the size and shape of the brain, the teeth, and a skull base that allowed better balance of the head at the top of a straighter spine. The great novelty of *Homo habilis* is the emergence of cultural behavior (Tobias, 1992) which in its turn heralds the birth of *homo symbolicus.*

The condition of being a biped and the upright position that left the hands free together played a fundamental role in the creation of culture. Moreover, when standing upright *Homo habilis* could focus his gaze on the surrounding environment, on distant horizons, on the natural landscape with its various features, all of which was essential for the symbolization process. The neck vertebrae gave him greater head movement, and this facilitated contemplation of the skies, which was a crucial element in psychic, intellectual, and religious growth.

Homo habilis and *Homo erectus* were the first men to have a vision of the cosmos, and this left an indelible mark on human symbolism: the vault of heaven. It is typically portrayed as the roof that covers and is supported by the earth; indeed, in various later cosmologies the disk of the earth is shown as surrounded by a chain of mountains, like columns supporting the dome of heaven. With pebble cutting archaic man expressed aesthetic awareness, since this involved choosing materials in relation to their colors. We can thus imagine the impact that

the colors of the sky, of dawn and sunset, or the rainbow must have made on him. And indeed, Franco-Cantabrian art offers some fine evidence of this influence. Moreover, there was also the movement of the the sun, moon, and stars, and the succession of day and night. This latter element began to feature with increasing importance with the flowering of the two great cultures of Mesopotamia and Egypt, where celestial and astral symbolism embraced cosmic, psychic, and religious values.

M. Eliade began his *Traité* (1954) with a study of the vault of heaven. In his view, mere contemplation of the sky provoked the sacred experience in archaic man: height is an inaccessible dimension for man; thus the sidereal zones acquired the prestige of eternity and transcendence.

207

207. *Reproduction of rock decorations made by the Frimont culture in Capitol Reef National Park, Utah (United States). The two male figures appear to be observing two half-crescents and two concentric circles. The vault of heaven seems to envelop the men.*

208, 209. *Pages 148-9: Reproduction from a Masai Bible made by the German Veterinary Sister Katharina Kraus in the 1970s and 1980s. She so closely identified with the life and culture of the Masai that she became convinced that their monotheism and mythology comprised elements that were remarkably close to biblical themes. She thus painted panels illustrating the Bible in a style that gained recognition in many countries. Left: Abraham is portrayed with many animals, a sign of great importance for the Masai, yet his face is turned toward the vault of heaven. Right: Jacob's dream with the ladder connecting sky and earth and angels climbing up and down it.*

38 The Discovery of Transcendency

THE CULTURE produced by *Homo habilis* and *Homo erectus* and the traces of fire and funeral rites left by the latter are evidence of an experience of the sacred. This experience postulates the discovery of transcendency. But just how did archaic man attain a perception of transcendency?

The historian of religions can turn to the comparative genetic method in his efforts to define and comprehend the influence of the heavenly vault on the psychic life of archaic man and his perception of transcendency. Starting from evidence derived from past and present peoples, it is possible to build an interpretative framework of religiosity based on the cult of the sky, the heavenly vault, and the various celestial cults. Moving backwards through history, scholars try to grasp the behavior of *Homo sapiens, erectus,* and *habilis* with the aid of what we know about prehistoric religious phenomena on the one hand and recent research into symbols and their workings on the other.

A particularly rich research area regards peoples without writing, now extensively documented in the works of a number of specialists: W. Schmidt and the ethnologists of the Vienna School (W. Schmidt, 1912-1954); R. Pettazzoni (1922), M. Eliade (1954 and 1979), and numerous other anthropologists and ethnologists. It has been shown that in Australia the supreme gods of the aboriginals inhabit the sky and keep up direct links with it. In India, Africa and Tierra del Fuego, the Supreme God is invested with distinctly celestial symbolism. Shang Ti is the heaven, the Supreme God of ancient China (M. Kaltenmarm, 1981). In several of the ethnic cultures of Siberia, the name of the Great God signifies heaven. *Tengri,* the archaic Turkish and Mongolian term, designates both the vault of heaven and the deity.

There is a second group of documents concerning the heavenly vault and its religious significance pertaining to the great religions of populations that had invented writing: Mesopotamia and Egypt. Next came the Indo-European peoples, for whom the day and night skies possessed essential religious functions. A third field of inquiry that is still under way regards the cave inscriptions. These provide us with abundant evidence of the praying man with his hands raised toward the heavens, as the Valcamonica inscriptions show.

Taking all this information into account, the historian of religions can work back to Neolithic man and *Homo sapiens,* whose funeral and fire rites and belief in the afterlife contribute to our knowledge of his religiosity and sense of the transcendent. In the course of the millennia, the conscious and subconscious mind of this archaic man were clearly shaped by contemplation of the sky both by day and at night. It seems reasonable to suggest that the source of man's discovery of the transcendency on which his religiosity is based might be the incessant interaction of subjective impulses and objective injunctions deriving from contemplation of the vault of heaven. The historian, the anthropologist, and the ethnologist continue their journey back toward the origins and *tempora ignota.* In so doing, they discover new cultural evidence of *Homo erectus* and *Homo habilis,* both of whom in their own ways justify the appellative of *homo symbolicus.* During the slow course of the millennia, as expansion of the symbolic faculty brought about improvements in pebble-cutting techniques, these men began to turn their attention to the celestial world: the vault of heaven and its form and colors, the sun's course, the nightly movement of the moon and stars. To use

M. Eliade's words, "a contemplation of this sort must have amounted to a revelation" (1954). Ancient man discovered transcendency not by means of a rational operation but through using his own imagination, his own symbolic faculty. Myths still played no role at this early archaic stage. They were to come later, as part of the collective memory of a sacred story of the origins. The symbolism of the vault of heaven is what allowed early man to live his first sacred experience.

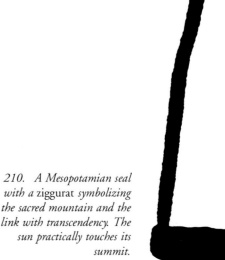

210. A Mesopotamian seal with a ziggurat *symbolizing the sacred mountain and the link with transcendency. The sun practically touches its summit.*

210

150

211. *Page 152: The Small Ararat seen from the south, in Iranian Azerbaijan. Since prehistoric times, the volcanic massif of Ararat has been considered a sacred mountain, possibly the foremost symbol of a sacred mountain in Eurasia. Even the split of the Rift Valley in Africa seems to point across the Red Sea to Mount Ararat.*

39 The Birth and Growth of Man's Religious Consciousness

DURING THE course of his research work, the paleoanthropologist Y. Coppens has drawn attention to a particular characteristic of *Homo habilis:* his role as a creator of culture. From the time of his earliest achievements man has never ceased to create and to make discoveries, since reflection on one discovery spurs on another. It was thus that man discovered the first signs of his destiny in the cosmos, his nature and origins through the light of his own reflections (Coppens, 1987).

Consciousness of the Sacred

The imagination of early man who created culture and observed his natural environment in order to understand his destiny must have related to the five basic symbols: the heavenly vault by day and by night, the solar symbols, the lunar symbols and the movement of the stars, the (chthonic) symbols of the earth and fertility, and the symbols of the natural environment, water, mountain, tree. Man's awareness was aroused by contemplation of the sky, by means of which he lived a sacred experience connected with the celestial hierophanies. In Eliade's view, his imagination hosted "a light of transcendency deriving from the outside." There is no doubt that this first experience of the sacred was to quicken his consciousness for thousands of years, gradually leading him to grasp the affinities and contrasts between sky and earth and to reflect on his condition in the cosmos in the light of his vision of the celestial heights. This first stage of the development of religious consciousness is related to the discovery of transcendency and the creation of a first rudimentary culture.

Awareness of the Mystery of Life, of Death, and the Afterlife

Contemplation of death, which implied an awareness of the mystery of earthly life and the afterlife, gradually led to the development of a second stage. The first funeral rites help us to identify this historical moment in the evolution of *Homo sapiens,* with the earliest signs of it appearing at the end of the *Homo erectus* period. Related to the Neanderthal and Qafzeh burials, the funeral rites constitute undeniable evidence of the existence of religious awareness. They bear witness to the fact that these men nurtured feelings of otherness and affection for the dead and believed in an afterlife, as witnessed by the offerings found in the graves and the care devoted to protecting the corpse. During the course of the Upper Paleolithic the number and arrangement of these graves, the ornaments, offerings and objects placed beside the dead and the regular use of red ochre as a symbol of blood and life together indicate a new development in the awareness of the afterlife of *Homo sapiens sapiens.* M. Eliade has insisted on the fetal position of numerous skeletons and the way they faced east. This latter rite suggests a particular intention on the part of the living: "to unite the fate of the soul with the course of the sun in hope of a re-birth, that is of an afterlife in another world" (Eliade, 1979). The shells set into the eye sockets confirm such a belief. The development of funeral rites, from Qafzeh to the end of the Upper Paleolithic, speaks for a parallel growth of religious consciousness based on the belief in an afterlife relating to the awareness of transcendency.

Awareness of a "Sacred Story" of the Origins

Franco-Cantabrian art expresses a third stage in the development of religious consciousness. The mythograms painted on the cave walls and ceilings and the adolescent footprints found in many decorated caves have suggested to historians of religion that initiation rites existed alongside the myths. Whatever the interpretation attributed to this art, the symbolism it embodies is extremely rich, which means

212. *Simplified reproduction of a fresco in the burial chamber of Tuthmosis III at Thebes (Egypt), late 14th century* B.C. *The tree has an arm that the pharaoh holds onto and a breast to suckle him with a sap that only the deity can give.*

that the individual and collective imagination must have been particularly fertile. The experience of the sacred relating to a distinct perception of transcendency is based on a religious memory that refers to origins, the cosmos, and the mystery of life. For the first time ancient man possessed a sacred story that belonged to the clan, for whom it served as a model of conduct. Thus the religious consciousness of a community made its first appearance within the context of a hunter-gatherer economy, before settlement began. The millennia that saw the flowering of cave art heralded a change in the individual and collective consciousness of humanity. This was the dawn of the birth of myths and awareness of a sacred origin story.

Images of the Deity

A fourth stage in the formation of man's religious consciousness coincided with the rise of Natufian civilization and the dawn of the Neolithic. The earliest evidence of this stage is to be found in the Near East, around the middle Euphrates and in Anatolia, for it was here that the first representations of the deity were made. The form was essentially human, with female features or sometimes those of a bull. These two symbols of the deity were common throughout the Mediterranean. Jacques Cauvin (187) has pointed out that thanks to these discoveries we are now sure of one of the primary vehicles of the spread of Neolithic culture. In his view the evidence no longer speaks for a mere perception of transcendency and the divine, but rather its symbolic translation and representation through meaningful signs. A profound change took place in the consciousness of Natufian *homo religiosus,* and this was expressed in divine images of the sort found at Mureybet and Çatal Hüyük. A new symbolism thus came into being to communicate new thoughts, evidence of an important change in the human imagination. For the first time man's relationship with the

deity was given visible expression: the praying figures with their arms raised toward the heavens. In man's religious consciousness the performance of prayer expresses something absolutely new (J. Ries, 1992). With the personification of the deity, belief in a Supreme Being allowed Natufian and Neolithic man to turn to his god or gods "through the power of prayer, represented by the upraised arms" (J. Cauvin, 1987).

Awareness of the Divine Presence

The personification of the deity and symbolic portrayals of it in the form of statues led ancient man to build temples, sanctuaries, and *ziggurats* where the faithful could meet their gods. This fifth stage in the formation of religious consciousness took place in the great religions beginning with Sumer, Accad, ancient Egypt, and Babylon. Aware of the divine presence, man kept his own god in the temples and sanctuaries where the divine statue, dressed and embellished with gold and precious stones, became the object of a cult performed for the king by his delegates, the priests. The temple was thus God's dwelling on earth, and the place it occupied was sacred land. Indeed, whenever necessary the edifice was rebuilt in exactly the same spot. In Babylon the *ziggurats* were the stairway by means of which encounters between man and God could take place. In pharaonic Egypt every morning the priest made the soul of the god or goddess descend on the statue present in the *naos.* A feast-day calender was drawn up: the faithful would accompany the divine statue on its journeys by land or in a barque on the Nile. The word of God was expressed through divination, oracles and intepretation of the movement of the stars. God spoke and the faithful listened. Through the thousands of tablets found in Mesopotamia and the written documents of ancient Egypt we are familiar with the texts of the prayers and divine oracles. The faithful knew that their life had to comply with the divine will (J. Ries, 1992).

Religious Consciousness among the Followers of the Three Great Monotheisms

Religious consciousness reached its sixth and final stage with the three great monotheisms. Man discovered the one God, a personal, spiritual and omnipotent being who created the cosmos, life, and men. God is revealed to the faithful and in his almighty power affects their life and history. With Abraham, hierophany gave way to theophany. Yahweh made a covenant with his people and intervened continually in their favor, speaking not through oracles but through revelation and the living Word. This God demands faith, a religious experience that implies obedience to him and his will. The prophets and their descendents were entrusted with the mission of guiding the faithful. Muhammad became conscious of his own particular mission and preached the one God and his teachings. The messianic prophecies were fulfilled by Jesus Christ, the Word of God present among men through the mysteries of incarnation and redemption. He founded the Church, entrusting it with the task of continuing his work and training generations of true worshipers of the Father in the light of the Holy Spirit (W. Kasper, 1982 and L. Giussani, 1991).

213. Reproduction of the design on an Etruscan bowl, now at the Louvre. The central character is caught between two trees: the tree of good and the tree of evil. Awareness of relationship with the deity gives a sense of good and evil.

Conclusion
40 From the Sacred Experience to the Appearance of the Great Religions

USING THE comparative genetic approach we have followed events in their historical order and then counterchecked them by working backwards to the origins. At this point we should take a last look at *homo religiosus*.

The Appearance of *homo religiosus*

In putting this book together we have focused on duly established facts. As the reader will appreciate, the basis of our analysis of cultural and religious phenomena, and indeed of our hermeneutics or interpretation of the facts and their meaning, is a comparative method that is both typological and genetic. Hermeneutics is the search for meaning. Since this volume has been compiled by a historian of religions, it contains precious contributions by other historians of religions as well as accounts of recent discoveries by paleoanthropologists. Moreover, it also comprises the work of comparative specialists, archaeologists, sociologists and hermeneuticists. The selective bibliography should help orient the reader in these various fields. The present book acts as a junction between the different branches of the human sciences.

Homo religiosus is one who believes in the existence of a transcendency located outside this world but manifest within it for the benefit of mankind. He is the person who lives the sacred experience. *Does homo religiosus exist?* (M. Meslin, 1992). The question is answered in this book. However, a much fuller and more explicit answer is to be found in the *Traité d'anthropologie du sacré*, the fruit of collaboration between approximately fifty or so scholars.

Since 1959, the progressive discovery of *Homo habilis* and Olduvaian culture has proved to be one of the happy surprises of twentieth-century paleoanthropology since it provides the missing link connecting the Australopithecines and *Homo erectus*. *Homo habilis* was a *homo symbolicus* who could experience the sacred in terms that were, however rudimentary, no less real than any other aspect of his culture. We have tried to distinguish him in what were still elementary cultural and "religious" activities by means of the symbolism of the heavenly vault. *Homo erectus* (1.6 million-300,000 years ago) has left us greater cultural and religious evidence. Chipping bifacial tools, funeral and fire rites, and other aspects of behavior are signs of an experience of the sacred that went beyond that of *Homo habilis*.

With *Homo sapiens* (300,000-35,000 years ago) humanity advanced toward the threshold of "modernity." Funeral rites grew in number and diversity, witnessing to belief in an afterlife and to cultural development that relied on a fertile imagination. The remarkable achievements of Franco-Cantabrian art give expression to the first myths and initiation rites that help us understand both the religious phenomenon and the way culture and the sacred experience were transmitted. The existence of a community provides a framework for new interpretations of the artistic heritage that acted as the cultural

horizon for *Homo sapiens sapiens* from 35,000 to 9,000 years ago. From *Homo habilis* to the caveman of the Upper Paleolithic, it was the imagination that drove cultural and religious growth. In the Old Stone Age this was to some extent based on initiation to the clan myths, symbols, and rites. Thus a religious tradition was born, which meant that the first institutions had been founded.

From the Neolithic to the Three Great Monotheisms

Around 10,000 years ago in Syria and Palestine man left the caves, created villages, and settled. The invention of farming and husbandry then followed. Settlement represents one of the great moments of human history. Within the sphere of our interests, it coincided with the appearance of the first deities, sign of a profound change in psychic life: "The birth of the notion of divinity is one of the principal characteristics of the spread of Neolithic culture" (J. Cauvin, 1987). Natufian civilization was the prelude to the "Neolithic revolution." From mere belief in transcendency man turned to representation of the deity: his religiosity became a religion, with its beliefs, religious ideas and cults: goddess worship, bull worship, the birth of a divine couple. A new posture is established: hands raised towards the vault of heaven and the divine figures. This is praying man, whose presence indicates the birth of the first liturgies.

The number of tombs increased, the first sanctuaries were created, and thousands of statuettes were made. Then, in the fourth millennium B.C., the invention of writing introduced another revolution. A literary and religious heritage was established, religious thought, prayers and rituals could be rapidly transmitted, temples and sanctuaries were built, and a vocabulary of the sacred came into being. By creating divine images, man expressed his desire to see the face of God. His belief in transcendency prompted the creation of thousands of images of the deity. Yet at the heart of these religions there is always the experience of the sacred and belief in the deity. The way is thus prepared for the creation of the great religions of Mesopotamia, the Near East, Egypt, India, Greece, and Rome.

From Hierophanies to Theophanies

For thousands of years, *homo religiosus* adopted a universe of cosmic symbols in order to fulfill his experience of the sacred: heavenly vault, sun, moon and stars; air, water and fire; animal and plant symbols and those reflecting man, woman and child. To these were added the myth with the symbols of height, ascension, the flight of birds and the celestial epiphanies: thunder, lightning, rain, rainbow, storm, and meteor. Man brought this wide-ranging symbolism into play in his search for the divine.

Four thousand years ago the divine appeared to man as a theophany, that is, without the mediation of the cosmos that had characterized the earlier hierophanies. Abraham received the message and the promise of the living, personal God. Instead of hierophanies, Israel received the message of Yahweh, the revelation of the divine name, and then the covenant of Sinai. Yahweh could intervene in the life of the people to whom he gave his Law, and he asked of them faith and holiness, signs of the covenant (P. Ricoeur, 1974). Later Muhammad arose, one of the three messengers of the one omnipotent, omniscient, living God. Israel had Torah, Islam the Koran. In their fear of idolatry, Israel and Islam did all they could to oppose the making of images of the one God (R. Arnaldez, 1983).

The third messenger of the one God was Jesus of Nazareth. He revealed the Father, announced the Spirit, and prepared the kingdom. In his discourse expressed in parables, Jesus adapted some of the cosmic symbolism to the announcement of the gospel and the kingdom: threshold, door, sower and seed, tree and bird. Moreover, he added allegories taken from daily life. Thus hierophany and theophany were reconciled. The historical event of the existence of Jesus is a theophany in the real sense of the word, and this very existence constitutes the greatest religious revolution in history. Having sent the Holy Spirit to his apostles, Christ continues to be present in history through the Church, his mystical body.

214. A theophany took place on Mount Sinai: God appeared directly to Moses, without the mediation of the cosmos ("hierophany"). Mount Sinai had probably long been a sacred mountain for the people of the region. Present-day Sinai (Mount St. Catherine) is generally accepted by Christians as the place where this theophany took place. However, there is no archaeological proof of it. After a number of expeditions at the end of the 1980s, E. Anati suggested that the Sinai of the theophany might be Mount Har Karkom in the Negev region, due north of the Paran desert in Israel. There is no doubt that this is an extraordinary sacred mountain, a place of worship for thousands of years, as archaeological surveys show. In the photo, the moon rises behind Har Karkom.

Bibliography

Works of General Interest

GARANGER J. (ed.), *La préhistoire dans le monde. Nouvelle édition de la préhistoire d'André Leroi-Gourhan*, PUF, Paris 1992. Bibliografia p. 3-86

LEROI-GOURHAN A. (ed.), *Dictionnaire de la préhistoire*, PUF, Paris 1988

POUPARD P. (dir.), VIDAL J., RIES J., COTHENET E., MARCHASSON Y., DELAHOUTRE M. (red.), *Dictionnaire des religions*, PUF, Paris 1985 (tr. it. *Grande Dizionario delle Religioni*, 2 vol., Cittadella-Piemme, Assisi-Casale Monferrato 1988, 1 vol., 1991)

RIES J. (dir.), *Trattato di Antropologia del Sacro*, in 6 volumi, Jaca Book–Massimo, Milano. Già pubblicati: vol. 1. *Le origini e il problema dell'Homo religiosus*, 1989; vol. 2. *L'uomo indoeuropeo e il Sacro*, 1991; vol. 3. *Le civiltà del Mediterraneo e il Sacro*, 1992

Chapter 2

MURPHY J., *The Origins and History of Religions*, University Press, Manchester (tr. francese *Origines et histoire des religions*, Payot, Paris 1951)

ANWANDER A., *Die Religionen der Menschheit*, Herder, Freiburg/Br. 1949 (tr. francese *Les religions de l'humanité*, Payot, Paris 1955)

ZAEHNER R. C., *At Sundry Times* (tr. francese *Inde, Israël, Islam, religions mystiques et révélations prophétiques*, DDB, Paris 1965)

BIANCHI U., *Saggi di metodologia della Storia delle religioni*, Ateneo, Roma 1979

ID., *History of Religions*, in M. ELIADE (ed.), *The Encyclopedia of Religion*, 16 vol., Macmillan, New York 1987, vol. 6, p. 404-7

Chapter 4

SCHMIDT P. W., *Ursprung und Werden der Religionen*, Münster 1930 (tr. francese *Origine et évolution de la religion. Les théories et les faits*, Grasset, Paris 1931)

LOWIE R., *Traité de sociologie primitive*, Payot, Paris 1936

LEVY-BRUHL L., *La mythologie primitive*, Paris 1935 (tr. it. *La mitologia primitiva*, Newton Compton, Roma)

ID., *L'expérience mystique et les symboles chez les primitfs*, Paris 1938

EVANS-PRITCHARD E. E., *Theories of Primitive Religion*, Oxford 1965 (tr. it. *Teorie sulla religione primitiva*, Sansoni, Firenze 1979)

Chapter 7

PINARD DE LA BOULLAYE H., *L'étude comparée des religions*, 2 vol., Beauchesne, Paris 1929

SLAWIK A., HAEKEL J., *Die Wiener Schule der Völkerkunde*, Berger, Wien 1956

ELIADE M., *La creatività dello spirito*, Jaca Book, Milano 1979

PETTAZZONI R., *L'essere supremo nelle religioni primitive*, Einaudi, Torino 1968

Chapter 8

COPPENS Y., *Le singe, l'Afrique et l'homme*, Fayard, Paris 1983 (tr. it. *La scimmia, l'Africa e l'uomo*, Jaca Book, Milano 1985)

PIVETEAU J., *L'apparition de l'homme. Le point de vue scientifique*, O.E.I.L., Paris 1986

FACCHINI F., *Le origini. L'uomo*, Jaca Book, Milano 1990

ELIADE M., *Trattato di storia delle religioni*, Einaudi, Torino 1954; Boringhieri, Torino 1986

Chapter 9

CAMPS G., *La préhistoire. A la recherche du paradis perdu*, Perrin, Paris 1982

FACCHINI F., GIMBUTAS M., KOZLOWSKI J. K., VANDERMEERSCH B., *La religiosità nella preistoria*, Jaca Book, Milano 1991

BINANT P., *La préhistoire de la mort*, Errance, Paris 1991

Chapter 10

LEROI-GOURHAN A., *Préhistoire de l'art occidental*, Mazenod, Paris 1965

ID., *I più antichi artisti d'Europa. Introduzione all'arte parietale paleolitica*, Jaca Book, Milano 1981

AA. VV., *Art et civilisations des chasseurs de la préhistoire*, Musée de l'homme, Paris 1985

NOUGIER L. R., *Les grottes préhistoriques ornées de France, d'Espagne et d'Italie*, Balland, Paris 1990

VIALOU D. (ed.), *La préhistoire*, Gallimard, Paris 1991

Chapter 11

LAMING-EMPERAIRE A., *La signification de l'art rupestre paléolithique*, Picard, Paris 1962

LEROI-GOURHAN A., *Les religions de la préhistoire*, PUF, Paris 1964 (tr. it. *Le religioni della preistoria*, Rizzoli, Milano)

ID., *Le geste et la parole*, 2 vol., Albin Michel, Paris 1964 (tr. it. *Il gesto e la parola*, 2 vol., Einaudi, Torino 1977)

ID., *Préhistorie de l'art occidental*, Mazenod, Paris 1965

ID., *I più antichi artisti d'Europa. Introduzione all'arte parietale paleolitica*, Jaca Book, Milano 1981

BERNOT L. (ed.), *André Leroi-Gourhan ou les voies de l'homme, Colloque 1987*, Albin Michel, Paris 1988

ELIADE M., *Storia delle credenze e delle idee religiose*, vol. I, Sansoni, Firenze 1979

ANATI E., *Origini dell'arte e della concettualità*, Jaca Book, Milano 1989

VIALOU D. (ed.), *La Préhistoire*, Gallimard, Paris 1991

Chapter 12

BREUIL H., *Quatre siècles d'art pariétal*, Centre d'études préhistoriques, Montignac 1952

NOUGIER L. R., *Premiers éveils de l'homme. Art, magie et sexualité dans la préhistoire*, Lieu commun, Paris 1984

LEWIN R., *Human Evolution*, Blackwell, Oxford 1984-89 (tr. francese *L'évolution humaine*, Seuil, Paris 1991)

MOHEN J. P., *Vous avez tous 400 000 ans*, Ed. Lattès, Paris 1991

Chapter 13

BREUIL H., LANTIN R., *Les hommes de la pierre ancienne*, Payot, Paris 1959, 1979

UCKO P., ROSENFELD A., *Palaeolithic Cave Art*, London 1967

VIALOU D., *L'art des cavernes. Les sanctuaires de la préhistoire*, Le Rocher, Monaco 1987

Chapter 14

MARINGER J., *L'homme préhistorique et ses dieux*, Arthaud, Paris 1958

PATTE E., *Les hommes préhistoriques et la religion*, Picard, Paris 1960

UCKO P., ROSENFELD A., *Palaeolithic Cave Art*, London 1967

ANATI E. (ed.), *Prehistoric Art and Religion. Valcamonica Symposium 1979*, contributi di C.BARRIÈRE e di Fr. JORDÀ CERDÀ, Jaca Book e Centro Camuno di Studi Preistorici, Milano 1983

VIALOU D., *L'art des cavernes. Les sanctuaires de la préhistoire*, Le Rocher, Monaco 1987

SAINT-BLANQUAT H. DE, *Mémoires de l'humanité. Enquêtes en Préhistoire*, Seuil, Paris 1991

Chapter 15

VALLA F. R., *Le Natoufien, une culture préhistorique en Palestine*, Gabalda, Paris 1975

CAUVIN J., *Religions néolithiques en Syrie-Palestine. Documents*, Maisonneuve, Paris 1972

ID., *Les premiers villages de Syrie-Palestine du IXème au VIIème millénaire av. J.-C.*, de Boccard, Paris 1978

AA. VV., La mort dans la préhistoire, in *Histoire et archéologie*, no. 66, Paris 1982

Chapter 16

MELLAART J., *Çatal Hüyük*, Thames & Hudson, London 1967

SREJOVIĆ D., *Lepenski Vir*, Beograd 1969

SREJOVIĆ D., LETICA Z., contributi in *Les religions de la préhistoire, Valcamonica Symposium 1972*, Centro Camuno di Studi Preistorici, Capo di Ponte, Brescia 1975, p. 87-104

CAUVIN J., L'apparition des premières divinités, in *La Recherche*, no. 194, p. 1472-80, Paris 1987

EVANS J. D., *Malta*, Thames & Hudson, London

1963 (tr. it. *I segreti dell'antica Malta*, Il Saggiatore, Milano 1982)

ID., *The Prehistoric Antiquities of the Maltese Islands*, Athlone, London 1971

ANATI E., *Missione a Malta*, Jaca Book, Milano 1988

Chapter 17

ELIADE M., *Mito e realtà*, Borla, Torino 1989

ID., *Storia delle credenze e delle idee religiose*, vol. I, Sansoni, Firenze 1979, p. 49-61

CAUVIN J., *Les premiers villages de Syrie-Palestine du IXème au VIIème millénaire av. J.-C.*, de Boccard, Paris 1978

SREJOVIĆ D., La cultura di Lepenski Vir, in *L'Umana Avventura*, no. 10, p. 73-79, Jaca Book, Milano 1988-89

Chapter 18

CAUVIN J., L'apparition des premières divinités, in *La Recherche*, no. 194, p. 1472-80, Paris 1987

MELLAART J., *Çatal Hüyük*, Thames & Hudson, London 1967

ID., *The Goddess of Anatolia*, Eskenazi, Milano 1989

GIMBUTAS MARIJA, *The God and Goddesses of Old Europe*, Thames & Hudson, London 1974

ID., Figurines of Old Europe (6500-3500 b.C.), in *Les religions de la préhistoire, Valcamonica Symposium 1972*, Centro Camuno di Studi Preistorici, Capo di Ponte, Brescia 1975

ID., La religione della dea nell'Europa mediterranea: sacro, simboli, società, in RIES J. (ed.), *Trattato di Antropologia del Sacro*, vol. 3: *Le civiltà del Mediterraneo e il Sacro*, Jaca Book, Milano 1992, p. 49-67

Chapter 19

ANATI E., *Evoluzione e stile nell'arte rupestre Camuna*, Centro Camuno di Studi Preistorici, Capo di Ponte, Brescia 1975

ID., *Valcamonica: 10.000 anni di storia*, Centro Camuno di Studi Preistorici, Capo di Ponte, Brescia 1980

ID., *I Camuni, alle radici della civiltà europea*, Jaca Book, Milano 1982

ID., *Le statue-stele della Lunigiana*, Jaca Book, Milano 1981

GUILAINE J., *La France d'avant la France. Du Néolithique à l'âge du fer*, Hachette, Paris 1980

RENFREW C., *Before Civilization*, London 1973 (tr. francese *Les origines de l'Europe*, Flammarion, Paris 1983)

Chapter 20

MARSHALL J., *Mohenjo-Daro and the Indus Civilization*, 3 vol., Probshain, London 1921

MACKAY E.J.H., *Further Excavations at Mohenjo-Daro*, Book Corporation, New Delhi 1938

MODE H., *Indische Frühkulturen*, Benno Schwabe, Basel 1944

WHEELER SIR M., *The Indus Civilization*, University Press, Cambridge 1960

CASAL, J.M., *La civilisation de l'Indus et ses énigmes*, Fayard, Paris 1969

ZABERN PH. VON, *Vergessene Städte am Indus*, Verlag von Zabern, Mainz am Rhein 1987

UNESCO COLLECTIF (ed.), *Civilisations anciennes du Pakistan*, Musées Royaux, Bruxelles 1989

Chapter 21

CAUVIN J., *Les premiers villages de Syrie-Palestine du IXème au VIIème millénaire av. J.-C.*, de Boccard, Paris 1978

ID., La mutation religieuse du Néolithique d'après les documents du Proche-Orient, in *Cahiers de l'Institut Catholique de Lyon*, no. 9, p. 69-82, Lyon 1983

ID., Mémoire d'Orient: la sortie du jardin d'Eden et la néolithisation du Levant, in *Cahiers de l'Institut Catholique de Lyon*, no. 17, p. 25-40, Lyon 1986

ID., L'apparition des premières divinités, in *La recherche*, no. 194, p. 1472-80, Paris 1987

Chapter 22

COPPENS Y., Commencement de l'homme, in *Le débat*, no. 20, p. 30-53, Gallimard, Paris 1982

ID., *Le singe, l'Afrique et l'homme*, Fayard, Paris 1983 (tr.it. *La scimmia, l'Africa e l'uomo*, Jaca Book, Milano 1984)

FACCHINI F., *Le Origini. L'uomo*, Jaca B[...] 1990

LEROI-GOURHAN A., *Le geste et la pa[...]* Albin Michel, Paris 1964 (tr. it. [...] *parola*, 2 vol., Einaudi, Torino 1977[...]

TOBIAS P.V., *Paleoantropologia*, Jaca B[...] 1992

ELIADE M., *Storia delle credenze e delle [...]se*, vol. I, Sansoni, Firenze 1979, p. [...]

CAUVIN J., Mémoire d'Orient: la sortie[...] d'Eden et la néolithisation du Levant[...] *de l'Institut Catholique de Lyon*, no.1[...] Lyon 1986

Chapter 23

BOTTÉRO J., *Mésopotamie. L'écriture, la r[...] dieux*, Gallimard, Paris 1987

BOTTÉRO J., KRAMER S.N., *Lorsque les dieu[...] l'homme. Mythologie mésopot[...]* Gallimard, Paris 1989

ROUX G., *La Mésopotamie. Essai d'hist[...]que, économique et culturelle*, Seuil, P[...]

CASSIN ELENA, *La splendeur divine. Intro[...] l'étude de la mentalité mésopota[...]* Mouton, Paris 1968

HOENN K., *Sumerische und akkadische[...] und Gebete*, Artemis Verlag, Zürich[...] 1953

SEUX J.M., *Hymnes et prières aux d[...] Babylonie et d'Assyrie*, Cerf, Paris 1974[...]

Chapter 24

BAUMGARTEL E., *The Cultures of Prehistori[...]* Oxford University Press, Oxford, vol. [...] vol. II 1960

MORENZ S., *Aegyptische Religion*, Kohlh[...] Stuttgart 1960 (tr. it. *Gli Egizi*, Jaca[...] Milano 1983)

DAUMAS FR., Amour de la vie et sens du div[...] l'Egypte ancienne, in *Magie des extrêmes*, Etudes Carmélitaines, DDB, Paris, Bruges 1952, p. 92-141

ID., *Les dieux de l'Egypte*, PUF, Paris 1970

RIES J., La religion de la préhistoire égyptienne. Les étapes de la recherche, in *Valcamonica Symposium 1972. Les religions de la préhistoire*, Centro Camuno di Studi Preistorici, Capo di Ponte, Brescia 1975, p. 293-312

ID., Il segno della vita come espressione del sacro nell'antico Egitto, in *L'Umana Avventura*, p. 93-101, Jaca Book, Milano 1986

Chapter 25

KALTENMARK M., *Lao-Tseu et le taoïsme*, Seuil, Paris 1965

LAO-TSEU, *Tao tö King*, tradotto da KIA-HWAY, Gallimard, Paris 1967

LARRE CL., *Le Livre de la Voie et de la Vertu*, Paris 1977

MASPERO H., *Le Taoïsme et les religions chinoises*, Gallimard, Paris 1971

VANDIER-NICOLAS NICOLE, *Le taoïsme*, PUF, Paris 1965

ZHENG CHANTAL, *Mythes et croyances du monde chinois primitif*, Payot, Paris 1989

Chapter 26

DUMÉZIL G., *L'idéologie tripartie des Indo-Européens*, Latomus 31, Bruxelles 1958 (tr. it. *L'ideologia tripartita degli Indoeuropei*, Il Cerchio, Rimini 1988)

ID., *La religion romaine archaïque*, Payot, Paris 1966 (tr. it. *La religione romana arcaica*, Rizzoli, Milano 1977)

RIVIÈRE J.-CL., *Georges Dumézil à la découverte des Indo-Européens*, Copernic, Paris 1979

Chapter 28

CAZELLES H., *La Bible et son Dieu*, Desclée, Paris 1989

AA.VV., *I volti di Dio. Il Rivelato e le sue tradizioni*, Edizioni Paoline, Milano 1992

C.E.R.I.T., *Les chrétiens et leurs doctrines*, Desclée, Paris 1987

PERROT CH., *Jésus et l'histoire*, Desclée, Paris 1979

RIES J., *Les chrétiens parmi les religions. Des Actes des Apôtres à Vatican II*, Desclée, Paris 1987 (tr. it. *I cristiani e le religioni*, Queriniana, Brescia 1992)

ARNALDEZ R., *Jésus fils de Marie, prophète de l'Islam*, Desclée, Paris 1980

DURAND G., *Les structures anthropologiques de l'imaginaire*, Dunod, Paris 1992[11] (tr. it. *Strutture antropologiche dell'immaginario*, Dedalo, Bari 1983)

ID., *L'imagination symbolique*, PUF, Paris 1984 (tr. it. *L'immaginazione simbolica*, Il Pensiero Scientifico, Roma 1977)

VIDAL J., *Sacré, symbole et créativité*, Centre d'histoire des religions, Louvain-la-Neuve 1990 (tr. it. *Sacro, simbolo e creatività*, Jaca Book, Milano 1992)

ELIADE M., *Trattato di storia delle religioni*, Boringhieri, Torino 1986

Chapter 32

PÉPIN J., *Mythe et allégorie*, Etudes augustiniennes, Paris 1976

SEZNEC J., *La survivance des dieux antiques*, Flammarion, Paris 1980 (tr. it. *La sopravvivenza degli antichi dei*, Boringhieri, Torino 1981)

LIMET H., RIES J. (edd.), *Le mythe, son langage et son message*, Centre d'histoire des religions, Louvain-la-Neuve 1983

ELIADE M., *Mito e realtà*, Borla, Torino 1989

ID., *La nostalgie des origines*, Gallimard, Paris 1971 (tr. it. *La nostalgia delle origini*, Morcelliana, Brescia 1980)

SCHELLING F.W., *Introduction à la philosophie de la mythologie*, 2 vol., Aubier, Paris 1945

Chapter 33

CAZENEUVE J., *Les rites et la condition humaine*, PUF, Paris, 1958

ID., *Sociologie du rite*, PUF, Paris 1971

ELIADE M., *Images et symboles*, Gallimard, Paris 1952 (tr. it. *Immagini e simboli*, Jaca Book, Milano 1981)

ID., *Le mythe de l'éternel retour*, Gallimard, Paris 1949 (tr. it. *Il mito dell'eterno ritorno*, Borla, Torino 1982)

RIES J. (ed.), *Les rites d'initiation*, Centre d'histoire des religions, Louvain-la-Neuve 1986 (tr. it. *I riti di iniziazione*, Jaca Book, Milano 1989)

LIMET H., RIES J. (edd.), *L'expérience de la prière dans les grandes religions*, Centre d'histoire des religions, Louvain-la-Neuve 1980

Chapter 34

RIES J. (ed.), *Trattato di Antropologia del Sacro*, vol. 1: *Le origini e il problema dell'Homo religiosus*, Jaca Book, Milano 1989

VIDAL J., *Sacré, symbole et créativité*, Centre d'histoire des religions, Louvain-la-Neuve 1990 (tr. it. *Sacro, simbolo e creatività*, Jaca Book, Milano 1992)

ELIADE M., *Images et symboles*, Gallimard, Paris 1952 (tr. it. *Immagini e simboli*, Jaca Book, Milano 1981)

BACHELARD G., *L'air et les songes*, Corti, Paris 1943

DURAND G., *Les structures anthropologiques de l'imaginaire*, Dunod, Paris 1992[11] (tr. it. *Strutture antropologiche dell'immaginario*, Dedalo, Bari 1983)

Chapter 35

BIANCHI U., *Storia dell'etnologia*, Abete, Roma 1971

EVANS-PRITCHARD E.E., *Theories of Primitive Religion*, Oxford University Press 1965 (tr. it. *Teorie sulla religione primitiva*, Sansoni, Firenze 1979)

ELIADE M., *Australian Religions*, Cornell University Press, Ithaca-New York 1973 (tr. it. *La creatività dello spirito*, Jaca Book, Milano 1979)

LÉVI-STRAUSS CL., *Mythologiques*, Plon, Paris: 1. *Le cru et le cuit*, 1964; 2. *Du miel aux cendres*, 1966; 3. *L'origine des manières de table*, 1968; 4. *L'homme nu*, 1971 (tr. it. Il Saggiatore, Milano: *Il crudo e il cotto*, 1980; *Dal miele alle ceneri*, 1982; *Le origini delle buone maniere a tavola*, 1971; *L'uomo nudo*, 1983)

SCHMIDT W., *Der Ursprung der Gottesidee*, 12 vol. Aschendorfsche Buchhandlung, Münster 1912-1954

ZAHAN D., SCHADEN E., HULTKRANTZ Å., *Les religions chez les peuples sans tradition écrite*, in PUECH H., *Histoire des religions*, Gallimard, Paris 1976, vol. 3, p. 545-988

Chapter 36

FACCHINI F., *Le origini. L'uomo*, Jaca Book, Milano 1990

TOBIAS PH.V., *Paleoantropologia*, Jaca Book, Milano 1992

LEROI-GOURHAN A., *Le geste et la parole*, 2 vol., Albin Michel, Paris 1964 (tr. it. *Il gesto e la parola*, 2 vol., Einaudi, Torino 1977)

COPPENS Y., L'origine de l'Homme; le mileu, la découverte, la conscience, la création, in *Revue des sciences morales et politiques*, p. 507-32, Paris 1987

Chapter 37

PERLÈS C., *Préhistoire du feu*, Paris 1977

VANDERMEERSCH R., *Dictionnaire de la préhistoire*, PUF, Paris 1988

COPPENS Y., *Le singe, l'Afrique et l'homme*, Fayard, Paris 1983 (tr. it. *La scimmia, l'Africa e l'uomo*, Jaca Book, Milano 1985)

AA.VV., *André Leroi-Gourhan ou les voies de l'homme*, Albin Michel, Paris 1988

ELIADE M., *Storia delle credenze e delle idee religiose*, vol. I, Sansoni, Firenze 1979

ID., *Traité d'histoire des religions*, Gallimard, Paris 1949 (tr. it. *Trattato di storia delle religioni*, Boringhieri, Torino 1986)

Chapter 38

KALTENMARK M., AA.VV., voce "Ciel", in *Dictionnaire des Mythologies*, 2 vol., Flammarion, Paris 1981, vol. 1, p. 188-99

Chapter 39   Capitolo 39

RIES J., *Il rapporto uomo-Dio nelle grandi religioni precristiane*, Jaca Book, Milano 1992

KASPER W., *Le dieu des chrétiens*, Cerf, Paris 1982 (tr. fr.)

GIUSSANI L., *Il senso religioso*, Jaca Book, Milano 1986/1991

Chapter 40

MESLIN M., L'homo religiosus existe-t-il?, in *Cahiers d'anthropologie religieuse*, 1, Presses de Paris-Sorbonne, Paris 1992, p. 7-18

RIES J. (ed.), *Trattato di Antropologia del Sacro*, in 6 volumi, Jaca Book–Massimo, Milano. Già pubblicati: vol. 1. *Le origini e il problema dell'Homo religiosus*, 1989; vol. 2. *L'uomo indoeuropeo e il Sacro*, 1991; vol. 3. *Le civiltà del Mediterraneo e il Sacro*, 1992

RICOEUR P., Manifestation et proclamation, in CASTELLI E. (ed.), *Le Sacré*, Aubier, Paris 1974, p. 57-76

ARNALDEZ R., *Trois messagers pour un seul Dieu*, Albin Michel, Paris 1983

DATE DUE

HIGHSMITH

DISCARDED

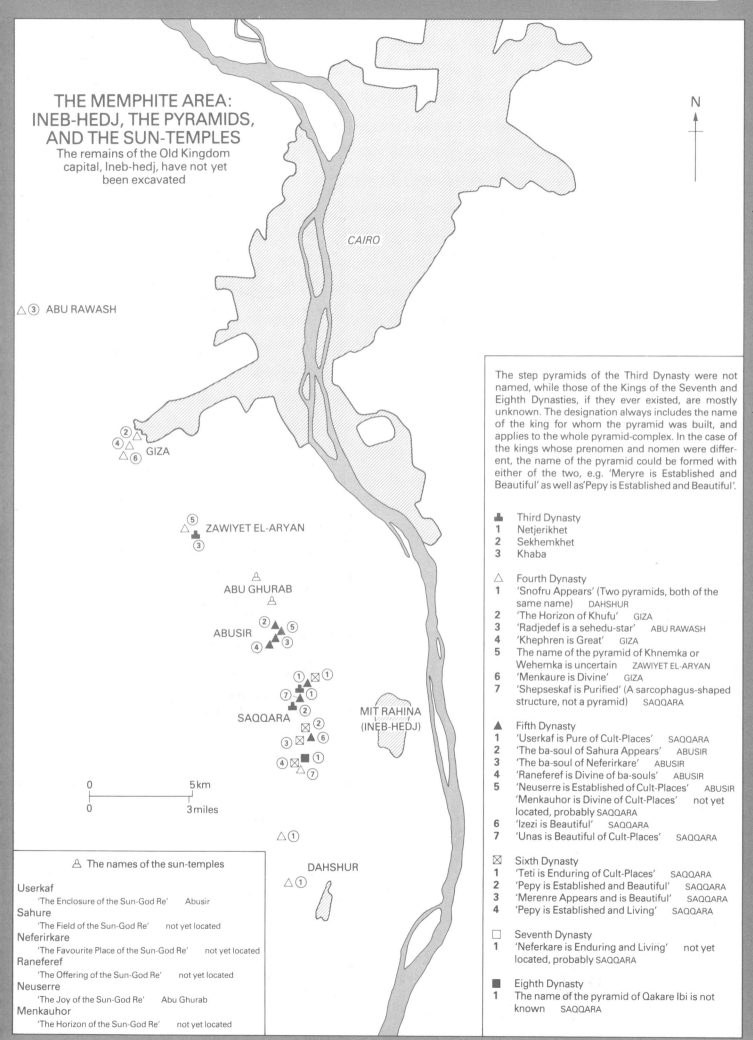

THE MEMPHITE AREA:
INEB-HEDJ, THE PYRAMIDS,
AND THE SUN-TEMPLES
The remains of the Old Kingdom
capital, Ineb-hedj, have not yet
been excavated

N

CAIRO

△③ ABU RAWASH

②
④ △ GIZA
△⑥

⑤
△ ▪ ZAWIYET EL-ARYAN
③

⚲
ABU GHURAB
⚲

② ▲▲ ⑤
ABUSIR
④ ▲▲ ③

① ⊠ ①
⑦ ▪▲ ①
▪▪
②
SAQQARA
⊠ ②   MIT RAHINA
③ ⊠ ▲ ⑥   (INEB-HEDJ)
④ ⊠ ▪ ①
⑦

0   5km
0   3 miles

△①

△① DAHSHUR

△ The names of the sun-temples

Userkaf
   'The Enclosure of the Sun-God Re'   Abusir
Sahure
   'The Field of the Sun-God Re'   not yet located
Neferirkare
   'The Favourite Place of the Sun-God Re'   not yet located
Raneferef
   'The Offering of the Sun-God Re'   not yet located
Neuserre
   'The Joy of the Sun-God Re'   Abu Ghurab
Menkauhor
   'The Horizon of the Sun-God Re'   not yet located

The step pyramids of the Third Dynasty were not
named, while those of the Kings of the Seventh and
Eighth Dynasties, if they ever existed, are mostly
unknown. The designation always includes the name
of the king for whom the pyramid was built, and
applies to the whole pyramid-complex. In the case of
the kings whose prenomen and nomen were different, the name of the pyramid could be formed with
either of the two, e.g. 'Meryre is Established and
Beautiful' as well as'Pepy is Established and Beautiful'.

⚲ Third Dynasty
1 Netjerikhet
2 Sekhemkhet
3 Khaba

△ Fourth Dynasty
1 'Snofru Appears' (Two pyramids, both of the
   same name)   DAHSHUR
2 'The Horizon of Khufu'   GIZA
3 'Radjedef is a sehedu-star'   ABU RAWASH
4 'Khephren is Great'   GIZA
5 The name of the pyramid of Khnemka or
   Wehemka is uncertain   ZAWIYET EL-ARYAN
6 'Menkaure is Divine'   GIZA
7 'Shepseskaf is Purified' (A sarcophagus-shaped
   structure, not a pyramid)   SAQQARA

▲ Fifth Dynasty
1 'Userkaf is Pure of Cult-Places'   SAQQARA
2 'The ba-soul of Sahura Appears'   ABUSIR
3 'The ba-soul of Neferirkare'   ABUSIR
4 'Raneferef is Divine of ba-souls'   ABUSIR
5 'Neuserre is Established of Cult-Places'   ABUSIR
   'Menkauhor is Divine of Cult-Places'   not yet
   located, probably SAQQARA
6 'Izezi is Beautiful'   SAQQARA
7 'Unas is Beautiful of Cult-Places'   SAQQARA

⊠ Sixth Dynasty
1 'Teti is Enduring of Cult-Places'   SAQQARA
2 'Pepy is Established and Beautiful'   SAQQARA
3 'Merenre Appears and is Beautiful'   SAQQARA
4 'Pepy is Established and Living'   SAQQARA

☐ Seventh Dynasty
1 'Neferkare is Enduring and Living'   not yet
   located, probably SAQQARA

▪ Eighth Dynasty
1 The name of the pyramid of Qakare Ibi is not
   known   SAQQARA

IN THE SHADOW
OF THE PYRAMIDS

IN THE SHADOW OF THE PYRAMIDS

Egypt during the Old Kingdom

Text by Jaromir Malek

Photographs by Werner Forman

University of Oklahoma Press
Norman and London

To J.J. and P. with love

But the iniquity of oblivion blindely scattereth her poppy, and deals with the memory of men without distinction to merit of perpetuity. Who can but pity the founder of the Pyramids?
(Sir Thomas Browne, *Hydriotaphia*, 1658)

Note on the rendering of ancient Egyptian words:

As in many cases we do not know with certainty how ancient Egyptian words were pronounced, they are given—with one or two exceptions—in the standardized form used by Egyptologists. The same applies to royal and private names. For one of the kings of the Fourth Dynasty I have, however, preferred the non-committal Greek form Khephren because the correct reading is still a matter of dispute.

Half-title page: Relief-decoration could be equally well applied to a wooden surface, in this case a stela (false-door), as to stone. The couple represented here are Iyka, a 'manager of the royal estate' (hut-aat) and 'royal priest', and his wife Iymert.

Title page: The familiar silhouettes of the pyramids of Khufu, Khephren and Menkaure at Giza, to the south-west of modern Cairo.

Copyright © 1986 by Orbis Book Publishing Corporation Limited.
Photographs copyright © Werner Forman 1986
First published in Great Britain 1986 by Orbis Book Publishing Corporation Limited, London.
Published in the United States by University of Oklahoma Press, Norman, Publishing Division of the University.
First edition 1986.
Manufactured in Yugoslavia.

Library of Congress Cataloging-in-Publication Data

Málek, Jaromír.
In the shadow of the pyramids.

1. Egypt – Civilization – To 332 b.c. I. Forman, W. (Werner) III. Title.
DT61.M29 1986   932'.012   86-40188
ISBN 0-8061-2027-4

CONTENTS

ONE

PROLOGUE

MANETHO, AN EGYPTIAN PRIEST living under the Ptolemies Soter and Philadelphus, compiled a history of Egypt based on old records and archive lists of kings. History-writing was a concept alien to Egyptian thinking, and although his was a good native name (*manehto*, 'horse-groom') and his origins from an important provincial town of Sebennytos in the central Delta were beyond reproach, it was a foreign culture and an un-Egyptian world outlook which inspired the work. Manetho's *Aigyptiaka* was written in Greek and has come down to us only in the form of excerpts made from it by later chroniclers, but it has exerted a lasting effect on the formal division of the political history of ancient Egypt and the way it is traditionally interpreted.

Following the usage of his time, Manetho divided the kings known to him into thirty dynasties or ruling houses, starting with the legendary Menes and concluding with the last native king, Nektanebos. Some of these divisions followed ancient king-lists, others seem to have resulted from his misunderstanding of the sources, or their imperfection, and several may have been introduced by him simply for convenience. Nevertheless, Manetho's dynastic division is still generally used and its author is deservedly regarded as the first Egyptian historian.

The ancient Egyptians did not record history for its own sake and our knowledge is, therefore, based on history's raw materials and on texts which were composed for other purposes. Yet the Egyptians were not entirely oblivious of their past. A rare insight into their awareness of it is still visible in a large memorial temple built by King Seti I for the perpetuation of his cult in the Upper Egyptian town of Abdju (Abydos) a thousand years before Manetho, around 1300 BC. In the maze of its chapels, columned halls, and vestibules there is a corridor known as 'The Gallery of the Lists.' In the relief carved on its east wall Seti I and his son, the future Ramesse II, are shown symbolically offering libation and incense to a large number of Egyptian deities represented by their names. On the opposite west wall the father and son appear in a similar scene before two long rows of cartouches containing the names of their royal ancestors. The list, by its nature, did not aspire to historical completeness.

The remarkable accuracy of pyramid construction and the mathematical properties of the design, which may sometimes involve the use of π (e.g. the height of the pyramid of Khufu = $\dfrac{\text{perimeter of the base}}{2\pi}$), can be rationally explained. However, the exact procedures of surveying and construction of these massive structures are not known to us because of the absence of contemporary written records.

7

An important type of sculpture which remained
unique to private statues was the representation
of the tomb-owner as a scribe. Literacy was an
essential qualification for a successful
bureaucratic career, and the scribe-statues which
were introduced towards the end of the Fourth
Dynasty quickly became very popular. They
show a man in the typical squatting posture of a
scribe, reading or writing on a roll of papyrus
spread on his lap. Most of these statues are very
ordinary pieces, but the 'Scribe du Louvre',
found in a late Fourth or early Fifth Dynasty
tomb at Saqqara, and known by its present
location, is probably the best private sculpture
made during the Old Kingdom.

It included only the groups of rulers regarded by its compiler as the most illustrious and worthy of commemoration, while the kings of the less famous periods of Egyptian history were simply omitted. At its beginning it presents a series of fifty-six names, introduced by that of Meni (Menes of Manetho), and is the most complete record of successive kings of the earliest part of Egyptian history.

To the eyes of an outsider the initial impression of ancient Egypt is one of unfamiliarity. The astonishment of the stranger encountering Egyptian civilization for the first time is nothing new. No one has conveyed it better than Herodotus who visited Egypt in the second half of the fifth century BC. 'In Egypt the women go to market and sell the produce, while the men remain at home weaving; and their weaving technique involves pushing down the weft, which in other countries is pushed upwards. Egyptian men carry loads on their heads, the women on their shoulders. The women urinate in a standing position, the men sitting down. . . . Elsewhere priests grow their hair long: in Egypt they shave themselves. The common custom of mankind in mourning is for the bereaved to cut their hair short: Egyptians in the event of bereavement let both their hair and beards (which they normally shave) grow long. . . . For writing and for counting with pebbles the Greeks move their hands from left to right, the Egyptians from right to left. And despite this practice they claim that their own writing is "rightwards", while that of the Greeks is "leftwards".'

Although the development of ancient Egypt can be followed in detail through written records over the unparalleled span of some 3000 years and through archaeological artefacts for even longer, the unfamiliarity of the culture makes it difficult to see it as other than static and permanent. Egypt's ideological and political concepts seem to have been remarkably impervious to change. Egyptian art of all periods strikes us by the peculiarity of its forms of expression and apparent rigidity of conventions. The principles of the hieroglyphic system of writing endured little affected by the passing of time, from its emergence towards the end of the Predynastic Period, around 3000 BC, to its last recorded instance in the temple at Philae near the first Nile cataract as late as AD 394.

Yet the first impressions are shown on closer examination to be mis-

Right: Although the technique of relief uses the
same conventions, and a similar approach to
portraying reality, as painting on a flat surface,
it is three-dimensional and thus sensitive to a
play of light. The third dimension of Egyptian
relief of the Old Kingdom, its height or depth,
amounted to no more than a few millimetres.
Depending on whether the represented feature is
above or below the surrounding plain, the relief
is 'raised' or 'sunk'. When the surface was
exposed to direct sunlight, sunk relief was
preferred because it relies on the strong contrast
between light and shadow. Raised relief was
chosen for decoration illuminated by diffused
light. The alabaster panel of Rawer of the mid-
Fifth Dynasty, decorated in sunk relief, was
found at the back of a niche in his tomb at Giza.

Old Kingdom sources are strangely and surprisingly silent about the Giza sphinx. It was only some 1,000 years after the Sphinx had been made, during the Eighteenth Dynasty of the New Kingdom, that it was mentioned. At this period it was thought to represent the sky-god Haremakhet ('Horus on the Horizon') or the Syrian deity Hauron.

Right: The eastern part of the enclosure containing Netjerikhet's step pyramid was occupied by stone replicas of kiosks and chapels for the celebration of the royal jubilee-festivals (heb-sed). It is likely that during the Old Kingdom these festivals took place at Ineb-hedj (Memphis), the first after 30 years of the king's reign. Netjerikhet's *heb-sed structures* were provided for the jubilee the king hoped to enjoy in afterlife. Parts of the cult temples of the developed pyramid-complexes may have served a similar purpose, but Netjerikhet's arrangements remain unique. Some of the elements of the buildings which are currently being restored at Saqqara are modern.

10

leading. Egyptology, the study of ancient Egypt, established itself as a scholarly discipline more than a century and a half ago when, on 29 September 1822, young Jean-François Champollion read to the Académie his 'Lettre à M. Dacier relative à l'alphabet des hiéroglyphes phonétiques' with the explanation of the system of the Egyptian hieroglyphic script. Since then most aspects of Egyptian civilization have been analysed, some with remarkable exactitude. The political, social, and cultural history of Egypt can now be divided into several clearly defined broad periods which with their varying causes and conditions are quite distinct.

Egypt's historic era started around 2925 BC, and the whole of the country had come under the authority of one ruler only a little earlier. The formative stage of the Egyptian state corresponds to the first two royal dynasties of Manetho and the first fourteen kings of the Abdju (Abydos) list, and was completed around 2658 BC. The Old Kingdom, which was thus ushered in without any perceptible break, produced and sustained the first flourishing of ancient Egyptian civilization in all its aspects. Egyptian society quickly achieved a high degree of economic prosperity as the result of the efficiency and organizational abilities of its officials, and a high cultural standard because of the skills and talents of its craftsmen and artists. It was a period of prosperity, stability, confidence, and self-assurance, an era during which the Egyptians first realized their ambitions and aspirations, and became the most advanced civilization of their time. Even the notoriously 'unhistorically'-minded Egyptians of later times used to look to the Old Kingdom for religious, cultural, and moral inspiration. For us, Old Kingdom pyramids and tombs, with their magnificent reliefs and paintings, statues and stelae, often epitomize the whole of ancient Egypt and the achievement of its civilization.

The Old Kingdom lasted for over 500 years (2658–2135 BC), and corresponds to the Third to Eighth Dynasties of Manetho. Its kings are represented by the fifteenth to fifty-sixth names of the Abdju list. The sharp decline at the end of the Old Kingdom and during the following period affected Egyptian society at all levels. When the collapse approached, the Egyptians themselves felt that their world was coming to an end. 'What had never happened has now happened' was how a sage called Neferti described it. 'The land turns round as does a potter's wheel' were the words of another prophet of doom, Ipuwer.

Above: Structures in wood and various perishable materials were faithfully and deliberately copied in stone in Netjerikhet's enclosure, but it would be wrong to assume that this was because stone architecture had at first to rely entirely on forms developed in other materials. Here it was a recognition of stone as the material in which to build for eternity, a concept which was to remain valid for the rest of Egyptian history.

Above left: While under construction, the design of Netjerikhet's traditionally conceived stone-built mastaba was modified five times, as if the architect was gradually becoming aware of the possibilities of the new building material and did not wish to miss the opportunity to capitalize on them as work progressed. It was changed as a result of an enlargement of its ground plan, but more importantly by a sudden adoption of a four-stepped, and later six-stepped, silhouette. Imhotep, the alleged architect in charge of the project, later became one of the few private persons deified in Egypt. His connection with Netjerikhet was confirmed by the discovery of the base of Netjerikhet's statue with Imhotep's name inscribed on it.

TWO

THE BEGINNINGS

In the vizier Mereruka's early Sixth Dynasty tomb at Saqqara, a papyrus thicket is dramatically depicted alive with animals and birds. The water is teeming with fish, and three baying hippopotami are harpooned by men in boats. Locusts resting on some rushes provide a haven of peace in the commotion which reigns all around them.

ANCIENT EGYPTIAN CIVILIZATION owed its existence to the unique combination of physical conditions found in the north-eastern corner of the African continent from *c.* 10,000 BC. About a half of the Black Land (*Kemet*), as it was called by its inhabitants, was little more than a narrow strip of an extremely fertile dark soil deposited by the nameless River (*iteru*) and annually replenished by the waters of the inundation. The stream flowed on its journey to the north through an extensive region of Nubian sandstone, but this in southern Egypt gave way to limestone beyond the present Esna. When it passed the Ineb-hedj district ('White Wall', later Mennufer or Memphis in Greek), it divided into a series of smaller branches which spread like the fingers of a hand before reaching the Mediterranean shore, thus creating the wide expanse of alluvial land known to us as the Nile Delta. It was a marshy area containing a large number of unstable river channels, and permanent habitation was only possible on the Delta's margins and on sporadically occurring sandy ridges ('turtle-backs') which remained out of reach of water even at the height of inundation. These watery regions were full of wildlife, and an almost obligatory scene in the Old Kingdom tomb-scene repertoire showed the tomb-owner spearing fish and hunting birds with a throw-stick from a small papyrus skiff in swamps.

The extent of marsh-land in the Nile valley itself was limited. A chain of oases to the west provided focal points for settlers, but otherwise only a poor and sparsely inhabited country stretched on either side of the Black Land. For much of the early history of ancient Egypt, until about 2350 BC, the deserts, particularly their borders and the tracts adjacent to the wadis, were not entirely arid and barren because of the generally moister climate with some periodic rainfall. These parts of the desert supported savanna-type vegetation with trees and shrubs, and were the habitat of a variety of wildlife. The most significant factor in the environmental changes which occurred in the Nile valley before the beginning of the Sixth Dynasty was man, whose farming activities deprived many of the animals and birds of their natural breeding grounds, and who purposefully tried to eliminate animals harmful to him or his crops.

Only reluctantly the Egyptians ventured outside the Nile valley. The hills in the desert to the east were rich in valued minerals and metals, in particular copper and gold. The same held true of Nubia, the land beyond the acknowledged southern frontier formed by the granite barrier of the first Nile cataract. In addition, Nubia also possessed the precious commodity of which Egypt was so painfully short—wood. In the north-east, the Sinai peninsula became the source of copper and the semi-precious

Forms of Predynastic pottery varied from simple bowls, cups, and tall vases to curious forms on feet, or pots consisting of two connected cylinders. Although usually made without the help of any mechanical device, the standard of Predynastic pottery was not surpassed in historic times.

stone turquoise, though both were perhaps at first imported rather than mined by the Egyptians. Goods from more distant countries reached Egypt by sea or overland through these desert regions, and the commercial routes had to be safeguarded. Military expeditions were sent out to deal ruthlessly with the occasional threat to the inhabitants of the Nile valley settlements posed by roving bands of the nomadic 'sand-dwellers' (*heryu-sha*) of the desert. On the whole, however, Egypt's safety in isolation within its natural geographical frontiers and its self-sufficiency in almost all respects were among the most important circumstances which influenced the formation of the character and attitudes of its inhabitants.

The annual inundation is caused by the summer monsoon rains outside Egypt, in the mountains of Ethiopia and the southern Sudan, though the

reason for it was never understood by the Egyptians. Most of the land in the valley and the Delta which was naturally flooded when the Nile rose, remained under water for some ten weeks between August and November. The difference between the highest and the lowest level of the Nile was over eleven metres (thirty-five feet) in southern Egypt, some seven metres in the Ineb-hedj district, and about three metres in the Delta. When the river left its natural bed, the heavier of the materials carried by its flood-waters were deposited first so that levees gradually formed close to the Nile banks in the valley and separated the main stream from the low-lying basins beyond. Water stayed in these seasonally flooded basins long after the inundation ended, and each year a fresh deposit of sediment rich in organic matter was left behind.

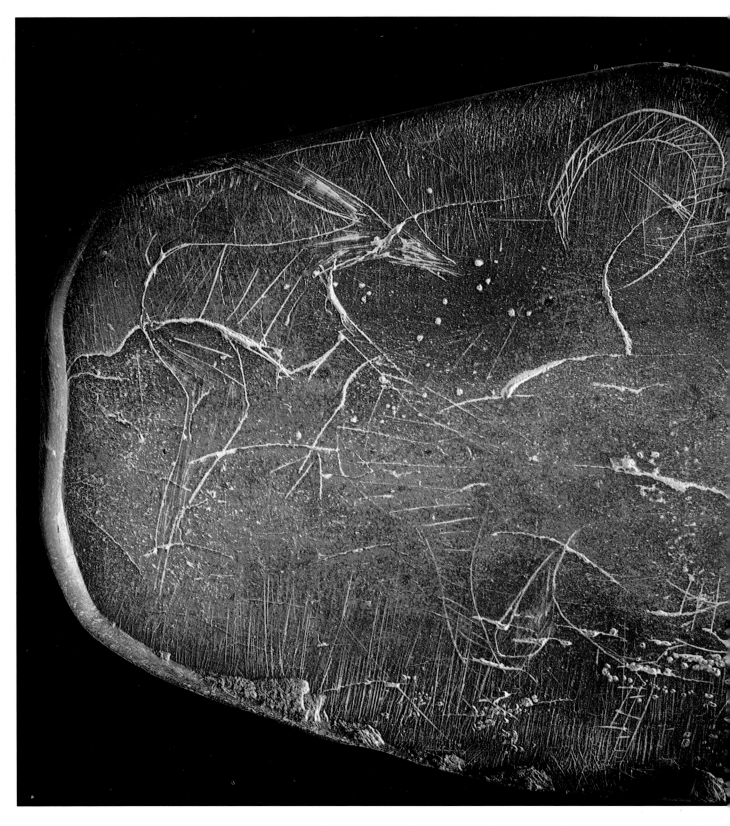

Predynastic (Nagada I Period) cosmetic palette with finely incised representations of desert animals. The drawings are in subject, style, and execution strongly reminiscent of the early rock art of the Eastern Desert and Nubia.

The Nile is very predictable, but the relationship between man and the river was so delicately balanced and his dependence on it so complete that an occasional deviation from its usual timetable and its normal volume of water had very serious consequences. Surprisingly, the Egyptians had no deity of the River as such, but the fertile aspects of inundation, *hapy*, were portrayed in the form of a grotesquely fat man with a huge paunch and pendant breasts, the image of well-being and prosperity.

There is little evidence that any of the changes which took place along the Nile before the beginning of the historic era were due to migrations of

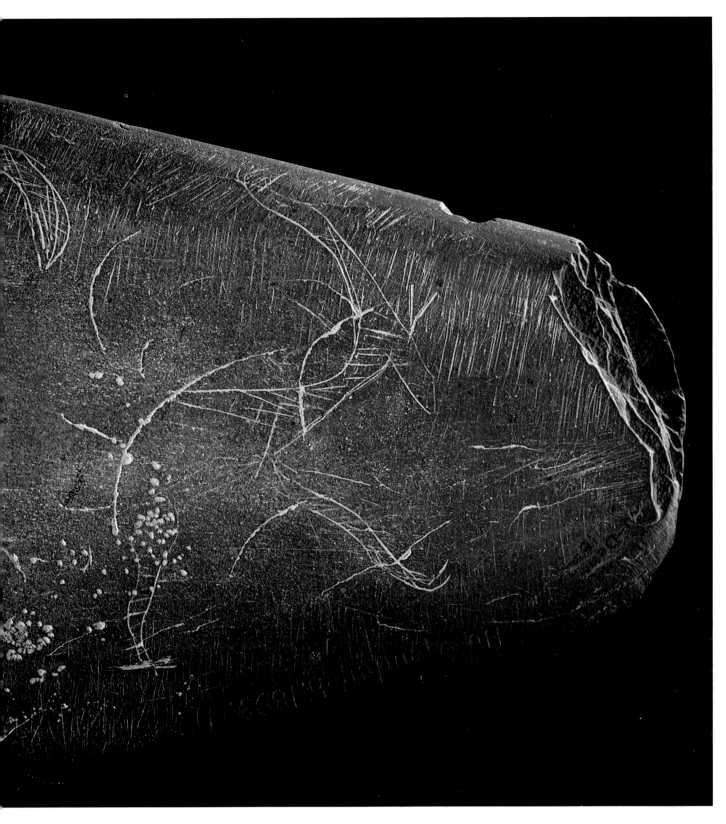

population from outside Egypt. On the contrary, it appears that basically the same, even if not homogeneous, physical types persisted throughout all of the prehistoric and historic periods. The environmental conditions in Shemau (the southern valley, or Upper Egypt) and Ta-mehu (the northern Delta, or Lower Egypt), were in sharp contrast. The geographical shape of the country was unique—nearly 900 km (600 miles) long, but in the valley only exceptionally as much as twenty km (twelve miles) wide. Along this frontier there would have been contacts with different peoples sufficient to produce variations attested in skeletal

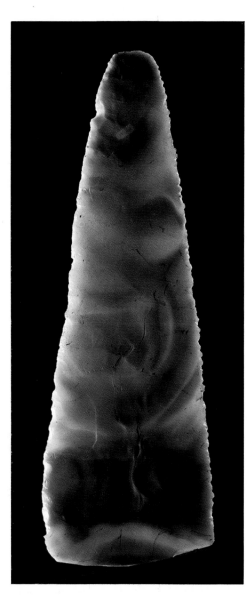

remains. The inhabitants of Upper Egypt were on the whole of a smaller, gracile type with long narrow skulls, compared with the taller and more heavily built mesocephalic Lower Egyptians. On monuments, all men have dark curly hair and their bodies are dark red to indicate the heavily sunburnt light-brown skin (brown was absent from the palette of the Egyptian artist). The conventional depiction of the lighter complexion of women was yellow.

A similar picture of population stability is obtained from an analysis of the Egyptian language, even though the variety of current opinions is as great as in the case of physical anthropology. Connections exist with ancient and modern Semitic languages of western Asia, as well as Cushitic, Berber and Chado-Hamitic languages of Ethiopia, Libya and the western Sudan. These, however, suggest a common origin rather than a super-imposition of one language upon another. The prehistoric inhabitants of Egypt and the historic Egyptians therefore spoke the same language in different stages of its development. It was only after proper texts (rather than names, titles, lists, or short descriptions accompanying representations) appeared during the Fourth Dynasty that we can study it in detail, but some of the features of the earlier phase of spoken Egyptian were preserved in the religious literature of the Old Kingdom.

The time between the Palaeolithic (Stone Age) civilization and the rise of the first Egyptian dynasty of kings is conveniently described as the Predynastic (Neolithic) Period. The most significant advance made at that time was the introduction of settled agriculture. Each year when the inundation receded, conditions in the Nile valley were suitable for primitive farming. The water which was left in naturally created flood-basins could with little effort be made to last for most of the growing season of any seed which may have been sown. The pattern of farming in the Predynastic Period varied from one place to another in order to exploit local conditions to the maximum, but for much of the early history of Egypt there was little need for large-scale artificial irrigation of the fields under cultivation and the matter was left in the hands of local communities. Even during the Old Kingdom the role of the

Above, this page and facing page: Implements made of flint were gradually increasing in number and quality to attain their peak before the end of the Predynastic Period, although copper was already used for the same purpose. In flint-making, high skills, and therefore specialization, were needed for mining the raw material and for the masterly craftsmanship displayed in some of the pieces found at late Predynastic and early Dynastic sites.

state in maintaining the irrigation system remained distinctly limited.

The agricultural techniques and implements required for this early form of cereal cultivation were simple, and the change to settled farming was probably made easier by previous experimentation involving wild grains. Among finds of the Predynastic cultures are flint blades with serrated edges which were inserted in wooden sickle-handles used for reaping, circular threshing floors, granaries lined with wickerwork for storing the grain, and simple stone querns, or hand-mills, for grinding it. Emmer wheat and barley were the cereals cultivated, and although Asia is usually thought to have been their origin, Ethiopia is also a possibility.

The regular occurrence of favourable conditions for agriculture encouraged the establishment of settlements, often on the levees, which stayed dry during the inundation, and on the margins of the floodplain. The earliest villages perhaps were only semi-permanent, with primitive huts constructed of poles, reeds, and mats, but towards the end of the Predynastic Period there were fortified 'towns' with brick-built rectangular houses consisting of a roofed room and an open forecourt. Nubt (modern Nagada) and Nekhen (Hierakonpolis, modern Kom el-Ahmar) were the two Upper Egyptian towns in the forefront of this development. The view that the settling of the Nile region resulted from rapidly growing desiccation is unfounded. The climatic conditions remained relatively stable during the Predynastic Period and those changes in food production which occurred were due to the early settlers' grasp and exploitation of the favourable circumstances along the Nile. The population growth resulted both from the rising birth-rate and the increasing number of people settling in the region on a permanent basis.

Cattle, goats, sheep, pigs, and donkeys were the domestic animals, as well as dogs, but at this early period there were as yet no cats. Most of these animals probably reached Egypt from Asia via Sinai, but the local contribution to their domestication seems to have been small. Hunting and fishing continued to play a significant, if gradually diminishing, part in the economy, and arrow-heads, throw-sticks, and fish-hooks are frequently found in excavations.

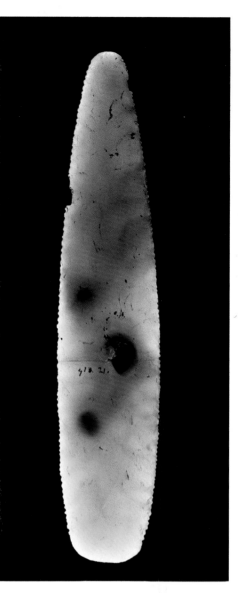

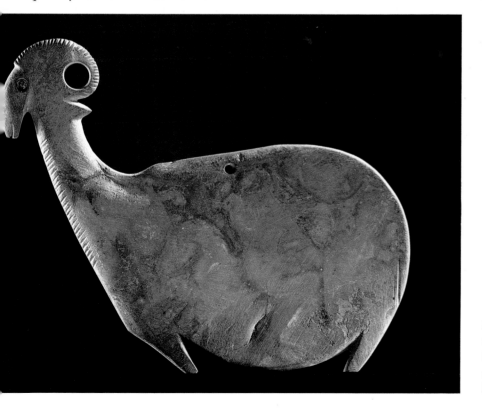

Flat cosmetic palettes ranged from simple rectangular shapes to elegant forms which imitated animals such as hippopotami, elephants, antelope, sheep, turtles, fish, and birds.

The most impressive element of some of the palettes is design in harmony with form. These patterns and solutions of spatial problems were imitated for the rest of Egyptian history. The 'Two Dogs Palette' was found at Nekhen (Hierakonpolis). Because of the haphazard distribution of the animals on the reverse of the palette, it is usually regarded as earlier than other pieces with a more orderly arrangement closer to the registers of Dynastic art. Such an explanation, however, may underestimate the sophistication of the design. For the Egyptians, the deserts bordering on the Nile valley were the home of wild animals and mythical beasts, and represented chaos. Within the symmetrically carved leaping dogs, the creatures of the desert present a mêlée of forms, postures, and movements, the very picture of disorder. Two long-necked animals are shown on the obverse.

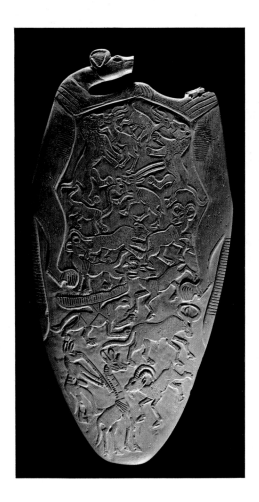

The earliest sites with Predynastic remains date from about 5000–4500 BC. From then on, the development of prehistoric civilization can be followed continuously until the beginning of the First Dynasty, but not everywhere and not in full at all archaeological sites so far located. The chances of preservation and the changes which have taken place in the appearance of the valley and the Delta since then account for the patchy pattern. The successive stages of this development, or archaeological cultures, are known by the names of the villages near which their cemeteries or settlements were first recognized, or where they are particularly well attested. The Predynastic Period of northern Egypt is poorly known, but much of the country soon displayed considerable cultural unity. Nagada was the main culture from about 4000 BC, though at first confined to the south. It is usually divided into phase I (formerly called Amratian, after the site of Amra) and the later phase II (formerly Gerzean, after Gerza), which immediately preceded the rise of the First Dynasty.

In the absence of written records we have to rely entirely on artefacts for our knowledge of Predynastic society and its level of material culture.

Whether metallurgy evolved in Egypt independently or whether it was introduced from Palestine is a matter of some dispute. In southern Egypt, copper was known from the very beginning of the Predynastic Period, but initially it was very scarce and only used for the manufacture of small decorative items such as beads, and was thus regarded as a precious rather than a useful material. During Nagada II it became sufficiently common for its uses to be extended, and the opportunity was eagerly seized, as attested by the finds of copper axes, adzes, knives, daggers, awls, pins, and needles. Other metals, such as gold, silver, and even meteoric iron, were mostly used for the making of personal ornaments. Metal-working was one of the earliest industries which required specialization and separated craftsmen from the vast majority of farmers.

Stone was used for the manufacture of implements as well as weapons, among which the disc-shaped and later pear-shaped maceheads were the most prominent. The production of stone vessels reached a remarkably high standard towards the end of the Predynastic Period when they were made in large quantities. A variety of materials were employed, some very hard, including porphyry, basalt, schist, alabaster, and limestone. Cosmetic palettes used for grinding malachite (copper ore), and to a lesser degree galena (lead ore), for preparation of the popular green or black eye-paint, were also made of stone, in particular green schist. In the Predynastic Period the knowledge of small-scale stone-working was wide-ranging. It provided a starting point for the development which culminated in the tremendously rapid advances when monumental architecture in stone appeared at the beginning of the Third Dynasty.

In pottery, coarse utilitarian 'kitchen' ware, as well as very fine vessels with incised, painted, or other decoration, is known from the Predynastic Period. Some of the decorated pots were specially made to be deposited in graves and can be seen as the earliest evidence for workshops specializing in the manufacture of objects for the necropolis. Flax was grown, and weaving is attested by finds of spindle whorls and surviving examples of coarse linen, but skins and leather were also used for making clothes.

The time preceding the first Egyptian dynasties may be characterized as a period of modest beginnings, but very able experimentation in Egyptian art. The variety of forms of artistic expression is surprising, and it was lack of opportunities and incentives to create on a larger scale rather than a lack of ability which restricted the artist.

At this early period the term 'art' has to encompass personal ornaments and applied art, i.e. decorated objects of everyday life. Religious and

aesthetic feelings went hand in hand from the very beginning of Egyptian civilization and cannot always be easily separated. Apart from the simple design and decoration of their 'kitchen' pottery, the personal feelings and preferences of ordinary Egyptians are revealed in the decorative items they wore on their bodies or clothes. These were very often made up of beads of various materials and can be reconstructed to form necklaces and belts or girdles. Shells were used for the same purpose. Bracelets and armlets of shell, bone, or ivory were worn, as well as rings, pendants, and small amulets, some of them representing animals, birds, or fish.

The obverse of the so-called Battlefield Palette shows standards of deities, represented by a hawk and an ibis which, provided with human arms, are escorting bound captives. Such a curious addition of human elements was already very characteristic of the late Predynastic Period, and similar artistic devices were common in later times. The bordered circular depression on the right is all that still reminds us that the original purpose of such objects was for grinding eye-paint.

Below: Elaborate hairdos must have been fashionable because ornamental haircombs and long pins, usually made of ivory and often crowned with a beautifully observed figure of an animal or bird, were common.

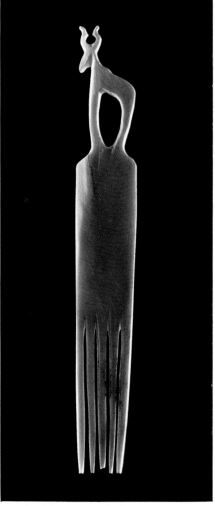

The other side of the palette-fragment shown opposite. A guinea-fowl (?) is represented above a long-necked animal, perhaps a gazelle rather than a giraffe. The animal is one of two which originally flanked a date-palm in a symmetrical fashion. This is probably one of the motifs which Egyptian art adopted from abroad at the end of the Predynastic Period.

A number of votive palettes and mace-heads show very sensitive modelling, such as can be seen here in a detail of the obverse of the same Battlefield palette. It shows a lion and vultures preying on bodies after a battle. The provenance of the object is not recorded, but the area of Abydos seems very probable. It is difficult to date items of this type. Nevertheless, it appears that one or two generations may have been sufficient for the new artistic concepts to be realized, as if pent-up potential had suddenly been given a means of expression; this is the feeling gained from observation of many other features of late Predynastic art.

Ornamental palettes used for the preparation of make-up, decorated containers, spoons, and ladles of bone or ivory also belong to the category of toilet articles.

Some of the artistic effort was directed towards grave goods and indicates developed ideas concerning life after death. Many of the pots from Nagada II graves are painted in red on a buff background with representations of people, animals, and in particular large boats propelled by many oarsmen. The boats may carry shrines with standards of local gods attached to them, but it is equally possible that we have here a reflection of the rudimentary ideas concerning funerary boat-voyages known from the Old Kingdom. A unique multicoloured tomb-painting on plaster was found in the so-called Decorated Tomb at Nekhen (Hierakonpolis). It was probably made for one of the local Predynastic chiefs, and its scenes show boats, with human figures and animals engaged in a variety of activities. The representations of people are primitive in their execution and similar to those known from rock-drawings in Wadi Hammamat and Nubia, and the spatial distribution of elements is as haphazard as on the pottery. Few features, such as the half-hearted attempt to place one group on a common base-line, can be even remotely connected with the conventions of Egyptian dynastic art.

Small statuettes of animals, such as lions, hippopotami, jackals, and hawks, and of people, made of clay, ivory, or stone, are occasionally found in Predynastic graves. They show a remarkably high degree of stylization and abstraction. A limited number of objects were made for the presumed primitive shrines or 'temples' intended for the worship of gods. One large structure which is interpreted in this way is an oval stone-built enclosure filled with clean sand at Nekhen (Hierakonpolis). It is similar in shape to the hieroglyph with which the name of the place was written. Even if its dating to the late Predynastic Period is correct, it represents a special local form of sanctuary which was not comparable to those existing elsewhere and could not have influenced their development.

The most accomplished specimens of art are votive palettes, mace-heads, and knife-handles, decorated in relief. These objects were made for the highest echelon of late Predynastic society as Egypt began to enter its historic age. The decorated slate palettes and limestone mace-heads had lost their original practical purpose, and now became a convenient medium for expressing some of the tenets of nascent state ideology. This early Egyptian 'court' art seems to have been concerned more with the king than the god for whose temple the votive object was intended, as if the ruler wanted to placate and impress the deity by his own status and thus tried to ensure for himself a continued success. This, rather than an attempt to record real historical events, probably inspired such early works of art.

Some of the motifs (a man dominating a pair of lions, long-necked animals, interlacing serpents, rosettes, a griffin) and details (headdresses and robes) can be sought in Mesopotamia, but this does not mean that the objects were made outside Egypt or that the artists were brought from abroad. At a time when the Egyptians were moulding their own style it would have been natural that their top artists, who were working for a very exclusive clientele, were more susceptible to outside artistic inspiration and more prone to experimentation than in later times when a tradition and style set in. Trade contacts would have been sufficient to account for this. With a few exceptions, these influences from outside Egypt can be detected only in the official art of the late Predynastic Period, and betray a substantial gap which had quickly developed between the very small ruling élite and the rest of the population. It was this 'court' art,

Opposite: The makers of early Predynastic statues knew as yet none of the conventions of later Egyptian three-dimensional art, which results in the curiously un-Egyptian impression their creations exert. This statuette, made of the hard basalt, is known as the 'MacGregor Man', after the Rev. William MacGregor in whose collection it was until 1922.

Below: Three colossi of the ithyphallic god Min were found at Gebtiu (Koptos, modern Qift). These statues, originally four metres (thirteen feet) tall, but now badly battered, are the only known examples of monumental temple sculpture of the late Predynastic Period, even though their dating is not as secure as one would wish. This way of portraying the god Min was to last for the rest of Egyptian history.

25

produced by professional artists/craftsmen, which eventually led to the creation of the characteristic Egyptian style, while the art of the people was left behind and ceased at this point to exert any further influence.

Several inventions are thought to have been introduced to Egypt from abroad (Palestine, Syria and Mesopotamia) during the late Predynastic Period, such as the cylinder seal, certain forms of pottery, and brick niche architecture ('palace façade'). Long-distance trade is well documented by finds of imported materials (obsidian, lapis lazuli, turquoise, copper, possibly silver, ivory, Red Sea shells, wood, etc.), but the routes along which these items arrived in Egypt at this time can only be guessed.

During the Predynastic Period the Egyptians successfully learnt to exploit conditions along the Nile and developed an economic system based on mixed farming which was capable of satisfying the basic material needs of everyone settled in the region. The society whose picture emerges from the disjointed pieces of information available to us was based on village communities. Communal granaries found at some sites suggest a certain degree of very early organization at a local level. The need to control the division of the land for agriculture each year after the flood, and the advantages which accrued from a joint planning and maintenance of local dikes and canals, led to the emergence of chiefs who exerted authority over limited areas.

In the absence of outside interference the stimuli for further changes and the eventual creation of the unified Egyptian state had to come from within existing society. Inner pressures for development became apparent towards the end of the Predynastic Period. Growing craft specialization significantly enlarged the small section of people who did not directly take part in food production, and helped to deepen the incipient social stratification of Egyptian society. In the Nagada II period the differences in the social status were clearly reflected in the types and sizes of graves and the quality of burial goods. The demands and expectations of the privileged group of local chiefs could only be satisfied through more advanced ways of social organization. At the same time, regional characteristics, such as more favourable farming conditions, proximity to mineral resources, or control of long-distance trade routes, created differences among local communities. These strains and contradictions led to conflict and the formation of larger political units towards the end of the Predynastic Period. The ease of communication by the river must have helped this development. The trend reached its logical conclusion when all desirable land along the Nile had been incorporated within the limits of control by one ruler. Although the precise steps of this process are not known to us, there is little doubt that it took place over a period of time and was one of gradual expansion and annexation rather than large-scale confrontation. The formation of an Egypt united in a political sense was accomplished at the latest around 2950 BC under King Narmer, and this situation was to last until the end of the Old Kingdom, more than 800 years later.

The sequence of events which led to the appearance of the Egyptian state towards the end of the Predynastic Period is often described as unification. The term must not be interpreted as conveying the idea of a struggle between two political entities which ended in the victory of the South (Upper Egypt) and the subjugation of the North (Lower Egypt). As on several occasions in later history, the initiative did, indeed, come from the South, where the stimuli for a change were always stronger. There is, however, no clear evidence for a showdown between two large kingdoms. The significance of the scenes on the decorated palettes and mace-heads is by no means certain, and although the distinction between

Predynastic statuettes strike us by their unusual portrayal of the human figure. Woman is often shown with a summarily indicated head, prominent breasts, a slender waist, and heavy hips. Sculptures of this type in ivory have no arms, but those made of clay show arms reminiscent of the wings of a bird raised above the head (hence the term 'bird deity'), as if supporting a vessel the woman may have carried on her head. The material from which the statuette was made no doubt caused the difference in style. Man, on the other hand, is usually represented as a squat rectangular block with a triangular bearded head and large eyes.

The completely preserved votive mace-head of Narmer is decorated with scenes arranged in registers. Standards with symbols of deities, as well as foreign captives and cattle and goats, are paraded before the enthroned ruler. Like the mace-head of King 'Scorpion' shown opposite, this object was found at Nekhen (Hierakonpolis).

Upper and Lower Egypt was stressed from very early times, this may have been a convenient administrative division—and one reflecting obvious physical reality—when the capital was established not far from the apex of the Delta at the beginning of the First Dynasty. One of the peculiarities of Egyptian thinking was the notion of dualism, i.e. a totality consisting of two elements in harmonious opposition. The concept was founded in Egyptian geography as well as early history. The country lends itself to such an approach easily: the known world = The Black Land (*Kemet*) + The Red Land (*Deshret*, the desert); Egypt = the valley (Upper Egypt) + the Delta (Lower Egypt). Historically, the earliest towns in Upper Egypt, where the idea would have developed, were Nekhen and Nubt, the homes of the rival gods Horus and Seth. Already Predynastic rulers wore two insignia on their heads, the White Crown and the Red Crown, and the royal title which was introduced in the reign of King Den of the First Dynasty and which was closest to our 'king' was *ni-sut-bit*, literally 'One who belongs to the Sedge (= Upper Egypt) and the Bee (= Lower Egypt).' This way of thinking must have appeared long before it found its reflection in iconography or texts, and to regard the occurrence of twin elements, such as the royal crowns, as evidence for the existence of two independent kingdoms in late Predynastic Egypt, amounts to looking at things through our own eyes, rather than seeing them the way the Egyptians did.

Interpretation of the very limited inscriptional evidence from the end of the Predynastic Period is difficult because of the primitive state of writing at the time, and it is unlikely that more informative sources will ever be found. Attempts to demarcate the stages leading to the creation of one Egyptian state from the geographical distribution of pottery bearing royal names hardly represents an infallible method. Trade invariably precedes conquest, and the pots with their contents could have been acquired by peaceful means. Political events are notoriously difficult to trace in ordinary archaeological material, and Predynastic Egypt is no exception to the rule.

Some areas were to be only gradually incorporated into Egypt. The region south of Nekhen may not have been annexed before the end of the Second Dynasty, and much of the north-eastern Delta did not form part of the Egyptian provincial system even during the Old Kingdom, probably because it was not thought to be economically viable. The political unification achieved in the late Predynastic Period thus did not represent the end, but only the most important phase, of a continuous dynamic process of establishing the natural frontiers of Egypt.

Manetho had at his disposal records of kings going back to King Menes, but this name may be completely fictitious and based on a word-play which was misunderstood as a royal name by the later compilers of king-lists. The first historic king in the Manethonian definition was Athothis, or Teti as he appears in the Abdju (Abydos) list, the second king of Manetho's First Dynasty. It was during his reign, in about 2925 BC, that the first year-lists ('annals') appeared, and that provided the earliest point of Egyptian history which Manetho, some 2650 years later, could trace. Hence it became the beginning of his history of Egypt. The traditional beginning of Egypt's First Dynasty and its historic era was thus fixed by the introduction of an administrative practice and perhaps compounded further by a misunderstanding, and had little direct connection with the appearance of the first Egyptian king, the creation of the Egyptian state, or the invention of script.

The more advanced of the votive palettes and ceremonial mace-heads of the late Predynastic Period already show a number of features usually associated with later reliefs: base-lines and rudimentary division of scenes into registers, intentional disregard for realistic relative sizes, and the typically Egyptian way of portraying the human figure. The two signs written next to the face of the king have been interpreted as his title and name, hence the term King 'Scorpion'. Such an interpretation, however, is almost certainly wrong. The scorpion is a large ceremonial image, as shown by the vertical projection probably representing a tang for insertion into a pole or mast, and does not record the king's name. If King 'Scorpion' is thus refuted, the likeliest candidate for identification with the figure on the mace-head is Narmer.

THREE

GATHERING PACE

The excellent quality of animal sculpture is one of the least known aspects of Egyptian art. The representational and other conventions imposed on the artist were less rigid when portraying animals, and so he was able to create more freely. The statue of a seated lion from Nekhen (Hierakonpolis) is a masterly combination of observation of live animals and of highly stylized features and motifs. The connection with the king is indicated by the bib-like mane falling on the chest of the animal, reminiscent of the lappets of the royal headcloth. Although the statue is made of pottery—an unusual material for this type of sculpture—the artist succeeded in conveying the vigour and ferocity of the beast. The piece probably dates from the Third Dynasty, but it may be earlier.

THE EGYPTIANS VERY EARLY EVOLVED A calendar based on a year of 365 days. When this happened, and the precise way in which it was arrived at is not known, but observation of several astronomical phenomena or the rising of the Nile over a period of time would have been sufficient for its calculation. For reasons which may have been closely connected with the provisioning of officials and the rudimentary system of collecting taxes, the new state bureaucracy soon felt the need for a dating system which distinguished between different years so that they could be recorded. The numbering of years starting from a fixed point was not known, and so each year was described, or named, by one or more of its outstanding events. This method required a centrally-kept list of such eponymous happenings in order that dates could be checked and computed; these year-lists ('annals') were started during the reign of King Aha (Manetho's Athothis, and Teti of other lists). More often than not the chosen occasions were of religious significance rather than of general interest, and the 'annals' cannot be regarded as an attempt to record history in the sense of later chronicles.

The creation of the unified Egyptian state introduced a new ideological framework and a new political organization of the country, but changed little in the material situation of the majority of the Egyptian farming population, and left the basic methods of agricultural production unaffected. Few of the cultural advances made at this time had a direct bearing on the lives of ordinary peasants. Centralized government brought a degree of safety and political stability, and its greater resources provided better security against the consequences of natural disasters such as famine, but the greatest effect of the change was in the sphere of manufacturing. Changes in society increased a demand for certain types of goods. The largest customer was the state itself, personified by the king and his immediate family, and many items of everyday life were now also made for the growing numbers of officials. Craftsmen and artists had easier access to raw materials, and were able to specialize as a result of the larger market for their products. When need arose, the state could mobilize a manpower which, in both number and quality, had been undreamt of by local chiefs of the Predynastic Period.

Arts and industries, inasmuch as the distinction between them was in Egypt always rather tenuous, now came to the fore. Metal-working and crafts which benefited from the use of metal implements made tremendous progress. The two main metals in which the Egyptians worked were copper and gold, but the latter was restricted to decorative items. Copper tools and weapons with their edges hardened by hammering were now in

The granite statue of kneeling Hetepdief is of an uncommon type, and represents a very early example of private sculpture: it probably dates from the end of the Second or the early Third Dynasty. On his right shoulder, Hetepdief bears the names of the first three kings of the Second Dynasty: Hetepsekhemui, Raneb, and Ninetjer. It is possible that the statue stood in the precinct of the temple of Ptah at Ineb-hedj and its owner, or his tomb, received through this statue a share of offerings which were destined for the Saqqara tombs of these kings. The names of the kings on the statue's shoulder were clearly visible and would have helped to jolt the memory of the priest in charge of the distribution of reversion offerings.

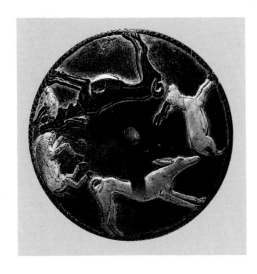

A gaming disc in black steatite, one of 45 made of various materials and variously decorated, found in the Saqqara mastaba of Hemaka, an official of King Den. The scene is in relief, and shows dogs chasing and despatching gazelles. The bodies of three of the animals are inlaid with alabaster.

common use by craftsmen, and vessels beaten out of sheets of metal were the chief innovation of the early dynasties. There was a variety of forms, including ewers, basins, and bowls, with their spouts and loop handles attached by rivets or wire.

Carpenters and cabinet-makers, working with native as well as imported woods, soon learnt all the essential techniques of joining. In addition to such prosaic items as doors, they manufactured household furniture, including beds, various chairs, stools, and chests, often decorated by fine carving or inlaid with ivory or faience. Leather upholstery of furniture was not uncommon, and the legs of chairs regularly terminated in ivory imitations of bull's hooves. Gameboards, some with pieces in the form of couchant lions, were very popular.

Jewellers used various materials, such as gold, copper, faience, shell, and ivory, together with a host of semi-precious stones, to make necklaces, bracelets, pendants, and amulets. Few of the more opulent examples are extant, but a remarkable discovery was made in the otherwise thoroughly plundered tomb of King Djer at Abdju (Abydos). A human arm swathed in linen in a primitive form of mummification, probably overlooked by robbers, was found with four bracelets still in place. One of the bracelets was made up of alternating gold and turquoise plaques shaped like a palace façade (serekh) with a hawk perched on top, symbolizing one of the royal names. The beads of various types in another bracelet included some made of amethyst and lapis lazuli.

Stone vessels of this period are the best from ancient Egypt, and are remarkable for their imaginative forms, often never to be repeated. Their makers were fond of imitating other materials, such as basketry, and although occasionally it may have been a simple adoption of a well-known motif, at other times it seems to have reflected a pure joy and exuberance in mastering the material and indulgence in showing off the creator's skill. A hand-held drill with a flint blade was the main tool of the trade, supplemented by a tubular drill and copper chisels. The flint industry continued to supply large quantities of blades for tools, particularly for everyday use by the poorer members of society.

Many specialized forms of mass-produced pottery were made, largely undecorated. Some were used for cooking, eating, and drinking, others

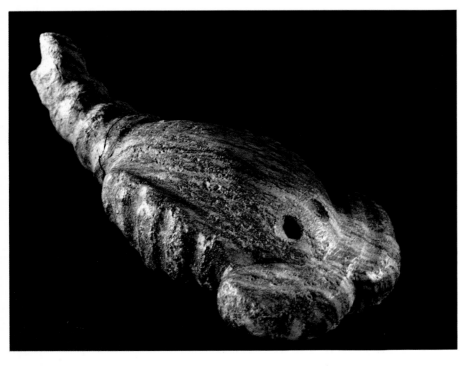

served for storage of solid foodstuffs, such as fruit, cheese, meat, and even bread, or as containers for liquids, including wine, beer, and milk, and yet others as moulds for baking bread and cakes. Grain was stored in large jars.

While crafts and applied arts thrived as never before, monumental sculpture, in the round and in relief, got off to a slow start. Only fragments of larger private statues in wood and of smaller pieces in stone have survived. The only known examples of royal sculpture in stone are two statues of King Khasekhem at the end of the Second Dynasty. Statues of animals, mostly lions and baboons, show features of abstraction and stylization in continuation of the Predynastic tradition. Much of these characteristics disappeared in the developed, more naturalistic, art of the Old Kingdom. Small sculpture in stone, ivory, and faience was common, and it is in these small figurines that we can follow the development from the Predynastic to the typical dynastic three-dimensional art.

Decorated palettes and mace-heads went out of fashion in the First Dynasty, together with any features which could be regarded as un-Egyptian. The art of relief-carving survived mainly in tomb-stelae (gravestones), but Egyptian monumental relief could only develop significantly when the changes in state ideology and religion, and the growing familiarity with the use of stone, found their expression in monumental building. As yet the opportunities offered were few, and until the situation changed in the Third and Fourth Dynasties, the ability displayed at the end of the Predynastic Period could not manifest itself more fully.

Our knowledge of official civil architecture, such as palaces, is almost entirely second-hand, based on their representations or presumed similarities in tomb architecture. The same is true of early temples, but we are well informed about tombs. Graves of ordinary people of the earliest period of Egyptian history were not richer or larger than their Predynastic counterparts, but tombs built during the First Dynasty for kings, close members of the royal family, and the highest officials of the state, now increased enormously in size. The area of their superstructure was regularly in excess of a thousand square metres (10,000 square feet), and although working with unbaked mud-brick, Egyptian architects and

The stela of King Djet, from his tomb at Abdju (Abydos), illustrates the difficult step from relatively small objects to monumental relief. A number of royal stelae of the first two Dynasties are known, one or two of them of excellent craftsmanship, but they are inscribed solely with the name of the king and carry no scenes.

work supervisors were acquiring the knowledge and managerial skills needed in large-scale monumental building of the Old Kingdom. The burial chamber and some of the magazines for tomb provisions were soon dug in the gravel and rock substratum, and during the Second Dynasty became a veritable maze of underground corridors and rooms. Above ground, the tombs of the First Dynasty, particularly, presented a striking appearance with their whitewashed niche façades painted in lively multi-coloured patterns in imitation of wall-matting.

The stelae with the names of the owners, which were found connected with some of these tombs, were their only decorated stone elements. The material was, no doubt, chosen for its durability. The knowledge of working in stone and appreciation of its possibilities as a building material led to an occasional use of stone elements for flooring, roofing, or wall-lining of rooms, and in the blocking of passages by portcullises. Not only limestone, but also the much harder granite from the southern Aswan region was employed.

At the beginning of the First Dynasty, a new administrative capital was founded and became known as Ineb-hedj, 'White Wall', presumably because of its appearance. A series of large tombs of high officials and some other members of the royal family were built in the desert cemeteries in this area, particularly at Saqqara. The site chosen for the capital was strategically located between the agriculturally important Delta with its contacts with western Asia, and the Nile valley with its access to gold and copper deposits and mineral resources, and was thus eminently suitable for administering both parts of the country. This caused some decline in the importance of the traditional centres in Upper Egypt, although they continued to enjoy religious prestige. The royal residence probably also moved to the north, but it is unlikely that the monarch remained at one place throughout the whole year. The kings of the First Dynasty, as well as Peribsen and Khasekhemui of the Second, were buried at Abdju (Abydos) next to several of their predecessors of the late Predynastic Period. The area and its local temple of the god Khentiamentiu (the 'Foremost of the Westerners', i.e. of the dead) may have already at that time been renowned as a religious centre, but this in itself would hardly have been a sufficient reason for the siting of royal tombs if there had not been other connections. It is likely that the Predynastic rulers whose successors eventually became kings of all Egypt originally came from this region. Royal tombs of the first half of the Second Dynasty probably were at Saqqara.

The king now enjoyed a unique status which elevated him above the rest of society. Ideologically, this must have represented a dramatic departure from the position held by the chiefs of the Predynastic Period. It is significant that no other figure which could be interpreted as being comparable to him appears on monuments before the beginning of the Old Kingdom. The concept of the king who is aloof, with only standards of deities accompanying and assisting him, emerged in Egyptian art at the time of unification. The king's duty was to govern the world and maintain its order.

The definition of the king's position in society had to reconcile his new royal status with some earlier concepts. One of these was the jubilee-festival (*heb-sed*), the original purpose of which was probably a periodic renewal of the powers and vitality of the local chief. Now it became a ritual replay of the beginning of the reign.

The distinction between the group which gave Egypt its early élite, the ruling *paat*, and the rest of the populace, the *rekhyt*, was the main division in Egyptian society at the beginning of the historic era. The origins of such social stratification, however, are not clear. It seems that at first all high officials of state administration were royal relatives, particularly princes, who to some extent shared the king's exalted position. The chasm which separated members of this élite from the rest of the population is graphically illustrated by the sizes of their tombs. Some of them, both royal and those of high officials, were found surrounded by smaller graves which contained burials of retainers: members of the household and the harim, craftsmen, dwarfs and entertainers, and even dogs.

The picture of the earliest Egyptian administration is detailed, but incomplete. Much of the evidence consists of official titles inscribed on vessels and found on seal-impressions, and does not lend itself easily to interpretation. The administrative system was, no doubt, diverse, and need not be regarded as particularly complex, thorough, or all-embracing. It was centred on the palace and the person of the king, with royal relatives acting on the king's behalf in the provinces, but many of the characteristics of the earlier chiefdoms had survived. The 'annals' show that a census of all Egypt took place every other year. It is likely that at first the king travelled the country by river during the 'following of Horus' and supervised the gathering of tribute. The 'treasurer of the king of Lower Egypt' (*sedjauty bity*) was in charge of this primitive form of personally enforced collection which eventually turned into more or less regular dispatches of produce to the royal palace. This official became the most important figure in the administration. The heights of inundation on cultivated fields, so meticulously recorded in the 'annals', may have been used for assessing the tax to be levied. Provisions for the palace and the royal tomb came from royal estates in the Delta which were the responsibility of *adj-mer* officials recruited from royal princes.

The departments called the 'White House' (*per-hedj*) and the 'Red House' (*per-desher*) functioned as the state treasury. The received produce was kept in specialized storehouses, and was used to pay officials, craftsmen, and retainers, and was perhaps also distributed as donations to local temples and primitive funerary cult institutions. It also served as a means of exchange in foreign trade and in any other way the king deemed desirable. The distribution was in the hands of the 'master of the largess' (*hery wedjeb*).

Village communities, although from the late Predynastic Period part of larger entities, continued to function as the smallest administrative units for the majority of the population. Theoretically, the political changes affected them profoundly because the king now claimed sovereignty over all land, in the same way as he was master over the fate of all people. In practical terms, this did not at first manifest itself beyond the need to comply with occasional fiscal and other obligations imposed by the king through his provincial representatives. If it is possible to accept the basic notion of inequality which underlies it, and which the newly created state now safeguarded, the political and economic system whose primitive form appeared in Egypt at the beginning of the historic era was ideally matched to the conditions of the country and its society. It was to be the most important factor in the further development during the Old Kingdom.

We can conjecture that each of the larger chiefdoms at the end of the Predynastic Period was connected with a cult-centre and a shrine or temple of the local deity. The fortunes of Egyptian gods waxed and waned with those of their home districts, and the development of relationships among deities went side by side with the creation of one state. The king of the unified Egypt identified himself with the god Horus of Nekhen, but the appearance of Seth of Nagada as well as the god Horus in

The centrepiece on this ivory comb from Abydos is a serekh *with the Horus-hawk (= the king) perching on top of it, and the name of King Djet written inside. Two was-sceptres symbolizing 'dominion', 'sovereignty', and an early form of the* ankh-*sign ('life') flank the* serekh. *Above, a bird's wings represent the sky, with a barque of an ancient form ferrying a hawk, perhaps the sun-god. Much of the symbolism in this group was employed by artists throughout the rest of Egyptian history.*

the names of two kings of the late Second Dynasty need not be a reflection of civil strife, because the relationship between politics and religion cannot be reduced to a simple equation. Almost all of the deities of later times were known during the earliest dynasties, usually in the forms of animals, birds, or fetishes. The 'annals' often mention religious festivals and the foundation of establishments which probably represent temples, but we have very little information about them from elsewhere.

It is not clear to what extent donations of votive objects to temples and funerary cult institutions were accompanied by consumable goods. Evidence for an early form of economic organization attached to temples comes from stone vessels dating to the Second Dynasty. They were found at Saqqara, and inscribed on them is 'The King of Upper and Lower

Egypt, the Two Ladies, Ninetjer. The food-provisioning [*djefau*] of the goddess Bastet. The first priestly guild [*wer*]'. The source of this food for the goddess is not known.

Statues of gods were commonly made, according to the 'annals', but none of them has survived.

Beliefs concerning life after death were complex even at this early time. Tombs were regarded as houses of the dead, and royal, and even some private tombs, were on occasion accompanied by funerary palaces or model estates. This interpretation was strengthened during the Second Dynasty to the point where we can distinguish bedrooms, bathrooms, lavatories, and stalls for cattle in the tomb. A chapel against the north face of the superstructure of a Saqqara tomb dated to the reign of King Qaa probably served for funerary cult. Religious ideas of a different kind may be the reason for boat-burials near some tombs. Their purpose was to provide a means of transport for the celestial voyages which the deceased would undertake in afterlife. The gravel or sand mounds in the super-structure of other tombs may be connected with the concept of resurrection and the primeval mound on which life appeared.

Egypt's early contacts with the world outside the Nile valley fall into three categories: punitive military raids aimed at protecting and consolidating the frontiers, expeditions in order to bring various kinds of stone only occurring outside the valley, and long-distance trade. Most of the evidence for the supposed military expeditions against the inhabitants of the deserts comes from the 'annals'. 'Dates' of packaging or bottling on small labels which were attached to containers of foodstuffs provide other examples. 'The smiting of the Iuntyu-tribesmen' or 'the first occasion of the smiting of the East', are, unfortunately, rather vague indications, and may refer to ritual occasions rather than real events. The same may be true of representations of the king slaying an enemy which may be symbolic. However, there is evidence of an early military expedition to Nubia as far as the second cataract, which is recorded on a rock at Gebel Sheikh Suleiman near Wadi Halfa.

Conifer and cedar timber, now used in the construction of tombs and wherever quality wood was required, were obtained from coastal Syria and the Lebanon. Finds of large amounts of Syro-Palestinian pottery are interpreted as evidence for imports of olive oil and perhaps wine. The rest of the goods which were obtained by long-distance trade from Asia or Africa belonged to the luxury category, and included ebony, ivory, resins, obsidian, and lapis lazuli. Routes overland as well as by sea must have been used, and the western Delta seems to have played a particularly prominent role in the latter.

Some fourteen hundred years later, around 1250 BC, an anonymous scribe was copying the names of kings of the past on to an old sheet of papyrus for verification of documents in his office. When he came to the name of Djoser, he changed his reed pen and wrote the name in red, thus acknowledging the reputation Djoser (Netjerikhet) enjoyed at that time. It was not an attempt to mark the beginning of a completely new historic era. Manetho's Third Dynasty starts with Nekherophes, a Graecized form of the name of Nebka whose claim to fame otherwise is slight. To find the reasons for the change between Manetho's Second and Third Dynasties is not easy. Historians, ancient and modern, have tried to impose formal limits and dividing lines on the development of Egypt which started with the beginning of settled life in the Nile valley, but none of these markers are satisfactory. At best, they represent only milestones in the relentless, uninterrupted march towards the civilization usually described as the Old Kingdom.

Small ivory statuettes found in the temple at Nekhen (Hierakonpolis) may represent the beginnings of the typical 'dynastic' style in sculpture in the round, but their dating has not yet been established. Like this female dwarf with a massive wig, some of them probably belonged to items of furniture.

FOUR

ESTABLISHED AND BEAUTIFUL

'Pepy is Established and Beautiful.'★

The family group of Sonb is a fine example of vigorous composition rather than an outstanding work of art. The diminutive figure of the squatting dwarf, his seated wife, and two small children, have been successfully combined to form a pleasing group in which the dwarf's small stature, though not concealed, is made inconspicuous. Sonb held the titles of a 'servant of the god' (hem-netjer) of King Khufu and his successor Radjedef, and the statue was found in his tomb at Giza. This may suggest that he lived during the Fourth Dynasty, but a Sixth Dynasty date is more likely for this type of private sculpture.

IN THE PRESENCE OF THE SPECTACULAR ART and architecture of the Old Kingdom, with pyramids and tombs, one could easily forget that Egyptian society was for its existence entirely dependent on the production of its farmers. The simple agricultural tools and techniques known from representations in Old Kingdom tombs continued scarcely changed for the rest of the country's history. They were found sufficient for the tasks in hand and there was little inducement to improve them.

A selective panorama of farming life, accompanied by short conversations between farmworkers, was included in the repertoire of reliefs of many private tomb-chapels. Thus in one of them, of Sekhem-ankh-ptah of the middle of the Fifth Dynasty, the tomb-owner is described as 'watching the work in the fields: ploughing in the seed, reaping, pulling flax, loading donkeys, threshing with donkeys on threshing-floors, and winnowing'. These activities are shown in several registers before him, and were the main stages of the telescoped agricultural year as depicted by the sculptors who carved tomb-reliefs.

It is unlikely that the Egyptians of the Old Kingdom were able to obtain more than one crop annually. The year started with sowing when the inundation receded at the beginning of winter (ancient Egyptian *peret*, literally 'coming out' of either fields from under water, or seed), our October/November. The names of the most important cereals which were cultivated can be found on the so-called slab-stelae set up against the east face of the superstructures of some of the tombs built near the pyramid of King Khufu at Giza during the Fourth Dynasty. The tomb-owner is represented seated at a table before a long list of offerings, part of which consists of compartments in the form of small granaries with a description of their contents. On one of these stelae, of a 'scribe of divine books' whose name is lost, there are six such granaries with two varieties of barley (Hordeum hexastichon), Upper and Lower Egyptian (*it shema* and *it mehi*), emmer (Triticum dicoccum, *bedet*), an unidentified grain or fruit *besha*, wheat (Triticum aestivum, *sut*), and dates (*bener*), the last included because they were used in brewing beer.

Reliefs show that seed was scattered by hand from small baskets which the sowers carried over their shoulders, and was trodden in by a flock of sheep or a herd of goats, or was ploughed in with a yoke of oxen or cows. The ploughman was usually accompanied by another man urging on the animals. 'Go! ho, go!' shouts the drover of the oxen while encouraging

---

★ *The name of the pyramid of Pepy I at southern Saqqara.*

39

This page and facing page: Desert and riverbank scenes in the tomb of Ptahhotpe, of the late Fifth Dynasty, at Saqqara: hunting with dogs, cutting out the roes of fish, rope-manufacture, making papyrus rafts, netting fowl, and boatmen returning from the marshes engaged in a playful jousting tournament. These are just several miniature episodes from the large panorama of country life unfolding before two large figures of Ptahhotpe on the east wall of his offering-room (opposite two false-doors). To the uninitiated the size of the figures may seem unexpectedly small: the total height of the decorated area of the wall is some 5 Egyptian cubits (c.260 cm), and each of the seven horizontal registers is only between 29 and 43 cm high. The conscious striving to fill the available space entirely by representations and texts is particularly apparent in this tomb-chapel.

them not too gently with a stick, and 'under you, team!', probably reminding them to watch where they are treading. The most versatile of Egyptian agricultural tools, the hoe (*henen*), consisted of a wooden handle with a wooden 'blade' inserted in it by means of a tenon, and strengthened by a rope cross-tie. It was already in use in the Predynastic Period. A hieroglyph representing a plough (*heb*), made entirely of wood, first appeared in the Second Dynasty.

The corn ripened before the beginning of the Egyptian summer, between our February and April. Reaping was done with sickles of the same type as in the Predynastic Period. 'I am telling you, men, the barley is ripe, and he who reaps well will get it,' says the overseer to whom a sample sheaf is being shown for inspection in the tomb of Sekhem-ankh-ptah. 'What is it, then, men? Hurry up, our emmer is ripe!' the overseer goads the reapers in the Fifth Dynasty tomb of Ty at Saqqara. The cut corn was tied in sheaves which were put into large sacks ready for transport. 'Ho! donkey-herd of 2500!' is written in the Fifth Dynasty tomb of the vizier Akhtihotpe over the scene of animals brought in at top speed by men wielding sticks. The laden donkeys were led, some of them reluc-

tantly, to improvised threshing-floors. 'Ho! go!' shouts one drover in the tomb of Sekhem-ankh-ptah, while a comrade advises him of a more effective method: 'Prod him in the rear, my friend!'

Flax-harvesting took place at about the same time, and representations of flax being pulled, tied into bundles, and transported on donkeys, often accompany the grain-harvest in Old Kingdom tombs.

Threshing was done by driving a herd of hoofed animals, usually cattle or donkeys, over sheaves of corn spread on a circular threshing-floor. The animals had to be kept on the move and not allowed to start helping themselves to grain, and the scene is usually one of seeming confusion, with men with sticks shouting at them and at each other at the top of their voices: 'Drive them round then!' 'Hey! I'll hit you if you turn round!' 'Watch what you are doing!'

Winnowing was done by sifting in hand-held sieves, or by tossing what was left on the threshing-floor, after the removal of straw, high in the air with wooden winnowing fans to allow a breeze to blow the chaff away. Unlike all the other agricultural tasks, this was carried out by women. 'Hurry up, my sister!' calls a farmhand at one of the women winnowing

Representations of mock-fights among pole-wielding crews of papyrus rafts returning from fowling expeditions are commonplace. The liveliness of the composition of such scenes is in marked contrast with the formality of the reliefs showing the tomb-owner.

grain in the Sixth Dynasty tomb of Ankh-mahor. 'I'll do as you like!' she says. 'Put your hand in this barley, it is still full of chaff!' a winnower rebukes her companion in the tomb of Ty.

The last stage, described in the tomb of Sekhem-ankh-ptah as 'measuring barley by the council', was carried out by the administrators of the estate: a 'crier' counting the number of measures of corn being stored in the granary, a 'scribe of the granary' recording it, and the 'overseer of the property' who was in charge of the farm, together with the 'keeper of the books of the official property'.

Ground emmer was used for baking many varieties of bread and cakes. Barley, wheat, and dates were the main ingredients for brewing beer.

Cattle-breeding, producing meat, milk, and hides, as well as providing draught animals, played a vital role in the economy of the Old Kingdom. The counting of cattle became the main part of the, initially biennial, and at the end of the Sixth Dynasty annual, census and taxation. An inspection of cattle is a common topic in tomb-reliefs. The vizier Akhtihotpe is accompanied by his eldest son and various officials while 'watching the cattle brought for the festival of the god Thoth from the estates of the spirit (*ka*) and the villages of the official property in Lower and Upper Egypt'. The 'estates of the spirit (*ka*)' were farms which supplied produce for Akhtihotpe's tomb. Herdsmen, some of whom are bringing calves or carrying bundles of fodder to induce the animals to move, are shown leading long-horned oxen (*gen* and *ren iwa*) decorated with large collars round their necks. These were animals to be slaughtered during the festival. The numbers of the inspected livestock are sometimes given; thus, in the Fifth Dynasty tomb of Rakhaef-ankh at Giza, they are 834 head of long-horned cattle, 220 head of hornless cattle, 2234 goats, 760 donkeys, and 974 sheep. Even for a well-to-do priest of the pyramid of Khephren these are very large numbers, and one may assume that they represent the holding of Khephren's cult establishment rather than that of an individual priest.

Parts of the Delta and elevated banks which separated the river from cultivated flood-basins were particularly suitable for grazing cattle. Herdsmen engaged in various bucolic activities often accompany marsh-scenes in tomb-reliefs. 'Herdsman! don't let that bull mount her!' is written above a representation of a man with a stick minding cattle in the Sixth

The hippopotamus was the fiercest and most powerful of the animals of the Nile, and the dangerous and exciting hippopotamus-hunt is sometimes shown in tomb-reliefs. The scene is usually just a cameo detail of a large composition, with the tomb-owner engaged in spearing fish or hunting birds with a throw-stick in the marshes. These were much more leisurely activities where the physical danger was reduced to falling off the papyrus raft. The hunting of hippopotami was an attempt to eliminate a potential danger to people and fields and, therefore, it cannot be properly described as sport. In this scene the prow of the papyrus skiff of the tomb-owner, Princess Sesh-seshet Idut of the Sixth Dynasty, is visible above the harpooned hippopotami.

Dynasty tomb of Khunes at Zawiyet el-Amwat. 'Hey! my darling, eat the bread!' a soft-hearted herdsman sitting on the ground beside a lying ox cajoles his charge on a relief in the Saqqara tomb of the vizier Ptahhotpe. Milking scenes occur, as well as depictions of cows suckling calves. 'Pull hard, herdsman, she is in pain!' an overseer commands in a calving scene where a cow with a swishing tail, a twisted head, and a bulging eye shows all the signs of distress.

Pigs were not represented in tomb-reliefs of the Old Kingdom. Attempts were made to breed, or at least keep in captivity, wild animals such as oryxes. This was caused by the traditional, by then outdated, requirements for certain offerings in the funerary cult, rather than by purely economic reasons. On one of the wooden panels which served as stelae (gravestones) in the Saqqara tomb of Hezyre, dating from the beginning of the Third Dynasty, 'sprinkling water', 'washing the hands', and 'burning incense', followed by 'wine', a stand with a bowl containing some unspecified food, 'a young oryx', and a joint of meat on a plate, are listed above the symbolic table with loaves of bread at which Hezyre sits.

Gardens supplied vegetables and fruit. 'Watering vegetable patches in

Herdsmen with cattle fording a canal in the late Sixth Dynasty tomb of Princess Sesh–seshet Idut at Saqqara.

the garden of the official property by a gardener' is among the scenes in the Fifth Dynasty Saqqara tomb of Niankh-khnum and Khnumhotpe. A carefully prepared bed of lettuce, with small channels bringing water to each plant, can be seen in the tomb of Mereruka. Gardeners are watering the vegetables from pots which they carry on a yoke across their shoulders, while others are harvesting the crop. Onions or garlic are pulled up by a kneeling man on a relief from the early Sixth Dynasty tomb of Niankh-nesut. Cucumbers, leeks, beans, lentils, and melons were also grown.

Fruit-trees and vines were cultivated. A royal decree issued for Metjen, who lived in the early Fourth Dynasty and had it recorded in his tomb at Saqqara, granted him a 'land property 200 cubits long and 200 cubits wide, enclosed by a wall, equipped, and planted with useful trees; a very large pond is to be made in it, and fig-trees and vines are to be planted'. Such an orchard-cum-vineyard is represented in the Giza tomb of Iymery of the Fifth Dynasty. Two men are scaring away birds, while another two are climbing trees picking figs and some other fruit. The four most characteristic processes of viticulture come next: men picking grapes from vines trained on trellises, treading them in a crushing vat, pressing

Hunting of desert animals, such as oryxes and gazelles, sometimes aimed at capturing animals alive, so that they could be used for breeding or as sacrificial animals. In other cases, particularly when hounds were used, hunting was a sport. This scene, which also shows a lion attacking a bull, is in the early Sixth Dynasty tomb of Mereruka at Saqqara.

must in a sack by twisting long poles attached to it, and finally filling wine-jars.

Figs and wine played the role of Egyptian food of the gods. The resurrected king is 'one of the four gods fashioned by the earth-god Geb, who traverse Upper Egypt and who traverse Lower Egypt, who lean on their staffs, who are anointed with unguent, who are dressed in red linen, who live on figs and who drink wine'. Dates were the most important among the other fruits, some only known by their names and as yet unidentified, which contributed to Egyptian diet during the Old Kingdom. Bee-keeping was practised, and a honey-harvest scene was among those in the sun-temple of Neuserre.

Groups of men netting fish and others trapping wild fowl were frequently represented episodes of life by the Nile. 'It is coming and it is bringing a good catch of fish!' exclaims one of the men heaving a large net which is alive with a variety of fish in the tomb of Ty. 'There are some good fish in it!' agrees his companion. 'What fishing, what a catch!' incredulously repeats one of the fishermen in the Fifth Dynasty tomb of Neferirt-nef. Reliefs show fish being cut open for drying and their roes extracted for the preparation of a relish (botargo), as well as being cooked on a spit over a fire.

Wild fowl was usually caught with large clap-nets. When the birds were enticed to settle down and feed on food scattered inside the net, it was closed with a rope pulled by men lying in wait. In the Sixth Dynasty tomb of Udjaha-teti at Saqqara the men, who have just vigorously closed the net and fallen over on the ground from the effort, tell each other with obvious pleasure: 'There are all kinds of catch in it!' In addition to catching wild fowl, there were also poultry-yards for breeding geese and ducks.

Bread and beer, supplemented by vegetables, fruit, and an occasional fish or fowl, with meat probably being an exceptional luxury, represented the diet of ordinary Egyptians. Offering-lists in Old Kingdom tombs give us some idea about the composition of the menu of upper-class Egyptians, but this was, no doubt, radically different from that of ordinary people in its range of food-items. Such a list appears above and in front of the table with bread-loaves at which Nikanesut is seated on a relief in his tomb at Giza. The list includes nineteen different kinds of bread and cakes, seven varieties of beer and two of wine, ten different cuts of beef, four species of fowl, seven types of fruit, wheat and barley, with onions as the only vegetable. Some of the entries in the list are repeated and probably represent varieties which were not further specified in the list, as in the case of wine, and so the number of items may be even higher.

Some of the foodstuffs produced by the farmers were used to satisfy their own needs. Much of the produce, however, was intended for the many temples and tomb-chapels serving the cult of the dead. The most spectacular of these were connected with pyramids. They represent the ultimate in Egyptian achievement in large-scale technology and organization. While, apparently, little attempt was made to distinguish the king's tomb by its size and form from those of his relatives and officials during

The old constructional principle of step pyramids, based on buttresses of masonry surrounding the central core, was retained even in true pyramids, and each of them thus contains a step pyramid inside its structure. These buttresses can be clearly seen on the tower-shaped ruin of the pyramid at Maidum. The Maidum pyramid was originally conceived as a step pyramid and subsequently modified to a true pyramid by additional casing, but the enormous pressures thus created were underestimated by its architect. This led to its partial collapse, though it seems that this did not happen until some time in the Middle Ages. The pyramid was originally built for the last king of the Third Dynasty and probably completed by Snofru.

the First Dynasty, we find the situation radically altered at the beginning of the Third. This impression of a sudden change is probably only illusory. The rock-cut substructures of the presumed royal tombs of the Second Dynasty at Saqqara have completely lost their brick-built buildings above ground, and if these reflected in any way the size of the galleries below ground, they would easily provide the missing link demonstrating the gradual increase in size in comparison with private tombs.

The ability to raise a large structure in stone appeared in Egypt at the beginning of the Third Dynasty. The earliest record of a stone building dates to the end of the reign of King Nebka, the first king of the Third Dynasty. One of his years in the 'annals' on the so-called Palermo Stone includes 'erecting [the building called] Men-netjeret in stone'. The structure has not yet been located. Shortly afterwards, a stone-built tomb was begun for his successor, King Netjerikhet, at Saqqara. It is not easy to be certain about the motive behind the departure in form from a mastaba, i.e. a flat-roofed tomb whose outside faces showed only a slight incline, to a stepped pyramid. It is possible that it was but a new presentation of an old concept. The core of some of the brick-built mastabas of the First Dynasty at Saqqara contained another superstructure in the form of a low and presumably truncated pyramid of many small steps above the burial chamber. This may have represented the original grave mound and been connected with the idea of the mythical mound on which life first appeared, while the mastaba's exterior, the niche façade, imitated the outward appearance of the royal palace. Mastabas of high officials, who at that time belonged to the royal family, and presumably also those of kings, thus combined a grave containing the body of the deceased with a dwelling for the continued existence of his spirit (*ka*). It would not have been uncharacteristic of Egyptian thinking to have preserved one within the other, and the fact that the concealed structure was not visible to human eyes was irrelevant. In the case of the step pyramid of King Netjerikhet both elements are present, but they are separated physically: the concealed mound is now freed and represented by the step pyramid, while the niche façade of the mastaba is now imitated by the niched enclosure wall of the whole complex.

The next significant change in the appearance of the royal tomb and its ancillary buildings occurred some seventy years later, at the beginning of the Fourth Dynasty. The innovations introduced at that time were so wide-ranging that they must have had their origins in the sphere of religion rather than technology. It is not improbable that other buildings, probably brick-built, were associated with step pyramids in the Nile valley, but none have been located so far. Pyramids of the Fourth Dynasty now had a monumental stone-built entrance (valley temple) at the edge of cultivation. This was connected by a causeway to a cult temple against the east face of the pyramid which stood in the desert. The cult temple was the main element of the now fully developed royal pyramid-complex, where daily rituals were conducted and token offerings presented to the spirit of the dead king. The pyramid was but a monumental sealed tomb which did not play a direct part in the maintenance of the cult. The pyramid-complex, the pyramid-town in the valley and its personnel, and the land and other possessions which constituted their economic basis, together formed the king's cult establishment.

At first, the cult temple had been situated to the north of the pyramid. Egyptian architects were, however, remarkably flexible and inventive in their approach to converting the demands imposed by religion into

Below left: Only one valley temple of the three pyramid-complexes at Giza, that of Khephren, can be visited. Khufu's valley temple is hidden under the houses of the village of Nazlet es-Simman to the east of the pyramid-plateau, and in view of the remarkably complete state of the rest of the complex its excavation sometime in the future offers a most exciting prospect. Menkaure's valley temple was unfinished at the time of the king's death, and the remains of its walls have, since its discovery, been once again covered by the sand. Khephren's valley temple impresses by the sobriety of its design, and is the best demonstration of the total dominance of straight lines—mostly at right angles—in Old Kingdom architecture.

Below right: The pyramid of Unas was the first in which the interior walls were inscribed with the Pyramid Texts. These inscriptions can be divided among some 750 utterances, or 2,300 shorter spells. Most of them appear in the six pyramids of kings and the three pyramids of queens, which contain the Pyramid Texts, but their selection and arrangement are not always the same.

reality. They were not afraid to improvise when forced to do so by circumstances: thus Userkaf's pyramid at Saqqara has its temple against its south face, presumably because of the presence of an earlier structure to the east, and the temple of Neuserre at Abusir was built off the central axis of the pyramid for the same reason. The changes in the orientation of the cult temple which took place in the Fourth Dynasty, accentuating the east–west axis of the complex, were of a different type and a more permanent nature. They were probably due to a modification of beliefs concerning the king's afterlife. The earlier notions of celestial voyages undertaken in the company of gods had been reflected in the predominantly northern orientation towards the north star. Now they were combined with the ideas about the kingdom of the underworld god of the west, Osiris, and confirmed by a western orientation.

One of the conspicuous features of ancient Egyptian mentality was the reluctance to abandon an old concept in the face of a new one. Combination of motifs and elements, and re-interpretation and syncretization of ideas were preferred. This was perhaps a reflection of a different approach to the notion of progress from that prevalent in modern societies. From the Fourth Dynasty on, the cult temple was regularly situated near the eastern face of the pyramid, but a small chapel continued to be built against the pyramid's northern face for the rest of the Old Kingdom.

The royal tomb itself changed its form from a step pyramid to a true pyramid at the beginning of the Fourth Dynasty. We have no solid evidence for the reasoning behind the change. It may have been the next logical modification to make in the development of the royal tomb, a true pyramid being the simplest and most perfect form which a structure with a rectangular ground plan can adopt, but it may have been an imitation of the summit of the obelisk associated with the sun-god Re of Iunu (Heliopolis). It was in the Fourth Dynasty, in the reign of Radjedef, that the royal epithets associating the king with Re appeared, and the name of the god now became a standard component of the king's *ni-sut-bit* name.

While each of the pyramids of the Fourth and Fifth Dynasties was of an individual design, all those of the Sixth Dynasty were, at least outwardly, of the same type: 150 by 150 cubits (78.75 metres, or about 250 feet) in ground plan, and 100 cubits (52.20 metres or 171 feet) high. Standardization was, as a rule, consciously avoided by the Egyptians, even though uniform tombs were built by Khufu for his family and officials at Giza. The state may have already experienced difficulties in undertaking large-scale projects, and pyramids of a standard size may have reduced the organizational problems. A pyramid of this size was still an impressive building, though modest in comparison with its predecessors, and would have simplified the planning decisions at the outset of the work.

The basic layout of the pyramid complex of the Fourth to Sixth Dynasties (valley temple, causeway, cult temple, pyramid) was imitated in sun-temples built during the Fifth Dynasty, and indicates that in the Old Kingdom there was a generally accepted concept of a purposefully designed and built temple. A large masonry obelisk (not monolithic) of the sun-temple served as the focal point of the upper temple. The open plan and decorative scheme stressed the beneficial influence of the sun-god and the ritual occasions of the reign, such as jubilee-festivals, sanctioned by him. Only two sun-temples, those of Userkaf and Neuserre, have so far been located with certainty and excavated, while another four, which are mentioned in texts, still await discovery.

Detailed information about the appearance of temples of local gods is almost completely lacking. With the possible exceptions of the temples of Re-Harakhti at Iunu (Heliopolis) and of Ptah at Ineb-hedj (Memphis),

The burial chamber of Ptah-shepses, the vizier of Neuserre, at Abusir. It contains a graffito which represents a method used by the stonemason to work out the measurements of the irregularly shaped lintel from data supplied by the architect. Egyptian geometry was entirely practical, and the author of the graffito was only as much a geometrician as a scribe adding and subtracting the number of bread-loaves in administrative documents was a mathematician.

the amount of royal building activities in these local temples probably remained limited throughout the Old Kingdom.

At Saqqara, royal tombs of the Second Dynasty and the step pyramids of the Third formed an isolated group some distance into the desert, with no tombs of lesser beings in their immediate vicinity. This was the concept of the original *ta djeser*, usually translated as 'sacred land', or 'necropolis', but which perhaps more accurately meant 'secluded region'. It was a continuation of the traditional arrangement of the earlier necropolis at Abydos. Non-royal tombs must have been built at some distance to the east, close to the valley. Such a strict separation of royalty and officialdom changed with the pyramid itself in the Fourth Dynasty. The area near the pyramid of the king now became crowded with tombs of members of the royal family, king's officials, priests, and craftsmen. The most prominent queens were buried in small subsidiary pyramids.

The king was at first deemed responsible for the provision of private tombs for the rest of the royal family and his officials. Snofru and Khufu carried out this duty in an exemplary fashion by laying out tombs for future use in a regular pattern in the neighbourhood of their pyramids as soon as space became available. The number of people who were able to secure a tomb in the royal necropolis grew, and the uniformity very quickly disappeared during the reigns which followed. Nevertheless,

Much of the stone required for building the Giza pyramids came from the vicinity of the site. This created a number of artificial rock faces which started in the reign of Khephren to be used for the complete or partial cutting of private tombs. Rock-cut tombs seem to have existed at northern Saqqara even earlier, so the idea was not new, but there natural rock cliffs were employed. Cost-saving was the main consideration. The tomb of Meresankh, one of the queens of Khephren, presents a combination of the rock-cut and free-standing techniques, with superstructure built over a rock-cut chapel. Some of the tomb features, including statues of the tomb-owner and relatives, were also cut in the living rock, and this method made the statues seem as if they were placed in niches.

proximity to the royal pyramid always remained an important consideration in the choice of the tomb-site for reasons of convenience and safety
from depredations. While, with only one exception, the rulers of the Old
Kingdom adopted pyramids for their burials, mastabas continued to
serve as private tombs. It is possible that the first stone-built private
mastaba at Saqqara was contemporary with the step pyramid of Netjerikhet, but it was not until the reign of Khufu that crews of royal workmen
built them in large numbers at Giza. The earliest Giza tombs with rock-
cut chapels, which opportunely used rock faces left after the quarrying of
stone for pyramids, are only a little later, but even there Saqqara may have
been in the forefront of development. Despite this, brick-built mastabas
continued to be used for the rest of the Old Kingdom on account of their
comparative cheapness and convenience.

To understand the formal development of the private tomb and its
elements in the Old Kingdom, it is necessary to go back to the beginning
of Egyptian history. Above ground, the mastabas of the First Dynasty
were solid structures with the underground burial chamber inaccessible.
The façade round these brick-built mastabas consisted of a series of niches
imitating doorways ('palace façade') among which one, in the eastern
face near the south-eastern corner, served as the focus for the posthumous
cult. We can conjecture that this was the place to which offerings required
by the spirit (*ka*) of the deceased were brought and where the ritual of
presentation was conducted. A person standing outside the mastaba in
front of this niche was facing west, the traditional Egyptian abode of the
dead, and although we have no textual evidence from this early part of
Egyptian history for this belief, already in the Predynastic Period most of

Individual private statues were by far the most common. Pair statues (man and wife, mother and daughter, etc.) and family groups were known, but really large groups were unique to statues cut in the living rock. This group of ten represents the women of Queen Meresankh's family at Giza, some probably shown more than once.

The pyramid-complex was surrounded by tombs which formed the pyramid cemetery. The workshops with craftsmen employed in the building of tombs and the maintenance of their funerary cults were located in the pyramid-town. There were precise reasons why a particular pyramid cemetery was chosen for the siting of a tomb. The tomb-owner may have served in the king's administration and the tomb or parts of it may have been royal gifts, or he may have been connected with the king's cult establishment. Family tradition and the place of origin were also of some importance. As a rule of thumb, it can be said that a man's tomb was built close to where his wealth and influence lay in his lifetime. Although of the Sixth Dynasty, Meryre-nufer Qar, who was 'overseer of the pyramid-towns of Khufu and Menkaure', and 'inspector of priests of the pyramid of Khephren', was buried in the old Fourth Dynasty cemetery at Giza.

the bodies were oriented towards the west. In the Second Dynasty a gravestone ('niche-stela') was placed at the back of this niche. In the Third Dynasty the niche developed into a small room approached by a narrow corridor, as if it had been withdrawn into the body of the mastaba for protection. This, indeed, was exactly what happened. A rudimentary one-room chapel was thus formed and the focus of the cult was now transferred from the outer face of the mastaba to the far wall of this chapel. The niche, formerly in the outer face of the mastaba, was now reproduced within the chapel itself. Such a transfer of function from one part of the structure to another without disturbing the underlying logic is characteristic of Egyptian thinking and can be observed time and again in burial customs. When the niche façade completely disappeared from outside the mastaba in the Second Dynasty, it re-appeared on the coffin which was also regarded as the house of the spirit (*ka*).

The fully stone-lined niche ('false-door' stela) was at first the only decorated feature of the chapel, but gradually reliefs started to take more and more space on its walls. The original single room within the body of the mastaba (though there may have been others outside) was added to until by the Sixth Dynasty virtually the whole superstructure was occupied in this way, thus in effect creating the semblance of a house. The burial chamber, which in the Old Kingdom was regularly at the bottom of a shaft dug in the rock substratum, was inaccessible, and it was only in the Sixth Dynasty that decoration extended there to even a limited degree. With the decrease in the number of large decorated chapels already becoming apparent, the burial chamber and particularly the coffin now took over some of the essential decorative elements of tomb chapels. When, during the general decline which followed the end of the Old

Kingdom, decoration virtually disappeared from tomb-chapels, it was only the false-door stela (i.e. the successor of the original niche in the façade) and the coffin which retained some of it, as if the cycle of development had been completed and only the essentials were left.

The original reason for the decoration of tomb-chapels was to provide the spirit (*ka*) of the deceased with the necessities of its continued existence in the after-life. On stelae of the Second Dynasty the tomb-owner is seated at a table above which is a list of offerings which could be read aloud if anybody wanted to make the 'presentation of offerings by voice'. As decoration extended to the walls of the chapel, some of the activities now shown in tomb reliefs were closely connected with the idea of provisioning, particularly the scenes of butchery. Others, depicting scenes taking place on the tomb-owner's estate or his household, represent an evolution of this concept: husbandry, netting fish and fowl, crafts, baking, cooking, brewing, and feasting. Other topics may have originally been of the same type, but now became traditional and perhaps were understood differently, e.g. the fowling and fishing in marshes. The tomb-owner is taking an active part in these scenes, rather than watching others as he does almost everywhere else. These activities may have been symbolic, and were not necessarily simple records of pleasure. Some of the scenes were included because they were associated with the main themes represented, though far from being essential: boatmen equipped with long poles are shown engaged in a jousting tournament beside netting fish, a flute-player accompanies reapers harvesting corn, and a pet baboon is 'helping' men pressing must by twisting poles attached to a sack of crushed grapes.

The tomb was built for eternity, and so it was a good place in which to record legal texts, particularly those concerning its endowment, letters

The chapel of the tomb of Meryre-nufer Qar was rock-cut; its mastaba-shaped superstructure, now lost, was stone-built. In the Giza necropolis such use of two different building methods was common. Some uniformity in the plans of tomb-chapels can be discerned during the Third and Fourth Dynasties, but later practically every tomb represented an individual combination of the prescribed tomb elements.

The greywacke triads (groups of three) of Menkaure were found in the valley temple of his pyramid-complex at Giza. The king is shown accompanied by the goddess Hathor (with the sun-disc and horns), who was the patron deity of the valley where the temple was located, and by a personification of an Egyptian district, in this case Hu (Diospolis Parva). Menkaure's valley temple contained a series of such statues, but it seems that not all the districts were represented. This creates some problems when we try to explain their presence in the temple. It is likely that their purpose was similar to that of reliefs showing district processions in other pyramid-complexes. The statues are relatively small, around 95 cm (37 inches) high, and this invariably comes as a shock to those conditioned by monumental works of art of the later periods.

received from the king, and autobiographical texts. Representations of funerals perhaps followed a pattern similar to that set by the decoration of temples by showing activities closely connected with the structure itself. As tomb decoration became varied, the craftsman/artist himself began to exercise greater personal influence over the selection of themes within the limits imposed on him by the purpose of the building.

The connection between reliefs and three-dimensional sculptures was very close. The style which can be observed in the art of the Old Kingdom had its roots in relief used in the court art of the late Predynastic Period. Sculptures in the round developed later. This is the picture obtained from excavated material, but the same sequence can be deduced from some of the characteristics of statues which show their origin in 'two-dimensional' relief. Already the earliest male standing statues invariably show the left foot advanced in the typically Egyptian 'flat-footed' posture. There are two reasons for this: the favourite 'main' direction in Egyptian two-dimensional art, as well as writing, was for figures and hieroglyphs to face right, while one of the basic representational rules was that none of the important elements should be obscured. For the Egyptians the ideas of completeness and perfection were almost identical. If we imagine two people of the same height, both facing right, represented side by side on the same base-line, it has to be the person farther away from us whose face is projected slightly forward of the face of the nearer person. If represented differently, the man's face, his most characteristic feature, would be obscured. In the case of the feet of a man standing facing right it is the left foot which is shown slightly advanced, even if the person is just standing, not striding. A sculptor started to make a statue by sketching its profile on a stone block from which he was going to carve, and thus introduced this element into three-dimensional sculpture.

Tomb-statues were deposited in *serdabs*, rooms made inaccessible to human beings for reasons of safety, but which were easily penetrable by the spirit. The statue's function as substitute abode for the spirit (*ka*) did not lead to attempts to produce a faithful likeness of the person in his or her tomb statues, because individuality was given them by the inscription of the tomb-owner's name.

Royal sculpture was of a much higher standard than private sculpture, and produced a larger variety of types. Many royal statues were innovative, and while some set patterns which were imitated for the rest of Egyptian history, others were not to be seen again. There is little doubt about their individuality, resulting from the attempt to portray the facial features of the king, as well as from the stylistic peculiarities of the sculptors or their schools.

Radjedef was the first king, and apparently also the last, to be represented with a small figure of one of his queens squatting by his legs. In sharp contrast, a pair statue of Menkaure and his queen, probably Khamerernebti II, standing by his side, is a study in dignity as well as affection. Both Radjedef's and Menkaure's sculptures served as the prototypes for many private statues of a husband and a wife.

Almost all statues were considerably less than life-size, and although colossal statues existed, they were quite exceptional. The material of royal statues varied greatly, with the more prestigious hard stone preferred, but even wood and copper were used. An entry in the 'annals' for one of the years of King Nebka of the Third Dynasty runs as follows: 'The year of: fashioning the copper statue called King Khasekhemui who is tall of the White Crown. The height of inundation on the fields: two cubits, six palms, two and a half fingers.' The sculpture was probably made of metal shaped by hammering and joined by rivets. Giving names to royal statues was a common Egyptian practice, and the episode shows that copper was still regarded as a very prestigious material. This sculpture has not been preserved, but similarly made statues of Pepy I and Merenre were found at Nekhen (Hierakonpolis).

Private statues were only very rarely made by sculptors capable of endowing them with individual features, even though we cannot always establish whether they are lifelike representations of their subjects. Some of the statues belonging to this category date to the Fourth Dynasty and were produced in royal workshops, e.g. the seated vizier Hemyunu dating to the reign of Khufu, or the bust of the vizier Ankh-haf, probably of the reign of Khephren. The apparent stagnation in the standard of private sculpture after the end of the Fourth Dynasty was because most statues were now ordered privately, and the ability of craftsmen available to a private individual was much lower than that of the top sculptors of the royal workshops who made some of the statues of the Fourth Dynasty.

The uniformity of types (seated, standing, scribe, and groups) was due to the fact that they were all tomb-statues, placed in *serdabs* and later in burial chambers, and thus performed identical roles. Several of them of different forms and materials may have been made for the same tomb. Private statues of the Old Kingdom are small, examples over fifty centimetres (twenty inches) in height being exceptional, and most of them were originally painted.

A greater variety occurred in the so-called servant statuettes. These were statuettes representing members of the tomb-owner's household performing various menial tasks, mostly connected with the preparation of food. Tomb provisioning, the same idea that inspired the earliest reliefs, must have led to the introduction of these sculptures in tombs.

Monumental architecture in stone is incomparably better known than domestic architecture in unbaked mud brick because its chances of preservation are much greater. Furthermore, continuous habitation in the cultivated area has largely obliterated traces of earlier dwellings. In the peasants' houses a corridor led to a rectangular walled open courtyard serving for a variety of purposes, such as a working area, a place for keeping animals, and probably also for cooking, with one or several

The earliest royal statue of the Old Kingdom was discovered in a closed room, serdab ('cellar' in Arabic), near the step pyramid of King Netjerikhet at Saqqara. The limestone statue is nearly life-size, and shows the king, enveloped in a tight-fitting cloak, seated on a massive throne, with his names inscribed on the front of the pedestal. The garment of Netjerikhet was the type worn during the jubilee-festival. Buildings erected for the festival were imitated in Netjerikhet's pyramid enclosure, and the festival was a frequent theme of decoration of royal temples. The present rather grim expression on the face of the king is due to the later plunderers of the temple gouging out the inlaid eyes.

roofed rooms at the back. The dwellings of settlers in the communally built 'pyramid-towns' present a surprisingly complex arrangement round a central court, with halls, bedrooms, a bathroom, and a storeroom.

The building of pyramids, temples, and tombs gave an enormous boost to the development of certain crafts, particularly those connected with the 'necropolis industry', but many of the products manufactured by crafts-men of the Old Kingdom were intended for everyday life. As before, metals worked were mainly copper and gold (or electrum). A metal-workers' shop, with various operations under way, is shown among the scenes on the walls of the causeway leading to the pyramid temple of King Unas at Saqqara. Electrum, an alloy of gold and silver, is the metal used by craftsmen in this scene, together with copper. Four kneeling men are cold-hammering the metal into sheets with stone hammers, while two of their colleagues are melting electrum in a crucible by blowing into long blowpipes in order to force the fire. The manufacture of metal vessels is shown next. One man is squatting on the ground either hammering a large bowl to shape over a wooden core or polishing it, and others are finishing a large vase and two spouted ewers and basins. The weighing of metal ingots and their recording takes place next to a metalworker with a blowpipe, perhaps casting the blade of an adze which his companion is shown sharpening.

Hammering remained the only method used to harden the cutting edge of cast tools. Copper implements found among the funerary equipment of Khufu's mother Hetep-heres I at Giza, perhaps uninten-tionally left behind by workmen, include a heavy chisel, a chasing tool ('punch'), and a knife in a decayed wooden handle. A copper ewer and a basin were found in the same tomb. The ewer was shaped by beating, but its spout was cast and fixed to it by cold hammering. Copper had its uses even in architecture. The drainage system of the pyramid temple of Sahure at Abusir employed hammered copper pipes, and a length of it was found still in situ when the temple was excavated.

Gold was cast as well as hammered. Sheet gold was used for covering objects made of wood, usually over a layer of plaster, and for plating other metals.

Carpenters and cabinet-makers manufactured a wide range of objects, in particular furniture and house-fittings, as well as items of tomb and temple equipment. On the relief in the Fifth Dynasty tomb of Ty at Saqqara a tall shrine, presumably for a standing statue, and a low chest on small legs, are being smoothed by two men with polishing stones (the plane was not known). This was the last stage of their manufacture, and most items being made by Old Kingdom craftsmen are shown like this, almost complete. A squatting man is shaping a plank with an adze, while another is vigorously sawing through a piece of timber attached in an upright position to a pole. 'Take another! It is hot!' is the advice given to him in the text concerning the large pullsaw. 'Polishing a bed of ebony by polishers from the official property' runs the description above two men busy with a bed, and 'a carpenter drilling a chest' above a kneeling man using a bowdrill.

Animal-legged beds, stools, and chairs, as well as chests and boxes, and also doors, door-bolts, and wooden columns for houses, and coffins and shrines for tombs and temples, were made by woodworkers. Axes, adzes, saws, bowdrills, and various chisels and mallets were the main tools used by Old Kingdom carpenters.

Several other crafts are shown next to metalworkers in the early Sixth Dynasty tomb of Ankh-mahor at Saqqara. Sculptors are busy carving and painting wooden statues. Four men are seated on the ground, each beside

The largest statue of the Old Kingdom is at Giza. The word sphinx may derive from Egyptian sheshep ankh, 'living image', i.e. statue. The sculpture, some sixty metres (about 200 feet) long, represents a creature with the body of a lion, and the head of a king wearing the royal nemes-headcloth. The concept is the exact opposite of the usual way in which many deities were represented, with a human body and an animal's head. The idea of a lion guarding the entrance to a temple was known even earlier, and the sphinx at Giza was probably intended to protect the approach to the pyramid-complex of Khephren. The skill with which the two elements were combined is remarkable, as is the ease displayed in working on an unprecedented scale. There is no evidence that the sphinx enjoyed any form of worship in its own right during the Old Kingdom.

a stone vessel, two of which are being drilled and another two polished. The range and quality of stone vessels declined during the Old Kingdom in comparison with the preceding period, and they seem to have been chiefly used as containers for materials distributed from royal storehouses or traded with abroad.

On the same wall, three leatherworkers are manufacturing leather sacks and containers. One is making a skin more pliable by passing it over a wooden trestle, while another is cutting a piece of leather. Dyeing of leather was known. Sandals, various bags, sacks, boxes, and furniture fittings were made, with goatskins serving as containers for water, and rawhide was used for lashing blades of tools to their handles or hafts, or for joining parts of furniture. Skins of wild animals were worn on special occasions.

Jewellers complete the contingent of Ankh-mahor's workshop. Dwarfs were often employed in the manufacture of jewellery, and three pairs of them are shown here seated at low tables making a broad collar and two large collar counterpoises (*menit*). Similar items, also made of beads, are strung by jewellers in the register below. Scenes in other tombs show beads for such collars being drilled.

Pottery-making is only infrequently represented, the Fifth Dynasty mastaba of Ty at Saqqara being one of the few exceptions. A large pottery kiln is shown, with its minder squatting in front of it shielding his face from the heat, together with a man shaping a pot on a slow wheel, and several others finishing pots by hand.

Monumental building used up huge quantities of stone which had to be quarried and brought to the site. Most of the material was limestone quarried locally, preferably in the immediate vicinity of the building site. Limestone of better quality, used for the outer casing of structures and for lining the interior walls of tomb-chapels, came from the quarries at Roau (Tura), and had to be ferried from across the river.

Other stone used in building and making sarcophagi, altars, and statues travelled long distances: red and black granite from Aswan and Nubia, diorite from near Toshka in the southern part of the Western Desert, alabaster from Hatnub and greywacke from Wadi Hammamat, both in the Eastern Desert. These quarries were not opened permanently, but special expeditions were sent to them to bring material when it was required. A graffito at Hatnub, dated to the 'year after the sixth census' of Teti, mentions a force of 300 men taking part in such an expedition, while another may refer to as many as 1000 men. The leader of a quarrying expedition was usually described as 'treasurer of the god' (*sedjauty netjer*) and 'overseer of the task force' (*imy-ra mesha*).

Quarrymen and stonemasons were organized in the same way as the contingent of a boat. The largest unit was a crew (*aper*) of some hundred men which, for administrative purposes, had a name, such as 'Great', 'Pure', 'August', 'Satisfied', but apparently also 'Drunk'. This was usually connected with the name of the king for whom the crew worked. The crew was divided into five watches (*za*): starboard and port bows, starboard and port stern, and rudder, each consisting of two gangs of ten men.

Egyptian communications and transport during the Old Kingdom relied almost entirely on river and canal traffic. Large ships built of wood appeared when monumental building in stone began and the need for bringing large quantities of heavy materials to the building sites arose in the Third Dynasty. Egypt always was a country short of quality wood, and although local woods such as sycamore and acacia were used for small boats, timber had to be imported from the Lebanon and coastal Syria for the construction of large craft. Even these were built in the typically ancient Egyptian manner which showed that their ancestors were papyrus rafts, and so their hulls had no keel. Boat-builders working on smaller boats for everyday use are shown in a number of tombs. Small rafts were made of papyrus, but they were of limited life and carrying capacity, and so they were only used by peasants and herdsmen for crossing canals and marshy areas, or possibly by noblemen during fishing and fowling expeditions.

Even the heaviest stone elements could be transported in boats. In the reliefs of Unas' causeway, large monolithic palm-capital columns of Aswan red granite for the pyramid-temple of Unas are shown being shipped to Saqqara. The Egyptian artist cannot be entirely trusted to have accurately rendered the relative sizes of the boats and the columns, but the barges are described as 'laden with granite columns of twenty cubits', i.e. about 10.5 metres or 34 feet. Two columns are shipped in each barge, and so it appears that these must have been over 30 metres (100 feet) long. None of the barges has been preserved, though a ceremonial barque over 40 metres (134 feet) long has been found near the pyramid of Khufu at Giza. All valley temples of pyramid-complexes of the Old Kingdom were connected with the river by canals which, while the structures were being built, served as the main means of approach for all traffic. According to a fragment of an autobiographical text of an official responsible for transport it took seven days to cover the river distance of over 900 kilometres (600 miles) from Aswan to the capital.

The Nile is very suitable for river traffic, and there was no need to build special harbours or landing places. The granite region of the first cataract south of Aswan presented a natural barrier to boats and attempts to cut channels which would have enabled even larger ships to pass are known to have been made.

Egyptian sea-going ships displayed special modifications in comparison with boats intended for river traffic. The most significant of these was a cable connecting the bows and the stern above the deck, so-called hogging-truss, which provided a longitudinal support and thus compensated for the absence of a keel. Egyptian sea-going ability cannot be disputed, but it is likely that during these trips Egyptian ships were hugging the Levantine or Red Sea coast rather than venturing on high seas.

Although the concept of the wheel was known and employed for several purposes, roads in our sense did not exist during the Old Kingdom. Light loads were carried on donkeys along narrow tracks skirting the cultivated fields. Donkeys were also the only animals known to have been ridden. Wheeled transport did not exist. Heavy objects, almost exclusively building materials and funerary items such as stone sarcophagi, were transported on wooden sleds, dragged by cattle along sand- or mud-covered paths specially prepared to reduce friction. Only short distances were, as a rule, covered in this way, the only notable exceptions being mining and quarrying expeditions sent deep into the deserts, in which human force probably played the decisive part.

Donkeys were the only animals known during the Old Kingdom which could be used for long-distance expeditions, but their limited carrying capability and the need for bringing a supply of water for them imposed limits on the length of such trips. The 'overseer of Upper Egypt', Harkhuf, describes several expeditions to the southern land of Yam in his tomb at Qubbet el-Hawa during the reigns of Merenre and Pepy II. Three hundred donkeys made up his caravan during one trip, and the duration of two of these trips is given as seven and eight months.

There is no evidence in the form of texts for the state of astronomical and advanced mathematical knowledge during the Old Kingdom, but

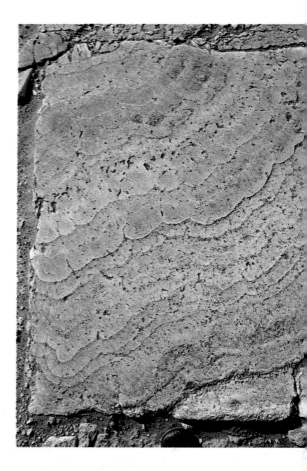

The attitude of the Egyptians towards stone in architecture seems to have been quite different from their approach to sculpture. Statues of the most visually attractive materials were, nevertheless, often painted. On the other hand, for temples a judicious choice was made of contrasting colours of polished alabaster, basalt, granite and quartzite.

59

the precise orientation and the accurate measurements of buildings show the Egyptians' ability to solve the practical tasks involved in constructing monuments. Their approach to mathematical problems and their solution was, no doubt, entirely empirical rather than theoretical.

The Egyptian calendar was a practical consequence of astronomical awareness. A state like Egypt, with a sophisticated bureaucratic system, needed a calendar for advance planning and a reliable dating system. The calendar year had 365 days divided into three seasons of four months, each of thirty days, with five extra (epagomenal) days. In theory, New Year's Day coincided with the arrival of the annual inundation and so introduced the first season, *akhet*. The heliacal (pre-dawn) rising of Sirius after a period of invisibility also took place for the first time around this date. Two factors, however, made sure that all these events rarely occurred on exactly the same day. Firstly, the river did not start rising at the same time every year, and the variation could be considerable. Secondly, the calendar year was about a quarter of a day shorter than the astronomical year, and since no provision (such as a leap year) had been made to rectify the error, the calendar and the seasons were getting more and more out of step, at the rate of one month every 120 years. At the end of the Old Kingdom the difference, as compared with its beginning, was some five months, and the date expressed in terms of a season, month, and day of the civil calendar lost all relationship to the real season of nature.

While, at first, the various occasions recorded in the 'annals' were used to describe years, the choice of these eponymous criteria was eventually limited to the (mostly) biennial census of cattle. The year was 'of the n-th occasion of the census' or it was the year 'after the n-th occasion of the census'. Towards the end of the long reign of Pepy II the census probably became an annual affair or was abandoned, because shortly afterwards the designation of the year seems to correspond to the actual numbering of the regnal years of the king.

Like mathematics and astronomy, medicine relied on empirical rather than theoretical understanding. Many of the physicians (*sunu*) known to us from the Old Kingdom were attached to the royal palace and were thus members of the large retinue looking after the king's welfare. Some display titles which suggest that there was a degree of specialization, such as 'physician of the eyes of the Great House' (*sunu irty per-aa*), i.e. oculist. Whether this is a correct interpretation, or whether this is just a typically Egyptian way of converting totality into its constituent elements and presenting them separately (a physician dealing with all diseases could also be described as oculist, dentist, etc. depending on the particular problem he might be treating) is not certain.

Some medical works of later times were credited with great antiquity, but we do not know whether the attributions are genuine or whether they were just introduced to enhance their value. Medical instructions and precepts certainly were written down as early as the Fifth Dynasty. When the vizier Wash-ptah was taken ill in the presence of King Neferirkare, the king summoned royal children, lector-priests, and chiefs of physicians, and ordered containers with books to be brought and presumably consulted, though apparently in vain. The badly damaged record of this event was inscribed in Wash-ptah's tomb at Saqqara.

The extent of medical competence is not known to us because no medical texts of this early period have been preserved. Whatever empirical surgical knowledge existed, it could not have been acquired as the result of attempts at primitive mummification. The embalmers and physicians belonged to different specialized groups and there is no evidence of any connection between them.

After the beginning of the Fifth Dynasty, private statues were frequently competently made, and often pleasing in appearance, but rarely outstanding works of art. The wooden statue known as 'Sheikh el-Beled' ('Headman of the Village' in Arabic), found at Saqqara, is a happy exception, showing a corpulent ageing man with a remarkably expressive shrewd, rustic face. Even if the statue is a type rather than a portrait of an individual, it is the work of a master sculptor who was capable of transcending his role as a craftsman. The work dates from the end of the Fourth or the early Fifth Dynasty.

By the beginning of the Fourth Dynasty the hieroglyphic script, used in tombs and monumental inscriptions carved in stone, had produced the first longer texts. Earlier it was mainly used for descriptive notices identifying representations, and the names of officials on their stelae, and offerings systematically arranged into lists. The earliest type of text commonly used in private tombs was the 'offering given by the king' (*hetep-di-nisut*) formula. It was a short prayer asking the god of the necropolis, at first Anubis, for a share of reversion offerings which were presented to him by the king, but gradually it grew into a more complex system of wishes.

As the decoration of tomb-chapels began to occupy large areas of walls, some of the texts recorded snippets of conversation between the people represented. The first real narrative appeared as an autobiographical text in which the tomb-owner described events in his life. The emphasis in many of the early texts is on the official's possessions and how they were acquired, often with their description. The text thus represents a permanent record which should ensure that the tomb-owner's entitlement to these possessions is not forgotten. Parts of these texts may be direct quotations of legal documents.

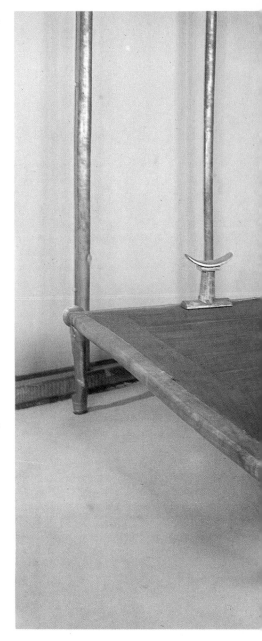

In the Fifth Dynasty autobiographical texts developed further to include episodes illustrating the tomb-owner's character and describe his memorable achievements. These texts were, of course, idealized and never mentioned any failings. At the same time, a tendency towards formalization of the laudatory passages appeared. 'I am one beloved of all people. Never have I said anything wrong to the king or a person of authority about anybody. I am one praised by his father, his mother, and his lords in the necropolis,' claims Nekhebu in his tomb at Giza. 'I gave bread to the hungry, and clothes to the naked,' says Pepynakht Heqaib at Qubbet el-Hawa. On the one hand, the mere existence of these statements can perhaps be seen as evidence that behaviour described in them was not necessarily universal, but on the other they indicate a generally accepted moral code according to which a person was expected to live. The concern about complying with it suggests that one's prospects for afterlife would have been impaired by ignoring it. The concept of a moral evaluation was new, and perhaps the result of new religious ideas, particularly the increased importance of Osiris, which became widespread during the Fifth Dynasty.

Texts concerning the acquisition of the tomb are common, as well as threats to those found guilty of impropriety. Thus Akhtihotpe of the Fifth Dynasty at Saqqara claims: 'As for any people who enter this tomb of mine in an impure state, or who cause damage to it, judgement will be held upon them for it by the Great God.'

The incentive for the introduction and development of texts in tomb-chapels was thus closely connected with striving to ensure one's afterlife and the continuation of one's cult, and was not dissimilar from the motives which led to the introduction of tomb decoration and statues.

Unlike the monumental texts in tombs, the so-called teachings (*sebayt*) represent a purely literary genre transmitted on papyri. The form of these compositions is that of advice given by the father to his son as a series of maxims or instructions concerning his life and career. These works are a curious mixture of theoretical moral principles and of their very pragmatic application based on previous experience, and were intended for the select group of literate officials. The alleged author of the teaching invariably is a famous person, such as Prince Hardjedef of the Fourth Dynasty, or Izezi's vizier, Ptahhotpe, but whether these attributions reflect reality is not altogether certain. 'Do not be arrogant on account of what you

know, and do not be over-confident because you are a wise man, but consult the ignorant as well as the wise. The limits of skills have not yet been reached, and no expert is a complete master . . .'

Official monumental inscriptions did not substantially differ from the formally very accomplished administrative records in style and contents.

The Pyramid Texts represent the only large corpus of religious texts set down during the Old Kingdom. With the exception of the *hetep-di-nisut* prayer, private tombs contained neither religious texts nor representations of gods. Contact with the gods was the prerogative of the king.

The earliest uninscribed sheets of papyrus, the material used for everyday administrative purposes, were found in the Saqqara tomb of Hemaka of the reign of King Den of the First Dynasty. The manufacture of this type of writing material was fairly complicated and must have taken some time to perfect, but none of the earliest papyri have been preserved.

Most of our knowledge of the Old Kingdom comes from tombs. Though representations in tombs of wealthy Egyptians are concerned with their owners' needs in the afterlife, and with their funerary monuments, they record incidents which took place in this world. The picture derived from them may be selective, but it does reflect everyday reality.

Remains of the furniture found in the Giza tomb of Hetep-heres I, the chief Queen of Snofru and the mother of Khufu, included a bed, a bed-canopy, a curtain-box, two armchairs, a palanquin, and several chests. They have copper fittings, and their decoration consists of chased sheets of gold, and inlays in gold, carnelian, and faience. The furniture on display in the Egyptian Museum in Cairo has been completely restored using the original materials found in the tomb.

FIVE

MANAGING THE ECONOMY

'As for the villages of my tomb endowment which the king has given me for my provisioning . . . offerings presented by voice will come for me from them in my tomb which is in the necropolis of the pyramid called Khephren is Great . . .'★

WHILE ECONOMIC EXPLOITATION OF PROVINCES outside the capital Ineb–hedj by the central authority had remained at a fairly primitive level during the first two dynasties, rapid progress was made at the beginning of the Third. The village communities, which at first formed the basis of Egyptian agricultural production, were now systematically transformed. The control exercised by the state administrative system was strengthened.

The profound changes which took place were spurred on by the inauguration of monumental building in stone. The programme of pyramid-construction and the creation of the royal cult establishments associated with the pyramids shaped the society and economy of the Old Kingdom more than anything else. Such projects encouraged technological and cultural advances and accentuated the differences between various sections of the community serving them. The pyramid was a material expression and affirmation of two of the basic tenets of state ideology and religion: the exceptional position and role of the king in the world, and the belief in continued existence after death.

It is customary to admire the unrivalled size and perfection of the massive structures raised at this early period of Egyptian history, but more impressive is the organizational and managerial genius of the men who were in charge of such enterprises, and their courage, imagination, and self-confidence in undertaking them in the first place. Large numbers of workmen were needed for handling stone blocks at building sites, and many more were engaged in their quarrying and transport, the building and maintenance of roads and construction-ramps, supply of workmen's tools, the care of draught animals, and provision of water, food, and other necessities of life. Many supervisors and scribes accompanied the labour force. Sculptors could only start their work on reliefs after the structures had been completed. The logistics of these operations must have been truly daunting. Even if much of the work which required a large work-force was carried out during the months of inundation when there was little to do in the flooded fields, the number of people whose provisioning

The burial chamber of the step pyramid of Netjerikhet, below ground level, was approached by a sloping shaft from the north.

★ *From a Fifth Dynasty text, now in Cairo Museum CG 1432, endowing a tomb at Giza.*

The appearance of large-scale building in stone at the beginning of the Third Dynasty accelerated changes in society as well as in arts and architecture. Seen from outside, Netjerikhet's enclosure walls imitated the appearance of the niched exterior of tombs of the First Dynasty, which themselves had probably adopted the exterior form of the royal palace. Engaged columns with the capitals in the shape of papyrus umbels were used in the heb-sed part of the enclosure. The step pyramid dominates the necropolis of Saqqara even now, and the enclosure walls as well as many of the buildings have been restored in years of painstaking research and work under the direction of J.-P. Lauer.

suddenly became the responsibility of the state was so large that the old system, geared towards the limited material requirements of the palace, could no longer cope unaltered. Most of the administrative changes which now started to take place in the organization of agriculture were due to the pressure to increase production.

From the beginning of the Third Dynasty new royal farming estates (*hut-aat*) were being created throughout Egypt. Many of them were founded during the reign of King Snofru, which saw an unprecedented increase in the volume of monumental building. An entry for one of his years in the 'annals' on the so-called Palermo Stone runs as follows: 'The year of: creating 35 estates with people and 122 cattle-farms; building a 100-cubit *Dua-taui* barque of conifer wood and two 100-cubit barques of cedar wood; the seventh occasion of a census; the height of inundation on the fields: five cubits, one palm, one finger.'

The monumental building of pyramids had a profound effect on Egyptian society and its economy. Cult and later also temple establishments now became an important element in the country's life. Their economic dependence on the central authority was gradually lessening. When royal cult establishments began to play a role in the material support of officials of state administration in the mid-Fifth Dynasty, it was an indication that the balance of economic power, based on land-ownership, had shifted very significantly. From then on these establishments represented a major economic force in the land, and acted as the main clearing houses for the distribution of national produce.

The king set out to prepare a pyramidal tomb for himself early in his reign, and also made legal arrangements for the theoretically indefinite maintenance of his posthumous cult in the temple adjacent to the pyramid. The main material requirement of a cult establishment was a guaranteed supply of provisions, such as bread, beer, meat, and fowl. Some of these were 'offered' to the spirit of the deceased king on the altar in the temple, while the rest was consumed by the temple personnel. Provisions came from various sources outside the temple. Remains of the papyrus-archive of the cult establishment called 'The *ba*-soul of King Kakai [= Neferirkare]' at Abusir show a high standard of book-keeping: 'Day 23. Brought from the Residence: 2 *des*-jars [contents not specified]; 4 jars of *zefet* [an unidentified liquid]; 1 loaf of *hetja*-bread; 2 loaves of *hetjat*-bread; 12 ducks. Brought from the storehouse of the valley estate [*ra-she*] of King Kakai: 3 *des*-jars; 1 loaf of *pezen*-bread; 1 loaf of another variety of bread. Brought from the chief physician Rakhuf: 1 duck.' On the following day, the 24th, exactly the same quantities of supplies were brought from the Residence. Other goods received that day were 'brought from the sun-temple called The Favourite Place of the Sun-God Re: 2 loaves of *hetja*-bread; 6 loaves of *hetjat*-bread; 2 loaves of *pezen*-bread, 1 cake, 10 ducks.' In each case the names of the men who came with these offerings were also recorded.

Not all provisions which were brought to the cult establishment remained there, because such an institution had its own 'clients' to whom it in turn re-distributed some of the offerings for use in their own tombs.

To safeguard his cult and make it economically independent, from the beginning of the Fourth Dynasty the king usually endowed his cult temple with land in the form of estates which then supplied it directly. Some of such land was in the valley not far from the lower part of the pyramid-complex, but most of the estates were situated in distant areas. Many of them were new foundations on territory previously unexploited, particularly in the Delta where free land was still available. To cultivate these estates peasants were re-settled from crown land elsewhere, to-

gether with cattle and equipment, and captives were brought from military campaigns abroad, particularly Nubia and Libya. The estates of Snofru's cult establishment are represented in the valley temple of his southern pyramid at Dahshur as a procession of peasant women, each carrying a symbolic tray with offerings. On their heads they have the hieroglyphic signs which read 'an estate of Snofru', and their names are written beside them. They are divided into groups preceded by the symbol of the district in which they were situated. This is a typically Egyptian device for presenting in a lively and visually attractive way what could have been a dry and rather dull copy of a systematically drawn-up legal document. Thus the standard of the Hare-district (the fifteenth of Upper Egypt) is followed by three such figures representing the estates called 'The Fishing Net of Snofru', 'The *pak*-bread of Snofru', and 'Snofru is Great'. The standard of the Oryx-district (the sixteenth of Upper Egypt) introduces a group of five estates, 'The Joy of Snofru', 'The Dancers of Snofru', 'The Road of Snofru', 'Snofru is Luscious of Pastures', and 'The Nurse of Snofru'.

In the second half of the Fifth Dynasty a noticeable increase in the occurrence of titles connected with pyramids shows that cult establishments had become an inseparable element of the central economic management of the country. Previously the personnel, supervised by an 'overseer of the pyramid' (*imy-ra mer*), had consisted of a lector-priest

The pyramid at Maidum represents the transitional stage of development from the step pyramid enclosures to the full pyramid-complexes. The valley of the complex, however, has not yet been excavated, and so we do not know whether there was a pyramid-town near the valley temple.

69

Inspection of cattle and fowl, including cranes, in the Fifth Dynasty tomb of Ty at Saqqara. The restored slit-aperture is one of three connecting the offering-room with the sealed serdab (statue-room) beyond.

who conducted the daily ritual, and his assistants, 'part-time' priests called *waeb* ('pure one') or *hem-netjer* ('servant of the god'). They had been organized into five 'guilds' (*za*) which served monthly in turn. The names of these 'guilds' were adopted from ship terminology. When not on duty, the priests had been craftsmen, cooks, farm-hands, and other skilled or semi-skilled workers who lived in the 'pyramid-town'. This was a settlement which had grown in the valley near the monumental entrance (valley temple) to the pyramid-complex. The social status of such people had hardly been elevated. Now, however, even the highest officials of administration began to hold offices connected with pyramids. Thus the vizier Akhtihotpe, who lived at the end of the Fifth Dynasty, is described in a scene in his tomb as 'chief justice and vizier, overseer of the broad hall, king's chamberlain, *iun-kenmut*-priest, judge and *adj-mer* official, priest of the goddess Maet, and overseer of the two towns and inspector of the two pyramids called Djedkare is Beautiful, and Menkauhor is Divine of Cult-Places'. It may have been the increased shortage of unexploited land which made the king use his cult establishment to support his officials or to provide for their tombs. A formal appointment to a 'salaried' nominal priestly function in such an establishment carried with it entitlement to income in kind from the temple's resources, or to the use of some of the temple's land in the form of one or more estates. These became one of the

Left and below left: A procession of semi-divine personifications, from Sahure's cult temple at Abusir, is led by the Lower Egyptian Hapy *(representing fertility), and includes* Nekhbet *(meaning 'budding', not connected with the goddess Nekhbet) and* Wadj-wer *('great green', probably meaning 'mass of water').*

Below right: Food articles brought to tombs include fish. There is no doubt that they were eaten, at least by ordinary people, yet they are not listed among the standard offerings. This must have been due to prohibitive religious precepts according to which fish was not 'pure' food. The offering-bearers shown here conclude a long procession of personifications of the estates of Nefermaet. His early Fourth Dynasty tomb is at Maidum.

The slaughtering of oxen or oryxes is shown in almost all tomb-chapels, but these are provisioning scenes which do not necessarily reflect everyday reality. Meat was a prestige food which the peasantry could hardly afford. This relief is in the Sixth Dynasty tomb of Princess Sesh-seshet Idut at Saqqara.

possible forms of the appointee's official ('ex officio') property for life, but had to be surrendered by his heirs. With each new pyramid a large area of cultivated land inevitably ceased to be directly available to the central authority, but this measure now meant that at least some of it was in fact used twice, as a donation to the royal cult establishment, and also for the support of the king's officials.

Two of the fourteen estates listed in the Fifth Dynasty tomb of the official Nen-kheft-ka at Saqqara were called 'The Ladder of Userkaf' and 'Userkaf is Beautiful of the Spirit', while another three were 'Hathor wishes that Sahure lives', 'The Spirit belongs to Sahure', and 'The Flood of Sahure'. Nen-kheft-ka's claim to these estates as his official property was, no doubt, due to the fact that, as his titles show, he was associated with the pyramids of Userkaf and Sahure in nominal priestly capacities.

The inroads into state resources made by the creation of royal cult establishments were deepened even more by the practice of issuing protective decrees which dispensed their members from taxation and state forced labour. Such a decree was made out in the year of the twenty-first census by Pepy I for 'the cult of the King of Upper and Lower Egypt, Snofru, in the two pyramids called Snofru Appears. The Majesty of Horus Merytaui [= Pepy I] ordered for him [i.e. Snofru] that this pyramid-town be exempt from carrying out any work of the administration of crown property and from paying any tax of any tax-department of the Residence, and from any forced labour of any department of forced labour, no matter who says so'. The decree then details possible demands which could be made on the inhabitants of the pyramid-town and specifically prohibits their imposition on this cult establishment.

During the Sixth Dynasty even very high officials were proud to display the humble title of 'settler' (*khenty-she*) of their king's cult establishment. Meryteti, the son of the vizier Mereruka and himself a vizier under King Pepy I, had the following titulary inscribed on the left side of the door to his tomb-chapel at Saqqara: 'Inspector of servants of the god of the pyramid called Meryre is Established and Beautiful, settler, king's son, count, sole companion.' The title of the 'king's son' was, of course, only honorific and bestowed on him in order to enhance his court rank. The greatest benefit derived from the title of 'settler' may have been exemption from various state obligations which the holder now enjoyed as a member of the royal cult establishment.

The complex arrangements made for the posthumous cult of kings were paralleled, albeit on a much smaller scale, by those in the privileged sections of society. The king's unique role carried with it an obligation to ensure the maintenance of the funerary cult of his officials and members of the royal family. The requirements were twofold: building the tomb, and supplying the necessary offerings and provisions. Graves of the vast majority of ordinary people continued to be dug in cemeteries on desert margins as before, and remained unaffected by the cult provisions made for the upper echelons of society.

At first, all tombs situated within the limits of the royal pyramid cemetery were probably built and provided as the king's favour by royal craftsmen. 'As for this tomb of mine, it was the King of Upper and Lower Egypt Menkaure—may he live eternally!—who ordered it to be made, when royal progress to the pyramid plateau took place in order to inspect the work done on the pyramid called Menkaure is Divine, with the royal architect, the two chief directors of craftsmen, and craftsmen in attendance on him, so that he could inspect the work on the building. Fifty men were detailed to work on it every day and assigned to prepare

The plan of the tomb-chapel of Ptah-shepses at Abusir includes a large pillared court. The centre of the court was open to the sky, but the now fallen architraves supported slabs which formed a roofed walk round its perimeter.

The division of the economic resources available for the maintenance of the funerary cult was reflected in the size and quality of the tomb, even though turning this into a simple equation cannot be justified. The people who could use their position in life to provide themselves with large and splendidly decorated tombs were not necessarily only those who held the most important offices in the state administration. Nor can we link increases or decreases in the sizes of tombs directly to the importance of the office. The mastaba of Neuserre's vizier Ptah-shepses dominates the whole necropolis at Abusir by its size and its architecture.

the purification tent of the place of embalmment. His Majesty ordered that none of them be taken away for any task except working on it until it was completed.' The damaged inscription mentions further 'bringing stone from the quarries at Roau in order to encase the building in limestone, and two jambs of the doorway to this tomb'. The rock-cut tomb of Debehni, whose construction is described in this text, can still be visited north of the causeway leading to the pyramid of Menkaure at Giza.

From the Fourth Dynasty onward, private enterprise started playing a significant role in tomb-building. 'The necropolis-workman Pepi is satisfied with the contract which I made with him', proclaims the treasurer of the royal granary Neferher-en-ptah on the lintel of the entrance to his tomb at Giza, dated to the Fifth or Sixth Dynasty. 'I had these statues made by the sculptor who is satisfied with the reward which I made him,' says the priest Memi in the inscription on one of the two statues found in his tomb at Giza. The craftsmen employed in the construction and decoration of the Saqqara tomb of Hetep-her-akhti 'made it for much bread, beer, cloth, oil, and barley', while Metjetji, of the end of the Fifth or the beginning of the Sixth Dynasty, claims about everybody who worked in his tomb: 'I made them satisfied—after they had completed the work on it—with copper belonging to me from my official property, while I also gave them cloth and fed them with bread from my official property.'

Tombs were provisioned in several ways which developed historically and often existed simultaneously. Supplies of offerings could be received from a royal property or a royal cult institution as an 'offering given by the king (*hetep-di-nisut*). The practical disadvantages of this method were considerable, and so from at least as early as the beginning of the Fourth Dynasty there is evidence for the 'offering given by the king' taking the form of land endowments. In its purest form (*hut-ka*, 'estate of the spirit') such an endowment consisted of an estate with land, people, cattle, and equipment, which was given outright to the tomb-owner to provide the required necessities for his tomb. A third method of securing offerings for the tomb was by 'reversion' (*wedjeb*) of provisions from royal cult or temple establishments or other tombs. Some of the revenue received by the original institution, in the most extreme case a tomb, was reverted, or re-directed, to be used as offerings in a secondary tomb. This was a characteristic way of legally arranging for the sharing of produce among several recipients, and one which can be seen in many forms at various levels of Egyptian society. A text in the Saqqara tomb of Persen, dating to the early Fifth Dynasty, provides an example: 'Bringing offerings for a presentation by voice, to the inspector of the Great House, Persen, consisting of reversion offerings of *hetja*-bread, *pezen*-bread, and *zefet* [an unidentified liquid], which come from the temple of Ptah South-of-his-Wall for the King's mother Neferhetpes daily eternally—given to him from it for a presentation of offerings by voice in the time of King Sahure.' Some of the revenue which the tomb of Queen Neferhetpes received from the temple of Ptah in the capital was reverted for Persen's own posthumous cult, perhaps because of a position he held in the queen's household. Such a re-distribution of offerings could take place several times over, because the tomb-owner could revert some of the income of his tomb yet again for use in tombs of his subordinates and lesser members of his household. This is the concept underlying the term *imakhu*, 'one provided for'. A man became *imakhu* by being promised a share of the offerings received by a god (i.e. from a god's temple) or a king, but also of those received by an important official or a member of the royal family with

Ptahhotpe, seated at a table piled with flat loaves of bread (represented upright), is holding a stone jar with a pleasantly smelling unguent to his nose. The space above and below the table is packed with offerings of food and drink. Ptahhotpe lived at the end of the Fifth Dynasty and his tomb is at Saqqara.

whom he was in some way connected. Netjer-punesut is in his tomb at Giza described as the 'possessor of provisioning' from Kings Radjedef, Khephren, Menkaure, Shepseskaf, Userkaf, and Sahure. At the end of the Old Kingdom a lowly official Khuen-ptah claimed to be 'one provided for by the hereditary prince Meri', thus indicating that he enjoyed, or hoped to enjoy, the privilege of receiving a share of offerings from the large Saqqara mastaba of the vizier Mereruka (Meri was his nickname) in whose vicinity he was buried. It was common practice during the Old Kingdom for the tomb-owner to describe himself as 'provided for by' the gods of the necropolis, such as Anubis or Osiris, or by 'his lord', i.e. the king. A woman could be 'provided for by her husband'. These cases, wishful epithets without any legal force, are yet another reflection of the Egyptian approach to personal dependence and patronage.

In the tomb, food and drink offerings were placed on a special stone table or in a basin in front of a stela (gravestone) which resembled a door with several sets of jambs and lintels ('false-door'), and the ceremony of 'presentation of offerings by voice' was then conducted by a lector-priest. If the tomb was endowed with its own land (*djet*), the people who worked on it were legally tied to it. They assisted in the tomb ritual and so were described as 'servants of the spirit' (*hem-ka*) and 'belonging to the endowment' (*ny-djet*).

If the tomb had no personnel of its own, 'servants of the spirit' could be hired in return for contractually specified benefits, often the use of land, though not its ownership. The eldest son and heir was usually in charge of the affairs of his father's tomb endowment, so that control over the

property remained in the same family, but it could be the widow who took control if there were no children. A 'brother of the endowment' (*sen djet*), in effect a professional manager, was appointed in the absence of a next-of-kin.

With the exception of the temple of Ptah in the capital, the temple of Re-Harakhti at Iunu (Heliopolis), and the sun-temples, there were few religious establishments whose economic importance matched their spiritual significance before the middle of the Fifth Dynasty. Donations made by the king for the maintenance of ritual in these temples could take the form of produce delivered from state storehouses or estates. A list of offerings presented to the sun-temple of King Neuserre at Abu Ghurab on the occasions of various religious festivals was inscribed on its gate and probably represented a copy of a document lodged in the royal archive. The list is, unfortunately, preserved in a very fragmentary state. For New Year's Day festival the offerings included loaves of *pezen*-bread, and also milk and honey. For the 'coming out', i.e. public festival procession, of the god Min the temple received 1000 loaves of *pezen*-bread, one ox, ten geese, honey, *sekhet*-grain, wheat, and 'all sweet things'. The annual total at the end of the list amounts to 100,800 'rations' consisting of bread, beer, and cakes, 7720 loaves of *pezen*-bread, 1002 oxen, 1000 geese, etc. Whether these figures include the offerings presented on special occasions, or whether they represent daily offerings, is not clear, but they do show the large quantities of food which passed through a single temple in a year. These products were not 'wasted' as offerings for the sun-god, but were consumed by the temple personnel and often re-distributed elsewhere.

An unusually eroded alabaster block can be seen in the middle of what used to be the pillared court in the eastern part of Teti's cult temple at Saqqara. It is all that remains of a large altar decorated with the king's names and personifications of Egyptian districts. Whether this particular altar was functional, or just symbolic, is not clear. We can be more certain about the purpose of another, similar, altar. This is now lost, but originally it stood in the inner, western, part of the temple, and offerings required in the funerary cult of the king were brought there and placed on it in front of the stela (false-door).

More important factors in Egyptian economy were donations of land made to these temples. The area of the land presented in this way could vary very considerably from one donation to another. According to the 'annals' on the Palermo Stone, the goddess Hathor, whose cult was connected with the valley part (ra-she) of the pyramid-complex of King Sahure at Abusir, received just over two arouras (setjat) of land, about half a hectare (about 1.2 acres), in the year following Sahure's second census. The god Re was given over 1704 arouras, i.e. nearly 470 hectares (1161 acres), as one single donation in the year after the third census of Userkaf. During the Fifth Dynasty such donations were made on a larger scale even to provincial temples. As a result, many officials in local administration benefited greatly from the priestly offices they held in their local temples, and this significantly strengthened their growing economic independence of the central government. The increasing number of tombs in the provinces towards the end of the Old Kingdom testifies to this trend, but did not reflect a tendency towards political autonomy.

Most of the land which did not belong to any of the numerous royal cult and temple establishments and tomb endowments, and which was not cultivated as official property by private individuals, was administered by the state as part of 'crown property'. This land was managed by the Residence (khenu), which also directed fiscal affairs and so concentrated most state income in its hands. Only a very limited area of land may have remained private, of either individuals or the remains of the original village communities.

Manpower required for a limited period of time for large building, quarrying, and other projects organized by the state was drawn from all people throughout the land. Only those who were exempt from state forced labour (wenwet or kat) by special royal decrees were able to escape this burdensome obligation. In this way the administration also raised temporary help with agricultural tasks, such as cattle-herding, on royal estates which suffered from shortage of manpower. A decree, issued for the temple of the god Min at Gebtiu (Koptos, modern Qift) by Pepy II in the year after the eleventh census, prohibits imposition of such duties on the temple's personnel: 'My Majesty does not allow: that they are put to work in cattle-pens, on farms of cattle, donkeys, and small cattle [i.e. sheep and goats] of the administration of herds, or any forced labour or any tax which may be imposed by crown property administration for the length of eternity.'

Taxation (medjed) in kind was directed towards institutions rather than individuals. The census of cattle was the most regular and comprehensive method which covered the whole country, but there were other forms, some perhaps of an occasional nature, which varied according to local conditions. When the decree of Pepy I, issued for the cult establishment of Snofru at Dahshur, exempts it from 'counting canals, ponds, wells, shadufs, and trees', we must assume that these served as criteria for tax-assessment.

The king's responsibility for supplies of provisions for the tombs of his officials and members of the royal family was only an extension of his obligation to provide their necessities in their lifetime. At first all important positions were held by members of the royal family who, because they themselves did not work on the land, received provisions directly from the royal palace. This was no longer possible when administration became more complex and covered all Egypt. A new and more efficient method of provisioning was based on assigning some crown land to royal relatives and officials for their use. The person owned this land, usually with people and cattle, for his lifetime. It was his official ('ex officio')

A new type of stela was introduced in the stone-built tombs which King Khufu built for his officials and royal relatives. Called slab-stelae for their shape (more wide than high), they were made in royal workshops and presented to the tomb-owner by the king, so they display an excellent standard of workmanship. They were only used at Giza for a limited period of time. This stela belonged to Princess Nefertiabt.

Craftsmen shown in the early Sixth Dynasty tomb of Mereruka at Saqqara include metalworkers and dwarfs employed in the manufacture of jewellery. To force the fire, metalworkers used blowpipes during the melting of metal in order to transform the mass extracted from the furnace into ingots.

property (*per-djet*) and represented his 'salary', but he was also expected to use it to maintain his large household and his professional subordinates, and thus to act on the king's behalf in supporting them. A direct grant of land represented the original form of official property, and members of the royal family particularly benefited from it. The same end was often achieved by appointing officials to nominal positions connected with royal cult establishments or estates of crown property, which then entitled them to such official property.

A man's private property thus usually came from several sources. In a scene in the late Sixth Dynasty tomb at Deir el-Gebrawi the owner, Ibi, describes how he has assembled provisions for his tomb: 'I have created it from the villages of my official property (*niuut djeti*), from my priesthood, from the 'offering given by the king' which the Majesty of my lord gave me so that I might acquire for myself fields . . . settled with the people of the endowment, furnished with cattle, goats, donkeys, and that which I acquired by my own arm—beside the property of my father—while I was manager of an estate of crown property [*per shena*] of 203 arouras of land which the Majesty of my lord gave me to make me wealthy.' Much of Ibi's accumulated possessions came from his appointment as manager of a royal estate, but a contribution was made by the income from his priestly office, an 'offering given by the king', and some property which he inherited from his father. 'That which I acquired by my own arm' may refer to property which was purchased by him. Such cases are not common, but occur already in the early Fourth Dynasty.

An illustrated version of the title deeds to one's estates was often represented in the tomb as a procession of women bringing offerings or leading animals. This was a method similar to that used in temples associated with pyramids. The nouns 'estate' and 'village' are of feminine gender in Egyptian, hence the sex of these offering-bearers. Meresankh, one of the queens of Khephren, had thirteen estates recorded on the east wall of her Giza tomb: one 'estate of Khufu' (*hut Khufu*), i.e. a farm newly created by the king, which she received because she was his granddaughter, ten villages of Khephren which she was given by her husband, one village of Radjedef whose presence can be explained by the fact that Radjedef was her stepfather, and one 'estate of the spirit' (*hut-ka*). The last estate constituted her tomb endowment and was to provide offerings for her tomb, in theory for ever, while the rest had to be surrendered after her death.

Three estates are shown in the Saqqara tomb of Metjen of the early Fourth Dynasty. One is called 'The Endowment of the Ram of Mendes', and probably represented Metjen's official property, but the other two are described as 'foundations of Metjen' called 'One who Comes when she Wishes' and 'The Mound of the God Sobek'. The mention of the tomb-owner in their names suggests that, unlike the first estate, these were specially created for Metjen and thus constituted his private inalienable property which he was allowed to dispose of in his will as he wished.

It is possible that some of these private estates represented in tombs did not belong to the tomb-owner exclusively, but rather supplied him only with some particular produce. This may explain some of their names, for example in the Fifth Dynasty tomb of Ty at Saqqara: 'The Wine of Ty', 'The Milk of Ty', 'The Fig of Ty', and others. These estates may even have been completely fictitious, but the evidence of tomb reliefs, unfortunately, is not detailed enough to enable us to distinguish such subtleties.

The Old Kingdom approach to the provisioning of the living and the methods used to achieve it were thus not unlike those for the provisioning

Part of the will in which Kaiemnefert endows his tomb in the necropolis of the pyramid of Khephren during the Fifth Dynasty. Kaiemnefert had the title of the 'adj-mer manager of the estate called Star of Horus Foremost of·Heaven', a vineyard in the Delta. It is, however, certain that this prestigious ancient title had become purely honorific by the Fifth Dynasty. The stone block was originally set up in Kaiemnefert's tomb at Giza.

Facing page: The exquisite low reliefs from King Userkaf's cult temple at Saqqara include some lively swamp scenes, perhaps connected with fishing and fowling. Although Userkaf also built a temple for the sun-god at Abusir, there is nothing to suggest that the state's economic resources were unduly strained: the quality of this work is very high.

of gods or the spirits of the dead. Despite different ideological motivation, they all represented means of securing distribution of the surplus national product among the privileged section of society in the most desirable way.

Internal trade had only a limited role to play in the country's economic life during the Old Kingdom. Peasants produced most of what they needed for themselves, and received other necessities, such as certain items of food (fish, fowl, salt, honey, oil), clothes, sandals, and perhaps some house fittings and furniture, from the owner of the land on which they were settled. Craftsmen were provisioned by the institutions for which they worked. Officials lived off their official property, mostly state land they were allowed to use in return for their services, or received goods directly from the state. Only a small amount of surplus produce was distributed through village markets, and apart from barter scenes in tombs there is no evidence to show how this worked.

Buying and selling of private property was a legally recognized practice which was recorded in documents. A few of these transactions are known to us in detail because, quite exceptionally, the records were copied on to stone. Tombs and their elements, including statues, as well as fields for one's tomb endowment, could be acquired by purchase, but also everyday necessities such as a house. 'I have bought this house from the scribe Tjenti. I gave him the value of 10 *shat* for it: four-strand cloth to the value of 3 *shat*, a bed of sycomore or jujube wood of the value of 4 *shat*, and two-strand cloth to the value of 3 *shat*.' There was no money as

The largest group of administrative documents known from the Old Kingdom concerns the affairs of the cult temple of King Neferirkare The papyri include accounts, rosters of duties, records of inspections, and inventories. Neferirkare's pyramid is the biggest at Abusir, and the documents were found in a room in the temple next to its eastern face.

such, and payment for goods and services was made in kind, and could thus be described as exchange. The term *shat* employed in Tjenti's document seems to represent a fixed official unit of value, expressed in terms of an amount of metal, in which transactions were calculated.

Egypt was almost completely self-sufficient in natural resources and most of the materials and products obtained through foreign trade belonged to the category of prestigious luxury goods. Timber from the Lebanon and Syria was the major exception. Commodities such as lapis lazuli, wine, and oils came from or through the same region, with Byblos playing an important role in maritime trade. Reliefs from the pyramid-temple of Sahure at Abusir show the return of Egyptian sea-going ships from such an expedition, bringing back bearded Asiatics who are represented as making obeisance to the king. A similar scene was also identified at the causeway leading to the pyramid of Unas at Saqqara. Whether these are records of actual events, or a genre of no historical relevance, is not clear, and we do not know the purpose of these expeditions. Tall-necked jars, presumably of oil, and bears, exotic animals for the Egyptians, are shown in Sahure's temple and may be connected with the trip to Asia.

Overland routes must have also been used.

Caravan routes remained the main links with the African regions lying beyond Nubia, which were the source of incense, hard woods such as ebony, oils, ivory, skins, ostrich feathers, and gold. Journeys to the land of Punt, probably situated inland from the Somali coast, were undertaken via the Red Sea. An entry in the 'annals' on the Palermo Stone for the 'year after the seventh census' of Sahure mentions the commodities 'brought from Punt', which included 80,000 measures of myrrh, 6000 units of electrum, 2900 units of wood, and 23,020 measures of unguent. The official Khnemhotpe recorded in the Sixth Dynasty tomb of Khui at Qubbet el-Hawa that he went with Khui and Tjetji, the 'treasurers of the god', to Punt and Byblos several (the figure not clear) times. A dwarf brought from Punt by the 'treasurer of the god' Werdedba in the reign of Izezi is mentioned in the letter of the young Pepy II to Harkhuf.

Egyptian exports seem to have been mostly manufactured goods, and included faience and stone vessels, probably filled with oils, and also clothes and furniture.

SIX

SOCIETY AND STATE

*'The order is great, its effectiveness endures. It has not been disturbed since the time of Osiris.'**

Alabaster was less commonly used for private sculptures, and the quality of the modelling of this statue is far above most Old Kingdom private works. It seems likely that it was produced in a royal workshop at the end of the Fourth or early in the Fifth Dynasty, and the woman may have been a king's relative or the wife of a high official. The exact provenance of the piece is not known.

THE SIZE OF THE EGYPTIAN POPULATION during the Old Kingdom is not known, but an estimate of about a million inhabitants, giving a relatively low population density, would probably not be far off the mark. Essentially it consisted of two main groups: the mass of peasants who worked on the land which they did not own, and the limited number of people broadly described as titled officials, who enjoyed the direct or indirect possession of land through one of the many forms which land-ownership could take. With the passing of time, craftsmen, particularly those belonging to royal cult establishments, emerged as a recognizable section of society because of the special status and privileges granted to them. Members of the royal family soon became, for ideological reasons, a group apart from the officials, as well as from the rest of the population. The apparent similarities to the situation of the late Predynastic Period and the first dynasties, with its division between the ruling *paat* related to the king, and the *rekhyt*, ordinary populace, would be misleading. The position of the king was, according to Egyptian state doctrine, quite exceptional, but other members of the royal family ceased to take an active part in the running of the state during the Fifth Dynasty and were relegated to supporting roles in the sphere of state ideology.

The king's relationship to gods (*netjeru*) was directly reflected in some of his names and titles. He was identified with the hawk-god Horus by the first and most ancient of his five names, related to the protective goddesses of Egyptian kings called Nekhbet and Wadjet ('The Two Ladies') by the second, and declared a 'son of the god Re', i.e. his heir, by his fifth name. All five names were conferred on him when he ascended the throne, even though the last was usually identical with that which he had used before he became king. He could be described as 'the young (or perfect) god' (*netjer nefer*), in comparison to the god Re. His 'divinity' was not the result of an accident of birth, but emanated from his office. It was assumed at his coronation, at which he was accepted as king by the gods of Upper and Lower Egypt; this marked a new beginning, a new 'joining of the Two Lands' and thus a re-enactment of the creation of Egypt after a period of chaos. This cyclical approach to progress and history had its origin in the geographical conditions of the country, with its never-ending regular fluctuation of the river and the change from inundation to the dry season, and the eternal progress of the sun-god through the repeated phases of day and night.

---

* *Papyrus Prisse, 88–9.*

Nevertheless, the Egyptian king was not regarded as another god, but rather as the custodian of the world who secured its smooth functioning. He played an important role which was recognized and acknowledged by the rest of society, and his performance affected everybody. He alone was invested with the authority to intercede with gods on behalf of men. The concept of a powerful and effective intermediary, and an action by proxy, permeates all Egyptian thinking. The Old Kingdom system of provisioning the tombs of *imakhu* is but one reflection of it. The king was thought to make all the offerings and donations to gods in their temples and, in return, to receive a continued approval and support for his rule.

Having been confirmed by gods, the king's supremacy over the world was theoretically absolute. All power and authority were vested in his person, and others could only exercise some of them if these were delegated to them by the king. However, even the king had to rule according to the god-decreed principles of *maet* and his freedom of action was thus restricted. *Maet*, literally 'truth', 'justice', 'righteousness', was a very general concept of 'order' in the world and established relationships in society, and had direct moral implications for each individual. It could be described as a social contract binding for all parties who entered into it in the belief that they would benefit from it. It was the main reason for much of the conservatism which governed Egyptian thinking, and for the reluctance to abandon earlier concepts.

The consequence of the king's position was that he was deemed responsible even for circumstances which were completely beyond his control, such as natural disasters, e.g. a low inundation. The king himself was not thought to have been able to remedy the situation directly, but a natural catastrophe would have been regarded as a failure on his part to perform his duty in maintaining the world's status quo.

The role of the king was, therefore, as much ideological as executive. The dogma concerning his position was proclaimed and re-affirmed by royal rituals, such as coronation and jubilee-festivals (*heb-sed*) while he was alive, and by the building of a monumental pyramidal tomb and the creation of his royal cult establishment for his existence after death. Such material expressions of state ideology soon came to play an essential part in the country's economy, but could only thrive while the premises of Egyptian kingship remained unquestioned. Their demise would have brought down the whole structure of the state.

The king's official dress included a kilt (*shendyt*), the Red (*deshret*) and White (*hedjet*) Crowns, both of different shapes, the crook (*heqat*) and flagellum (*nekhakha*), a ceremonial beard, and a bull's tail attached to the waist.

The king's prime claim to ascend the throne was as his father's son, reflecting the situation of an ordinary family. Ideally, he was the eldest surviving son by the most senior of the queens. There was no automatic right to succeed, and there was no 'divine dynasty' of kings. The blood ties within the royal family can only infrequently be studied in detail and are further complicated because of habitual intermarrying. Unlike their officials and the rest of the population, kings of the Old Kingdom regularly had several consorts, but the term 'harim' which is in general use suggests, wrongly, a large number of concubines. There is, in fact, no evidence for the latter.

Strife and conspiracy may have taken place within the royal family. Thus Weni, an official of the Sixth Dynasty, mentions in a somewhat cryptic fashion in his autobiographical text a trial involving an unnamed queen of Pepy I: 'When the proceedings against the queen, *weret hetes* (a title of queens), were instituted in the royal harim, His Majesty appointed

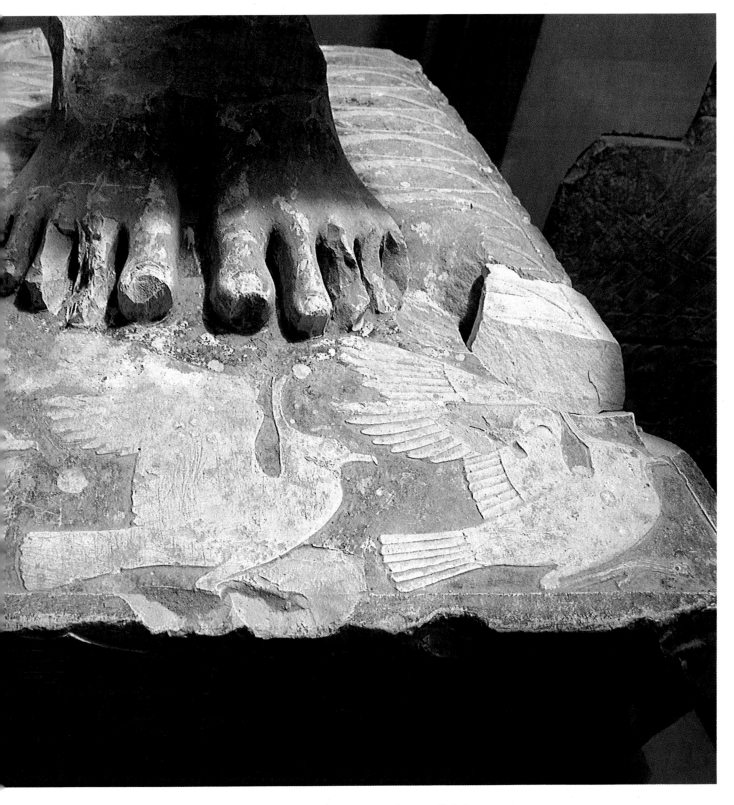

me to hear it privately, with no vizier and chief justice and no official being present except me alone.' The king could choose a queen of non-royal blood, the best-known case being again that of Pepy I who married two daughters, both called Ankh-nes-meryre, of an official Khui from Abdju (Abydos).

The Old Kingdom was a centrally planned and governed bureaucratic state whose theoretical base was the assumption that the king was the guarantor of the existence of the system, but the day-to-day running of the state was in the hands of professional administrators (*seru*, 'officials'). These did not form a special caste but, at least in theory, could be recruited

The feet of King Netjerikhet resting on the 'Nine Bows', representing Egypt's outside enemies, as well as the 'Lapwings' (rekhyt), symbolizing the Egyptian populace, perhaps originally mainly that of the Delta. The king had to dominate both the 'Bows' and the 'Lapwings' in order to fulfil his ideological role in the world. The feet, the base, and some fragments are all that remain of this life-size statue.

89

Ipi was a relatively humble 'manager of the estate' (heqa hut). Here he is carried in a palanquin, accompanied by attendants and men with sunshades, on a relief from his Sixth Dynasty tomb at Saqqara.

from any social group. Promotion could be rapid and parvenus may have occasionally posed problems of behaviour, as shown by the following advice from the literary work known as *The Teaching of Ptahhotpe*: 'If you are of humble origin and serve a prominent man, let all your conduct be good before god when you know his former lowly rank. Do not be haughty towards him on account of what you know about his past, but respect him for what has accrued to him, inasmuch as possessions do not come of their own.' Ability and knowledge, but also compliance and

submission, were the best recipe for success and advancement: 'Bend your back to your superior, your overseer of royal administration, then will your house endure in its property, and your rewards will be as they should.' Ethics of the officials of the Old Kingdom were very pragmatic and aimed at ensuring success in this world. They reflected the contemporary understanding of progress, with a return to the same starting point at each new beginning and the maintenance of the status quo. The 'established order' of the Old Kingdom was, according to the prevailing doctrine, perfect and incapable of further improvement, and man's duty was to conform. At the same time, Old Kingdom ethics insisted on correct behaviour and demanded a developed sense of social conscience in the attitude towards the poor and weak.

There are no long genealogies in Old Kingdom tombs displaying the owner's ancestry on which he would have staked a claim to his position in society, and in most cases not even the names of the parents are mentioned. The overall impression is that it was a period of opportunities, when a capable and determined man was appreciated and could make his mark in the world.

The peasants (*meret*) of the Old Kingdom were settled on the land which they cultivated. This could be administered by the state, belong to one of the royal cult or temple establishments, or form part of a tomb endowment. Some of the peasants may even have been attached to privately owned estates. Our information about the details of their legal position is very scanty, but it is clear that they were tied to the land on which they worked and which provided their own living, and had no say in the matter when the land changed hands. They were not free to leave or offer their work elsewhere. At the same time, there is no evidence that they would have been legally regarded as separate items of property and sold as slaves. The Egyptians of the Old Kingdom never really divorced these two elements, the land and its cultivators. It is at least to some extent possible to perceive why. When new farming estates were founded on previously unexploited land, the king had the power to settle them with people from elsewhere. The land presented by him to cult and temple establishments or given as tomb-endowments was already settled, because without people to cultivate it its value would have been limited. On the whole, there was a shortage of labour due to the creation of new estates and the movement of people from farming to other activities. The Egyptian administrative system was so thorough that, almost certainly, all inhabitants were registered so that it was easy to keep check on any population movements. Officials had the use of their 'ex officio' property, but were not allowed to dispose freely of it. This also applied to the personnel settled on the land. Estates of cult and temple establishments and tomb endowments 'belonged' to the deceased kings and officials and to gods, and so they were legally inalienable by the living. The possibilities of transactions involving only people were, therefore, very limited.

War was the only significant source of fresh manpower. We have no precise information on how captives were used and how they were treated. Some were probably settled on the newly recovered land or distributed among existing royal estates, while others may have been employed in quarrying and building. To these people, labour brought by force from abroad, it would be tempting to apply the term 'slaves', though this would be misleading. These prisoners of war did not produce a permanent social group among the Egyptian farming population and did not provide an alternative to the existing method of organization of agricultural production; on the contrary, they were gradually assimilated into the rest of the population.

91

Craftsmen were attached to institutions, such as the palace or temples. In a royal cult establishment they also doubled as part-time priests. Like the peasants of the establishment with whom they may have shared the 'pyramid-town', they benefited from exemptions granted to their settlement by the king, but unlike them they were in a position to use their free time for private gain. The craftsmen who had to be 'satisfied' in return for work done on private tombs came, no doubt, from royal cult establishments. Their position in society was somewhat ambiguous. They were not their own free agents because they were tied to the cult establishments to which they belonged, but unlike peasants whose surplus produce was probably creamed off most efficiently by their institutions, they were able to accumulate private property.

The only section of Old Kingdom society whose way of life can be reconstructed to some extent is officialdom, including some members of the royal family, because only their tombs contain enough inscriptional and visual evidence concerning daily life. The circumstances of the lives of ordinary peasants and craftsmen are known to us only insofar as they appear as participants in scenes shown in officials' tombs. Their houses have hardly ever been found in excavations. Comparable information concerning the king is completely lacking. The few extant administrative documents deal almost exclusively with affairs of cult establishments, temples, and tomb endowments, and while this information is invaluable for understanding how these institutions worked, it sheds little light on the lives of their ordinary personnel. The texts and decoration of pyramid temples and later the pyramids themselves had matters other than everyday life as their main theme.

Nikanesut was an official of the Fifth Dynasty whose titles suggest that he was in the personal service of the king. He also held several priestly titles, and was a 'king's son of his body', almost certainly an honorific court rank. The closest members of the household of this official are shown in the reliefs of the only decorated room in his tomb-chapel at Giza. Two 'overseers of the property' (imy-ra per) called Wehemkai and Kaiemnefert were in overall charge of Nikanesut's estates, though not necessarily simultaneously, and they were supported by eleven 'scribes' (zesh). A 'director of the workforce' (kherep iset) organized the peasants in the fields, while two 'directors of the dining hall' (kherep zeh), two 'overseers of linen' (imy-ra sesher), a 'seal-bearer', three butchers, two bakers, one cook, and five butlers looked after the well-being of the tomb-owner at home. Twelve 'servants of the spirit' (hem-ka) are shown in the tomb. As in the case of people living in pyramid towns and serving royal cults, 'servants of the spirit' combined ordinary jobs connected with the tomb endowment with part-time assistance at simple ceremonies connected with the maintenance of the funerary cult of the tomb-owner. Another fifteen men of Nikanesut's household represented in his tomb are without an indication of their profession. Other tombs add details to this insight into the organization of an official's property. A 'manager of the estate' (heqa hut) was responsible to the 'overseer of the property' for the daily running of each estate, and 'overseers' of 'the stalls' (imy-ra medjet) and 'the herds' (imy-ra tjesut) for the tomb-owner's cattle. An 'overseer of the storeroom' (imy-ra per-shena) supervised the household proper.

Domestic scenes show the tomb-owner at banquets, entertained by music made by flautists and harpists, and by singing and dancing, some of it bordering on acrobatics, or playing the snake (mehen) and senet board games. His wife—one only, though it seems that there was no specific prohibition regarding polygamy—and his children are often shown

Two circumstances make the identification of this beautifully finished, but uninscribed, greywacke head difficult. Firstly, the number of royal statues of the Old Kingdom unequivocally identified by texts is small, and so for most kings we have few or no comparisons to work with. Secondly, both the White Crown and the Red Crown were worn by gods and goddesses as well as kings, and so the possibility that the head belongs to a statue of a deity cannot be discounted. The sculpture was found near the sun-temple of King Userkaf at Abusir, and probably represents this king. Nevertheless, it is difficult to see in it many similarities with the colossal granite head, also thought to represent Userkaf, from his cult temple at Saqqara.

prominently by his side, accompanied by personal servants and entertainers, some of them dwarfs, and pet dogs and monkeys. Women did not take part in Egyptian administration, but many of those related to officials served as priestesses (*hemet*) of local gods. It seems that legally the position of women in society was not inferior to that of men, and the material well-being of married women was secured by written contracts.

In tomb-scenes, the owner is invariably a dignified, but passive, spectator of activities unfolding in registers before him. Almost the only exceptions are the occasions of hunting fowl in the marshes, where he is standing in a small papyrus raft about to hurl a wooden throw-stick at birds rising out of a papyrus thicket, or fishing, with several fish already impaled on a long barbed spear. These scenes may have soon become a genre rather than a faithful reflection of reality, and so they need not be taken at their full face value, but at the same time their veracity cannot be dismissed completely.

The inauguration of large building projects organized by the state from the beginning of the Third Dynasty led to the creation of a professional administrative system. While previously all high offices were held by the king's relatives, mostly royal princes, commoners now began to be appointed to all but a few positions in administration. Imhotep, the legendary figure reputed to be the architect of Netjerikhet's step pyramid, may have been the first of the eminently capable officials of non-royal blood who now came to the fore.

This development was, no doubt, a consequence of the vast increase in the size of bureaucracy required by the tightly governed centralized state, but it also represented an important change in administration's ideological basis. Royal princes had been able to exercise authority because of their blood relationship to the king, while the power of new officials was delegated to them and was conferred on them through their appointment. A crack separating the executive role of the state and the ideological function of the king and his relatives appeared for the first time in Egyptian history.

The highest Old Kingdom office was that of chief justice and vizier (*taity zab tjaty*) whose control extended over all departments of state administration and the judiciary, and who was directly responsible to the king. The origins of the office are obscure. The votive palette and mace-head of the Predynastic King Narmer show a person described as *tjat*, close to the king, and the etymology of this term is sought in the word (*we*)*tjat*, 'to beget'. Indeed, until the Fifth Dynasty, viziers were exclusively royal princes or their sons. The first vizier known to us by name is Menka, probably of the reign of Netjerikhet, but it was not until the Fourth Dynasty that the office acquired its full status while held by the sons of Kings Snofru, Khufu, Khephren, and Menkaure. When in the Fifth Dynasty even this office passed into the hands of commoners, royal relatives ceased to exert direct influence on the management of state affairs.

The title of vizier underwent a further development first noticeable at the end of the Fifth Dynasty. Some of the titles of Old Kingdom officials were not functional, but conveyed their court rank. The concept probably goes back to the times when the authority to carry out a task on the king's behalf sprang from the official's blood relationship to the king, i.e. his court standing or 'rank'. The importance may not have been purely theoretical and concerned with court protocol, but may have also carried some very practical advantages in the form of benefits to which the holder of such a rank was entitled. Some of the titles which fell in this category soon lost their original meaning and began to be used as rank

indicators. Even the title 'king's son' could be used in this way. Khufu's vizier Hemyunu had the title 'king's son of his body', although it is almost certain that his father was prince Nefermaet. The title of a prince was then conferred on Hemyunu in order to give him the court rank customary for a vizier. By an extension of this idea the title of vizier came to be regarded as a court rank indicator towards the end of the Old Kingdom, and its holders, particularly those who resided in provinces, were not always acting viziers.

An official like a vizier, with his all-embracing powers and complete control, was required because of the extreme fragmentation and complexity of the system of management and the existence of several chains of command. At the same time, individual officials usually concentrated several positions in their hands. This probably enabled them to shortcut procedures and strengthened the overall unity of the system, but it makes it difficult for us to follow how this worked. Officials of state administration were involved in the management of the state treasury, granary, and arsenal, the collection of revenue through taxes and its re-distribution, the imposition of forced labour, the organization of provinces, and various judicial tasks. Many of them played a more immediate economic role in the running of the crown property estates and workshops, or the organization of mining and quarrying expeditions. At the same time, some of them may have held offices connected with the king's household and personal service from which state administration developed in the first place. They may also have been connected in various capacities with royal cult

The concept of the king's right and duty to subjugate foreign lands found early artistic expression on the bases of royal statues which show the heads of prostrate captives. Usually made of a hard stone, in this case granite, these sculptures have been variously dated, but most of them are now attributed to the Third Dynasty. This piece comes from San el-Hagar (Tanis) in the north-eastern Delta, where it had probably been taken for re-use from elsewhere.

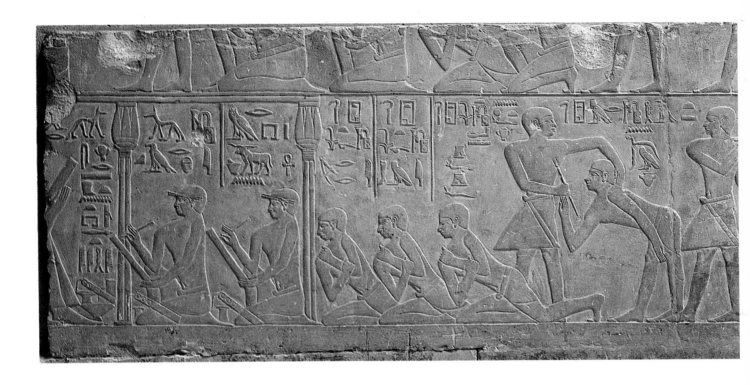

Estate managers (heka hut) are brought before a council and scribes in order to render accounts of their farms in the early Sixth Dynasty tomb of Mereruka at Saqqara.

establishments, sun-temples, or temples of local gods. To what extent they were answerable to the vizier in these respects is not clear.

The state treasury, with an overseer (*imy-ra per-hedj*) in charge, collected revenue produced at royal estates and, to a lesser degree, received as taxes. This mostly consisted of various articles of food, but also clothes, tools, furniture, wood, etc., each kept in a special section of the treasury. The storage of grain was administered separately by the state granary (*shenut*), as probably were the arsenal and magazines of oil. The goods kept in these establishments were used to satisfy the requirements of the palace household, but also to pay workmen of the royal workshops. They provided donations in kind presented by the king to pyramid and temple establishments, as well as 'offerings given by the king' to tombs of officials and members of the royal family. All these departments of state administration had large staffs of scribes, and the degree of control over even the smallest transactions must have been considerable. Unfortunately, none of these documents has so far been found.

The idea of justice and administering the law was closely connected with the concept of the world order (*maet*). There were no written laws during the Old Kingdom, but royal decrees issued for institutions as well as to private individuals were recorded and kept in royal archives. The vizier was the supreme judge, and among his titles were 'overseer of the six great courts' (*imy-ra hut-weret issau*), in whose capacity he was in charge of all lawsuits, and 'priest of the goddess Maet' (*hem-netjer maet*). An 'overseer of the great court' (*imy-ra hut-weret*) presumably conducted the legal proceedings, while 'judge and keeper of Nekhen' (*zab iry-nekhen*) was an ancient title of an official who was often involved in special legal proceedings. Only the most important criminal cases were tried in this way. Administration of justice for minor offences, particularly those involving property or dereliction of duty, was probably left in the hands of councils, i.e. the bodies of administrators of each institution. Physical punishment of those found guilty of misdemeanour or negligence, particularly where agricultural production was concerned, was within the confines of a property (*per-djet*) carried out by a body of the 'sons of the property' (*zau-per*).

In the provinces, the organization of royal estates, with the older villages (*niut*) subordinated to them, replaced the loose regional groupings headed by *adj-mer* officials of the first dynasties, which themselves reflected the Predynastic chiefdoms. The district (nome) organization of provinces during the Old Kingdom in which they were gradually transformed is shown almost already fully developed in the reliefs of the valley temple of the southern pyramid of King Snofru at Dahshur. Initially, each district was the responsibility of an 'overseer of commissions' (*imy-ra wepwet*). In the Fifth Dynasty the title of this administrator changed to 'overseer of the district' (*imy-ra*, followed by the hieroglyph of the appropriate district), and in the Sixth Dynasty to 'great overlord of the district' (*hery-tep aa en* + the district sign). The office of an 'overseer of Upper Egypt' (*imy-ra shemau*) with special responsibilities for the southern districts far from the capital, was created in the Fifth Dynasty.

There were twenty-two districts in the valley south of the capital, starting with Ta-sety (present Aswan), while the Delta consisted of fifteen. With the exception of parts of the Delta, particularly the north-eastern and coastal regions, the area administered was much the same as in later times. The provincial capitals of these districts never developed into large urban centres during the Old Kingdom, and their administrative and religious importance far outweighed their size.

Scribes in the Saqqara tomb-chapel of Princess Sesh-seshet Idut of the Sixth Dynasty.

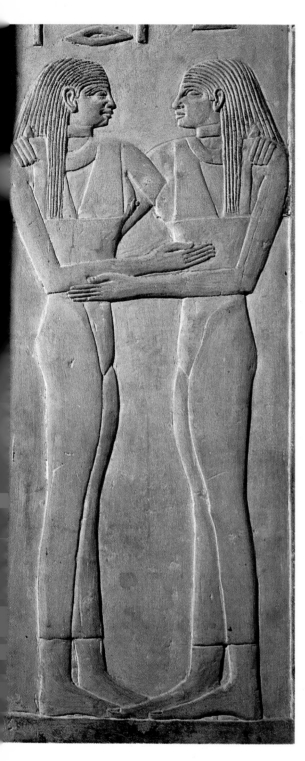

The decoration of the false-door of Nikaure, who was a 'priest [hem-netjer] of the god Re and of the goddess Hathor in the sun-temple of King Neferirkare', displays several unusual features. Relatives are sometimes represented with the tomb-owner, but here Nikaure's mother-in-law Hetepheres and his wife Ihat are shown embracing on the left outer jamb.

There is no evidence of serious social unrest during the Old Kingdom, but we must be aware of the fact that the sources of information at our disposal would probably not reflect them in any case. The Old Kingdom did not know a specialized permanent lawkeeping force or army, though there were some frontier fortresses and garrisons. Their personnel was mostly probably recruited from mercenary Nubians, whose duty was to perform tasks of a small-scale military or police nature. The danger of the military interfering in the affairs of the state was thus non-existent. The approach to any emergency which required a larger military force was the same as in the case of quarrying and mining expeditions. A body of men was conscripted and they were led by their own superiors, with an official appointed by the king in overall charge. The title 'overseer of the task force' (*imy-ra mesha*) applied to the leaders of military as well as peaceful expeditions. Towards the end of the Old Kingdom the same trend appeared as that detectable in trade expeditions, and military enterprises were no longer organized centrally by the state, but were delegated to local officials in border areas.

Throughout the Old Kingdom Egypt enjoyed almost complete safety from foreign intervention, and there was no need for military fortifications within the country. Its superior weapons, but in particular its organization, ensured that nomadic tribes of the deserts on both sides of the Nile soon ceased to present a military threat to its security. Nubia, south of the first Nile cataract, was probably the only area which witnessed vigorous successive campaigns at the beginning of the Old Kingdom, but their motivation was economic and the situation was resolved early in the Fourth Dynasty. Only during the Sixth Dynasty did reports of military actions start to multiply as Egypt's commercial interests and its access to natural resources came under threat, but this never amounted to endangering the existence of the state itself. The only more serious problem which started developing in the north-east during the reign of Pepy I was, apparently, dealt with successfully.

The plunder and the number of captives brought back from expeditions to Nubia in the reign of Snofru are so conspicuously large that they may have been the Egyptians' main motivation. During the early Old Kingdom the Egyptian state embarked on an imperialistic policy of the crudest type directed towards the inhabitants of the Nile valley south of the first cataract. In the Fourth Dynasty an Egyptian settlement existed at Buhen, near the second Nile cataract, but no attempt was made to colonize Nubia or to incorporate it into the general Egyptian administrative system, presumably because of the relatively poor conditions for farming and the shortage of people in Egypt proper. Instead, it was regarded as a source of manpower, cattle, wood, and minerals at the time when Egypt's economy was stretched to the limit because of the monumental building projects. All these resources were exploited to the utmost. The inhabitants of Nubia may have presented problems to Egyptian trade and access to natural resources, but there is nothing to indicate that they would have threatened Egypt's safety at any time. The result was almost complete depopulation of the Nile valley in Nubia, which lasted until the beginning of the Sixth Dynasty, with the inhabitants reduced to migrant nomadic groups.

The situation changed radically in the Sixth Dynasty as the result of population pressures which developed in the south and the abandonment of the previous policy towards Nubia by the Egyptians. The Nubian valley was once again settled. Relations were, at least at first, amicable. Weni, an official of Pepy I, recruited some of the troops for his Asiatic campaign from among 'the Irtjet-Nubians, the Medja-Nubians, the

Yam-Nubians, the Wawat-Nubians, and the Kaau-Nubians'. A rock inscription in the Aswan area records that King Merenre in person received Nubian chiefs there in the 'year of the fifth census', during which 'the chiefs of Medja, Irtjet, and Wawat were kissing the ground and were giving very great adoration'. Weni was actively helped by the Nubians during the same reign: 'His Majesty sent me to excavate five canals in Upper Egypt and to build three barges and four boats of acacia of Wawat, while the chiefs of Irtjet, Wawat, Yam, and Medja provided wood for them. I achieved it all in a single year.' Relations deteriorated towards the end of the Sixth Dynasty: Egypt's might was on the decline, while the power of Nubian chiefs was ascendant. Armed clashes and retributive expeditions led by administrators of the southernmost district of Egypt were frequently reported.

Two women playing the harp and singing are represented in another small scene on Nikaure's false-door. Although dating to the first half of the Fifth Dynasty, the false-door adopted some of the themes of decoration of the chapels, and so anticipated trends more common towards the end of the Old Kingdom.

Children playing games, from the early Sixth Dynasty tomb of Mereruka at Saqqara.

Although the record of an enormous Libyan booty accompanies a relief in the pyramid temple of Sahure at Abusir, its value as historical evidence is in doubt. With some exceptions in the Fourth Dynasty, military actions against the tribes living to the west of the Nile valley must have been very limited. The reason for this lack of interest on the parts of the Egyptians was that this region possessed a relatively small economic importance.

Egypt's relations with the areas to the east and north-east were of a more aggressive nature, aimed at securing access to the resources of the Sinai. Clashes with the nomads inhabiting the Eastern Desert and Sinai are listed on the Palermo Stone, and their subjugation symbolically proclaimed in rock inscriptions at Sinai.

Large-scale campaigning took place in Palestine during the reign of Pepy I and was described in the autobiographical text of Weni: 'His Majesty sent me to lead this army five times in order to destroy the land of the sand-dwellers every time they rebelled, with these troops.' It seems that the preventive measures taken by the Egyptians were caused by security considerations of a more serious nature, because they required a large number of troops. In two private tombs of the Sixth Dynasty, those of Kaemhest at Saqqara and of Inti at Dishasha, there are representations of a siege of a fortified town which may reflect these campaigns. For the first time in Egyptian military history we even get a glimpse of tactics employed in the engagement against desert raiders. Weni describes it as follows: 'I crossed in boats with these troops and landed behind a hill of a ridge to the north of the land of the sand-dwellers, while half of this army of mine was on the road. I came, captured all of them, and killed every raider among them.'

Facing page: The vizier Ptahhotpe carried in a palanquin, on the left outer jamb of the stela (false-door) in his tomb at Saqqara.

SEVEN

GODS
AND TOMBS

'Look up, you gods who are in the netherworld! King Unas has come, having become the great god, so that you may see him.' ★

King Unas suckled by an unknown goddess, on a relief from his cult temple at Saqqara. In most cases, the decoration of the cult temples is known to us only from isolated and very incomplete scenes. The temples, which have yielded more substantial areas of the original decorated surface, are those of Sahure at Abusir, and of Pepy II at Saqqara, but even they are in a very dilapidated state.

EACH SECTION OF THE EGYPTIAN POPULATION had its own ideas and beliefs, representing attempts to come to terms with the forces of nature and society beyond man's understanding. The official dogma concerning the king, reflected in the reliefs of the royal pyramid-complexes and the texts inscribed inside the pyramids, had little in common with the spiritual life of the majority of the Egyptian population and would have been scarcely comprehensible to them. The relationship of the individual to the state, embodied in the king, or to the local gods, as well as ideas about continued existence after death, affected the life of everyone, but to varying degrees. In Egypt different aspects of spiritual life were inextricably fused into one. Although we use terms such as 'religion', 'ideas about life after death', and 'state doctrine', to try to disentangle them is impossible. These ideas developed historically and were subjected to much re-interpretation, and did not form a perfect system without contradictions. The overall picture of the situation during the Old Kingdom presented to us by the available sources is very incomplete and unbalanced, and we are to some extent dependent on assumptions drawn from later times.

The belief in a local god, connected with a particular area and with limited powers, and local myths, was at the root of Old Kingdom religion. The Egyptian pantheon was thus a complicated system of deities of varying nature and significance, with little resembling a strict hierarchical order. Different gods originally played similar roles in various parts of the country, and there were varying approaches to the concepts of creation and cosmology. With the appearance of a unified state came attempts in the main religious centres, such as Iunu (Heliopolis) and Ineb-hedj (Memphis), to rationalize this situation, but they never developed further during the Old Kingdom, and the precise stages of this process are not clear.

The importance of the gods and their mutual relationship changed as did their local areas. Some of the local deities were recognized and accepted, even outside their home districts, by the top intellectual section of Egyptian society, but they almost certainly played no part in the spiritual life of humbler people. It was only the local god, and perhaps a few other deities associated with him, who was really significant for an ordinary individual whose religious outlook remained confined to the area where he lived. In the case of officials, the reasons for this limited outlook could be of a more materialistic nature, such as serving as a priest in the local god's traditional temple. It is likely that the peasant population

---

★ *Pyramid Texts, §272.*

also worshipped a host of minor deities about whom we know little because of their 'semi-official' nature. These found little reflection on monuments which are rarely associated with the lowest stratum of Egyptian society. Our awareness of them is based on material of later periods.

Nearly every god of the earliest part of Egyptian history was visualized in the form of an animal, bird, or even an inanimate object. Thus Bastet, the local goddess of the town Bast (modern Tell Basta) in the eastern Delta, became associated with a lioness, the god Thoth of Khemenu (Hermopolis Magna, modern El-Ashmunein) with an ibis, Khnum of the first cataract region with a ram, the goddess Hathor, whose worship was known from several places, with a cow, and the god Sobek with a crocodile. The precise reasons for such associations are not clear, but natural logic seems to have influenced the choice. Thus, the cults of the bull were popular in the cattle-grazing area of the Delta, a crocodile cult was known from the marshy Faiyum, etc. The god could adopt the form of an animal in order to become manifest, but this did not mean the animal itself was regarded as a deity. An unsophisticated mind prefers to think in terms of visual images rather than abstract concepts, and the system of local deities reflects the earliest stages of the development of Egyptian religious thought.

Attempts to endow gods, in particular the ancient god Min of Gebtiu (Koptos, modern Qift) and Ptah of Ineb-hedj (Memphis), with human forms date to the end of the Predynastic Period or shortly afterwards. This may have been due to their relatively late rise to prominence, or to the need to devise a more accessible image for these deities. So the ithyphallic god Min, one of the most ancient and most important local gods of the Old Kingdom, had previously been worshipped as a curious harpoon-like object (fetish), the precise nature of which is not clear. And when the capital moved to the north, the god Ptah benefited greatly from his connection with the area and became the most prominent among local gods of the Old Kingdom. The image of a deity represented with human characteristics shows a completely different understanding of the nature of gods because previously the contrast between man and the forces of nature was the very basis of primitive religion.

A combination of human and animal features in one form, e.g. the representation of the goddess Bastet as a woman with the head of a lioness, was a typically Egyptian artistic device, rather than a religious development in its own right. It became the usual form in which the deity appeared in official reliefs and statues, but did not contain additional significance. For most people, to whom official temples were closed, the fully zoomorphic idea of their local god remained the deity's main manifestation.

Two gods, originally connected with particular localities and thus local deities, became closely associated with the concept of kingship and the person of the king, and acquired special status. Horus and Seth were the two most influential gods of the earliest part of Egyptian history, the former represented as a hawk (*heru* means 'one who is distant' or 'one who is high'), the latter as an obscure animal which at first resembled a donkey. They were the local gods of the Upper Egyptian towns Nekhen and Nubt, and their connection with the early kings thus had a historical justification. It seems, however, that by the time the religious significance of these towns became reflected in the court art of the late Predynastic Period their former political importance was already a thing of the past. The unique position of these gods in no way implied a popular worship.

Most of the local gods, recognized by the state and regarded as representatives of their home districts, are attested from the earliest dynasties. Because of the role the king played in the world he alone could, as an intermediary, communicate with gods on behalf of men. This meant that monuments directly reflecting the attitudes of officials and still humbler people to these gods are practically non-existent during the Old Kingdom. Our information derives mostly from such meagre sources as personal names (e.g. the common name Ptahhotpe can be translated as 'The God Ptah is Satisfied', Nefer-her-sokar as 'The Face of the God Sokar is Beautiful', and Ankh-hathor as 'May the Goddess Hathor Live!'), the priesthoods held by tomb-owners and their relatives, the names of their estates recorded in tombs, and the names of gods listed in offering-texts on stelae and elsewhere in tombs. At his coronation, the king had to secure approval from local gods for his reign, and in addition to being responsible for the welfare of men on earth and in the afterlife, he was expected to maintain the shrines of local gods and to provide offerings for them and provisions for the upkeep of their priesthood.

This 'official' popular religion of the Old Kingdom, supported by the king, was very much based on the carrying out of rituals. The shrines were served by semi-professional 'servants of the god' (*hem-netjer*), recruited from local officials. The buildings, with their mud-brick walls and no relief decoration, were modest affairs, and this explains why so little of them has survived. They were situated in towns, not in the desert like royal cult temples and sun-temples, and thus fell victim to later alterations and re-building. The making of cult-statues for these sanctuaries is recorded in the 'annals', but hardly any have survived. This may be due to the fact that often their material, such as metal or wood, was re-used in later times. It is likely that the daily ritual in these temples was

For most people, it is the pyramids which symbolize the achievements of the Old Kingdom civilization. Their silent massive structures inspire awe and wonder, but standing before them we hardly feel that we are in direct contact with the thought and work of living people of a bygone age. The reconstructed wooden barque, originally found dismantled in a 'boat-pit' near the south-eastern corner of Khufu's pyramid, has the power to produce such an effect. Thousands of years of religion, mastery over the material, and nautical skill, are contained in this beautiful craft. Almost all the materials used in the boat's reconstruction are ancient. The shape is that of a sacred barque (wia), with a tall prow and stern, and the boat was probably used during Khufu's funeral. Yet another boat may still rest in a similar pit further to the west.

quite simple and consisted of taking the image of the god out of its shrine, cleansing, clothing, and anointing it, and offering it symbolic food and drink. Religious festivals were celebrated, and it was probably only on these occasions that ordinary people, who otherwise did not have access to the temple, had a chance to see the image of the local god.

At first, the main beneficiaries of the king's favours were the religious centres near the capital, and it appears that it was only in the Fifth Dynasty that temples even in the provinces began to receive land donations which turned them into economically independent institutions. It is possible that this was at first little more than a convenient substitute for the previous method of provisioning, but it proved of great importance for the growing economic self-reliance of the officials who were attached to these temples in priestly capacities. The king's greater interest in the shrines of local gods could have been the consequence of an earlier development. It seems that the official dogma concerning the king's relationship with the gods was re-defined and systematized during the Fourth Dynasty in order to make him part of a system with the creator sun-god Re (or, in a syncretized form, Re-Harakhti, 'Re-Horus of the Horizon') of Iunu

'Boat-pits' are often situated near Old Kingdom pyramids. They are of two types: those which imitate the shape of ceremonial barques, as e.g. the 'boat-pit' near the south-eastern corner of Radjedef's pyramid at Abu Rawash, and the rectangular pits which contain dismantled wooden boats. The stone replicas of barques are presumably connected with the idea of sky voyages on which the king was to accompany the sun-god. There can be several such boats round a cult temple and pyramid.

(Heliopolis) at the head. The rise in importance of the sun-god led to his recognition as the main state-god of the Old Kingdom, and the appearance of the name of the god in royal names and titles reflected it. The king, while still being called Horus, now became a 'son of the god Re'.

The first three kings of the Fifth Dynasty, according to a later popular tradition, originated in the union of the sun-god and the wife of a priest of Re. A series of sun-temples was built for the god's worship. From Userkaf to Menkauhor—except for the ephemeral Shepseskare—each king made a new sun-temple on a fresh site near the capital and not far away from his pyramid. This was a concept entirely different from the building or enlargement of temples of local gods on traditional locations, and was unique to the Fifth Dynasty. It was clearly regarded as each king's duty during his reign. The god Re as the chief state god was treated in the same way as the king, his representative on earth. The king built a pyramid and a cult establishment for himself, and a sun-temple for the worship of the state god where he stressed the god's relationship to his own reign. These temples received large donations of offerings and land, had their own personnel, and for much of the Fifth Dynasty were the most important economic institutions in the country after the state.

The increased influence of pyramid establishments in the second half of the Fifth Dynasty followed the decline and cessation of the building of sun-temples. The reasons behind this decline were very likely purely economic, rather than ideological, the system no longer being able to sustain the demanding construction schedule of both projects and the endowing of both institutions during a single reign.

Apart from the local god one other deity with local connections figured very prominently in the thoughts of the Egyptians of the Old Kingdom. It was the god of the local necropolis, such as Khentiamentiu at Abdju (Abydos) and Sokar in the Ineb-hedj (Memphis) region, and universally Anubis, usually associated with the jackal, and later Osiris. At a man's death one of the elements of his personality, 'vital force' or 'spirit' (*ka*), continued to exist in the tomb, while the deceased himself became an *akh*-spirit after the accomplishment of the prescribed funeral rites. The body was deemed necessary for the *ka*'s continued existence, and attempts to provide a substitute abode for it led to the introduction of tomb statues. The same belief prompted the first experiments with artificial preservation (mummification). The *ka*'s material needs were similar to those of

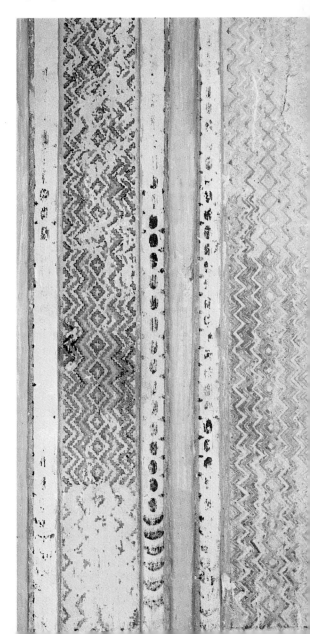

The chapel (i.e. the part of the tomb which was above ground and accessible) of a large mastaba of the Fifth or Sixth Dynasty could consist of a number of porticos, corridors, halls, courts, store-rooms, etc. The most important among them was the offering-room with a false-door. Unusually, in the mastaba of Mereruka the pillared hall contains a niche with an offering-table and a statue of the tomb-owner.

the living, and food and drink offerings were brought to the tomb's chapel which was the only part publicly accessible. In the absence of real offerings, these could be provided symbolically by representations on the stela (false-door) or tomb walls, or by recitation of prescribed formulae. The activities represented in Old Kingdom tombs which are connected with such provisioning are thus meant to be taking place very much in this world, not in any version of an Egyptian paradise.

The god of the necropolis was regarded as the ruler of the dead buried in his area. The provisioning of officials' tombs was originally seen as a transaction involving the king as the donor, the necropolis-god as the main beneficiary, and the tomb-owner as a participant allowed to share some of the offerings with the necropolis-god. No gods except those connected with the necropolis played any part in the ideas concerning afterlife reflected in private tombs of the Old Kingdom, and scenes involving gods were never shown in them. The strict division between the king and ordinary men in this world was thus continued in the arrangements made for the afterlife.

While ordinary spirits continued to exist in the realm of the god of the local necropolis, the king was originally thought to depart after his death to the polar star in the sky, the celestial region of the goddess Nut, and the abode of gods whom he joined there. He could adopt various forms and use various means to reach the sky, where he accompanied the sun-god in his barque in order to traverse the sky with him. The beliefs concerning this form of afterlife, probably closely related to the sky and solar concepts of Iunu (Heliopolis), are known to us from the Pyramid Texts. These were the texts inscribed inside the pyramids of kings and several queens from the end of the Fifth Dynasty. The Pyramid Texts contain religious and funerary spells and parts of myths of various dates and thus represent a mixture of widely differing concepts. They were probably included in an attempt to ensure that the king had them to hand if knowledge of them was required in his existence after death. Some of these texts may have been recited during the ceremonies accompanying the funeral.

The dead king is, however, in the Pyramid Texts also identified with the god Osiris. Osiris was originally a chthonic deity. At first, he perhaps assimilated the god Anedjti, and became connected with the town of Djedu (Busiris) in the central Delta, and very early on also Iunu (Heliopolis). His importance grew rapidly, and he may have, as early as the Fourth Dynasty, influenced the changes in the royal pyramid-complexes. In private tombs Osiris began to be mentioned in the Fifth Dynasty, which is also the earliest date at which he was represented in human form. He quickly acquired the status of the universal god of the nether-world, with Djedu (Busiris) and Abdju (Abydos) as his main cult centres. In Abdju, he assimilated the original god Khentiamentiu. Throughout the Old Kingdom only the king was identified after death with the god Osiris.

Much of the mythology known to us from later periods of Egyptian history must have already existed during the Old Kingdom. The myth of Seth's killing his brother Osiris, of the goddesses Isis and Nephthys' mourning over his body, and his eventual vindication by Horus, is already suggested in the Pyramid Texts.

Although a vast body of material is available for the student of religion during the later periods of Egyptian history, information concerning the Old Kingdom is very limited. No papyri with religious texts have been found, and only afterlife aspects are stressed in private tombs. Royal pyramid-complexes are almost the only source of reliefs showing gods, and the Pyramid Texts represent the only large corpus of inscriptions. Temples of local gods are virtually unknown.

In private tombs, the west-oriented stela (false-door) was thought to be a link connecting the world of the living and the world of the dead. The ka of the tomb-owner partook of the offerings of food and drink brought to the false-door which was the focal point of the tomb-chapel. The false-door invariably carried several representations of the tomb-owner in relief, but exceptionally one or more of these were made three-dimensional, probably influenced by statues which became an integral part of rock-cut tombs. This figure of Idu, half-emerging from the ground in his Sixth Dynasty tomb at Giza, strikes us as rather absurd in its concept, but it is interesting both for the imagery which inspired it, and because it demonstrates the close relationship between 'two-dimensional' reliefs and three-dimensional statues.

EIGHT

TOMB-ARTISTS AND THE WORLD

'The draughtsman of the temple of the goddess Matit, Pepy-sonb, whose real name is Nesu.'★

All statues of the Old Kingdom were functional, i.e. made to play a particular role in a temple, pyramid-complex, or tomb. With a few exceptions, art for art's sake did not exist, and artistic development was thus nothing but the search for a better way of fulfilling the sculpture's formal role or, at best, working within tightly prescribed limits. Sometimes statues were part of the decorative programme of a temple or a tomb. At other times they were regarded as an embodiment of the physical characteristics of the king or the tomb-owner, in order to provide an abode for the spirit (ka) if anything should happen to the corpse. The statues of Prince Rahotpe shown on page 113 and his wife Nofret pictured here come from their early Fourth Dynasty tomb at Maidum. Although made separately, they were intended as a pair.

SINCE MUCH OF OUR KNOWLEDGE of everyday life in Egypt during the Old Kingdom derives from reliefs in tomb-chapels, an understanding of the conventions of tomb art of this period and an appreciation of the limits of the artist's creative freedom are essential for interpreting this evidence.

The Egyptian canon, or fixed system of proportions according to which the human body was represented, appeared in a rudimentary form in late Predynastic court art. The same was true of the conventional way in which the body was seen: face and mouth in profile, eye and eyebrow in full view, chest and shoulders in front view, but waist and legs again in profile. The picture of the human figure is thus a composite view which could never be seen by one pair of eyes at one time. The Egyptian artist, however, sought a compromise in this approach to the portrayal of reality, and while he adhered to the concept that all essential parts must be represented and shown in their most characteristic views, he assembled these elements in a way which was as close as possible to how he normally saw them as a whole. Sometimes even such paradoxical combinations as joining the left arm to the right shoulder and vice versa seemed a small price to pay in order to reconcile the two contradictory methods. This prescribed way of showing human figures applied rigorously to the protagonists in tomb scenes, but to a lesser degree to the representations of minor participants. The greatest freedom of expression the artist enjoyed was in the portrayal of animals.

The same 'mosaic' approach can be seen in the composition of large scenes. The relative heights of figures were important inasmuch as they helped to distinguish between protagonists and participants, and since the whole scene was approached through its individual elements, the difference in sizes was not felt to disturb the balance of the composition. A large seated figure of a man may be accompanied by a diminutive representation of his wife squatting by his legs, or the tomb-owner may be shown absurdly large in comparison with the small figures of his sons.

Egyptian art did not develop a concept of perspective similar to ours, although some points of agreement may be found. Distances from the viewer were indicated by the relative positions of partly overlapping representations along the horizontal rather than the vertical axis, but these remained on the same base-line. In a large composition the area was

★ *Artist's signature alongside the staff held by the official Djau in his late Sixth Dynasty tomb at Deir el-Gebrawi.*

divided into several horizontal registers delineated by such base-lines. The orientation of the scenes within each register was determined by the large figure in the composition, e.g. if the scene was one of 'inspection' carried out by the tomb-owner, the smaller figures in the registers were bringing the inspected goods or animals towards him. In the absence of a protagonist who could serve as a focal point, the orientation was subordinated to the tomb's architecture, e.g. the false-door stela, to which the scenes were oriented.

Symmetry and inner logic also played an important part. Large representations of the tomb-owner on door-jambs are always symmetrically arranged, and the logic manifests itself by the tomb-owner always coming out of his tomb to 'meet' the visitor. In pillared halls, with representations of the deceased often occupying all four faces of the pillars, the route the visitor is to take is virtually signposted in this way.

Actions, or a continuous series of occurrences, were recorded by a selection of typical situations or phases. The lowest register on the wall usually contained the most recent episodes or those concluding the cycle. This arrangement, albeit operating along the temporal rather than spatial axis, is to some extent comparable to our notion of perspective.

The themes into which the decoration is divided do not always correspond to individual walls of the tomb-chapel, and corners of rooms thus do not necessarily represent dividing lines. Certain walls became associated with specific subjects, but because of the great diversity of the plans of chapels only very general rules developed. Texts which accompany the scenes may describe the action represented, record the conversation of the participants, or give their names and those of the objects shown, but in many cases they only serve as a convenient way of filling space. Large empty areas were regarded as failings on the part of the designer and sculptor.

The designer of the decoration of a tomb-chapel was thus subjected to restrictions of several types. The proportions and the way figures were portrayed were firmly established, as were the general principles of the spatial distribution of scenes on the wall. The main themes of decoration were more or less obligatory, and also their position in the chapel was indicated if not prescribed. The techniques and the choice of colours were in most respects the same in all tombs. All this was the consequence of the very pragmatic function of tomb decoration in securing the tomb-owner's afterlife. The designer was not allowed to put this at risk by giving a free rein to his artistic inclinations or by experimenting. His task was to execute the required design which had proved its effectiveness in the past. Yet there are no two tomb-chapels with identical decoration, and the number of wall-scenes which are similar to the point of identity could be counted on the fingers of one hand. This shows beyond any doubt that the artist had some freedom to create, and that this freedom was consciously sought, the opportunities seized, and new solutions to old problems perhaps even demanded by those who paid for the work.

Each theme which appears in the decoration of Old Kingdom chapels can be broken up into a number of smaller episodes. Thus the agricultural theme may include ploughing, sowing, treading the grain, reaping, filling sacks with sheaves, bringing a donkey-herd, loading donkeys, transport of grain to threshing floors, threshing, winnowing, and storing grain in granaries, to mention just the more common topics. The first freedom of choice the artist was able to exercise was in the matter of composition. As a rule, more than just one theme appeared on the same wall, and the artist was able to decide how he was going to divide the

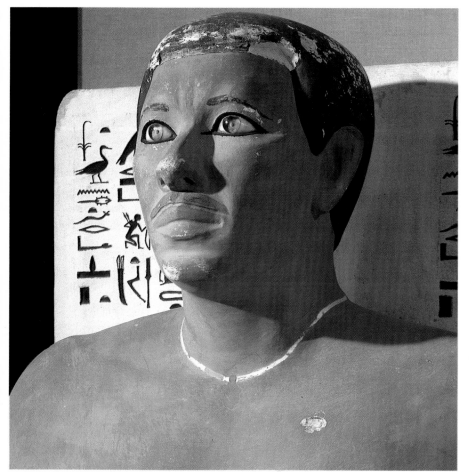

Above: The materials of private statues varied as much as those of royal sculptures, but the majority of them were made of the most accessible, limestone and wood. In the stone statues of the Old Kingdom it is still possible to discern the influence of the shape of the original block of material, but some wooden statues were now freed of the rigidity of the block: arms and hands were no longer attached to the body, and the sceptre and the staff were held in the hands in a natural way, not pressed against the torso. The material thus exercised a considerable influence over the development of form. This Sixth Dynasty statue of Meryre-haishtef was, unusually, carved of a single piece of ebony wood, and comes from Sidmant in Middle Egypt.

Left: A statue's uniqueness was guaranteed by its inscription. The text above the right shoulder of Rahotpe's statue is arranged in three vertical columns (hieroglyphs could be written horizontally as well as vertically), and describes him as 'overseer of the task force', 'director of bowmen', and 'King's son of his body'. The last five signs at the bottom of the left column record his name.

The 'overseer of sculptors' Niankhptah left a portrait of himself in the chapel of Ptahhotpe at Saqqara, whose reliefs he may have carved.

available space among them. Secondly, he had to select the episodes of each of the themes to be included. Thirdly, he chose how they were going to be shown. Even the most banal episodes, such as in the scenes of butchery, occur in countless varieties. The artist may have learnt to treat a particular episode in a number of different ways during his training, or he may have had patterns at his disposal from which he copied on the wall. The most attractive and probably the likeliest idea is that during his apprenticeship he had learnt to draw detailed elements of these episodes. A hand could be shown as holding a butcher's knife, or a flint knife-sharpener, or a leg of the slaughtered animal. A bent figure of a butcher might be completed to show him cutting off a leg of the slaughtered animal or extracting the heart. An upright figure could be supplied with various cuts of meat to carry. The artist's freedom thus in most cases consisted of being able to choose and combine prescribed elements of scenes in his own individual way to achieve the expected overall effect. Sometimes the artist's originality may have shown itself in an entirely new feature of his own added to the existing repertoire, and this was then adopted by others and became a standard element, while outdated and no longer fashionable scenes may have been abandoned. The distinction between a craftsman faithfully following a well-trodden path and a creative artist was very fine indeed, and often blurred.

Men responsible for the design and carving of tomb reliefs and statues were regarded in the same way as those who built the tomb or made its funerary equipment. The work on the construction of a tomb is never represented, but sculptors carving statues are often shown next to men making stone vessels, as well as carpenters and other craftsmen. In most cases they remained completely anonymous. Inscriptions in the Fourth Dynasty tomb of Nebemakhet at Giza, accompanying representations of two men, state that 'it was the painter Semerka, one rewarded by him (i.e. by the tomb-owner), who made his tomb', and 'it was Inkaf, one rewarded by him, who executed the work on his tomb'. They are very exceptional. A more common ploy was to introduce the figures of the artists among the small representations of offering-bearers. The most flagrant of such cases perhaps is that of the sculptor who was responsible for the magnificent reliefs in the Fifth Dynasty tomb of Ptahhotpe at Saqqara. On the north wall of the chapel, next to the scene of three papyrus rafts with boatmen engaged in a mock battle, is a small skiff showing the 'overseer of sculptors' Niankh-ptah well supplied with food and helping himself freely from a large jar of beer offered to him by a small boy. This artist, at least, seemed to have been quite content with his inconspicuous lot.

Statues formed a very important feature of private tombs, and scenes showing them dragged on sleds to the tombs are not uncommon in reliefs. Pictured here is a Sixth Dynasty mastaba of Princess Sesh-seshet Idut at Saqqara.

NINE

THE COLLAPSE

'Indeed, the ship of the southerners has gone adrift; towns are destroyed and Upper Egypt has become empty wastes.'★

WHEN PEPY II ASCENDED THE THRONE AT the age of six in 2247 BC, Egypt had been suffering from deep-rooted inner weaknesses for some time. Nevertheless, the tremendous momentum acquired during the uninterrupted progress from the beginning of the Predynastic Period carried the country onward until the compounded effects of the general malaise ripped apart the fabric of its society at the end of the Sixth Dynasty. The full impact of this became apparent during the First Intermediate Period.

The looming threat materialized shortly after Pepy II's immensely long rule of over ninety years. The strife for his succession created a political crisis which was reflected in the very short reign of one year and one month of one of his many sons, Merenre-Nemtyemzaf. It was followed by the probably unprecedented installation of a woman, Queen Neitiqert, on the Egyptian throne. The next seventeen rulers of the Seventh and Eighth Dynasties of Manetho shared only some sixteen years between them. Confusion must have permeated the whole system, until eventually the country came to be split into two large areas controlled by the rulers from Henen-nesut (Herakleopolis, modern Ihnasya el-Medina) and Waset (Thebes, modern Luxor).

Monumental building slowly ground to an almost complete halt. The pyramid of Pepy II was the last really large undertaking of the Old Kingdom. Only one of the pyramids of the following years has been located at Saqqara, and its reduced size and very simple construction are a telling illustration of the diminished royal power. Private tombs built near the capital from the mid-Sixth Dynasty onward became smaller and their decoration was frequently restricted to their painted burial chambers, and thus reflected a comparable trend in the declining prosperity of officialdom.

The body of Ankh-nes-pepy, a minor queen of Pepy II and the mother

A profound knowledge of history or architecture is not necessary in order to date Old Kingdom pyramids. It is enough to look at their present silhouettes: the step pyramid of Netjerikhet is of the Third Dynasty, while the pyramids proper which present a clean and sharp outline against the sky date from the Fourth Dynasty; those of the Fifth and Sixth Dynasties are now ragged shapes resembling huge piles of stone blocks and rubble. Less careful work, in particular the use of smaller blocks, is the reason for this decline. In this view of northern Saqqara, the pyramids, from the left, belong to Netjerikhet, Userkaf, and Teti.

★ *Papyrus Leiden 344 recto, 2,11.*

117

of one of his successors, was found buried in a re-used sarcophagus, a sad comment on the conditions which affected even the highest-ranking members of the royal family at this time. The last dated inscription at Wadi Maghara in the Sinai is of Pepy II's second census, probably his third year. The lack of later inscriptions was due to the government's reduced ability to finance large-scale mining expeditions and to the fall in demand for exclusive materials. Also the dangers of attack by hostile tribesmen seem to have increased dramatically, at least partly because the policing of border areas was less assiduously pursued. Pepynakht Heqaib describes in his tomb how he was sent to the country of the Aamu in order to bring back the body of an official 'building a ship there for a journey to Punt when the Aamu of the sand-dwellers killed him together with the troops who were with him'. The situation was particularly serious in Nubia and required measures reminiscent of the drastic military actions at the beginning of the Old Kingdom. The same Pepynakht describes one of these raids: 'The Majesty of my lord sent me to hack up the countries of Wawat and Irtjet. I did as my lord praises. I killed there a large number, including chief's children and commanders of élite troops. I brought a large number from there to the Residence as captives while I was at the head of a large and mighty army as a hero.'

Climatic conditions started worsening around the beginning of the Sixth Dynasty, and the disastrous consequences of this, particularly of the lower level of Nile inundations, became fully apparent when the central government disintegrated. Many texts of the period which followed the end of the Old Kingdom describe the famine which raged through the land. Ankh-tifi, the 'great overlord of the districts of Edfu and Hierakonpolis' during the Seventh or Eighth Dynasty, describes the desperate situation which developed in the south: 'Upper Egypt in its entirety was dying of hunger, everybody eating his children, but I never allowed it to happen that anyone died of hunger in this district.'

The conditions which existed in parts of Egypt during this unhappy period may have served as inspiration for two later literary works, the *Admonitions of Ipuwer*, and the *Prophecies of Neferti*. Both of them were composed for propagandist reasons, and the desperate situation provided them with a contrast for the happier times to come. Because of this, it is sometimes difficult to accept their vivid imagery as a faithful reflection of reality. It is also their poetic language which makes them remarkable, 'A man goes out to plough with his shield.' 'Indeed, many dead are buried in the river. The stream is a tomb, and the place of embalmment has become a stream.' 'Indeed, laughter has perished, and is no longer made, and it is grief which is throughout the land, mixed with lamentation.' Behold, he who was ignorant of the lyre now owns a harp.'

There are many factors to be taken into account when we look for the causes of Egypt's sudden decline during this period. The Egyptian state of the Old Kingdom was created and existed because of certain ideological preconditions which had their roots in the preceding periods. State and religious ideology, fused into one, had to be maintained by material means if the state was to survive with its basic characteristics intact. This entailed the monumental building of pyramids for the deceased kings and, even more important, the endowment of their cult establishments. Similar provisions, though on a much smaller scale, had to be made for the rest of the ruling hierarchy. Gigantic building enterprises used up huge amounts of contemporary resources and, no doubt, created economic strains. Such use of resources, however, was ideologically essential, and to direct the effort differently, towards more productive objectives, e.g. irrigation, was not an option which was really available in the framework

of the existing society. The endowment of royal cult establishments in itself did not represent a material loss because the surplus was re-distributed in various ingenious ways to filter through to larger sections of society. If certain practical difficulties could be overcome, it is conceivable to envisage a society whose total national product is first applied to satisfying the needs of the dead, and then used to sustain the living.

Nor can it be said that the growing power of temples, resulting from endowments and exemptions of their properties from state obligations, caused any losses in real terms. The Egyptian method of 'offering' to deities did not involve extensive waste of material and the numbers of the professional priesthood were very small.

The Old Kingdom was not brought to its knees by an upheaval caused by a popular uprising. The graphic descriptions of Ipuwer and Neferti depict chaotic conditions during a period of social instability, but hardly an attempt by the exploited class to change the social system. For the majority of the Egyptian population the question of the ownership of the land on which they worked was of limited consequence. Even such things as exemption from state duties and forced participation in state enterprises were of more concern to the landowner than to the peasants.

No large-scale invasion of the country from abroad took place at the end of the Old Kingdom. The increased insecurity in border areas, due

The fertile soil under cultivation can change into the barren sand of the desert virtually in a few yards. These were the most sensitive areas of the Black Land (Kemet) where even temporary neglect or lack of water had an immediate effect. The valley temples and the pyramids at Abusir could, to all appearances, be located in two different worlds.

Facing page: The starving people on this relief, almost certainly from the causeway of Unas at Saqqara, are not necessarily inhabitants of the Nile valley. Similar scenes, however, must have become commonplace even in Egypt, particularly in the south, at the end of the Old Kingdom.

The Great Pyramid seen through the crumbling superstructure of the Old Kingdom Mastabas.

to the failure of the weak administration to police them, at no point escalated into a decisive attack. The situation in Nubia was caused by climatic and ethnic pressures outside Egypt's sphere of influence, but it is likely that a strong government would have been able to safeguard its interests even there.

Egypt had had problems with royal succession even earlier, e.g. in the second half of the Fourth Dynasty, but these were always overcome and left no permanent scars on its society. The long reign of Pepy II, which in its last years probably was rather ineffectual, must have aggravated the situation, but could not have been its cause.

The worsening climatic conditions, in particular repeated low Niles, would have been a serious blow to Egypt's economy and would have caused considerable hardship at any time. The area of fields under cultivation diminished, the size of the harvest decreased, and the numbers of livestock were reduced. Yet it is difficult to accept even this as the single decisive factor which would have brought the Old Kingdom down. The changes were taking place slowly over a period of years. A well-functioning state would have been able to alleviate the worst consequences of natural disasters and organize countermeasures. It is hard to imagine that an administration which was capable of organizing projects such as pyramid-building would not have been able to instigate further intensive reclamation of land in the Delta, the Faiyum, or to inaugurate irrigation programmes in other areas.

What was it, then, that caused the first Egyptian civilization to disintegrate? Was the collapse which ensued inevitable? The seeds of the decline of the Old Kingdom were already present at its birth, and the dynamics of the process were contained in the system itself. The gradual shift in the ownership of land from the central authority to cult and temple establishments, as well as to private tomb endowments, was undermining the very foundations on which the state stood. These changes were not affecting agricultural production, but, by weakening the royal authority, they were slowly preparing conditions for a return to a situation comparable to that before the creation of one state. The consequences of this policy caused irreparable damage to state ideology because its chief representative could no longer live up to its expectations. This in turn made the state economy, in particular its system of official ('ex-officio') property which was now being transformed into private property, unworkable. There was no repressive apparatus effectively available to the king to enforce its continuation.

The eventual disintegration of the political structure which emerged at the beginning of the Third Dynasty from the chrysalis of the Predynastic Period and the first dynasties, was then unavoidable. Pepy II's long reign contributed to the decline, and Egypt's inability to maintain its influence outside its borders was a symptom of the malaise. The worsening of climatic conditions, unfortunately, came at a time when Egyptian administration was no longer in a position to react, and so it delivered the decisive blow. Without such intervention, Egypt would probably have gradually transformed into a conglomeration of smaller territorial entities. In the absence of foreign interference, these could have existed reasonably prosperously until inner pressures built up within society to such an extent that a new political solution was required. This would not necessarily have led to the type of state which eventually emerged as the Egyptian Middle Kingdom. Unfortunately, this was not to be. When new moves towards political unity appeared during the First Intermediate Period, it was, inevitably, again the Old Kingdom pattern which was sought and imitated.

TEN

EPILOGUE

THE OLD KINGDOM EXPERIENCE left an indelible mark upon Egyptian consciousness and found its expression in pessimistic literature whose theme was the futility of worldly pursuits. In the Middle Kingdom text known as *The Man Who Tired of Life*, the soul (*ba*) says to man: 'The builders in granite, those who erected halls in beautiful pyramids in fine work—when the builders become gods, their offering-tables are destroyed as if they were the weary-ones who are dead on the river bank for lack of a rescuer.' Spiritual achievements may make man's name live longer than his material provisions for afterlife. The song of a harpist in the Eleventh Dynasty tomb of Intef made a similar point: 'The gods of the past rest in their pyramids, the blessed nobles likewise are buried in their tombs, but the cult-places of the builders of mansions are gone. What has become of them? I have heard the words of Imhotep and Hardedef recited as their sayings in full. Yet what about their cult-places? Their walls have crumbled, their cult-places are gone as if they had never been.' These are signs of a profound ideological crisis which must have shaken Egypt's very foundations.

Even though many of the features of Old Kingdom administration, religion, literature, arts, and architecture, were eagerly studied and copied in later times, in reality there was no way back. Egypt had new periods of prosperity yet to come, but like a child suddenly matured by a harrowing experience, it could never regain the same self-assurance and blind confidence in its own resources and abilities displayed earlier. The times had changed and new forces appeared which made sure that the old economic and political model could not be resurrected. Old Kingdom pyramids and temples became things of the past, only to be visited and admired. A graffito at Saqqara records such a visit: 'The scribe Ahmose, son of Yeptah, came to see the temple of Djoser. He found it as though heaven were within it, with the sun rising in it, and he said: Let bread, oxen, fowl, and all good and pure things be given to the spirit of the justified Djoser, may heaven rain fresh myrrh, may it drip incense.'

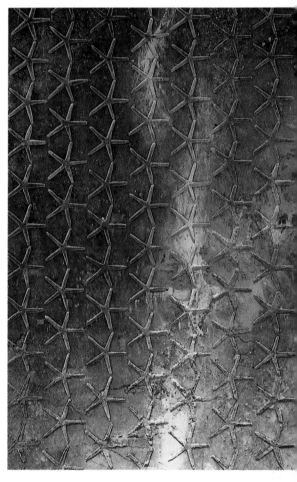

The star-covered ceiling of the interior of the pyramid of Teti at Saqqara. To become an 'indestructible star' was one of the king's aspirations in afterlife.

More than any other Egyptian monuments, the Giza pyramids of the three famous kings of the Fourth Dynasty never ceased to fire people's imagination. Their burial chambers had almost certainly already been plundered during the period of chaos and disorder which followed the end of the Old Kingdom. Some attempts were made to restore at least their interiors and contents during the Ramessid and Late Periods.

CHRONOLOGICAL TABLE

As no safely astronomically fixed dates are available from Egypt during the 3rd millennium BC, absolute chronology (i.e. in years BC) can still be subject to corrections. These might be of the order of some 150 years for the first two dynasties (and more for the Predynastic Period), and up to some 50 years for the Old Kingdom. Relative chronology (i.e. the order of kings) is, with one or two minor exceptions, secure.

In the Old Kingdom the king had five names. The oldest, the Horus-name, was usually written in a *serekh* ('palace façade'), and is given here for the kings of the first three dynasties whenever possible. The kings of the Fourth to Sixth Dynasties are listed by both their *ni-sut-bit* ('prenomen') and the 'son of Re' (birth name or 'nomen') names when these are different. They used to be written in cartouches (oval frames). The names of the kings of the Seventh and Eighth Dynasties are quoted, except for those indicated by ★, in the form in which they appear in the Abdju (Abydos) king-list.

PREDYNASTIC PERIOD	*c.* 5000/4500–2925 BC
united Egypt	at least as early as 2950 BC
Narmer (probably same as King 'Scorpion')	*c.* 2950–2925 BC

FIRST AND SECOND DYNASTIES *c.* 2925–2658 BC

FIRST DYNASTY:
- Aha (Teti of Abdju king-list, Athothis of Manetho)
- Djer
- Djet
- Den
- Andjib
- Semerkhet
- Qaa

SECOND DYNASTY:
- Hetepsekhemui
- Raneb
- Ninetjer
- Weneg (*ni-sut-bit* name)
- Send (*ni-sut-bit* name)
- Sneferka
- Sekhemib-perenmaet, perhaps same as Peribsen (= 'Seth-name')
- Khasekhem, perhaps same as Khasekhemui-nebuihetepimef (= 'Horus-and-Seth name')

THE OLD KINGDOM
(THIRD TO EIGHTH DYNASTIES) 2658–2135 BC

THIRD DYNASTY	2658–2584 BC
Zanakht (*ni-sut-bit* Nebka, Manetho's Nekherophes)	2658–2639 BC
Netjerikhet (Djoser of later tradition)	2639–2620 BC
Sekhemkhet	2620–2614 BC
Khaba	2614–2608 BC
Qahedjet	2608–2584 BC
FOURTH DYNASTY	2584–2465 BC
Snofru	2584–2560 BC
Khufu	2560–2537 BC
Radjedef	2537–2529 BC
Khephren	2529–2504 BC
Khnemka or Wehemka (reading uncertain)	2504–2499 BC
Menkaure	2499–2471 BC
Shepseskaf	2471–2467 BC
Thamphthis (name only known from Manetho)	2467–2465 BC

FIFTH DYNASTY	2465–2322 BC
Userkaf	2465–2458 BC
Sahure	2458–2446 BC
Neferirkare Kakai	2446–2436 BC
Shepseskare	2436–2429 BC
Raneferef (= Izi?)	2429–2419 BC
Neuserre Iny	2419–2388 BC
Menkauhor (also Ikauhor)	2388–2380 BC
Djedkare Izezi	2380–2352 BC
Unas	2352–2322 BC
SIXTH DYNASTY	2322–2151 BC
Teti	2322–2292 BC
Meryre (Neferzahor) Pepy I	2291–2254 BC
Merenre I Nemtyemzaf	2253–2248 BC
Neferkare Pepy II	2247–2154 BC
Merenre-Nemtyemzaf II (from Abdju king-list)	2153–2152 BC
Neitiqert	2152–2151 BC
SEVENTH DYNASTY	2151–2145 BC

SEVENTH DYNASTY (continued):
- Netjerkare
- Menkare
- Neferkare★
- Neferkare-neby
- Djedkare-shema
- Neferkare-khendu
- Merenhor
- Neferka-min
- Nikare
- Neferkare-terer
- Neferkahor

EIGHTH DYNASTY 2145–2135 BC
- Neferkare-pepysonb
- Neferka-min-anu
- Qakare Ibi★
- Neferkaure
- Neferkauhor
- Neferirkare

The period which follows, 2134–2040 BC, is known as the First Intermediate Period, and is succeeded by the Middle Kingdom.

BIBLIOGRAPHY

The list contains selected monographs and larger works dealing with various aspects of the Old Kingdom and the preceding period. Much of the discussion concerning some of the topics covered in this book has been conducted on pages of specialized journals, not readily accessible to non-specialists. References to such articles have been omitted here, but the works cited below include them in their own bibliographies.

The main source for hieroglyphic texts of the Old Kingdom still remains Kurt Sethe's *Urkunden des Alten Reichs*, 2nd ed. Leipzig 1933, even though many new inscriptions have become known since its publication. For references to Old Kingdom material from the Memphite area see B. Porter, R. L. B. Moss, E. W. Burney, and J. Malek, *Topographical Bibliography of Ancient Egyptian Hieroglyphic Texts, Reliefs, and Paintings*, III, 2nd ed. in 2 vols., Griffith Institute, Ashmolean Museum, Oxford 1974 and 1981. It also lists references to excavation reports and publications of material not included in our Bibliography.

ALDRED, Cyril *Egypt to the End of the Old Kingdom* (Thames and Hudson, London 1965)

ARKELL, A. J. *The Prehistory of the Nile Valley* (Handbuch der Orientalistik, 7.1.2A.1, E. J. Brill, Leiden/Köln 1975)

ATZLER, Michael *Untersuchungen zur Herausbildung von Herrschaftsformen in Ägypten* Hildesheimer Ägyptologische Beiträge, 16, Gerstenberg Verlag, Hildesheim 1981)

BAUMGARTEL, Elise J. *The Cultures of Prehistoric Egypt*, 2 vols. (Griffith Institute, Ashmolean Museum, Oxford 1955 and 1960)

BAUMGARTEL, Elise J. *Predynastic Egypt* (Chapter IXa of *CAH*³ i, Pt. 1, Cambridge University Press 1970, pp.463–97)

BAER, Klaus *Rank and Title in the Old Kingdom. The Structure of the Egyptian Administration in the Fifth and Sixth Dynasties* (The University of Chicago Press 1960)

BEGELSBACHER-FISCHER, Barbara L. *Untersuchungen zur Götterwelt des Alten Reiches im Spiegel der Privatgräber der IV. und V. Dynastie* (Orbis Biblicus et Orientalis, 37, Universitätsverlag Freiburg, Schweiz/Vandenhoeck & Ruprecht, Göttingen 1981)

BUTZER, Karl W. *Early Hydraulic Civilization in Egypt. A Study in Cultural Ecology* (Prehistoric Archaeology and Ecology, The University of Chicago Press, Chicago and London 1976)

EDWARDS, I. E. S. *The Early Dynastic Period in Egypt* (Chapter XI of *CAH*³ i, Pt. 2, Cambridge University Press 1971, pp.1–70)

EDWARDS, I. E. S. *The Pyramids of Egypt* (Penguin Books, Harmondsworth 1985)

EMERY, Walter B. *Archaic Egypt* (Penguin Books, Harmondsworth 1961)

FAKHRY, Ahmed *The Pyramids* (The University of Chicago Press, Chicago and London, 2nd ed. 1969)

GOEDICKE, Hans *Königliche Dokumente aus dem Alten Reich* (Ägyptologische Abhandlungen, 14, Otto Harrassowitz, Wiesbaden 1967)

GOEDICKE, Hans *Die privaten Rechtsinschriften aus dem Alten Reich* (Beihefte zur Wiener Zeitschrift für die Kunde des Morgenlandes, 5, Verlag Notring, Wien 1970)

GOEDICKE, Hans *Die Stellung des Königs im Alten Reich* (Ägyptologische Abhandlungen, 2, Otto Harrassowitz, Wiesbaden 1960)

HAYES, William C. (ed. by SEELE, Keith C.) *Most Ancient Egypt* (The University of Chicago Press, Chicago & London 1965)

HELCK, Wolfgang *Die Beziehungen Ägyptens zu Vorderasien im 3. und 2. Jahrtausend v. Chr.* (Ägyptologische Abhandlungen, 5, Otto Harrassowitz, Wiesbaden, 2nd ed. 1971)

HELCK, Wolfgang *Geschichte des Alten Ägypten* (Handbuch der Orientalistik, 1.1.3, E. J. Brill, Leiden/Köln 1968)

HELCK, Wolfgang *Untersuchungen zu den Beamtentiteln des ägyptischen Alten Reiches* (Ägyptologische Forschungen, 18, Verlag J. J. Augustin, Glückstadt–Hamburg–New York 1954)

HELCK, Wolfgang *Untersuchungen zu Manetho und den ägyptischen Königslisten* (Untersuchungen zur Geschichte und Altertumskunde Aegyptens, 18, Akademie-Verlag, Berlin 1956)

HELCK, Wolfgang *Wirtschaftsgeschichte des Alten Ägypten im 3. und 2. Jahrtausend vor Chr.* (Handbuch der Orientalistik, 1.1.5, E. J. Brill, Leiden/Köln 1975)

HOFFMAN, Michael A. *Egypt before the Pharaohs. The Prehistoric Foundations of Egyptian Civilization* (Routledge & Kegan Paul, London & Henley 1980)

JACQUET-GORDON, Helen K. *Les noms des domaines funéraires sous l'Ancien Empire égyptien* (Bibliothèque d'Étude, XXXIV, I.F.A.O., 1962)

KANAWATI, Naguib *The Egyptian Administration in The Old Kingdom. Evidence on its Economic Decline* (Aris & Phillips Ltd., Warminster 1977)

KANAWATI, Naguib *Governmental Reforms in Old Kingdom Egypt* (Modern Egyptology, Aris & Phillips Ltd., Warminster 1980)

KEMP, Barry J. *Old Kingdom, Middle Kingdom and Second Intermediate Period c. 2686–1552 BC* (Chapter 2 of TRIGGER, B. G.; KEMP, B. J.; O'CONNOR, D. and LLOYD, A. B. *Ancient Egypt. A Social History*, Cambridge University Press 1983, pp.71–182)

LAUER, Jean-Philippe *Histoire monumentale des pyramides d'Égypte, i. Les pyramides à degrés (IIIe Dynastie)* (Bibliothèque d'Étude, XXXIX, I.F.A.O., Cairo 1962)

LAUER, Jean-Philippe *Le mystère des pyramides* (Presses de la Cité, Paris 1974)

MARTIN-PARDEY, Eva *Untersuchungen zur ägyptischen Provinzialverwaltung bis zum Ende des Alten Reiches* (Hildesheimer Ägyptologische Beiträge, 1, Verlag Gebrüder Gerstenberg, Hildesheim 1976)

MRSICH, Tycho *Untersuchungen zur Hausurkunde des Alten Reiches. Ein Beitrag zum altägyptischen Stiftungsrecht* (Münchner Ägyptologische Studien, 13, Verlag Bruno Hessling, Berlin 1968)

POSENER-KRIÉGER, Paule *Les archives du temple funéraire de Néferirkarê-Kakaï (Les Papyrus d'Abousir). Traduction et commentaire*, 2 vols. (Bibliothèque d'Étude, LXV, I.F.A.O., Cairo 1976)

RANSOM WILLIAMS, Caroline *The Decoration of the Tomb of Per-ñeb. The Technique and the Color Conventions* (The Metropolitan Museum of Art, New York 1932)

SCHENKEL, Wolfgang *Die Bewässerungsrevolution im Alten Ägypten* (D.A.I. Abteilung Kairo, Verlag Philipp von Zabern, Mainz/Rhein 1978)

SMITH, William Stevenson (revised with additions by SIMPSON, William Kelly) *The Art and Architecture of Ancient Egypt* (Penguin Books, Harmondsworth 1981)

SMITH, William Stevenson *A History of Egyptian Sculpture and Painting in the Old Kingdom* (The Museum of Fine Arts, Boston, 2nd ed. 1949)

SMITH, William Stevenson *The Old Kingdom in Egypt and the Beginning of the First Intermediate Period* (Chapter XIV of *CAH*³ i, Pt. 2, Cambridge University Press 1971, pp.145–207)

TRIGGER, B. G. *The Rise of Egyptian Civilization* (Chapter I of TRIGGER, B. G.; KEMP, B. J.; O'CONNOR, D. and LLOYD, A. B. *Ancient Egypt. A Social History*, Cambridge University Press 1983, pp.1–70)

ZIBELIUS, Karola *Ägyptische Siedlungen nach Texten des Alten Reiches* (Beihefte zum Tübinger Atlas des Vorderen Orients, Reihe B[Geisteswissenschaften], 19, Dr. Ludwig Reichert Verlag, Wiesbaden 1978)

The sources of the quotations at the beginnings of the Chapters are as follows: p. 7, the name of the pyramid of Pepy I at southern Saqqara; p. 14, a Fifth Dynasty text endowing a tomb at Giza, now in Cairo, Egyptian Museum, CG 1432; p. 18, Papyrus Prisse, 88–9; p. 22, Pyramid Texts, §272; p. 25, artist's signature alongside the staff held by the official Djau in his late Sixth Dynasty tomb at Deir el-Gebrawi; p. 26, Papyrus Leiden 344 *recto*, 2,11.

INDEX

ACKNOWLEDGMENTS

Werner Forman and the publishers would like to acknowledge the help of the following museums in permitting the photography shown on the pages listed:
The British Museum: 18 below, 23 below, 27, 86, 113 top. The Ashmolean Museum, Oxford: 16, 17, 18 top, 19, 20, 21, 22, 24, 25, 28, 29, 30, 33 left, 36, 37. The Louvre, Paris: 8, 34, 121. The Egyptian Museum, Cairo: 9, 14–15, 32, 33 right, 35, 38, 54, 55, 58, 61, 62, 63, 71, 78, 82, 83, 88–89, 90–91, 92, 94–95, 98, 99, 102, 110, 112, 113 bottom, 115 bottom.

Werner Forman would also like to thank the following for their help:
T. G. H. James and Dr A. H. Spencer, British Museum; Dr Mohamed Saleh, Egyptian Museum; Dr Wafaa Taha El Sadeek, Cairo; Dr Helen Whitehouse, Ashmolean Museum; Nassif Hassan, Dr Ahmed Kadry, Dr Mohamed Ibrahim Aly, Cairo; Mme C. Belanger, Mlle Harlé, Mlle Delange, Jean-Louis Hellouin de Cenival, Louvre.

Jaromir Malek wishes to thank Dr Graham Piddock for the translation of the passage from Herodotus, Book II, 35–6, quoted in the Prologue. He would also like to use this opportunity to express his appreciation of the help received from the staff of the Ashmolean Library (Griffith Institute), Oxford.

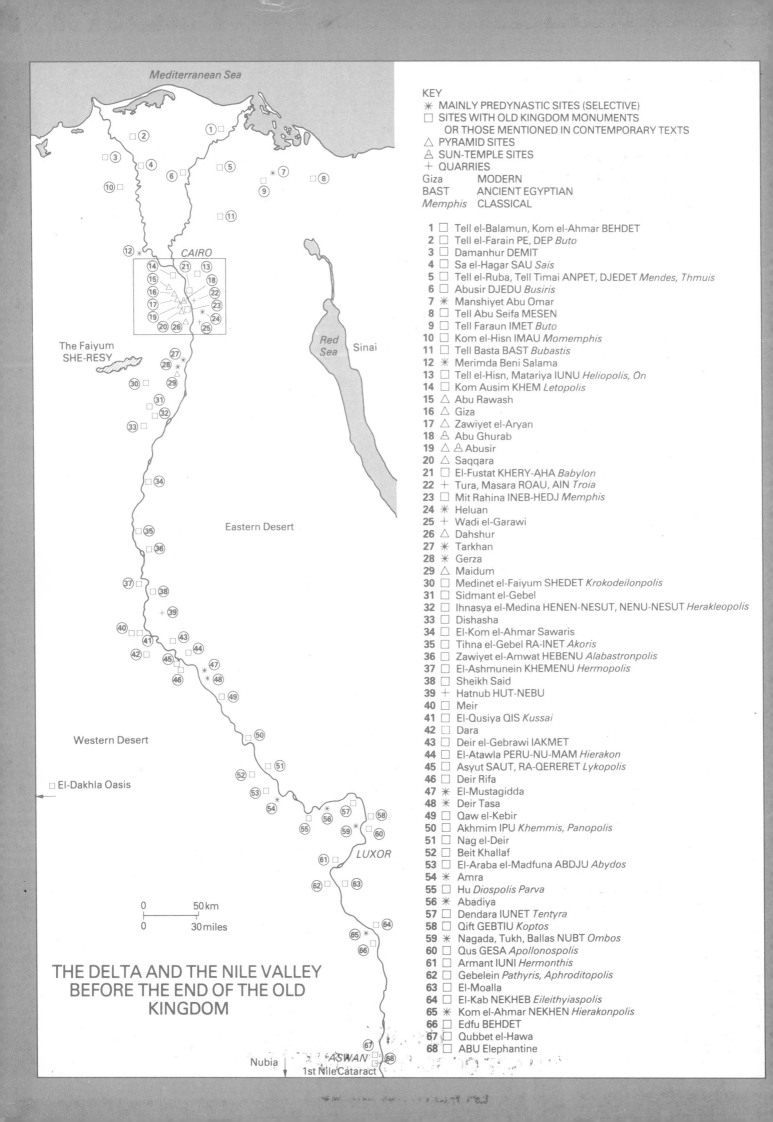

Mediterranean Sea

CAIRO

The Faiyum
SHE-RESY

Red Sea

Sinai

Eastern Desert

Western Desert

El-Dakhla Oasis

LUXOR

Nubia

ASWAN
1st Nile Cataract

KEY
* MAINLY PREDYNASTIC SITES (SELECTIVE)
□ SITES WITH OLD KINGDOM MONUMENTS
  OR THOSE MENTIONED IN CONTEMPORARY TEXTS
△ PYRAMID SITES
⌂ SUN-TEMPLE SITES
+ QUARRIES

Giza   MODERN
BAST   ANCIENT EGYPTIAN
Memphis   CLASSICAL

1 □ Tell el-Balamun, Kom el-Ahmar BEHDET
2 □ Tell el-Farain PE, DEP *Buto*
3 □ Damanhur DEMIT
4 □ Sa el-Hagar SAU *Sais*
5 □ Tell el-Ruba, Tell Timai ANPET, DJEDET *Mendes, Thmuis*
6 □ Abusir DJEDU *Busiris*
7 * Manshiyet Abu Omar
8 □ Tell Abu Seifa MESEN
9 □ Tell Faraun IMET *Buto*
10 □ Kom el-Hisn IMAU *Momemphis*
11 □ Tell Basta BAST *Bubastis*
12 * Merimda Beni Salama
13 □ Tell el-Hisn, Matariya IUNU *Heliopolis, On*
14 □ Kom Ausim KHEM *Letopolis*
15 △ Abu Rawash
16 △ Giza
17 △ Zawiyet el-Aryan
18 ⌂ Abu Ghurab
19 △ ⌂ Abusir
20 △ Saqqara
21 □ El-Fustat KHERY-AHA *Babylon*
22 + Tura, Masara ROAU, AIN *Troia*
23 □ Mit Rahina INEB-HEDJ *Memphis*
24 * Heluan
25 + Wadi el-Garawi
26 △ Dahshur
27 * Tarkhan
28 * Gerza
29 △ Maidum
30 □ Medinet el-Faiyum SHEDET *Krokodeilonpolis*
31 □ Sidmant el-Gebel
32 □ Ihnasya el-Medina HENEN-NESUT, NENU-NESUT *Herakleopolis*
33 □ Dishasha
34 □ El-Kom el-Ahmar Sawaris
35 □ Tihna el-Gebel RA-INET *Akoris*
36 □ Zawiyet el-Amwat HEBENU *Alabastronpolis*
37 □ El-Ashmunein KHEMENU *Hermopolis*
38 □ Sheikh Said
39 + Hatnub HUT-NEBU
40 □ Meir
41 □ El-Qusiya QIS *Kussai*
42 □ Dara
43 □ Deir el-Gebrawi IAKMET
44 □ El-Atawla PERU-NU-MAM *Hierakon*
45 □ Asyut SAUT, RA-QERERET *Lykopolis*
46 □ Deir Rifa
47 * El-Mustagidda
48 * Deir Tasa
49 □ Qaw el-Kebir
50 □ Akhmim IPU *Khemmis, Panopolis*
51 □ Nag el-Deir
52 □ Beit Khallaf
53 □ El-Araba el-Madfuna ABDJU *Abydos*
54 * Amra
55 □ Hu *Diospolis Parva*
56 * Abadiya
57 □ Dendara IUNET *Tentyra*
58 □ Qift GEBTIU *Koptos*
59 * Nagada, Tukh, Ballas NUBT *Ombos*
60 □ Qus GESA *Apollonospolis*
61 □ Armant IUNI *Hermonthis*
62 □ Gebelein *Pathyris, Aphroditopolis*
63 □ El-Moalla
64 □ El-Kab NEKHEB *Eileithyiaspolis*
65 * Kom el-Ahmar NEKHEN *Hierakonpolis*
66 □ Edfu BEHDET
67 □ Qubbet el-Hawa
68 □ ABU Elephantine

0   50km
0   30 miles

THE DELTA AND THE NILE VALLEY BEFORE THE END OF THE OLD KINGDOM